ALLEN D. GRIMSHAW
SOCIOLOGY DEPT

W9-CFO-307

LANGUAGE
SPREAD

LANGUAGE SPREAD

Studies in Diffusion and Social Change

Edited by Robert L. Cooper

INDIANA UNIVERSITY PRESS • BLOOMINGTON
in cooperation with the
CENTER FOR APPLIED LINGUISTICS • WASHINGTON, D.C.

Copyright © 1982 by Center for Applied Linguistics

All rights reserved

No part of this book may be reproduced or utilized in any form
or by any means, electronic or mechanical, including photocopying
and recording, or by any information storage and retrieval system,
without permission in writing from the publisher. The Association
of American University Presses' Resolution on Permissions constitutes
the only exception to this prohibition.

Manufactured in the United States of America

Library of Congress Cataloging in Publication Data
Main entry under title:

Language spread.

"Papers . . . prepared for an international conference . . . convened by the Center for
Applied Linguistics . . . held at the University College of Wales, Aberystwyth, September
12–14, 1978"—Pref.
    Includes index.
    1. Language spread—Congresses. 2. Social change—Congresses. I. Cooper,
Robert Leon, 1931–   .
II. Center for Applied Linguistics.
P40.5.L37L3   401'.9   81–47567
ISBN 0–253–32000–3   AACR2
1 2 3 4 5 86 85 84 83 82

CONTENTS

Preface

This volume is the first collection of theoretical articles and case studies devoted to language spread, the phenomenon whereby the uses or the users of a language increase. The papers were initially prepared for an international conference on the topic, convened by the Center for Applied Linguistics, supported by the Ford Foundation and the International Development Research Centre (Ottawa), and held at the University College of Wales, Aberystwyth, September 12–14, 1978. Although work on language spread had been undertaken before, particularly in some of the research supported by the Ford Foundation, the conference was a major stimulus for the emergence and crystalization of this phenomenon as a field of inquiry. On behalf of my colleagues at the Aberystwyth conference, I want to thank the aforementioned institutions for organizing and supporting the conference and for helping to make the production of this book possible. In particular our thanks go to Elinor Barber of the Ford Foundation, to Kenneth King of the International Research Centre, to Dora E. Johnson, Sirarpi Ohannessian, Rosemary Tripp, and G. Richard Tucker of the Center for Applied Linguistics, and to Carl Dodson of the University College of Wales.

Robert L. Cooper
Jerusalem

Introduction

Bernard Barber

It is a pleasure and privilege to write a brief foreword to this excellent volume on language spread. I should like to make comments from two perspectives, first, that of the sociology of science, and second, that of systematic sociological analysis and research. From both perspectives I want to urge that sociologists could profit a great deal from paying more attention to, and working more frequently in, the area of sociolinguistics, a new scientific specialty in which language spread is a new subspecialty.

THE PERSPECTIVE OF THE SOCIOLOGY OF SCIENCE

Although like all new scientific specialties, it has its prehistory or early history, sociolinguistics has emerged as a flourishing, intensely cultivated field of study only since the 1960s. It was in the 1960s that the first paradigmatic statements and research appeared at conferences attended by what were then "pioneers" and are now "establishment figures" for the field. One of the organizational turning points for the emerging specialty of sociolinguistics occurred in 1964 at the summer seminar sponsored by the Social Science Research Council on Sociolinguistics in conjunction with the Summer Linguistic Institute of the Linguistic Society of America. From that "beginning" there have come all the products and indicators of a maturing scientific specialty: a rapidly increasing amount of research, leading figures and other associated specialists, conferences, associations, journals, "invisible colleges" (informal communication networks among specialists), and an increasing differentiation and specialization of topics within sociolinguistics, one of which is the subject of this book. In a recent review of work on

1

language in society, Allen Grimshaw, a sociologist who is himself a specialist in the field, has said, "perhaps as many books on sociolinguistic topics have been published since 1973 as had ever been published previously" (Grimshaw, 1973; see also Grimshaw, 1974). On a small scale, this remark echoes Derek Price's statement that ninety percent of all the scientists who have ever lived are still living. For science as a whole, and probably for recent sociolinguistics, there are periods when the growth rate is exponential.

Because of near-exponential growth rates at certain periods, scientific specialties can mature very rapidly. Sociolinguistics is now a mature specialty and there can be no better evidence of that maturity than this volume. A distinguished group of specialists, reporting extensive and solid research, using a variety of paradigms (at the frontiers of any scientific specialty is there ever complete consensus on a single paradigm?), move at once to the solution of certain problems and to the posing of new theoretical and research and methodological questions. There is discovery here, but also the frustration of present limited theoretical and methodological resources, with both discovery and frustration carried forward by the excitement that prevails in a newly mature but not yet rigidified specialty.

New specialties get recruits both from novices coming fresh to a discipline, that is, graduate students, and also from established specialists who are attracted to the new field and move over from their old specialty. Because it is an exciting and important field, sociolinguistics and its subspecialties like language spread ought to appeal to both types of recruits from the broad discipline of sociology. While there are already some sociologists who specialize in sociolinguistics, including a few of the pioneer and leading figures, sociology itself and the specialty of sociolinguistics would both profit from more mobility into this field.

Before taking up my second perspective, one last word from the perspective of the sociology of science may be useful. The sociology of science attempts not only to describe the structures and processes of emerging scientific specialties, but also to explain why they emerge at particular times and places. Why has sociolinguistics emerged and come to maturity in the last twenty years? The answer to this question deserves more careful study than I have given it, but perhaps it is reasonable to suggest two interdependent causes for its emergence at this time. On the one hand, during this period language has come to be recognized as a "social problem" that exists in just about every country in the world in some form or another. The present volume indicates many, though even then not all, of the ways in which language is a "social problem," something that some people think requires change and reform of some kind. And social problems are sometimes powerful pointers or guides or incentives for scholars to work on particular scientific and practical questions. Further research on the origins of sociolinguistics as a specialty should investigate the extent to which various social problems have been sources of scientific concern with this field.

Social problems, of course, often exist without any consequences for scientific specialties. They can have consequences only when the second cause for the emergence of a scientific specialty is present, namely the existence of the theoretical, methodological, and other technical knowledge resources essential for carrying on scientific inquiry in the new area of interest. In the 1960s the technical knowledge resources necessary for establishing sociolinguistics were available in its two parent fields, linguistics and sociology. It is the interactive combination of technical knowledge and new social problems that probably led to the emergence of sociolinguistics in its time and place.

THE PERSPECTIVE OF SYSTEMATIC
SOCIOLOGICAL ANALYSIS AND RESEARCH

Language is obviously one of the indispensable and universal components of the cultural system of all societies. As such, it should be a major focus of sociological concern. The sociology of language should be as much a sociological specialty, a course taught in sociology departments, as the sociology of science, law, religion, ideology (to mention some other universal cultural components) and as the sociology of the family, of stratification, of education, and of the polity (to mention only some universal social-structural components of society). It is my impression, which could be checked by some simple research, that before World War II the sociology of language was a more widespread and standard field in sociology, both as a specialty and in introductory courses and texts, than it has been since that time. However, as the two excellent review articles of the sociology of language by Grimshaw indicate (1973, 1974), the tide is turning again toward more serious and general concern with this important subject. In anthropology, of course, the study of language has always been a central and continuing concern, both for practical and theoretical reasons.

Systematic sociological analysis and research can not afford to neglect language as one of the essential components of societies as social systems. Language systems, their structure, processes, and patterns of change, are interesting in their own right, as are the other systemic components of society, but they are also interesting for their patterns of interdependence with these other systemic components: language with the polity, or the economy, or with stratification structures, and so forth. Language systems, in these interdependencies, are now the independent variable, now the dependent variable. And if anyone needs any convincing about any of these several propositions I have offered for the sociological importance of language, all s/he needs to do is read any of the essays in this volume on language spread. This volume will demonstrate to any sociologist what is already here and what s/he has been missing: the sociology of language. The time should be soon when research and courses in the sociology of language exist in all first-rate sociology departments and when every textbook of sociology has a chapter on language as a cultural and social phenomenon.

REFERENCES

Grimshaw, Allen D. 1973. "On Language in Society: Part I," *Contemporary Sociology* 2, 575–85.
Grimshaw, Allen D. 1974. "On Language in Society: Part II," *Contemporary Sociology* 3, 3–11.

A Framework for the Study of Language Spread

Robert L. Cooper

There are numerous examples of language spread, from the diffusion of Sumerian, Akkadian, and Aramaic in ancient Mesopotamia (Paper, this volume), to the celebrated expansion of Greek, Latin, and Arabic within the empires associated with those languages (Brosnahan 1963), to the spread of Spanish in the New World (Heath 1972; Heath and Laprade, this volume), to the present-day spread of Arabic in the southern Sudan (Mahmud, this volume), Amharic in Ethiopia (Cooper 1976), Hindi in India (Misra, this volume), Russian in the Soviet Union (Lewis 1972 and this volume), Mandingo in West Africa (Calvet, this volume), Swahili in East Africa (Whiteley 1969; Mazrui and Zirimu 1978; Scotton, this volume), and English globally (Fishman, Cooper, and Conrad 1977).

What do such diverse examples have in common? What are the psychological, social, and linguistic phenomena which, in interaction, account for language spread? Do languages spread in the same way as single items of vocabulary, pronunciation, or grammar? Do languages spread according to the same laws as innovations more generally? What variables entering into what equations can predict the rate and extent of spread of a given language among a given group of speakers?

The answers to such questions are of undeniable interest. We are only beginning to see the shape of the answers, however, in part because we have only begun to ask such questions, in part because social-change theory is in general not well developed, and in part because studies of language spread, which have been marked by differing substantive preoccupations and methodological orientations, lack a common frame of reference within which the results of different studies might be compared. Furthermore, many of these studies have been

5

carried out in isolation from other relevant research traditions. Thus it is difficult to relate language-spread studies not only to one another but also to studies undertaken within related traditions. The present paper attempts a definition of language spread, then discusses the relevance of related research traditions, and finally proposes a checklist of variables to be employed in the study of language spread.

TOWARD A DEFINITION OF LANGUAGE SPREAD

Language spread may be defined as *an increase, over time, in the proportion of a communication network that adopts a given language or language variety for a given communicative function*. We can discuss this definition in terms of (1) what is spreading, (2) the notion of spread as a time-dependent phenomenon, and (3) the medium through which language spread occurs.

What Is Spreading

Although we speak of *language spread*, the expression is of course metaphorical. Languages do not acquire speakers. It is speakers (or readers and writers) who acquire and use languages. When we refer to language spread, then, we are referring to the spread of behaviors. The behaviors which spread can be approached from three points of view: form, function, and pervasiveness.

Form refers to the linguistic diversity of the language which is spreading as well as to its structural similarity to the other languages known by adopters or potential adopters. Swahili, for example, consists of a number of dialect clusters, some of which are mutually unintelligible. While the standard form of the language (the variety spoken in Zanzibar town) appears to be the variety spreading most rapidly, there are a number of upcountry dialects being acquired as an additional language (Whiteley 1969:4–7). To what extent do these different forms constitute a single "item" for purposes of analysis? Is it "Swahili" which is spreading or "Standard Swahili" or, for example, Ki-Ngwana (a group of dialects spoken in parts of the eastern Congo) or Ki-Settla (a variety or varieties developed in contact with European settlers)? For some analytical purposes we may want to include all varieties, in which case we may speak of the spread of a "language." For other purposes we may wish to analyze the spread of particular varieties separately, especially where there are attitudinal differences associated with different varieties or when there is variation in their resemblance to other languages the learners know.

The language or language variety, of course, may not remain the same during its spread. Language change, found in all language varieties, is probably accelerated by the process of spread, inasmuch as spread implies accelerated language contact, one source of language change. Thus, for example, the Swahili upcountry dialects emerged as a consequence of interaction between Swahili-speaking traders from the coast and initially non-Swahili speakers from the interior. Clearly differences in form will themselves be a dependent variable when the investigator's purpose is to describe the impact of spread upon language structure.

Function refers to the purpose for which a language or language variety is spreading. If a language is spreading for two different purposes, is one item spreading or are two? In Israel, for example, English appears to be spreading for several purposes. It is used as a medium of scientific texts and reference works assigned and consulted at the universities, as a lingua franca with visitors from abroad, a medium for belles lettres and for international pop culture, and a medium for written exchange between Israeli firms and their foreign customers and suppliers (Nadel, Fishman, and Cooper 1977; Cooper and Seckbach 1977). Have the spreads of these different functions proceeded simultaneously, via the same channels, at the same rate, and to the same extent? It seems unlikely that they have. Mahmud (this volume), for example, suggests that Arabic is spreading in the southern Sudan at different rates for different functions. In any event, we have as yet little to say about the factors promoting or impeding the spread of different types of language function. Thus it seems proper that a definition of language spread specify that what is spreading refers to a *given communicative function*. If a language is spreading with respect to two communicative functions, we will treat it as two items of spread.

Defining language spread in terms of a given communicative function is not without its problems. On what basis do we determine the functions a language is playing? In Kampala (Scotton 1972), for example, the most important lingua francas are Swahili and English. Almost everyone in Kampala knows some Swahili, which is learned outside school. English, however, is learned mainly at school and is a marker of educated status. Persons who choose to use Swahili with a stranger can be sure of being understood but they give up the opportunity to identify themselves as educated. Speakers who choose English, on the other hand, identify themselves as educated, but they run the risk of offending the stranger if the latter turns out not to know English. Swahili therefore tends to be used in situations in which the speaker wishes to emphasize solidarity and English in situations in which status differentials are stressed. Do English and Swahili then fulfill the same function or different functions when they are used as lingua francas in the rounds of everyday life in Kampala? If the extensive literature on bilingual usage has taught us anything, it is that language choice is systematic, i.e., that when speakers can use either of two varieties, their choice reflects the social identities and social values which the speakers wish to stress in any given interaction. One can argue, therefore, that a speaker can never use two languages for the same purpose, in a context in which either would be understood, because the choice of one language rather than another signals communicative intent, e.g., intimacy versus social distance, formality versus informality, ingratiation versus insult.

Can speakers be said to be using two languages for the same purpose when they use each with monolingual speakers (i.e., where no choice is possible)? In linguistically diverse Ethiopian markets, for example, there is some evidence that transactions are facilitated by the multilingualism of the sellers, who appear to use the languages of the numerically most important groups who come to the market (Cooper and Carpenter 1969). If vendors use Oromo to sell to monolingual Oromo speakers and Amharic to sell to monolingual Amharic speakers, are they using Amharic and Oromo here for the same function (trade) or two different functions (trade with Amharas, trade with Oromos)? Inasmuch as the seller may well treat representatives of each group differently, e.g., with respect to bargaining conventions, one could argue that the functions are separate.

However, one can endlessly subdivide functions. The problem here is to group together interactions which share enough features to make it reasonable to treat them as "the same" with respect to their communicative function, so as to make it possible to compare language spread in one context with language spread in another. We thus offer a classification based on three variables. The first is the skill or skills required by the function, i.e., listening, speaking, reading, writing. The inclusion of this variable as a basis for classifying communicative function is justified by the common-sense observation that (1) channels of written and spoken communication are typically different, (2) acquisition of literate skills typically depends upon formal education, access to which is distributed differently in different sociolinguistic contexts, and (3) it typically requires a longer time to acquire productive skills (speaking and writing) than receptive skills (listening and reading).

The second basis for classifying communicative function is whether the language is spreading for between-group or for within-group purposes. It is common in the United States, Canada, and Australia, for example, for immigrants initially to restrict their use of English to interactions with members of the host community, using their mother tongue with fellow immigrants. In time, however, English takes on many of the functions fulfilled by the mother tongue. For these immigrant communities, then, English first spreads for between-group purposes and later for within-group purposes. Languages which originally spread for between-group purposes can spread for within-group purposes not only among an immigrant population but among an indigenous populaton as well, as for example the spread of English in Ireland. Inasmuch as between-group and within-group interactions can usually be distinguished with respect to frequency as well as with respect to the norms appropriate to communicative behavior, and inasmuch as communicative interaction is likely to be crucial for the spread of language (as of any innovation), it seems reasonable to employ the distinction between between-group and within-group communication as a basis for classifying communicative function.

The third basis which can be used to classify the function for which a language spreads is suggested by Mazrui and Zirimu's (1978) analysis of the spread of Swahili. These analysts distinguish three functions for which Swahili has spread in eastern and central Africa: economic, political or administrative, and religious. According to Mazrui and Zirimu, Swahili's spread for economic purposes has been "the most spontaneous and the most natural of its three historic functions" (427) and the spread of this function has depended least on formal education.

> Where Kiswahili is needed purely for purposes of trade, marketing, and employment, the language has not fired the imagination of educators. . . .
> It is when Kiswahili is needed either for a political function or for religious purposes that educational policy makers become inspired, and governments or missionaries move with despatch toward giving the language a role in the formal structures of training and socialization. (427–8)

The distinction which we want to emphasize here is not the authors' classification of functions into commercial, administrative, and religious, but rather their distinction between horizontal and vertical integration.

> We define horizontal integration simply in terms of social communication and interaction across geographical and ethnic divisions of the society as a whole. We define vertical integration as a process of interaction between different strata of the society, especially between the elite and the masses. To the extent that Kiswahili served as the main language of trade unionism and organized labor, and facilitated social communication between workers and peasants from different geographical areas and ethnic groups, the language was performing horizontally integrative functions. (439)

They point out that Swahili spread as a lingua franca for horizontal integration

> in spite of the relative indifference of educational policy makers, and quite
> often in spite of their actual hostility to Kiswahili. What all this reveals
> once again is how economic necessity for a particular language in a given
> sociological situation could generate the spontaneous spread of the language, notwithstanding the formal educational system. The marketplace as
> an arena of linguistic spread can certainly be decisively independent of the
> classroom. But when a language is needed for vertical integration, especially in the sense of facilitating social communication between the rulers
> and the ruled, the educational system becomes once again a favored
> medium for dissemination. (440)

When there is little vertical integration, and thus little opportunity for social mobility, the spread of official languages (e.g., English in Anglophone Africa) is impeded because those without opportunities for social mobility see little value in learning the language (Scotton, this volume).

Just as the social interactions constituting within-group communication are likely to be different from those constituting between-group interaction, so are the interactions involved in horizontal integration likely to be different from those involved in vertical integration. The nature of these differences and their influence upon language spread are, of course, questions which it will require considerable ingenuity to investigate but which seem to be well worth the effort required to answer them.

It can be asked at this point why we do not use domains such as commerce, administration, and religion as a basis for classifying the functions for which a language spreads. The domain of social interaction is, after all, an important sociolinguistic theoretical construct. There are certain problems involved in the use of domain in the study of language spread, however, and these will be discussed in the section on language maintenance and language shift below. In any case, domain refers to the *location* of the function rather than to the function itself.

Pervasiveness refers to the degree to which speakers adopt a language or language variety for a given communicative function. Alternatively, it can be regarded as the type of adoption or the type of dependent variable used to represent adoption. There are at least two precedents for employing different "levels" of adoption as dependent variables: research on persuasion and research on the diffusion of innovations. In research on persuasion, the different dependent variables which are used form a scale of pervasiveness of attitude change, or, alternatively, a scale of the degree to which a persuasive message has succeeded: attention to the communication, comprehension of its message, yielding to or agreeing with the message, retention or memory of the message, and action in accordance with the message (McGuire 1969). There seems to be no widely accepted single scale of dependent variables for research in the diffusion of innovations. However, researchers in that field often distinguish between knowledge and use of the innovation. They investigate the diffusion of knowledge about the innovation as well as the diffusion of its use. Thus for example they compare the characteristics of early and late knowers as well as those of early and late users. Also, some researchers distinguish between first use and sustained use, and others distinguish trial from adoption (Katz, Levin, and Hamilton 1963). Rogers and Shoemaker (1971) propose five stages of acceptance of an innovation: awareness (first knowledge that the innovation exists), interest (gaining knowledge about the innovation), evaluation (gaining a favorable or unfavorable attitude toward the innovation), small-scale trial, and decision to adopt or reject the innovation.

In research on language spread, we may distinguish among several classes of criterion variables, ordering them along a scale of behavioral pervasiveness:

1. *Awareness*. The speaker learns that the language or language variety exists and that it can (or must) be used for a particular communicative function.

2. *Evaluation*. The speaker forms a favorable or unfavorable attitude towards the *personal usefulness* of the language for a particular function. Evaluation here is *not* equivalent to favorable or unfavorable feelings about speakers of the language. English, for example, spread throughout Ireland in spite of Irish antipathy towards the English (Macnamara 1973). "It is worth remembering," as Whiteley (1969:13) pointed out, "that the desire to learn another's language springs only very rarely from a disinterested wish to communicate with one's fellow humans." Thus evaluation here refers to the speaker's opinion that knowledge of the new language for a given function will or will not assist him in attaining valued goals. If the language will not help speakers to attain such goals, they are unlikely to learn it, or, having learned it, to use it.

3. *Proficiency*. The speaker is *able* to use the language for a given communicative purpose. The criterion of spread here is defined not in terms of grammatical or phonetic accuracy or in terms of fluency but rather in terms of the extent to which the speaker can use the language for a given function.

4. *Usage*. The speaker uses the language for a given function. One can describe usage in terms of absolute and relative frequencies. Thus, for example, two Israelis may read an English-language daily newspaper, but only once a week. The first also reads a Hebrew daily newspaper every day, whereas the second reads no other newspaper. Their frequency of usage, with respect to the English daily, is the same, but the exclusiveness of their usage is different. The first reads newspapers mainly in Hebrew whereas the second reads newspapers exclusively in English. The pervasiveness of English, with respect to newspaper reading, is greater for the second Israeli than for the first.

Not all who become aware of a language for a given purpose form positive evaluations of its personal usefulness; not all who form positive evaluations learn it; and not all who learn it use it. Thus, for example, in a survey of language proficiency, usage, and attitudes in the Ethiopian provinces of Kefa and Arusi (Cooper, Singh, and Abraha 1976), a substantial proportion of Amharic mother-tongue respondents mentioned English as a language they would like to know, although the opportunity for learning it was small and the opportunity for using it smaller still. To cite another example, it is not possible to do without knowledge of written French in France but "it is possible to have only a few opportunities for its practice" (Tabouret-Keller 1968:109). While less pervasive behaviors may be necessary if not sufficient conditions for more pervasive behaviors, more pervasive behaviors may well strengthen less pervasive ones. For example, increased usage may improve proficiency as well as evaluation. Thus it would seem useful to employ all four indices of adoption, where possible, so as to describe the rate and extent of their spread, to explain differences in their spread, and to show how the spread of one influences the spread of others.

To sum up our discussion of *what* is spreading, our definition suggests that we specify the form of the language which is spreading, the communicative function for which it is spreading, and the pervasiveness of the behavior that serves as the criterion of adoption.

Spread as a Time-Based Phenomenon

Language spread, like any social change, occurs over time. While the diffusion of any innovation requires time, it is likely that the spread of proficiency (if not awareness, evaluation, or usage) of a language requires more time than do most of the innovations whose diffusion is typically studied. While some functions for which a language spreads may require minimal knowledge, others may require years before a learner has acquired sufficient proficiency.

Katz et al. (1963) point out that, strictly speaking, it is the *time* of adoption rather than adoption itself which is the dependent variable of interest to researchers. If time of adoption can be determined, then the characteristics of early and late adopters can be compared, and diffusion curves, showing the number of adopters as a function of time of adoption, can be drawn. Many diffusion studies report S-shaped curves (Warner 1974), i.e., the percentage of potential adopters to accept an innovation rises slowly at first, then gathers speed, and then slackens off until it reaches a ceiling, with the proportion that has accepted the innovation remaining stable thereafter. Both Lieberson (this volume) and Scotton (this volume) refer to Greenberg's (1965) description of the spread of a lingua franca as having a dynamic of its own. As more people learn the language it becomes more useful as a lingua franca, thus encouraging even more people to learn it. The increase then slackens off either as the proportion of additional speakers requiring a lingua franca approaches zero or as the language encroaches upon the boundaries of another lingua franca. Thus diffusion curves for lingua francas may well be S-shaped. Such a curve is illustrated in Figure 1. It would, of course, be of great interest to compare diffusion curves for the different criteria of language spread and for different languages, not only with one another in contrasting sociolinguistic settings, but also with other types of innovation.

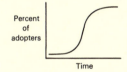

Percent of adopters

Time

FIGURE 1. An S-shaped diffusion curve.

According to Katz et al. (1963), relatively few diffusion studies take systematic account of time, partly because of difficulty in obtaining data. These writers identify three methods for determining the time of acceptance of an innovation: recall, records, and inferences. An example of the use of recall in diffusion research is Fliegel and Kivlin's (1966) study. Working with a sample of farm operators in a Pennsylvania county, they asked respondents when they first began to use each of thirty-three modern farm practices as well as how they perceived each innovation in terms of fifteen attributes (e.g., initial cost, saving of time). With this information the researchers were able to determine which characteristics of innovations were related to speedy adoption. An example of the use of records in determining time of adoption is Coleman, Katz, and Menzel's (1957) study of the adoption of new

drugs by physicians. These investigators were able to inspect the pre-
scriptions on file in pharmacies, making it possible to date each doctor's
first use of a new drug. Katz et al. point to archeological dating methods
of stratigraphy or Carbon-14 as examples of inferential methods of determining time of adoption in diffusion studies. Paper's (this volume)
discussion of language spread in the Middle East relies on data obtained
by such methods.

While it is always dangerous (because often wrong) to state that no
study whatsoever of a given sort exists, the present author knows of no
study of language spread which plots, as a function of time, the number
or proportion of potential adopters who accept a given language. Thus
we know little if anything about the shape of diffusion curves in language spread. This is not to say that studies of language spread ignore
time completely. Mahmud (this volume), for example, asked his respondents at what age they first spoke Arabic. Thus a diffusion curve
could be drawn from his raw data. In most studies, however, little if any
attempt is made to document change over time. Rather the change is
assumed and an attempt is made to explain it. Fishman, Cooper, and
Rosenbaum (1977), for example, correlated the status of English, in
approximately one hundred countries in which the bulk of the population does not speak English natively, with various characteristics of
these countries (e.g., status as former Anglophone colony, degree of
linguistic diversity).

Those studies of language spread which do present evidence with
respect to change over time present cross-sectional data gathered at
either one point of time or at several points in time. An example of the
former is found in Lewis (1972:103), who, citing, the 1959 Soviet
Union census, compared for urbanized non-Russian nationalities in
Central Asia, the percentage of all ages who have learned Russian with
the percentage of the ten- to nineteen-year-old age group who have
done so and found that on the average twice as many of the ten- to
nineteen-year-olds had learned Russian as for all ages combined, data
consistent with the hypothesis that Russian is spreading within these
nationalities. Similarly, Tabouret-Keller (1972) presented data showing
variation with age with respect to knowledge of French and the dialect
among rural school children in the Pays d'Oc and in Alsace. In the Pays
d'Oc virtually all children are fluent in French by age eight, whereas
knowledge of the dialect is learned slowly and, at age fourteen, by no
more than 40 percent of the children. In Alsace, most children are
fluent in the dialect at age eight; knowledge of French, acquired at
school, rises steeply until, by age fourteen, almost all the children have
learned it. "In one case, the standard language has taken over as the
native language for children of the rising generation, replacing the Occi-

tan which was native for those of fifty and over, whereas in the other this has not happened. In Alsace the situation is still homogeneous and the distribution of the dialect as a first language does not vary from generation to generation" (366). In a third example of the use of cross-sectional data gathered at one point in time, Hofman and Fisherman (1971), citing the 1961 Israel census and the work of Bachi (1956), point out that age at immigration and length of residence in Israel are each correlated to the degree to which immigrants to Israel use Hebrew. The younger the immigrant at the time of arrival and the more time spent in the country, the higher the index of Hebrew usage.

While we can expect a correlation between number of years of exposure to a language and proficiency or usage in it, languages do not necessarily spread more rapidly among younger people than among older ones. When the language can be learned at school, and when educational opportunities are expanding, we can expect to find a greater percentage of adopters among younger people than among older people. But when the language is not learned at school, but learned informally, there is no reason to expect younger persons to adopt more readily than older persons unless access to the interactions which promote adoption is related to age. Thus, for example, in the Ethiopian survey of Kefa and Arusi cited above, it was found that younger Oromos were more likely to know Amharic than older Oromos, in part because of expanding opportunities to attend government schools, in which Amharic is the only medium of instruction. In contrast, older Amharic mother-tongue speakers were more likely to know Oromo than younger Amharic mother-tongue speakers. Oromo is learned only outside of school. Older persons presumably had had a longer period in which to learn.

Data collected at two or more points of time, of course, provide more compelling evidence of language spread (or its absence), than data collected only once. Lieberson (1970), for example, citing the four decennial Canadian censuses between 1931 and 1961, showed that there were only slight changes in the percentage of the population able to speak each of the official languages or in the percentages of the population claiming each as mother tongue. However, citing Arès (1964a, b), he pointed out that in all provinces except Quebec, English was replacing French as the language of the French Canadian ethnic group. Arès examined the proportion of the French ethnic group claiming French as mother tongue and the proportion claiming that they could only speak English, in 1931 and in 1961, and found that the former proportion declined and the latter rose in all provinces except Quebec, where the ratios were stable.

While such data are useful, we would prefer to have valid data indicating the *time* of adoption. How can such data be obtained? Records are ordinarily not available, although it might be possible to seek published data such as (1) the first date on which firms publish newspaper advertisements seeking personnel with given language skills, (2) the first date on which firms insert bilingual entries in the "yellow pages" of the telephone directory, (3) the percentage of students at successive dates who enroll in beginning classes teaching a given language. More direct data would be desirable if these can be obtained. One can, of course, ask respondents when they first became aware of, wanted to learn, learned, and used a given language, but it remains to be seen how accurate such information can be. Longitudinal studies would probably yield the most valid information, at least with respect to individuals. We could ask (or observe or test) the same respondents, at several points in time, with respect to their awareness, evaluation, proficiency, and usage of a given language. However, because language spread may proceed for decades, indeed centuries, most longitudinal studies could cover only a portion of the total time frame involved. On the other hand, changes observed over a period as short as a decade (short from the perspective of language spread but long from the point of view of investigators and the agencies which fund their research) ought to lead to generalizations which could be applied to longer periods. Although there are undoubted difficulties in gathering data about time of adoption, it seems clear that we must make the effort if we are to advance our understanding of language spread.

The Medium Through Which Language Spread Occurs

If we consider language spread as a geographical phenomenon, then language spread represents an increase, over time, in the area over which a language has been adopted. If, for example, three maps were prepared showing the area in which Amharic was spoken for the middle of the fifteenth, nineteenth, and twentieth centuries respectively, we would see first a constriction and then an expansion in the area in which Amharic was spoken. The constriction was caused by the great Oromo migrations, which, beginning in the fifteenth and sixteenth centuries, pushed the Amharas toward the center of the Abyssinian plateau, displacing or swamping them along the plateau's edges (Ullendorff 1965). The later expansion of Amharic was facilitated by the military successes of the Amhara Emperor Minilik toward the end of the nineteenth century, consolidated and expanded by Emperor Haile Selassie in the twentieth century. The geographical expansion of Amharic was in part the result of the migration of Amharic-speaking settlers to the newly conquered or reconquered territories, which created pockets in which Amharic was spoken natively. But the expansion also resulted from the indigenous inhabitants of these territories beginning to adopt Amharic as an additional language. Whereas the Amharic-speaking migrants were a small minority among the non-Amharic indigenous population, the Oromo migrants, beginning in the sixteenth century, came in tremendous numbers, changing the ethnic composition of the areas in which they settled. The Oromo westward and northward migrations were caused by pressures from the Somalis and Danakils to the east, in the Horn of Africa. It is hard to know to what extent these migrations spread Oromo geographically, resulting in there being a larger area in which the language was found, or simply moved the area in which it was found, without causing an increase in this area.

The study of language spread as a geographical phenomenon can be rewarding. A glance at a map showing the mother-tongue composition of Ethiopian towns, for example, shows the striking geographical dispersion of Amharic throughout the country (Cooper and Horvath 1976:198). In all fourteen provinces there are towns in which Amharic is spoken natively by at least one quarter of the population, even though more than 95 percent of the country's Amharic mother-tongue speakers are found in only five of these provinces (Bender, Ferguson, and others 1976). It can also be seen that the urban concentration of Amharic mother-tongue speakers is higher in towns situated on roads. From this map we can hypothesize that Amharic is spreading partly as a function of urbanization and the development of the transportation network. Another example of the usefulness of maps in the study of language spread can be seen in Heine's (1970) maps of the distribution of African lingua francas, in which we can see that the boundaries of most lingua francas are contiguous with the boundaries of others, illustrating Greenberg's (1965) observation that nothing stops the spread of a lingua franca more surely than the existence of a rival lingua franca.

While it is possible to map the geographical dispersion of a language, showing the proportion of the population claiming it as first language or as an additional language, the study of geographical dispersion is really a means toward our understanding of language spread and not an end in itself. We tend to become bound by our terms and forget that the term *language spread,* conjuring up as it does visions of a physical phenomenon, like a river overflowing its banks and flooding the lowlands, or a wind passing over a field of wheat, is only a metaphor. A language does not expand, except metaphorically. It is the relative number of people *in contact* with the language which expands, whether this contact be specified as awareness, evaluation, knowledge, or use. Thus the geographical dispersion of a language is the geographical dispersion of *people* in contact with it. Therefore dispersion, over time, among people rather than in space is the primary focus of the study of language spread.

If the primary focus of language spread as a field of inquiry is on dispersion, over time, among people, rather than in space, our primary datum is not an increase in the absolute number of people in contact with the language but rather an increase in the *relative* number of people in contact with it. That the absolute number of speakers of language A is growing faster than the number of speakers of language B solely because the birthrate of mother-tongue speakers of A is faster than the birthrate of mother-tongue speakers of B, while of importance for the spread of A among speakers of B, is not itself a phenomenon to be explained by the study of language spread. However, if we are concerned with an increase in the relative number of people in contact with the language, we must define the population for whom the proportion of those in contact with the language is to be computed.

How is the population among whom the language is spreading to be defined? One approach is to define the population in terms of a particular social structure, i.e., a set of individuals who share the same norms and values but who are differentiated by status and role and by frequency and type of interpersonal interaction. This is the tack taken by Katz et al. (1963), who define the spread of an innovation in terms of its diffusion through a social structure.

One problem with using social structure to define the population through which language spreads is that language spread is not confined by the societal boundaries implied by social structure, although the characteristics of social structure, e.g., frequency of interaction, degree to which social networks are open or closed (Gumperz 1964), degree of social mobility, may speed or retard the diffusion of a language within that structure. We may liken language spread to a forest fire. A language's spread may be retarded by social boundaries just as a fire's spread may be retarded by rivers, lakes, and unwooded sections. Nonetheless, languages do spread across social boundaries just as fires spread across firebreaks. If we confine the study of language spread to a single social structure, we would miss the opportunity to investigate language spread across structures and to learn about the permeability to language spread of different types of social boundary.

A second problem with confining the study of language spread to a single social structure is that when usage of a language is spreading for between-group communication, it does so as a function of between-group interaction. A language cannot spread as a lingua franca without the opportunities and incentives to communicate implied by between-group contact. How can we account for the influence, on language spread, of different types of between-group interaction if we confine our investigations to interactions which occur *within* the boundaries imposed by social structure? We must also look *across* boundaries.

If we do not confine ourselves to a single social structure as the population through which a language spreads, how should that population be defined? The solution proposed here is to define that population as a communication network.

A communication network is a set of verbal, interactional links among persons, each network set off from others by sparsity of interaction. In Figure 2, in which the arrows between pairs of persons (A and B, B and C, etc.) indicate verbal interaction (whether oral or written) between them, we can see two communication networks: ABCD and EFGH. Though these two networks are connected because D and E interact with one another, there is more interaction within networks than between them. Communication networks can be subdivided into smaller networks corresponding to different bases of association (e.g., village, trade union, ethnic group, market, mass communication medium, speech community) and differing with respect to their structural and functional properties. Among the properties which are likely to be of interest for the study of language spread are (1) the number of persons in the subset, (2) the linguistic homogeneity or diversity of persons in the subset with whom the average member is in contact, (3) the average frequency of interaction between each member and those with whom he or she is in contact, (4) the average duration of such contact, and (5) the function of such contact. By using the communication network, with its constituent subnetworks, as the population through which language spreads, we can study language spread both as a within-group and as a between-group phenomenon, and we can study the facilitating or retarding effects of different types of subnetwork on language spread. While it may be difficult to operationalize the concepts of communication network and subnetwork, one can argue that they are no more difficult to operationalize than the notion of speech community, which has been of considerable heuristic value in the sociology of language.

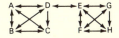

FIGURE 2. Two Communication Networks.

In the spread of innovations, diffusion occurs at a macro level whereas adoption occurs at a micro level (Zaltman and Stiff 1973:417).

Thus in the spread of languages, diffusion is the summation of innumerable individual adoptions. Most studies of the diffusion of innovation have considered the spread of items which are adopted by individuals, although some innovations require groups, e.g., telephone, fluoridation (Katz et al. 1963). Among group-oriented innovations, a further distinction is made, according to Katz et al., between items which permit an individual to adopt or not (telephone) and items where the group adopts as a unit (fluoridation). Language, of course, is a group-oriented innovation par excellence. A language which the speaker can use only with himself (i.e., a private language) can not spread. We can follow the distinction made by Katz et al. between a language adopted by individuals and a language adopted by groups. An example of the latter would be the adoption by schools or school systems of a given language as subject or medium of instruction. Thus we might be able to study the rate and extent to which Canadian schools or school systems provide French-medium classes for Anglophone pupils. While the spread of such classes is clearly relevant to the spread of French among Canadian Anglophones, the spread of these classes seems in principle amenable to study in the same fashion that any educational innovation, e.g., open classrooms, the new math, can be studied. The study of the spread of educational innovations is, in fact, a well-defined tradition within the study of the spread of innovations more generally. It can be argued, moreover, that the spread of any type of institutional adoption with respect to language, e.g., American cities' use of Spanish on municipal forms, can be studied within the framework of the study of the diffusion of innovations more generally. Thus it would seem useful to restrict the study of language spread to the phenomenon of individual adoptions and not to include the spread of institutional adoptions, although the latter ought clearly to be considered as a factor promoting the former.

THREE RELEVANT RESEARCH TRADITIONS

The research traditions most relevant to the study of language spread are research with respect to the diffusion of innovations, language maintenance and language shift, and language change.

Diffusion of Innovations

There is an immense literature on the diffusion of innovations. Most of this is in sociology (general sociology, rural sociology, and medical sociology), although a substantial number of innovation studies are found in anthropology, economics or marketing, education, mass communications, and public health. While the distinction between material and nonmaterial innovations is recognized (Ogburn 1922), most studies have been focused on the diffusion of material or physical products or processes. Language spread, which, of course, involves a nonmaterial innovation, has been largely ignored by students of diffusion. In Rogers and Shoemaker (1971), the standard text on the subject, there is no entry for language in the index. Of the approximately 2,750 publications in the Diffusion Documents Center at the Institute for Communication Research, Stanford University (see Rogers, Williams, and West 1977 for a bibliography of the collection), only two items concern the spread of linguistic innovations, both drawn from the 1949 volume of *American Speech,* one a single word, "shivaree" (Davis and McDavid 1949), the other a collection of lexical items used by oil workers (Boone 1949).

One of the major problems in diffusion research is the lack of a generally accepted scheme for classifying innovations so that the results obtained for one item are generalizable to others. "The trouble is that nobody is quite sure what dimensions of an item are relevant, and very little research has been done to try to find out" (Katz et al. 1963:244). Among the dimensions which have been suggested in diffusion research, in addition to the traditional distinction between material and nonmaterial, are (1) initial cost, (2) extent of anticipated profitability, (3) divisibility for trial (the possibility of using the innovation on a trial or limited basis), (4) complexity, and (5) pervasiveness (the extent to which adoption of the innovation creates ramifications in other spheres of life). Some of these can perhaps be applied to language. (For a different set of characteristics to classify a spreading language, see Scotton, this volume, who proposes the use of distinctive features, e.g., plus or minus "official.")

Initial cost might be operationalized as the amount of time required to learn the language for the purpose for which it is spreading. "Time required," in turn, might be related in part to the similarity between the structure of the languages the learner already knows and that of the spreading language. Thus, for example, one reason suggested for the success of Swahili is that most of its users have spoken Bantu languages to which it is related. Amount of time required to learn the language would also be related to the degree of proficiency required by the function for which the language is spreading as well as to the opportunities available for learning.

Extent of anticipated profitability could perhaps be operationalized as the degree to which the learner claims knowledge of the language for a given function will help advance him toward personally valued goals. A study of language attitudes among Israeli high school students (Cooper and Fishman 1977), for example, found that respondents who believed that knowledge of English helped them to reach important personal goals (e.g., making a good impression on other people, having interesting work to do) tended to know English better and to use it more than those who viewed English as being less helpful. However, this characteristic might better be viewed as a dependent variable—a form of adoption.

Divisibility for trial or "trialability" might be relevant to language spread in terms of the extent to which a learner feels free or unembarrassed to use the new language imperfectly. In Kampala (Scotton 1972), for example, no social stigma attaches to the use of broken Swahili whereas the use of broken English implies that the speaker has not gone to school long enough to learn the language well. It is plausible that this difference in social evaluation encourages the use of Swahili and discourages the use of English in Kampala.

Complexity can refer both to the language being learned and to the function which accompanies it. The item is presumably more complex when (1) the function for which the language is spreading as well as the language itself is new, (2) the degree of proficiency required by the function is high, and (3) the structural dissimilarity between the learner's language and the spreading language is high. Although "complexity" and "initial cost" ought to be highly related for language spread, they would not be perfectly related, inasmuch as individual differences in language-learning aptitude or in opportunities to learn would cause individual differences in cost but not in complexity.

Pervasiveness could apply to the frequency of the interactions for which the language is spreading, from the point of view of individual adopters. Thus a language spreading for interactions at work or at home would be a more pervasive item than a language spreading for domains in which the interactions are less frequent.

Katz et al. (1963) recommend that students of the diffusion of innovation pay attention to "value systems," as one set of factors related to an innovation's acceptance. Value systems refer to attitudes, values, and personality traits of individuals and of the groups to which they belong. The central importance of value systems is that of "compatibility" between the culture of a group or the personality of the individual, on the one hand, and the innovation on the other.

That value systems may be crucial for language spread seems clear. Mazrui (1971), for example, writes that the spread of English met initial resistance among Muslims south of the Sahara, in part, because of a tendency to associate English with Christianity. Inasmuch as Islam was

revealed through Arabic, and inasmuch as mission schools were important agents for the transmission of English, it was natural to assume that
English was the language of Christianity as well as a vehicle for its promotion. This association plus a general defensiveness toward European
culture created suspicion toward English. Similarly, the ancient association of Amharic with Coptic Christianity may have retarded the spread
of Amharic among Ethiopian Muslims. In contrast, Swahili's association
with Islam may have helped that language to spread because it has symbolized "a trans-national cultural pride and sense of dynastic historical
grandeur" (Mazrui 1971:195). While these examples have referred to
the perceived compatibility of the culture or group symbolized by the
language, compatibility can also refer to the function for which the language is spreading if the function is also new. Thus, for example, Syrian
missionaries helped to spread Giiz in ancient Abyssinia, and it is reasonable to suppose that groups for whom Christianity was relatively
compatible adopted Giiz earlier than groups for whom Christianity was
relatively incompatible.

The tradition of research on the diffusion of innovations is clearly
relevant to the study of language spread, particularly with respect to the
characteristics of the item which is spreading and the item's compatibility with group values. Language spread is, after all, the diffusion of an
innovation. The classical paradigm employed in diffusion research
seems, however, to be inappropriate for the analysis of language spread.
The basic model appears to consist of "two types of actors, an advocate
of change and a potential acceptor of change; the situations in which
these actors operate; communication between the actors; and the subject of that communication, a new idea or thing" (Fliegel and Kivlin
1966:235–36). In the words of Rogers (1962:13–14), "the diffusion
process consists of (1) a new idea, (2) individual A who knows about
the innovation, and (3) individual B who does not yet know about the
innovation. The social relationship of A and B has a great deal to say
about the condition under which A will tell B about the innovation and
the results of this telling." This paradigm emphasizes the channels of
communication along which information and persuasion flow. Thus the
work of Katz and Lazarsfeld (1957) on personal communication has
stimulated research on the two-step flow of communication, in which
mass media messages are followed by word-of-mouth communication
(Pool 1973). Rural sociologists have posited a two-step flow from
county agent to influential farmer to other farmers in the diffusion of
new farm practices (Katz et al. 1963), and students of mass communications have typically found that mass media channels are relatively
more important for imparting knowledge about an innovation and in-

terpersonal channels are more important in persuading the potential adopter to accept the innovation (Rao 1971).

The relevance of information and persuasion seems clear for innovations which must be accepted or rejected consciously, e.g., hybrid corn, chemical fertilizer, birth control practices, kindergartens, a new toothpaste. Is language such an innovation? Undoubtedly there are contexts in which the language spreads because of the conscious decision of people to learn it, particularly when adopters must enroll in classes or engage a tutor in order to do so. More than 115,000,000 persons are currently studying English in 106 non-English mother-tongue countries, excluding China (Gage and Ohannessian 1974), for example. Although for many of these students, the study of English is imposed (i.e., it is the sole medium of instruction or a required subject of instruction), for millions of others it is an elective subject, either within a course of other studies, or as a sole subject as, for example, in night-school classes for adults.

The spread of a language with respect to its usage may also be the result of conscious decisions. For example, many Jews in Palestine at the turn of the century, who used Hebrew for liturgical purposes and who occasionally used it as a lingua franca, began, for ideological reasons, to use Hebrew as the language of the home and as the language of their everyday interactions.

However, language proficiency and usage may spread without conscious attention on the part of adopters. When Swahili was penetrating the African interior, borne along trading routes by Swahili-speaking traders, it is likely that many who learned it, simply "picked it up" without conscious attention. The degree of proficiency required for its use in trade would not have been great, the language was related to others that the learners knew, and learners could probably speak it poorly without embarrassment. The learning could have been so gradual that learners may not have been particularly aware of their own accomplishment. If it is wrong to characterize the spread of Swahili for trade as operating below the level of consciousness (and this suggestion is obviously not made for its spread as a medium of instruction or political administration), it is probably also wrong to characterize it as the result of a deliberate decision, made in response to a flow of information and persuasion, analogous to a Colombian farmer's adoption of chemical fertilizer.

Of course the degree of consciousness involved in historical cases of language spread must usually remain a matter of speculation. But it is reasonable to suppose that languages can and do spread in a fashion for which the conventional diffusion paradigm is inappropriate. In Ireland, for example, after the solid establishment of English rule in the seventeenth century, the Irish "decided that there was no future in Irish and that, if they were to better themselves, they needed to know English. So they learned it" (Macnamara 1971:65). To explain the spread of English in Ireland, can we use a model in which individual A knew about English and individual B did not and in which A told B about it, after which B decided to accept or reject English? Even if B encountered many As and even if B's acceptance or rejection was not immediate, the model seems faulty. In the case of English in Ireland, the conclusion that "there was no future in Irish" is more likely to have come as a gradual awareness, implicitly recognized, than as an explicit decision whose implementation was planned. Further, the acceptance of English may have proceeded without a conscious attempt to seek or evaluate information about the language, whose usefulness, in any case, must have been obvious. Finally, B may have acquired English without any attempt by A to inform or to influence the potential adopter. B probably learned English by interacting with speakers of English who were indifferent as to whether A learned it or not. In short, B's acquisition and usage of English probably unfolded and developed gradually in response to the demands of the complex sociolinguistic contexts in which B participated, rather than in response to the flow of information and persuasion posited by the conventional diffusion model. Thus, to the extent that the model treats adoption as an explicit, conscious decision based upon information and persuasion transmitted interpersonally or through the mass media, it appears inappropriate for at least some cases of language spread.

Even if the classical paradigm were appropriate, however, there are several reasons for suggesting that language spread be studied in its own right. First, it is a nonmaterial innovation, whereas most items studied in diffusion research are material innovations. Second, language spread typically occurs over longer periods of time than most other innovations which are studied. Third, language spread involves a pervasive social change, whereas the innovations which are commonly studied are of less importance, although they may themselves trigger important social changes. Finally, the study of language spread can contribute not only to diffusion research but also to the sociology of language in general and to language maintenance and language shift in particular.

Language Maintenance and Language Shift

In the latest version of his seminal paper on language maintenance and language shift, Fishman (1972:76) defines the field as "the relationship between change (or stability) in language usage patterns, on the one hand, and ongoing psychological, social or cultural processes, on the other hand, in populations that utilize more than one speech variety for intra-group or for inter-group purposes." Whereas there can be no language spread without language shift, there can be language shift without language spread. A population which abandons a given communicative function or context (e.g., literacy, liturgy, contact with a given group) may abandon the language associated with it (if that language serves only that function for the population) without replacing the language with another. Although language shift can occur without language spread, most studies of language maintenance and language shift have focused on situations in which one language was advancing or threatening to advance and another language was retreating or under threat.

The two fields of inquiry differ on several grounds. First, studies of language maintenance and language shift usually focus upon the threatened language whereas studies of language spread focus upon the waxing language (Fishman 1977). Second, whereas the basic datum of language shift is "that some demonstrable change has occurred in the pattern of habitual language use" (Fishman 1972:76), language spread has several basic data: changes in awareness, evaluation, and proficiency, as well as in use. It is true that students of language maintenance and language shift are interested in changes in language attitude (including awareness and evaluation) and proficiency, but this is so because such changes are related to changes in language usage, either as antecedents or as consequences. Thus scholars of language maintenance and language shift employ attitudinal and proficiency variables to predict, explain, or reflect language shift rather than as dependent variables in their own right. A third difference is that language-maintenance and language-shift studies tend to be carried out in immigrant settings, whereas language-spread studies tend to be carried out among indigenous populations, although this difference is not a necessary one and there are exceptions to this generalization.

The contextualization of bilingual usage, which Fishman has stressed in his formulation of language maintenance and language shift as a field of inquiry and in his own research strategies, is important for the study of language spread. Fishman has pointed out that language usage may vary as a function of medium (written, read, and spoken language), role (encoding, decoding, inner speech), formality, and domain. It is the notion of domain which has perhaps had the greatest impact on language-maintenance and language-shift studies. A domain, according to Fishman, is a constellation of social situations (encounters defined by the intersection of the setting, the time, and the role-relationships of participants) that are constrained by a common set of behavioral rules. While *a priori* domains of social interaction may be offered, such as home, work place, formal education, and religion, their existence must be verified empirically for any given speech community. The usefulness of contextualization for the description of bilingual usage has been shown clearly (see especially Fishman, Cooper, and Ma 1975), and it is for this reason that the present paper has stressed the importance of treating separately each function for which a language is spreading.

The problem with applying domain analysis to the study of language spread is that domains are peculiar to a given speech community whereas language spread can be a between-group as well as a within-group phenomenon. If the population within which the language spreads is treated as a communication network, we could perhaps posit two types of domain: within-group and between-group domains. A between-group domain would be a set of social situations in which participants from different groups interact with one another and which are regulated by the same set of behavioral norms. Thus, if a communication network is composed of two groups, the contexts in which members of these groups participate could be classified into three sets: those peculiar to group A, those peculiar to group B, and those peculiar to between-group interaction. Whether or not domain analysis can be usefully applied to the study of language spread, work in language maintenance and language shift suggests to us the importance of finding some way to clarify and composite the myriad social interactions through which a language spreads.

One of the topical subdivisions of language maintenance and language shift is what Fishman (1972) calls behavior toward language. Part of this subdivision deals with organized efforts on behalf of language. Whether the locus of such efforts is found in official language-planning agencies or in voluntary organizations founded as part of "language movements," the activities of such bodies may accelerate or retard language spread. Those interested in language spread will therefore attempt to discover the impact of different types of effort (e.g., standardization, modernization, purification, elaboration, agitation, and policy decisions with respect to institutional use of language in, for example, schools, the police, the courts, parliament) on behalf of both the threatened and the spreading language. Also of interest will be the effects of different sorts of implementation of these efforts (e.g., the use of different types of mass media campaign, the use of field workers to disseminate neologisms) on language spread.

Language Change

A third research tradition relevant to language spread is the study of language change. Whether or not one subscribes to the notion of "language drift" (Sapir 1921), whereby a language changes in accordance with the unconscious selections of speakers of those random variations which follow a direction predetermined by the structure of the language and its history of development and change, all language change can be viewed as the outcome of diffusion. In some cases the innovations may arise from language borrowing, which Haugen (1950:230) defines as "the process that takes place when bilinguals reproduce a pattern from one language in another." In other cases, the innovations may arise from variation in the speech of monolinguals. Whether or not the innovations arise from languages in contact, innovations introduced by some speakers are adopted by others. We know little about the social circumstances which promote or retard the spread of linguistic innovations, although linguists have hypothesized that such changes spread as a function of degree of verbal interaction and the relative prestige which one speaker has for another. Bloomfield's (1933:46–47, 403) statement is perhaps the prototype of this view:

> The most important differences of speech within a community are due to differences in *density of communication* . . . imagine a huge chart with a dot for every speaker in the community, and imagine that every time any speaker uttered a sentence, an arrow were drawn into the chart pointing from his dot to the dot representing each one of his hearers. At the end of a given period of time, say seventy years, this chart would show us the density of communication within the community . . . We believe that the differences in density of communication within a speech-community are not only personal and individual, but that the community is divided into various systems of sub-groups, such that the persons within a sub-group speak much more to each other than to persons outside their sub-group. Viewing the system of arrows as a network, we may say that these sub-groups are separated by *lines of weakness* in this net of oral communication. The lines of weakness and, accordingly, the differences of speech within a speech-community are *local,* due to mere geographical separation, and *non-local* or as we usually say, *social.* . . . The most powerful force of all in fluctuation works quite outside the linguist's reach: the speaker favors the forms which he has heard from certain other speakers who, for some reason of prestige, influence his habits of speech. . . . In the ideal diagram of density of communication, we should have to distinguish the arrows that lead from each speaker to his hearers by gradations representing the prestige of the speaker with reference to each hearer. If we had a diagram with the arrows thus weighted, we could doubtless predict, to a large extent, the future frequencies of linguistic forms.

Bloomfield's schema prefigures the work of communication theorists in its description of a communication network ("sub-groups are separated by lines of weakness in this net of oral communication"). And in his specification of interpersonal relationships as crucial for the process of change, he anticipates as well the work of researchers in the diffusion of innovation. One of the rare studies that tested his notions about change was that of Gumperz (1958), who described the relationship between dialect differences and social stratification in Khalapur, a village in North India. Gumperz found that simple frequency of social interaction could not account for the different dialects spoken in Khalapur. "Among Sweepers," who speak the most divergent dialect, "women devote most of the day to cleaning the houses and cattle compounds of the village, and much of that time is consumed in gossiping with and listening to the conversations of their employers," who speak the majority dialect (679). Gumperz believed that dialect differentiation in that village can best be explained on the basis of informal, friendship contacts. Thus it is not frequency but type of interaction, not relative prestige but friendship which appear to have been operating in Khalapur.

Labov's work (1963, 1966, 1972) also supports the importance of solidarity values in the maintenance or change of linguistic features. Identification with one's own group can either facilitate or retard change depending on which contributes more to the maintenance of group distinctiveness.

Most students of language change have focused on linguistic properties as sources and mediators of change. Relatively few have studied the social contexts in which language change occurs, which may explain why students of diffusion have ignored the vast literature on language change. However, most students of language change have also ignored the literature on the diffusion of innovations. One exception is Afendras (1969), who proposed that mathematical models of diffusion, based on density of communication, be used to describe the diffusion of linguistic items and to predict the relative influence that the structure of one language will have on another.

Another exception is Allony-Fainberg's (1977) work on the acceptance of neologisms proposed by the Academy of the Hebrew Language. She studied the characteristics of Israelis who were most likely to have accepted neologisms as well as the characteristics of terms which were most likely to have been accepted. She found greater acceptance among women and the better educated and lesser acceptance among the young. With respect to characteristics of the innovations themselves, she found that word length was not related to acceptance but that the number of words built on the same root was related to acceptance. Innovations formed from roots on which relatively few or relatively many *other* words were built tended to be accepted less than innovations formed from roots on which an intermediate number of other words (four or five) were built. She suggested that neologisms based on roots with relatively few words were less conspicuous and thus less readily learned whereas neologisms based on roots with relatively more words may tend to become confused with their cognates. Her work explicitly recognizes the acceptance of neologisms as an example of the diffusion of innovation and it draws on this tradition in employing different types of dependent variable marking acceptance (claimed awareness, claimed knowledge, claimed usage, claimed attitude, and tested knowledge).

The study of language spread can benefit from the study of language change to the extent that the latter concerns itself with social as distinguished from purely linguistic variables. Both language spread and language change involve the diffusion of innovation. In both cases the innovation is linguistic. In both cases, the innovation may acquire symbolic associations which can either retard or promote its spread. There may be of course important differences with respect to the rate of spread, the shape of diffusion curves, and the processes underlying spread. Until we know more than we do about either of these diffusionary phenomena, however, we cannot be sure what those differences are.

A CHECKLIST FOR THE STUDY OF LANGUAGE SPREAD

We are probably at a primitive enough stage of our understanding of language spread to be content with seeking answers to questions about relationships, although our ultimate purpose is to understand the reason for the observed relationships. Thus, for example, Brosnahan (1963) has suggested four factors as being positively associated with the spread of Arabic, Greek, and Latin: military conquest, duration of military authority, linguistic diversity of the population through which the language spreads, and material advantages associated with knowledge of the new language. Fishman, Cooper, and Rosenbaum (1977) found that the variables related to the status of English in approximately one hundred non-English mother-tongue countries included, in addition to Brosnahan's variables, urbanization, economic and educational development, and religious composition, although the direction of the relationship depended on the dependent variable employed, whether enrollment in English classes in the country as a whole or the use of English by state institutions.

We can perhaps summarize our questions about relationships as follows: (1) What variables are related to the extent and rate of language spread? (2) With what variables are differences in the shapes of diffusion curves associated? (3) What variables distinguish early adopters, late adopters, and nonadopters? (4) To what extent do the answers to questions 1–3 above differ for the diffusion of innovations in general and from the diffusion of linguistic (e.g., phonological, syntactic, lexical) innovations in particular? For each of these questions we can ask about the individual contribution of each variable as well as about the joint or cumulative contribution of all variables to the prediction of the criterion variable. Each of these questions can of course be asked for communication networks of varying sizes and types. We can collapse these four questions into a single summarizing question that serves as a framework for the study of language spread: *who adopts what, when, why, and how?*

This framework provides us with rubrics for topics of research that are relevant to language spread. Some of these topics are listed below.

1. *Who*

a. What characteristics (e.g., position within the communication network, need-achievement, openness to change) distinguish adopters from nonadopters and early adopters from late adopters?

b. What characteristics (e.g., linguistic heterogeneity, size, complexity) distinguish communication networks through which a language spreads rapidly from networks through which it spreads slowly or not at all?

2. *Adopts*

a. Do different levels of adoption (awareness, evaluation, knowledge, usage) spread at different rates and to different extents?

b. Do the levels of adoption necessarily form a scale whereby awareness serves as a prerequisite for evaluation, evaluation for knowledge, and knowledge for usage?

3. *What*

a. What structural characteristics (e.g., diversity of the variety that must be learned, similarity to varieties in the potential adopter's verbal repertoire) are associated with differences in the extent and rate of adoption?

b. What functional characteristics (e.g., skills required, between-group versus within-group interaction, interaction with respect to horizontal versus vertical integration) are associated with differences in the extent and rate of adoption?

4. *When*

a. How much time is required for a given language variety to be adopted by a given communication network under given conditions?

b. What characteristics are associated with differences in the shape of diffusion curves?

5. *Where*

a. What kinds of social interaction within what types of societal domain promote or retard the acceptance of innovation?

b. What are the characteristics of those individuals who are likely to be influential as agents of change with respect to what types of adopter and for what levels of adoption?

6. *Why*

a. What national and personal incentives for planners to promote (or hinder) language spread are related to differences in the extent and rate of spread?

b. What incentives for potential adopters to accept (or reject) a language variety are related to differences in the extent and rate of spread?

7. *How*

a. What language-planning activities are most likely to be successful for different types of adopter at different levels of adoption, through different types of change agent, and under different sociopolitical and economic conditions?

While it may be difficult to operationalize some of the variables which are employed in these questions, particularly when studied in connection with large social aggregates, it seems worth the effort, inasmuch as such operationalization will enable us to compare the results of different studies of language spread to each other and to studies of diffusion more generally. We cannot know what variables will be revealing unless we develop a common framework for their use. The framework presented here is offered as a contribution toward that end.

REFERENCES

Afendras, Evangelos A. Sociolinguistic history, sociolinguistic geography and bilingualism. In Second International Congress of Social Sciences of the Luigi Sturzo Institute, *International Days of Sociolinguistics*. Rome: Luigi Sturzo Institute, 1969. Pp. 663–82.

Allony-Fainberg, Yaffa. Linguistic and socio-demographic factors influencing the acceptance of Hebrew neologisms. Unpublished doctoral dissertation. Jerusalem: The Hebrew University of Jerusalem, 1977. (in Hebrew)

Arès, Richard. Comportement linguistique des minorités françaises au Canada-I. *Relations*, 1964a, April, 108–10.

Arès, Richard. Comportement linguistique des minorités françaises au Canada-II. *Relations*, 1964b, May, 141–44.

Bachi, Roberto. A statistical analysis of the revival of Hebrew in Israel. *Scripta Hierosolymitana.* Vol. 3. Jerusalem: The Hebrew University of Jerusalem, 1956. Pp. 179–247.

Bender, M. Lionel, Charles A. Ferguson, and others. Introduction. In M. L. Bender, J. D. Bowen, R. L. Cooper, and C. A. Ferguson (Eds.), *Language in Ethiopia.* London: Oxford University Press, 1976. Pp. 1–19.

Bloomfield, Leonard. *Language.* New York: Holt, 1933.

Boone, Lalia P. Patterns of innovation in the language of the oil field. *American Speech,* 1949, 24, 31–37.

Brosnahan, L. F. Some historical cases of language imposition. In J. Spencer (Ed.), *Language in Africa.* Cambridge: Cambridge University Press, 1963. Pp. 7–24.

Coleman, James S., Elihu Katz, and Herbert Menzel. The diffusion of an innovation among physicians. *Sociometry,* 1957, 20, 253–70.

Cooper, Robert L. The spread of Amharic. In M. L. Bender, J. D. Bowen, R. L. Cooper, and C. A. Ferguson (Eds.), *Language in Ethiopia.* London: Oxford University Press, 1976. Pp. 287–301.

Cooper, Robert L. and Susan Carpenter. Linguistic diversity in the Ethiopian market. *Journal of African Languages,* 1969, 8 (part 3), 160–68.

Cooper, Robert L. and Joshua A. Fishman. A study of language attitudes. *The Bilingual Review,* 1977, 4, (1 and 2), 7–34.

Cooper, Robert L. and Ronald J. Horvath. Language, migration, and urbanization. In M. L. Bender, J. D. Bowen, R. L. Cooper, and C. A. Ferguson (Eds.), *Language in Ethiopia.* London: Oxford University Press, 1976. Pp. 191–212.

Cooper, Robert L. and Fern Seckbach. Economic incentives for the learning of a language of wider communication: a case study. In J. A. Fishman, R. L. Cooper, and A. W. Conrad, *The Spread of English: The Sociology of English as an Additional Language.* Rowley: Newbury House, 1977. Pp. 212–19.

Cooper, Robert L., B. N. Singh, and Abraha Ghermazion. Mother tongue and other tongue in Kefa and Arusi. In M. L. Bender, J. D. Bowen, R. L. Cooper, and C. A. Ferguson (Eds.), *Language in Ethiopia.* London: Oxford University Press, 1976. Pp. 213–43.

Davis, Alva L. and Raven I. McDavid. 'Shivaree': an example of cultural diffusion. *American Speech,* 1949, 24, 249–55.

Fishman, Joshua A. Language maintenance and language shift as a field of inquiry: revisited. *Language in Sociocultural Change.* Stanford: Stanford University Press, 1972. Pp. 76–134.

Fishman, Joshua A. The spread of English as a new perspective for the study of 'language maintenance and language shift'. In J. A. Fishman, R. L. Cooper, and A. W. Conrad, *The Spread of English: the Sociology of English as an Additional Language.* Rowley: Newbury House, 1977. Pp. 108–33.

Fishman, Joshua A., Robert L. Cooper, and Andrew W. Conrad. *The Spread of English: the Sociology of English as an Additional Language.* Rowley: Newbury House, 1977.

Fishman, Joshua A., Robert L. Cooper, and Roxana Ma. *Bilingualism in the Barrio.* Second edition. Language Science Monographs. Vol. 7. Bloomington: Indiana University Publications, 1975.

Fishman, Joshua A., Robert L. Cooper, and Yehudit Rosenbaum. English the world over: a factor in the creation of bilingualism today. In P.A. Hornby

(Ed.), *Bilingualism: Psychological, Social, and Educational Implications.* New York: Academic Press, 1977. Pp. 103–39.

Fliegel, Frederick C. and Joseph E. Kivlin. Attributes of innovations as factors in diffusion. *The American Journal of Sociology*, 1966, 72, 235–48.

Gage, William W. and Sirarpi Ohannessian. ESOL enrollments throughout the world. *The Linguistic Reporter*, 1974, 16, (1), 13–16.

Greenberg, Joseph H. Urbanism, migration, and language. In H. Kuper (Ed.), *Urbanization and Migration in West Africa.* Berkeley: University of California Press, 1965. Pp. 50–59, 189.

Gumperz, John J. Dialect differences and social stratification in a North Indian village. *American Anthropologist,* 1958, 60, 668–81.

Gumperz, John J. Linguistic and social interaction in two communities. In J. J. Gumperz and Dell Hymes (Eds.), The ethnography of communication. *American Anthropologist*, 1964, 66, 6 (part 2), 137–54.

Haugen, Einar. The analysis of linguistic borrowing. *Language*, 1950, 26, 210–31.

Heath, Shirley Brice. *Telling Tongues: Language Policy in Mexico: Colony to Nation.* New York: Teachers College Press, 1972.

Heath, Shirley Brice and Richard Laprade. Castilian colonization and indigenous languages: the cases of Quechua and Aymara. This volume.

Heine, Bernd. *Status and Use of African Lingua Francas.* Munich: Weltforum Verlag, 1970.

Hofman, John E. and Haya Fisherman. Language shift and language maintenance in Israel. *International Migration Review*, 1971, 5, 204–26.

Katz, Elihu and Paul Lazarsfeld. The two-step flow of communication: an up-to-date report on an hypothesis. *Public Opinion Quarterly*, 1957, 21, 61–78.

Katz, Elihu, Martin L. Levin, and Herbert Hamilton. Traditions of research on the diffusion of innovation. *American Sociological Review*, 1963, 28, 237–52.

Labov, William. The social motivation of a sound change. *Word*, 1963, 19, 273–309.

Labov, William. *The Social Stratification of English in New York City.* Washington: Center for Applied Linguistics, 1966.

Labov, William. The linguistic consequences of being a lame. *Language in the Inner City: Studies in the Black English Vernacular.* Philadelphia: University of Pennsylvania Press, 1972. Pp. 255–92.

Lewis, E. Glyn. *Multilingualism in the Soviet Union: Aspects of Language Policy and Its Implementation.* The Hague: Mouton, 1972.

Lewis, E. Glyn. Bilingualism and bilingual education: the ancient world to the Renaissance. In J. A. Fishman, *Bilingual Education: an International Sociological Perspective.* Rowley: Newbury House, 1976. Pp. 150–201.

Lewis, E. Glyn. Movements and agencies of language spread: Wales and the Soviet Union compared. This volume.

Lieberson, Stanley. *Language and Ethnic Relations in Canada.* New York: John Wiley and Sons, 1970.

McGuire, William J. The nature of attitudes and attitude change. In G. Lindsey and E. Aronson (Eds.), *The Handbook of Social Psychology.* Second edition. Vol. 3. Reading: Addison-Wesley, 1969. Pp. 136–314.

Macnamara, John. Successes and failures in the movement for the restoration of Irish. In J. Rubin and B. H. Jernudd (Eds.), *Can Language Be Planned?*

Sociolinguistic Theory and Practice for Developing Nations. Honolulu: The University Press of Hawaii, 1971. Pp. 65–94.

Macnamara, John. Attitudes and learning a second language. In R. W. Shuy and R. W. Fasold (Eds.), *Language Attitudes: Current Trends and Prospects.* Washington: Georgetown University Press, 1973. Pp. 36–40.

Mazrui, Ali. Islam and the English language in East and West Africa. In W. H. Whiteley (Ed.), *Language Use and Social Change: Problems of Multilingualism with Special Reference to Eastern Africa.* London: Oxford University Press, 1971. Pp. 179–97.

Mazrui, Ali and Pio Zirimu. Church, state, and marketplace in the spread of Kiswahili: comparative educational implications. In B. Spolsky and R. L. Cooper (Eds.), *Case Studies in Bilingual Education.* Rowley: Newbury House, 1978. Pp. 427–53.

Nadel, Elizabeth, Joshua A. Fishman, and Robert L. Cooper. English in Israel: a sociolinguistic study. *Anthropological Linguistics*, 1977, *19*, 26–53.

Ogburn, William F. *Social Change.* New York: Viking Press, 1922.

Paper, Herbert H. Language spread: the ancient Near Eastern world. This volume.

Pool, Ithiel de Sola. Communication systems. In I. de Sola Pool, F. W. Frey, W. Schramm, N. Maccoby, and E. B. Parker (Eds.), *Handbook of Communication.* Chicago: Rand McNally, 1973. Pp. 3–26.

Rao, L. J. Generalizations about the diffusion of innovations. In E. M. Rogers and F. F. Shoemaker, *Communication of Innovations: a Cross-Cultural Approach.* Second edition. New York: Free Press, 1971. Appendix A.

Rogers, Everett M. *Diffusion of Innovations.* New York: Free Press of Glencoe, 1962.

Rogers, Everett M. and F. Floyd Shoemaker. *Communication of Innovations: a Cross-Cultural Approach.* Second edition. New York: Free Press, 1971.

Rogers, Everett M., Linda Williams, and Rhonda B. West. *Bibliography of the Diffusion of Innovations.* Council of Planning Librarians Exchange Bibliography 1420, 1421, and 1422. Monticello (Illinois): Council of Planning Librarians, 1977.

Sapir, Edward. *Language: an Introduction to the Study of Speech.* New York: Harcourt, Brace & World, 1921.

Scotton, Carol M. *Choosing a Lingua Franca in an African Capital.* Edmonton and Champaign: Linguistic Research, 1972.

Scotton, Carol M. Learning lingua francas and socioeconomic integration: evidence from Africa. This volume.

Tabouret-Keller, André. Sociological factors of language maintenance and language shift: a methodological approach based on European and African examples. In J. A. Fishman, C. A. Ferguson, and J. Das Gupta (Eds.), *Language Problems of Developing Nations.* New York: John Wiley and Sons, 1968. Pp. 107–18.

Tabouret-Keller, André. A contribution to the sociological study of language maintenance and language shift. In J. A. Fishman (Ed.), *Advances in the Sociology of Language.* Vol. 2. The Hague: Mouton, 1972. Pp. 365–76.

Ullendorff, Edward. *The Ethiopians: an Introduction to Country and People.* Second edition. London: Oxford University Press, 1965.

Warner, Kenneth E. The need for some innovative concepts of innovation: an examination of research on the diffusion of innovations. *Policy Sciences*, 1974, 5, 433–51.

Whiteley, Wilfred. *Swahili: the Rise of a National Language.* Studies in African History, 3. London: Methuen, 1969.

Zaltman, Gerald and Ronald Stiff. Theories of diffusion. In S. Ward and T. S. Robertson (Eds.), *Consumer Behavior: Theoretical Sources.* Englewood Cliffs: Prentice-Hall, 1973. Pp. 416–68.

Forces Affecting Language Spread: Some Basic Propositions*

Stanley Lieberson

Language spread is nothing more than a reshaping of the existing pattern of language acquisition and usage. It sometimes occurs because new functions are created, for example, the communication needs generated in airplane traffic control, but usually it occurs because one language replaces another either for some specific existing function or in a broader more general fashion, covering a wide variety of domains. What causes a language to expand? This is a question for which propositions and principles may be sought. It is very different from the task of explaining the specific set of linguistic usages observed in a given setting, because the present-day social correlates of an established and stable pattern of language practices need not account for its origins. Although it is almost certain that changes in the pattern of language usage can ultimately be traced back to societal shifts, it does not follow that the current social correlates of a relatively stable set of linguistic usages will provide very many clues to understanding the earlier *changes* that led to the present pattern of language usage.

This seeming paradox is due to a simple but overlooked fact, namely the social causes of linguistic phenomena need no longer be present after the language pattern is firmly established. In other words the products of social events have a life of their own. Once a language acquisition and usage pattern is established, then a set of norms, traditions, and expectations is generated about the language used in the marketplace, or the language given prestige and esteemed, or whatever. But these expectations and notions of propriety are not necessarily the

*Support from the Ford Foundation is gratefully acknowledged. My initial formulation of the problem benefited from helpful discussions with Adrienne Lehrer, Department of Linguistics, University of Arizona.

forces which initially created the language pattern. It is certainly interesting to know the nature of the societal shifts occurring after a linguistic change takes place, but the current set of social expectations did not necessarily precede and cause the linguistic shifts covered under the phrase "language spread." Put another way, those social events preceding a linguistic shift are different from those which follow from the shift, and merging the two can only cause confusion. The origins of a given language pattern cannot be exlained through the social facts associated with its present use. It is the past causes that have led to the present-day acceptance that are of significance, not the current social processes which maintain it.

It follows that the study of language spread is concerned with empirically determining which forces disrupt an existing set of language acquisition and usage patterns. This determination may take several paths, none of which is easy to pursue. One way is to explain the broad non-linguistic changes that in turn will significantly influence the existing set of language usages in the area under consideration—whether that be the community, a region, a nation, or indeed the world. Such a task is likely to take one into the realm of major social, political, technological, demographic, and economic changes—activities which are best left to those with specialized skills and knowledge. A second task takes these societal changes as "givens" and, without seeking to explain their origins, tries to comprehend the ways in which such shifts affect the existing pattern of language acquisition. One does not generate notions of what causes nationalism, industrialization, changing intergroup relations, etc., because this would be too massive a task, but rather one asks how such events affect the existing set of language usage patterns.

A third possible course is to study linguistic shifts that occur as a consequence of other linguistic shifts. For example, if language A is now used by an increasing proportion of the population of As because of nationalism or some other cause, then non-As may be forced to learn and use the tongue as well, which will have further linguistic consequences, and so forth. Or the usage of language B by the prestigeful members of the community may have consequences for the likelihood that B will be employed by members of other groups. There are a multitude of such interesting questions about the further linguistic consequences once a given linguistic change is generated by societal forces.

Unfortunately, it is more difficult than one might think to determine the linkage between societal cause and linguistic effect. Suppose, for heuristic purposes, it is assumed that no societal changes will occur henceforth. How long would it take for a linguistic equilibrium to become established such that the pattern of language acquisition and usage remained stable in every setting? It would probably not be until some distant point in time because presumably some of the events that occurred in recent decades (and possibly much longer ago than that) would not have worked themselves out yet in terms of their linguistic consequences, for example, the influence of an earlier literacy or education drive on language acquisition. Moreover, the linguistic shifts that occur as a consequence of other linguistic shifts might not have developed fully yet. Thus, one faces a serious problem in any attempt to study linguistic spread over time, to wit, one is dealing with the consequences of both past and more recent societal changes and it is extremely difficult, indeed probably close to impossible, to sort out empirically what is going on unless one has a very clear understanding theoretically of what to expect.

It is the second and third tasks that I wish to pursue here. Working primarily with international data, I wish to suggest several processes and linkages of the most elementary sort between societal change and the spread of language, including both the direct influence of social organization as well as the indirect influence that occurs when one linguistic change generates another change in the existing pattern of acquisition and usage.

THE CONSERVATION OF
LANGUAGE USAGE

Once established, the existing pattern of language usage will tend to perpetuate itself in situations which, had they existed earlier, would never have generated the same language pattern. This is because a series of expectations and adaptations is created which then perpetuates the language pattern. Once language A is established as the medium of communication in the marketplace for speakers of B and C, then simple shifts in the numbers of A, B, and C speakers will not generate a comparable change in the marketplace language pattern, because a set of understandings has arisen which tends to perpetuate A. It is these forces which generate what might be called the conservation of language usage.

Consider, for example, the role of French, English, and Spanish in international conferences. Latin had served as the lingua franca in the western half of the Roman Empire (Greek in the eastern half) and continued to serve as such in western Eruope well into the Middle Ages (Encyclopaedia Britannica, 1975, p. 656). By the seventeenth century, the language of diplomatic interchange was French. (The processes by which it succeeded Latin and edged out Italian and Spanish are well worth studying in terms of the questions at hand.) According to Butler and Maccoby (1928, p. 35), eighteenth-century negotiations were held almost exclusively in French. At the Congress of Vienna, the victors employed French not only in dealing with the defeated France, but also among themselves—indeed the treaty was written in that language. It was only at the close of World War I that English received important recognition as an equal to French in diplomacy. At the first assembly of the League of Nations, it was proposed that Spanish should also be made an official language, along with French and English, but this was defeated. Why did French enjoy this powerful position long at the expense of English? Secondly, why was Spanish still unable to move into a position of equality?

The linguistic patterns of "third parties" are a key factor in the conservation of language usage in the face of any potential change in existing patterns. Neither the number of native speakers nor the number of nations with French as the official language would have given that tongue a particular claim or advantage over English or Spanish as a medium of communication in the League. However, the neutral parties were crucial: French had become the established and accepted international language, and hence persons with neither English nor French mother tongue were far more apt to learn the latter language. Once established, there was little reason to shift. In 1920 English was spoken in the League of Nations Assembly by delegates from six nations in which English was not an official language, whereas French was used by delegates from twenty-four nations besides those from France, Haiti, Belgium, Canada, and Switzerland (Shenton, 1933, p. 381). By 1927, the numbers were even less favorable to English, with only two countries using that language, in addition to those from nations with English as an official language. (These and other remarkable statistics on language usage in international conferences were gathered by Herbert Newhard Shenton, a professor of sociology at Syracuse University and an advocate for an international auxiliary language.)

The defeat of Spanish as an international language may likewise be viewed in terms of the alternative linguistic systems already established. Of the eighteen nations in the first assembly of the League of Nations proposing that Spanish should be one of the official languages, all but four were Spanish-speaking countries (see World Peace Foundation, 1921, p. 27). Why was there such indifference to Spanish on the part of other nations? (Curiously, three of the four non-Spanish nations signing this proposal had French as an official language—Belgium, Haiti, Switzerland, as well as Denmark.) A clue may be had by looking at the linguistic practices of the sixteen original members of the League whose official language was neither English, French, nor Spanish. As a rough measure of their linguistic policy, I looked at the language(s) used for publishing official census volumes (chosen because the titles to such volumes are readily available to me in a series of books published by the Population Research Center, University of Texas). Information on the languages used in the census reports of China and Thailand in the late nineteenth and early twentieth centuries is not available from this source (see Population Research Center, University of Texas, 1966, p. 10-1 and p. 41-1). But for the vast bulk of the remaining "third party" nations, linguistically speaking, French is used along with the national language in the census titles. This is the case for Poland, Iran, Czechoslovakia, Greece (as early as 1870), Japan, the Netherlands, Norway (as early as 1835), Yugoslavia, and Sweden. It was not the case for Brazil, Denmark, Italy, Portugal, and Rumania. But in each of these cases, no other language was used besides the national one. In other words, it is clear that French had gained widespread acceptance and usage for such international functions. In turn, these "third-party" nations help to prevent change.

The conservation of language usage, in summary, is brought about not merely because a set of rules, understandings, and norms evolves after a language adoption occurs, but in addition because rival languages must compete not only with native speakers of the established tongue(s), but also with those linguistic "third parties" who also have a stake in the maintenance of the existing usage pattern. It is often the case that these third parties develop almost as much linguistic commitment to one language as do the native speakers. For example, in the past the non-English and non-French immigrants to Quebec very strongly favored English over French in their acquisition of an official mother tongue (Lieberson, 1970). Consequently, the French Canadians are now attempting to force those new immigrants who speak neither English nor French to become French-speaking.

POWER AND PRESTIGE: GENERAL OBSERVATIONS

Obviously, despite these conservative influences, the patterns of language usage do change; there are forces which overcome the inertia which exists in each sociolinguistic setting. Languages do not differ among themselves in their inherent power, but the users of languages do. Accordingly, the carriers of different languages differ in their ability to alter the existing language-usage pattern, thereby affecting the spread of languages. The term "power" and related concepts must be used with great caution. First, it is of little value simply to label situations of linguistic change as being due to changing power relations, even if there is good reason to believe they are due to such changes. Rather it is important to have a clear understanding of the precise mechanisms whereby such influence occurs, bearing in mind at all times that the power need not have been explicitly exercised. In applying the power concept one runs the risk of generating circular arguments that, on the surface, appear to explain the spread of a given language, but which in reality offer no explanation whatsoever. Such circular reasoning occurs when the investigator determines, without an independent empirical measurement of power, that shifts in language usage and adoption are due to changes in power among the speakers, nations, or other corporate bodies associated with these tongues. The reasoning employed is circular in that the very shift in language usage is taken to be evidence of differential power among the groups involved.

There are, of course, circumstances in which pure and naked power does operate to affect language usage—the events leading up to the League of Nations being an example. The observations of David Hunter Miller, a Technical Adviser to the American Mission which prepared the Covenant creating the League of Nations, are of great value here (1928a, b). Not only was the role of English rather enhanced by the fact that the United States and Britain were on the winning side, but moreover the usage of English as an equivalent to French was very much due to the position of influence enjoyed by Woodrow Wilson, the American President. "Almost all the diplomats present from countries other than Great Britain, the United States and Japan, spoke and understood French" (Miller, 1928a, p. 505). Earlier, he observed:

> The formal decision that "the Peace Treaty should be printed in French and English languages, which should be the official languages of the Treaty" was made on April 25 by the Council of Four. Much as the French wished otherwise, the British and American participation in the War and in its settlement and the presence of President Wilson in Paris made it inevitable that the English language should be an official language of the Treaty of Peace. Naturally the decision was one which the French greatly regretted not only in itself but also because the writing of the Treaty of Versailles in French and in English of equal validity made those two languages the official languages of the League of Nations and also the official languages of the Permanent Court of International Justice, and perhaps to some extent marked the passing of French as the chief medium of diplomatic intercourse. (1928a, p. 505)

Incidentally, the fact that the United States never did join the League of Nations and that its preference for English was hence totally irrelevant is further evidence for the contention made earlier that a given set of linguistic practices may continue on long after the disappearance of the events which initially caused the practice. At any rate, it is necessary to give a very close and precise consideration of the various ways by which power affects changes in linguistic usage—merely waving the term about is of little analytical value.

As for the prestige enjoyed by a language and the consequences this has for its diffusion, I am inclined to believe that such rankings are a function, not of any inherent qualities of the tongues, but for the most part of the speakers of such tongues or of the groups associated with the languages. For the most part we have learned that certain languages (or dialects within a language) are attractive, appealing, and generate our admiration and bestow prestige on its speakers. These responses are so thoroughly socialized that we are apt to attribute certain inherently esthetic qualities to some languages and inherently unattractive ones to others. But the social origin of these responses is no different from those determining the responses different foods generate in a given society, with some highly appealing, others relatively neutral, and others absolutely repulsive. One can conclude that attitudes towards a given language reflect a set of intergroup relationships, that are either on-going or that existed in an earlier period. As such, attitudes towards specific languages are essentially intervening variables in the case of language spread rather than fundamental causal factors. If there are radical attitudinal shifts towards a language which affect its spread, it is almost certain that underlying such attitudinal changes are shifts in intergroup relations, nationalism, and the like.

INTERACTION

Changes in the frequency and nature of the interaction between and within language groups is one of the major ways through which the existing pattern of language usage is altered. Because increased interaction exposes a group to the influence of other languages, while at the same time expanding the potential impact of its language on other speakers, as a general rule the existing pattern of language usage will change as interaction changes. Indeed the power of a group to influence language usage is only a *potential* force if the group is completely isolated; it is only through interaction with other populations that this potential is transformed into events which alter the existing language practices and thereby affect the spread and contraction of different tongues.

Interaction both within and between nations has increased dramatically in recent decades, due to technological improvements in transportation and communication. Consequently, one would expect changes in language usage that reflect the new intensity of interaction. Higher standards of living coupled with newer and cheaper forms of communication and transportation have made it possible for increased contact within and between nations. The post-World War II era has been marked by a massive expansion in the role of English in a variety of domains, particularly in science and business. To a striking degree, one can show that this shift in language usage, namely the expansion of English, is closely linked to the changes in the intensity and nature of commercial interaction. I will consider some of these financial changes, because I believe they help to suggest a number of hypotheses about the role of interaction in language spread. Although my concern here is primarily with international forms of interaction, the hypotheses are applicable to interaction on the local and subnational plane as well.

In the pre-World War I period, among the twenty-nine leading nations in international trade, there were nine English-speaking countries which received slightly more than one-third of the entire world's imports (Australia, Canada, British India, Ireland, British Malaya, New Zealand, South Africa, United Kingdom, and the United States). By contrast the four nations that can be classified as French-speaking in the list (Belgium, Canada—which is included for both English and French—France, and Switzerland) accounted for 16.7 percent of the world's imports. The two major German-speaking nations, Germany and Switzerland, received 13.8 percent and five Spanish-speaking nations (Argentina, Chile, Cuba, Mexico, and Venezuela) received 4.0 percent. Clearly the English-speaking world was the most significant international market, as measured by the value of their imports (ignoring, for the moment, the intralanguage imports that occur). The prominence of English increased by 1927 to the point where these same nine countries received 40.6 percent of the world's imports. French declined to 13.1 percent and German declined to 11.3 percent, with Spanish increasing slightly to 4.4 percent (all of these figures are computed from data reported in United States Department of Commerce, 1928, p. 742). By 1938 the English-speaking figure had dropped somewhat to 37.2 percent (based on data reported in United Nations, 1976, Special Table A).

The expansion of English as a commercial language during the post-World War II period was not accompanied by an expansion in the importance of such English-speaking nations in world trade. In point of fact, the nine nations in which English was either an official language or had been an official language during the colonial period accounted for only 27.9 percent of the world's imports in 1974, a rather considerable drop from the figures earlier in the century (which ranged from 35 to 41 percent). By contrast the French-speaking figure had actually increased somewhat from 1927 to 15.3 percent—albeit still below the 1911–13 level. German in 1974 amounted to 11.1 percent (figures based on the same source as used for 1938). In other words, the importance of English as a world trade language increased during a period in which these English-speaking nations declined as importers. How does one explain this? Certainly the English-speaking component of world trade is not the only indicator of international commerce. Moreover, non-English speakers may have been influenced by other factors in their shift to English, for example, the growth of English as a language for science and technology. Perhaps the dominant influence of the United States immediately after World War II was responsible for getting English going.

One major force for the expansion of English as a commercial language during the post-World War II period was the changing level of interaction. Although the role of these English-speaking nations declined, the importance of world trade itself increased considerably. This tremendous growth in world trade is illustrated with some index figures provided by the United Nations (1976, p. 96). Between 1948 and 1974, the value of all exports in the world was multiplied by more than six, from an index of 22 to an index of 139. By contrast the production of primary commodities merely doubled (from an index of 55 to 108) and even manufacturing was only multiplied by four during the period (from an index of 30 to 121). Clearly international trade became increasingly important to the nations of the world. In other words, the intensity of interaction went up even though the relative importance of English declined. International trade was more important than ever before, and hence the relevance of learning additional languages was greater than earlier. English was still by far the single most important language, and thus its power or strength increased through increasing interaction. In this regard, a modest correlation in the expected direction of .38 is reported by Fishman, Cooper, and Rosenbaum (1977, p. 91) between the relative importance of exports to English-speaking nations and a composite measure of English language behavior within the nation.[1] If these propositions about interaction are correct, it leads to the paradoxical conclusion that a language can become increasingly used and important at the same time as the source of its initial strength (the native speakers) declines. This is because increased interaction intensifies the relevance of a language. The weakness of Russian and Chinese for world communication, we shall see, is due to their low levels of interaction—not their inherent weakness.

FURTHUR EVIDENCE ABOUT
THE LEVEL OF INTERACTION

In the post-World War II period, there has been an incredible expansion in international banking, with major banks establishing branches in the far-flung corners of the earth to a degree unprecedented in earlier decades. Much of this is due, of course, to the expansion of world trade and the growing importance of multinational corporations (see, for example, Reimnitz, 1978), as well as to complex tax laws which make it desirable to establish branches in certain locations, the Eurodollar market (Mayer, 1974, Part 5), and a wide variety of other factors (Baker and Bradford, 1974; Robinson, 1972). The growth of international banking represents an intensification of interaction and, according to the principle suggested at the end of the preceding paragraph, increased interaction intensifies the relevance of language. Differentials between language groups in their relative advantage as a second language become increasingly relevant as the interaction pattern intensifies the need for nonnative language acquisition and usage.

To be sure, there have been international banking centers for many centuries. Earlier in this century, London was the premier banking center, with other leaders being New York, Paris, and, to a lesser degree, Berlin. In 1933, British banks had 62 foreign branches in Europe, 224 in the Near East, 98 in South America, and 73 in the Far East (Baster, 1977, p. 245). Likewise, there was a rather large number of foreign bank branches located in such cities as Hong Kong and Cairo in 1933 (my data for branch banks are derived from the Rand McNally *Bankers Directory* for the following years: 1933, 1947, 1965, and 1976. This is a standard reference for world banking and, although no doubt errors are inherent in such analyses—such as overlooking affiliates, the difficulty in determining headquarters, and the like—these *Directories* provide a superb opportunity for roughing out the changes in international banking networks during the period).

Zurich and Geneva, at present magnets for banks from throughout the world, had virtually no foreign banks in 1933. In Zurich in 1976 about a dozen different U.S. banks alone were represented, as well as various institutions from every part of the world. Japan is perhaps an even better example. In 1933 there were only a handful of foreign banks located in Tokyo, or for that matter, anywhere in the nation; two Dutch banks, one French, a Hong Kong institution, one United States bank, and a British bank were represented (in some cases with several branches). Represented in Tokyo in 1976 are thirty-one United States banks, ten from Great Britain, four each from France and Germany, ten from elsewhere in Europe, as well as four from Australia-New Zealand, five from Canada, four from Latin America, and at least one from Thailand, India, Korea, Taiwan, Singapore, and the Philippines.

Beirut provides another spectacular example of the intensification of international (and hence cross-linguistic) interaction on a financial and commercial plane. In 1933 there were a total of six different banks in Beirut; three were branches of Paris institutions, one was headquartered in Rome, and two were apparently local institutions. By 1965 there were at least twenty-five different foreign banks located there (I say "at least" quite intentionally since it is always possible that some bank that appears to be headquartered in Beirut or elsewhere in Lebanon is actually an unrecognized affiliate of a foreign institution). In turn, by 1976 there were sixty-four different foreign banks located in what had become a major international financial center.

Incidentally, coinciding with this great expansion in international banking has been an extraordinary shift among United States banks. The two largest Chicago banks had no foreign branches at all in 1947. By 1965, both had representatives in London and Tokyo, with one also in Zurich. One of these banks was represented in thirty-one different countries in 1976 with the other trailing close behind with twenty-eight. The Bank of America, the largest bank in the United States, had only one foreign branch in 1933 (in London), whereas by 1976 it had branches or some form of representation in over fifty nations—a number exceeded by the two largest New York City banks. To be sure there were some New York banks with overseas activities in 1933. The most extensive network that I found involved branches in some twenty-five nations. But for the most part, this type of international banking was not very extensive for American institutions until the last decade or so.

Some Linguistic Ramifications. Before moving on to analyze the relevance of this intensified contact for language spread, examining some changes that occurred in the banking practices will illustrate rather nicely the shift toward English. In both 1933 and 1941 a number of the Japanese institutions used the term *Ginko* rather than "bank" or some similar word in their name (the 1947 *Directory* gave the listings for Japan as of 1941). This practice disappeared almost completely in the post-World War II period, reflecting both the American occupation as well as a greater sensitivity to foreigners by an industry that was increasingly internationally minded. (Since the *Directory* is published in English, one might well expect a propensity to translate their names into the appropriate English common nouns, but this was of course a constant bias throughout the period and hence cannot explain the timing of the shift.) I might mention that banks located in French, Italian, and Spanish and Portuguese areas almost without exception stick respectively to *banque, banca,* and *banco* in their titles rather than use "bank." These tongues appear to be well established, and their practices do not change as readily as those among other language groups.

On the other hand the expansion of English is found in the practices exhibited by banks in both Athens and Beirut. I restrict my analysis to banks that are, so far as I can determine, locally based in the country. This allows one to avoid the complications that might occur through the inclusion of foreign institutions. At any rate, in Athens in 1933, *banque* was clearly the preferred term, with thirteen local institutions using it in their title (of which three put "bank" in parentheses in their listings). By contrast there were three *banks* (one of which was a "banque" in parentheses) and one *banca.* Practices in 1947 still favored the French word, with ten listed as *banque,* three of which include "bank" in parentheses. There were no institutions listed exclusively as *banks,* but there were three which used *bank* in the title but were followed by "banque" in parentheses. Again there was one *banca.* By 1965 it was all but over for the French word, with nine local *banks,* three of which had "banque" in parentheses. No *banques* were listed exclusively in French, although there was one that included the English term in parentheses. In 1976 there were no local *banques* at all, with or without the English in parentheses. The vast majority of the local institutions using the English word did not bother even to include the French term in parentheses (8 out of 12).

The chart below gives the language usage in 1976 of banks headquartered in Beirut, cross-classified by the year in which they were established.

Year of Establishment	Language Used in Bank Name	
	English	French
1880–1954	0	11
1955–1964	8	11
1965–1976	4	1

Since Lebanon had been under French control, it is not surprising to see the initial propensity to use French in naming banks in the period between 1880 and 1954 (bear in mind that these data refer to the language practice of banks surviving to 1976, not to their practices in earlier periods or of banks that no longer existed by 1976). English almost reached a parity with French between 1955 and 1964, with the latter falling behind among the small number of new Lebanese banks established in recent years.

INTERACTION: NUMBER OF SPEAKERS
VS. NUMBER OF UNITS

Every facet of language shift is influenced by the sheer demographic context of linguistic behavior; the present size of a language group has a profound bearing on the future with respect to its maintenance and spread (for an early quantitative study of the influence of language composition on bilingualism, see Weinreich's 1957 analysis of bilingualism in India). This is a simple and very clear point. It is also obvious that linguistic behavior is more than a pure product of demographic size. Hence, for example, bilingualism is also affected by the social institutions, employment opportunities, power, government policy, and the like. Compare, for example, the rates of bilingualism among French and English when in analogous demographic situations in Canada (Lieberson, 1970, pp. 46–50).

Also modifying the demographic impact on language maintenance and spread is the number and structure of units involved and their effect under a given set of social conditions. Such languages as English and Spanish enjoy certain advantages in the competition between tongues that are derived not merely from each claiming a large number of speakers in the world, but from the fact that these speakers are important in a large number of political units. By contrast, the impact of Chinese, Russian, Hindi, and Japanese that might be expected on the basis of the world-wide number of speakers of these tongues is in some circumstances modified and reduced because of the concentration of such speakers in a minimal number of nations. The contrast between French and German is interesting in that regard. Although the number of native speakers of German is greater than the number with French mother tongue, the former is an official language in Germany, Switzerland, and Austria, whereas the latter is official in France, Switzerland, Belgium, Canada, Haiti, and a large number of former colonies in Africa.

Unfortunately it is rather hard to separate the influence of number of political units from many other factors which operate; for example, it is unlikely that the position of Hindi is purely a function of the fact that it is a national language in only one political unit. Likewise, a comparison between the mere number of French and German units ignores the earlier forces which established the role of French. A continuum is of help here, ranging from those circumstances in which it is simply the sheer number of persons that determines the support base for a language to other circumstances in which individuals are not units but rather nations or some other corporate aggregate, and in which the number of persons belonging to each unit has no bearing on the number of representatives it gets. For the economics of publishing, the sheer number of potential underlying readers is crucial and the number of units much less important. On the other hand, in circumstances where each unit has the same number of delegates, at the United Nations, for example, the number of units with each language becomes far more important than the number of speakers represented by each unit. To be sure, interaction in all cases is between individuals, but their numbers are by definition relatively more significant in the purely demographic situation than in one where a unit form of representation exists.

Needless to say, English enjoys an enviable position since it is both a demographically important language and, at the same time, is an official language in a relatively large number of the world's nations. The relevance of the unit influence compared with a purely demographic influence is determined by the degree to which the interaction is between persons or between units. It is therefore helpful to distinguish between individual- and unit-based interaction, for example, tourist flow, as opposed to interaction between aggregate units such as nation-states or corporations. Changes in interaction will always affect the relative importance of different languages, but it is crucial to consider whether this involves individuals or units.

INTERACTION: RUSSIA AND CHINA

Two of the great languages of the world, in demographic terms, have effectively left themselves out of the competition in some domains because of the political and ideological factors involved. I refer here to the domains of international finance and, to a lesser degree, international trade. The 1976 edition of the Rand McNally *Bankers Directory* lists a total of two foreign banks in the People's Republic of China (p. F175): the Hongkong and Shanghai Bank, headquartered in Hong Kong; and the Chartered Bank, a British international bank with headquarters in London. Both of these banks have offices in Shanghai, but nowhere else in the People's Republic. In the 1933 *Directory*, there were a large number of foreign banks in both Shanghai and Peiping, as well as a number of other Chinese cities; for example, banks from Belgium, Germany, Japan, Italy, the United States, France, India, the Netherlands, and so forth. Mainland China, then, is one of the few instances in which the recent trend towards greater interaction fails to occur; indeed movement is in the opposite direction. To be sure, this is not the case for Taiwan—moreover, Hong Kong has become a great international banking center. Still, the kind of role that one might expect for Chinese due to the sheer number of speakers is greatly undercut because of the limited number of political units involved, compounded with the relative absence of interaction between mainland China and the rest of the world.

The Soviet Union, like China, has been relatively isolated from international finance. To be sure, the Soviet Union has not been above international capitalistic ventures; the Moscow Narodny Bank, established in London in 1919, lists many of the great New York City banks as its correspondents. Moreover, according to Mayer (1974, p. 455) the Eurodollar was invented at their bank in Paris, and the Russians have had a Swiss bank since 1966. Nevertheless, Soviet banking interaction has been quite limited, although increasing in recent years. There were about a dozen foreign banks in Moscow in 1976: three from the United States; two each from Italy and France; one each from Sweden, Yugoslavia, the United Kingdom, a branch of their own Moscow Narodny Bank (which is headquartered in London); and the International Bank for Economic Cooperation, which is essentially an iron-curtain bank representing the governments of Bulgaria, Czechoslovakia, East Germany, Hungary, Mongolia, Poland, Rumania, and the Soviet Union. Obviously, under other circumstances, the Soviet Union would be a much more significant center for international banking. As is the case for mainland China, its relative isolation means not only that its linguistic influence is vastly reduced in this domain, but it permits other languages to play an even more pronounced role. In that sense, one can argue that both China and the Soviet Union indirectly support the widening international role of English.

In similar fashion, the concentration of Eastern European trade within the Warsaw Pact nations as well as the relatively minimal international trade thus far exhibited by mainland China have reduced the broader significance of Russian and Chinese. To be sure, Russian has thereby become extremely important within the Warsaw Pact nations (Conrad and Fishman, 1977, p. 48), but this restricted trade minimizes its world role. The other "Centrally Planned Economies" in Europe, defined by the United Nations as Albania, Bulgaria, Czechoslovakia, the German Democratic Republic, Hungary, Poland, and Rumania, accounted for 53 percent of Russia's exports in 1975 (United Nations, 1976, p. 983). It would be interesting to know more about Cuba's linguistic policy, incidentally. From about 75 to 80 percent of Cuba's exports in the period between 1913 and 1938 was directed to the United States (United States Department of Commerce, 1928, p. 189; United Nations, 1951, p. 67). The Soviet Union, which had been such a minor market for Cuba that it was not even listed among the 35 most important customers for Cuba in the early post-World War II period (United Nations, 1951, p. 67), accounted for 41 percent of Cuba's exports in 1973 (United Nations, 1976, p. 291).

There are even fewer foreign banks represented in other Eastern European nations. Bulgaria listed one (a Lebanese bank), only a Yugoslavian bank was represented in Czechoslovakia, there was none in Hungary, one Italian and one U.S. bank had representation in Poland, and only one foreign bank (American) was represented in Rumania (based on the Rand McNally *Bankers Directory*, 1976). In short, the restricted interaction of Russia and mainland China vastly minimizes their potential international role that could occur through demographic types of interaction, that is, interaction that occurs on the basis of relative numbers. Those outcomes affected by the relative number of units would be less seriously altered by increased interaction because there are so few Russian- and Chinese-language nations anyway.

THE MECHANISM THROUGH WHICH LINGUISTIC PLURALITIES ARE CONVERTED TO LINGUISTIC MAJORITIES

One of the papers prepared for this volume (Scotton) cites Greenberg's observation of a "dynamic quality to the spread of a lingua franca" such that its usage at some point tends to accelerate (Greenberg, 1965, p. 52). Using international trade and banking data, I wish to suggest some mechanisms through which this occurs. Earlier I observed that a set of the leading English-speaking industrial nations of the world account for a smaller proportion of world commerce now than they used to. Nevertheless, in linguistic terms for many nations of the world English-speaking countries comprise their single most important international market. Hence, given the growth in world trade (in effect, interaction has gone up), one can readily understand the expansion in the significance of English for these countries. But what about other nations, ones in which customers with some other language are more important? Would the spread of English be expected to occur there as well?

Shown below is a set of hypothetical data representing export markets of four different nations, A, B, C, and D. For the first three of these nations, E is the most important market, consuming 30 percent of their exports. E consumes none of the exports from nation D, however, whereas B and C each receive 30 percent of D's exports. At first glance,

E is the optimal language for anyone in A, B, and C to learn. By learning E, members of A, B, and C will share a common language with their customers 30 percent of the time—not a felicitous figure, but still higher than could be obtained with any other language. By contrast the optimal language for someone in D to learn at first glance appears to be either B or C.

Language of Importer	Exporting Nation			
	A	B	C	D
A	—	20	20	20
B	20	—	20	30
C	20	20	—	30
D	10	10	10	—
E	30	30	30	0
F	10	10	10	10
G	10	10	10	10
Total	100	100	100	100

In point of fact, members of A, B, and C can now communicate with far more than 30 percent of their international customers. Although nobody in C has learned B and nobody in B has learned C, because in each case E was initially somewhat more desirable, members of C and B can communicate with each other through their common knowledge of E. Given these assumptions about A, B, and C, then it will also become optimal for members of D to learn E even though no trade occurs with the E nation. Because Bs and Cs will have acquired E themselves, an E-speaking member of group D will be able to communicate with far more customers than if either B or C is learned. In other words, we can see how a language will spread as interaction increases to the point where its earlier spread encourages even further learning.

Language Markets for a Sample of Nations. In order to consider the relevance of this process, I took a small sample from the *Yearbook of International Trade Statistics, 1975* (United Nations, 1976)—every fifteenth nation listed, including Zambia at the end since it was one short of inclusion anyway and I had only one other African country. For ten leading customers of each nation, I determined their official language(s) using the information sketched out in Urdang (1975). In nations such as Belgium, Canada, and Singapore, there is more than one official language and I credited each tongue accordingly. Hence, it is possible for the figures to sum to more than 100 percent because some nations contribute to more than one official language. In many cases the figures add to less than 100 percent because we are only dealing with ten large foreign markets for each nation that was sampled.[2]

A striking feature is precisely the plurality for English described earlier. English-speaking countries formed less than a simple majority of the export market in all of the nations sampled.[3] However, in seven of the ten nations, English was the largest single market. This amounted to only 19 percent for Bolivia's exports and 21 and 24 percent respectively for India and Zambia, but in other countries English was the market for a considerably larger part of the exports (Costa Rica, French Guiana, South Vietnam, and Uganda). Incidentally, the important role of English for South Vietnam in 1973 was not due to the United States, which received only 4 percent of the exports, but was due to the markets for their exports provided by Hong Kong (26 percent) and Singapore (12 percent). The data for Poland provide a good example of the confinement of iron-curtain countries to within the Eastern European sector to a degree that probably reflects more than the influence of transportation costs.

One can see precisely how English would be the single most desirable language for a large number of countries. And the operation of a simple feedback effect should lead to an even more significant role for the language. The figures also show an important worldwide role for a number of other European languages. German makes up 10 or more percent of the export market for four of these nations sampled. French is likewise a very important market in several cases. The minimal role of Russian and Chinese, discussed earlier, is nicely illustrated by Table 1. Except for Poland, Russia is an important customer only for India and, to a much smaller extent, Bolivia. Likewise, Chinese is significant only for South Vietnam—and that is due to the influence of Singapore and Malaysia rather than to that of mainland China.

DISTANCE, TRANSPORTATION, AFFLUENCE, AND INTERACTION

As a general rule, interaction has a cost, that is, there is a friction or resistance due to the time and distance involved in the movement of persons, goods, or messages across space. As a consequence, inventions in transportation and communication which reduce either the time or cost of such movements will tend to increase interaction. Likewise, greater affluence will have the same consequence by reducing the impact of transportation costs. Since the expansion and decline of international languages, just like those within a nation, is affected by changes in interaction, it is important to recognize some standard forces which influence interaction and see how these, in turn, affect language spread.

The ease with which people move across great distances has been greatly affected by the widespread use of air transportation in recent decades. Likewise, new technologies such as television and communication satellites have greatly facilitated the movement of messages. These are not trivial factors to consider in trying to understand the growth of English, and they will be highly relevant for future language shifts. Particularly important is the way such transportation changes and their widespread use have brought the massive numbers of English-speakers from the United States into the communication network. First, consider the intensification of interaction generally. There were 4,717 international conferences during the nearly one hundred years between 1840 and 1931 (Shenton, 1933, p. 26). Observe the incredible increase by decades in their number:

1840–49	9	1890–99	510
1850–59	20	1900–09	1,062
1860–69	77	1910–19	516
1870–79	168	1921–29	1,517
1880–89	311	1930–31	501

Except for a drop-off during the first World War, one finds extraordinarily steady growth in the number of international conferences. The first peaceful decade after the War was marked by a new record even though the year 1920 was not included. The period under study by Shenton ends with two years, 1930 and 1931, during which there were more international conferences than were held during the first forty years under consideration.

For the 1923–29 period, Shenton was able to tabulate the locations of 1,415 conferences (pp. 76–80). Europe is far and away the most important locale, with France in first place (275 conferences), followed by Switzerland (204), England and Scotland (122), Germany (109), Italy (103), and Belgium (101). The Western Hemisphere is relatively insignificant, with the United States holding 42, Canada 7, Cuba 6, Brazil 4, and Argentina 3. This is a period in which cross-Atlantic travel would have been both much slower and more expensive than today.

Not surprisingly, French was the official language in more conferences than any other tongue during this post-World War I period, being used officially by 220 organizations, compared with 160 using English, 132 choosing German, and with Italian occupying a weak fourth place with 22 (Shenton, 1933, p. 255). Although the United States was represented at a surprisingly large number of these international conferences, given the difficulties of travel at that time, it was tied with Austria for eleventh place in the rankings. France attended the greatest number of conferences, followed by Great Britain, Belgium, Switzerland, the Netherlands, Germany, Czechoslovakia, Italy, Poland, Sweden and then the United States and Austria (Shenton, 1933, p. 119).

Changes in the barriers of space alter the role of distance and its influence on interaction. I believe developments in recent decades have greatly favored English insofar as they have made it much easier for numerically important English-speaking populations located away from Europe to participate in international conferences in sizable numbers. Since French was not handicapped to the same relative degree (the only serious handicaps were those faced by French speakers in Africa), changes in the direction of bringing the world closer together have differentially affected the pace of interaction for language groups. What the future changes will be in transportation and communication cannot be predicted, but one can be certain that they will alter the probabilities of interaction for various language groups and this alteration will have an impact on language spread and maintenance.

IMPLICATIONS

If the principles and mechanisms described above are valid, then they should be relevant for understanding future situations in which social change causes various languages to gain or lose power and influence. The tendency towards the conservation of language usage observed at the outset is an extremely important notion because it means that shifts in the power of language groups or in their numbers or in other forces that might be expected to affect language spread will not necessarily have such effects. This is because the role of a language, once established, will tend to be perpetuated long after the disappearance of conditions which were initially necessary for its generation. Hence, it is quite possible for the English-speaking nations to decline in economic, political, or other types of power without a concomitant drop in the role of the English language. It also follows, then, that speakers of other languages can make significant gains in these domains without making an immediate linguistic gain. The role of neutral, third-party language

TABLE 1
Export Markets, Classified by Language, for a Sample of Nations

Official Language of the Importing Nation	Exporting Nation									
	Bolivia (1975)	Costa Rica (1974)	French Guiana (1975)	India (1975)	Lebanon (1973)	Netherlands (1975)	Poland (1974)	South Vietnam (1973)	Uganda (1975)	Zambia (1973)
English	19	31	46	21	10	12	8	46	47	24
German	8	13	—	3	—	32	16	2	6	10
Dutch	6	9	4	—	—	14	—	—	2	—
Japanese	8	—	—	10	—	—	—	24	8	—
Italian	4	3	—	2	2	6	4	1	3	12
Spanish	9	26	—	—	—	1	—	1	—	—
French	3	3	41	3	—	25	3	16	4	8
Russian	5	—	—	12	—	—	29	—	—	—
Other	—	3[a]	8[b]	12[c]	52[d]	4[e]	13[f]	65[g]	5[h]	10[i]

Source: United Nations, 1976, Table 3 for each exporting nation.
— Signifies no representation in the leading markets for that nation.
[a] Finnish
[b] Portuguese
[c] Persian (8 percent); Bengali (2 percent); Polish (2 percent)
[d] Arabic
[e] Swedish (2 percent); Danish (2 percent)
[f] Czech (7 percent); Hungarian (3 percent); Bulgarian (3 percent)
[g] Chinese (38 percent); Malay (15 percent); Tamil (12 percent)
[h] Arabic (2 percent); Serbo-Croat (3 percent)
[i] Portuguese (5 percent); Swedish (1 percent); Chinese (2 percent); Serbo-Croat (2 percent)

groups as a conservative force has been demonstrated to be extremely important. On the other hand, where it is the third-party language that becomes a competitor, then its conservative influence is lost since the initial support base will disappear. In other words, the impact of a decline in the power of English-speaking nations relative to, say, Chinese, will be minimized by "third-party" language groups such as the Japanese- or Spanish-speaking groups who have already made a commitment to English. But if one of these third-party groups becomes a competitor, then its support will quickly fall away. Thus if Japanese or Spanish were to begin to compete sociolinguistically with English, then the present bilingualism of such speakers would no longer work to slow down change.

Of special significance in altering language usage are changes in interaction patterns. There are several areas in which very significant interaction changes could occur. The Soviet Union and the People's Republic of China are far more isolated now than may be the case in the future. Increased interaction would make the potential power of these nations a greater reality, since changes in interaction affect the actual influence of a language group on other language groups.

On this score, Latin American nations at present do not interact nearly as much among themselves as one might expect. The export data for the two Latin American nations shown in Table 1 are by no means atypical for the Spanish-speaking part of the Western Hemisphere. This absence of interaction tends to undercut the potential strength of Spanish and, at the same time, serves to support English since the United States has such an important level of interaction with these countries. No Latin American country had a bank branch or representative in Lima, Peru, in 1976, whereas there are five United States banks represented, along with two each from Switzerland and Spain; and France, the United Kingdom, Japan, and Germany each have one bank represented. Likewise, in Caracas, Venezuela, there are two non-Venezuelan Latin American banks represented as well as two from Spain. But, on the other hand, fourteen different United States banks are represented in that city. São Paulo, Brazil has become a major banking center. There are nine different Japanese banks represented there, along with five from both Germany and Italy, four from Switzerland, three from France, and twenty from the United States. Although Spanish is relatively close to Portuguese, the only Latin American representation consists of a single bank from each of three different countries: Mexico, Argentina, and Ecuador. Likewise, Buenos Aires has one Brazilian bank, and the only international Spanish influence is due to the representation of four banks from Spain. By contrast, there are thirteen U.S. banks, nine from Germany, seven Swiss institutions, five each from France and Italy, and lesser numbers from the Netherlands, Belgium, the Bahamas, Israel, the United Kingdom, Canada, and Japan. Shifts due to industrialization and other factors could greatly reduce the power of English in Latin America and this, in turn, would both strengthen Spanish and reduce a "third-party" support base for English.

In closing, I should at least mention that the linkage between language and commerce sometimes runs in the opposite direction, namely language bonds can affect economic bonds. The post-World War II expansion of United States banking, for example, has led to further maintenance of London's dominant role in banking, since it appears to be the first city that American banks select for an overseas office. The common English language apparently affected this decision (Mayer, 1974, p. 466). Likewise, I find a banking linkage between Latin America and Spain that probably is not entirely due to international commerce. *Banco Nacional de Mexico*, with more than 400 branches in Mexico, has foreign offices in six cities, one of which is Madrid, but none in the United Kingdom. The *Banco de Comercio*, a large Mexican bank with 558 offices in the nation, has international representation in five cities, again Madrid is one of these. Similarly, Madrid is one of the six foreign offices for *Banamex*, and is the only European office for *Banco Comercial Mexicano*. Likewise, although I have not emphasized the fact, one still finds British and French banks playing a pronounced role in their former African colonies.

SEVEN PROPOSITIONS

This analysis of language spread can be summarized in seven propositions:

1. The origin of a given language pattern need not be found in the forces currently operating to maintain the pattern. A language pattern, once established, has a life of its own which may continue long after the initial causes have disappeared. Indeed, there is every reason to expect a set of intervening factors such as attitudes and norms to develop from some more basic underlying cause, but these should not be confused with the initial causes.

2. There is a conservation of language usage. Once language practices are established, they will tend to perpetuate themselves in situations which, if existing earlier, would never have generated the same language pattern.

3. The conservation of language usage is abetted by "third parties," namely groups for whom neither the existing dominant language nor its

potential competitor are native languages. Because they have little reason to shift from the second language already used to a new second language, third parties play a key role in the conservation of language usage. Once such neutral groups become bilingual in an existing dominant language, they develop a vested interest in that tongue with an intensity almost equal to that of the native speakers.[4]

4. An existing language usage pattern can be altered through changes in the frequency and nature of the interaction within and between language groups. Indeed, without interaction, the political, economic, social, scientific, and other sources of power and influence for speakers of a language group are only matters of potential rather than forces operating to affect behavior.

5. Two basic distinctions are necessary in analyzing the role of interaction. First, it is necessary to distinguish between changes in *potential* as opposed to *actual* influence (the two can change independently of one another and hence in opposite directions). Second, it is necessary to recognize that interaction ranges on a continuum from the purely demographic form, in which the number of each population is the crucial consideration, to an aggregate form in which each unit has equal participation regardless of the underlying population represented.

6. There are certain inherent mechanisms in language shift which, when operating by themselves, would tend to convert linguistic pluralities into linguistic majorities. As the number of persons acquiring a given language increases, this in turn increases the pressure for others to acquire the same second language even if their interaction patterns remain unchanged. It is through this mechanism that we can understand Greenberg's observation (1965, p. 52) of a dynamic and accelerating quality to the spread of a lingua franca.

7. Changes in the technology of transportation and communication will alter the levels of interaction. Because the consequences of such technological changes will not be the same for all language groups, the existing linkage between potential and actual influence will not change equally for all tongues. This in turn means that the existing patterns of language acquisition will tend to be altered when major differentials in interaction are generated through such technological changes.

NOTES

1. This is the only such effort I know of to correlate the role of exports with language behavior and hence is an important development, but a serious caution is necessary. Although the investigators claim that they measure "the percentage of exports sent to English-speaking countries" (Fishman, Cooper, and Rosenbaum, 1977, p. 85), inspection of their data source (United States Department of State, 1972) indicates that the figures refer only to trade with the United States and hence does not fully measure the role of English-speaking markets for various nations.

2. Although the ten markets listed for each nation were the largest in recent years, in some cases they did not overlap exactly with the largest ten for the year specified. For the most part, this had a minor influence on the results. The reader should bear in mind, however, that the proportions given in Table 1 are of exports to *all* nations, not merely those directed to the countries specified.

3. Incidentally, there are such countries in which more than half of their exports go to English-speaking nations.

4. Such groups, of course, are often disposed to shed the acquired language in favor of their own native tongue, but they are usually resistant to giving up one acquired second language for a new one.

REFERENCES

Baker, James C., and M. Gerald Bradford. 1974. *American Banks Abroad*. New York: Praeger.

Baster, A. S. J. 1977. *The International Banks*. New York: Arno Press.

Butler, Sir Geoffrey, and Simon Maccoby. 1928. *The Development of International Law*. London: Longmans, Green.

Conrad, Andrew W., and Joshua A. Fishman. 1977. "English as a World Language: The Evidence" in Joshua A. Fishman, Robert L. Cooper, and Andrew W. Conrad, *The Spread of English*. Rowley, Massachusetts: Newbury House.

Encyclopaedia Britannica. 1975. *The New Encyclopaedia Britannica, Macropaedia, Volume 10*. Chicago: Encyclopaedia Britannica.

Fishman, Joshua A., Robert L. Cooper, and Yehudit Rosenbuam. 1977. "English Around the World" in Joshua A. Fishman, Robert L. Cooper, and Andrew W. Conrad, *The Spread of English*. Rowley, Massachusetts: Newbury House.

Greenberg, Joseph H. 1965. "Urbanism, Migration, and Language" in Hilda Kuper, ed., *Urbanization and Migration in West Africa*. Berkeley: University of California Press.

Lieberson, Stanley. 1970. *Language and Ethnic Relations in Canada*. New York: Wiley.

Mayer, Martin. 1974. *The Bankers*. New York: Weybright and Talley.

Miller, David Hunter. 1928a. *The Drafting of the Covenant, Volume 1*. New York: Putnam.

————. 1928b. *The Drafting of the Covenant, Volume 2*. New York: Putnam.

Population Research Center, University of Texas. 1965. *International Population Census Bibliography, Latin America and the Caribbean*. Austin, Texas: Bureau of Business Research.

62   *Stanley Lieberson*

------. 1966. *International Population Census Bibliography, Asia.* Austin, Texas: Bureau of Business Research.
------. 1967. *International Population Census Bibliography, Europe.* Austin, Texas: Bureau of Business Research.
Rand McNally. 1933. *Bankers Directory, 1933.* New York: Rand McNally.
------. 1947. *Bankers Directory, 1947.* New York: Rand McNally.
------. 1965. *Bankers Directory, 1965.* New York: Rand McNally.
------. 1976. *Bankers Directory, 1976.* New York: Rand McNally.
Reimnitz, Jurgen. 1978. "German Banks Follow German Investment," *Euromoney* (June), 91.
Robinson, Stuart W. 1972. *Multinational Banking.* Leiden, Netherlands: Sijthoff.
Scotton, Carol Myers. "Learning Lingua Francas and Socioeconomic Integration: Evidence from Africa." This volume.
Shenton, Herbert Newhard. 1933. *Cosmopolitan Conversation.* New York: Columbia University Press.
United Nations. 1951. *Yearbook of International Trade Statistics, 1950.* New York: United Nations.
------. 1976. *Yearbook of International Trade Statistics, 1975, Volume 1.* New York: United Nations.
Urdang, Laurence, editor. 1975. *The CBS News Almanac, 1976.* Maplewood, New Jersey: Hammond Almanac.
United States Department of Commerce. 1928. *Commerce Yearbook, 1928, Volume 2.* Washington, D.C.: Government Printing Office.
United States Department of State. 1972. *World Data Handbook.* Washington, D.C.: Government Printing Office. (Department of State Publication 8665, General Foreign Policy Series 264)
Weinreich, Uriel. 1957. "Functional Aspects of Indian Bilingualism," *Word* 13: 203–33.
World Peace Foundation. 1921. "The First Assembly of the League of Nations," *A League of Nations* 4:27.

Learning Lingua Francas and Socioeconomic Integration: Evidence from Africa

Carol Myers Scotton

INTRODUCTION

This essay[1] will relate the spread of lingua francas to socioeconomic integration in a nation-state. Socioeconomic integration is characterized by a gradual, rather than a sharp, slope in the socioeconomic curve that accommodates separate groups within a nation. Position on this curve defines each group's control of the socioeconomic resources of the nation. With a gradual slope in the curve, mobility is possible; that is, entire groups or individuals have the potential to change their socioeconomic positions.

African data will be emphasized, and a hypothesis will be developed to explain the low amount of informal acquisition—and indeed, formal acquisition—of official languages in Africa. (The phrase "official language" will be used in this essay to mean "main official language"; many nations have several secondary official languages as well as a main official language.) However, this hypothesis is related to a number of general hypotheses regarding the interrelationship between the spread of lingua francas and other societal elements in any society. These general hypotheses are:

1. Language spread can be best explained in a framework which treats both a person's linguistic repertoire and the individual linguistic varieties it includes as societal elements, alongside other societal elements such as educational attainment, educational systems, political cultures, political parties, ethnic group membership, etc.

2. The acquisition of the same lingua franca performs different roles for different persons, depending on the specific configuration of societal elements a person already controls before that acquisition.

63

3. At any time, there is the possibility of change in a societal element in three areas: change in the content, or change in the power of a particular element, or change in the interrelationship of that element with other elements.[2] This essay, of course, is most concerned with possibilities for change in the content, power, and interrelationships of lingua francas as societal elements.

The case of the Akan cluster of languages in Ghana illustrates change in the content of a language. The relatively recent development of a pan-Akan identity among the more than 40 percent of the Ghanaian population that speaks one of the Akan dialects as a mother tongue has broadened the content of Akan as a linguistic category. Previously Akan subgroups such as the Ashanti, the Fante, and the Akin did not accept Akan as a primary linguistic or cultural identity (Smock 1975:169–70).

Change in the content of a language invariably entails change in the language's power. For example, the change from English to Swahili as the official language of Tanzania in 1967 represented a change in the content of the element "official language" and a change in the power of both Swahili and English, with Swahili gaining power. In a similar way, the change in Lusaka, Zambia, from Nyanja to English as the medium of public primary grades in the late 1960s is an example of a change in the content of the element "official school language." This change made Nyanja's status relative to other major indigenous languages spoken in Lusaka—notably Bemba—more problematic in certain areas of the city and therefore represented a change in the power of Nyanja as an element (Serpell 1978a:152).

The example of Swahili in Kampala, Uganda, illustrates the interrelationship of societal elements. Although Swahili is the national language of Uganda, it is taught in only a few schools. Therefore, Ugandans do not associate knowledge of Swahili with evidence of education. Since English, the official language, is compulsory in the schools, a relationship between speaking English and being educated is perceived (Scotton 1977a and 1977b).

The specific hypotheses which deal with Africa are these:

1. There is a relationship between the degree of socioeconomic integration that exists in a nation and the acquisition of the main official language, if that language is a second language for large parts of the population. In many African nations, a minimal degree of socioeconomic integration exists (for example, see Young 1976). If socioeconomic integration is restricted and if persons do not already possess the other societal elements recognized as crucial in power (e.g., at least a secondary school diploma, "right" ethnic group membership, etc.), then they see little advantage in learning the official language. This official

language may well be recognized as one of the important societal elements, the language of those who are socioeconomically mobile. However, the interdependence of societal elements is crucial. The potential language learners recognize this. They see adding the official language as but one piece of a socioeconomic picture puzzle. Unless one already controls other pieces (the powerful societal elements with which the language will interlock), a single, new piece will not allow the holder to design a successful socioeconomic picture. "The actual mobility of individuals depends, of course, not only on their incentives to move but also on the capabilities of doing so" (Blau 1964:295).

2. More and more people in Africa will learn nonofficial lingua francas (or secondary official lingua francas) through informal acquisition in the situations in which the language is used. Two changes in the power of these languages as societal elements are possible. If there is no change in the potential for socioeconomic mobility, involving entry into the upper strata, then pressure from below will bring about more indigenization of a wider range of activities so that secondary lingua francas will spread into new contexts. If the potential for socioeconomic mobility does change and attempts are made to equalize access to education and other societal resources, then the present official languages will spread downwards into more middle-range activities; and the extent of usage of secondary lingua francas may diminish as more and more people command the official language.

The argument will focus on the role of language as a social symbol. The emphasis is not simply on the conventional one of language as a symbol of group identification; rather, the emphasis is on language as a symbol of relationships. Language is a social symbol because people use it (usually subconsciously) to organize interactions. Language is one of the symbols which inaugurate and maintain social relationships.

Within the context of this essay, language's most important role as a social symbol is both as a societal resource and as an investment. A resource is something that can be turned to for help or support. An investment is something to which people commit themselves for future advantage; adding a language is an investment of effort and identity. The premise of this argument is that the same language may not turn out to be a true resource for all learners and therefore may or may not be a good investment. The power or performance of a language as a resource determines whether or not a person will seek to learn it. Languages which are added are valued not in terms of their specific content, then, but rather in terms of how they "work" (or do not work); that is, they are valued in terms of their interrelation with the other societal elements to which learners have access.

LANGUAGE AS A SOCIAL SYMBOL

The Yale University Computer Center identifies itself in Latin on each of its print-outs: *Centrum Computorum Universitatis Yalensis*. When the Chancellor of West Germany and the French Premier meet officially, it is reported they converse in English. A noted Belgian Africanist-linguist, lately deceased, was Flemish, but—as an educated Belgian—a fluent speaker of French. He insisted on English as the medium at international conferences with a long-time colleague, a French Africanist-linguist (personal communication—Pierre Alexandre). In Kenya, a group of Luyia school teachers, seated in a cafe in a town in the heart of Luyialand, greeted in English a passing Luyia who is a headmistress in a secondary school in another district and therefore not often met. After a few sentences, someone initiated a switch to a Luyia dialect, their mother tongue (personal communication 1977). The menu at a hotel in Luxor, Egypt, an Arabic-speaking nation, is printed entirely in French.

What do all these examples of the use of lingua francas have in common? In each case, language is being used as a social symbol either to make concrete or at least to assert claims of status. Although there also is simply an element of whimsy in programming a computer to print out Latin, the Yale Computer Center asserts by its use of Latin its membership in the academic community of letters and denies its status as a mere collection of hardware. The German and French heads of state and the Belgian linguist are asserting equal status by opting for English, a neutral code in their contexts. Using the lingua franca avoids unacceptable deference to anyone's mother tongue. A special way of asserting status is to identify or mark boundaries (Barth 1969). The shift to Luyia was not made by the Luyia school teachers until their use of English had marked them as educated to all within earshot. The French menu in Luxor is a boundary: only those who are "cultured" can cross it.

In all these cases, the use of a lingua franca is an overt symbolization of group membership. These cases support Abner Cohen's explanation of the use of social symbols:

> One of the most important of [the functions of symbols] is the objectification of relationships between individuals and groups. We can observe individuals objectively in concrete reality, but the relationships between them are abstractions that can be observed only through symbols. Social relationships develop through and are maintained by symbols. We "see" groups through their symbols. (1974:30)

Language, then, is figuratively one of the most visible means by which people are identified as members of groups and by which people negotiate for memberships. Language externalizes statuses by offering an objective criterion for group identification; language is in some senses outside the individual. When a language is so used, it need not be a lingua franca, of course. Traditionally, language is the most important single criterion of origin, hence the term *mother tongue*.

But negotiating for entry into *new* groups—perhaps the primary act of modernization—often requires learning a new language, especially if the new group is heterogeneous. If a new language is learned, this will be a lingua franca since, by the usual definition, a lingua franca is any language used among persons who do not share the same first language. A lingua franca may be the first language of any group member—but not of all members—or it may be alien to the entire group.

Adding a lingua franca, then, is part of the negotiation of new boundaries by an individual or a group for a new set of relationships in the society in which they operate. The process of learning the lingua franca is an investment, with the hope that the lingua franca itself will prove a valuable resource. The act of learning the new lingua franca (whether conscious or unconscious) becomes then part of the symbol that entry into new groups, that changes in status, are possible. Within the context of this paper, which lingua francas are learned symbolizes what types of changes are perceived as possible.

MEMBERSHIP IN WIDER COMMUNITIES AND NATIONAL INTEGRATION

In most parts of Africa, both individuals and governments increasingly have felt the need to enter wider communities than those into which they were born. In Ethiopia, for example, non-Amharas may seek the wider society of salaried employment in urban areas. In adding this identity as urban workers, they must almost certainly learn Amharic as a lingua franca (Cooper 1976). Ability to speak Amharic is a visible symbol of the aspirant's qualification, at least in one respect; therefore, he is anxious to learn this lingua franca.

Governments, too, have been anxious to have their citizens acquire languages that might be construed as symbols of the citizenry's membership in the wider, national community. Such languages must be lingua francas in the multilingual society. Nationalism, according to Karl Deutsch, is "a state of mind which gives 'national' messages, memories and images a preferred status" (1966:208). In order for citizens to accord this preferred status to nonlocal messages, they need at least the sense of membership in the nation, a sense which knowledge of the language of the wider, national communication can symbolize for them.

Ali Mazrui has argued persuasively that English served the cause of nationalism in colonial Africa by acting as a unifying force among ethnically diverse Africans. Within the context of language as a social symbol, one could say that the lingua franca, English, objectified the values and abstract concepts of nationalism. In a sense, a language is tangible, and English made nationalism tangible.

Mazrui wrote:

> By helping to produce agitating "scholars" the English language, directly or indirectly, helped to make the tribesman dissatisfied with his colonial status. We might also note how English helped to make it possible for, say a Lobi-speaking tribesman to think of the Nzima-speaking Nkrumah as a leader of more than the Nzima-speaking peoples. To accept Nkrumah as a fellow "Gold Coaster" was one thing: to accept him as a *leader* of *all* "Gold Coasters" was quite another. . . . The role of the English language in this case was to facilitate the sheer feasibility of trans-tribal leadership. (1975:97)

The naming of Swahili as not just the national but also the official language of Tanzania in 1967 served a similar symbolic purpose. Making Swahili official objectified supraethnic unity on an African basis and made Tanzania tangible as a nation. This act was, as W. H. Whiteley said, "an ideolized imperative, inducing a state of mind towards the language as one of the behavioral corollaries of the national ethos" (1971:151).

Few African nations, however, have the equipment in terms of a medium of communication to accomplish national integration. In the multilingual nations of Africa, this equipment is necessarily a lingua franca. Few lingua francas now have sufficient spread to facilitate such integration, with a few exceptions: Swahili (in Tanzania and in most of Kenya), Amharic (in Ethiopia), Wolof (in Senegal), Sango (in Central African Empire), and perhaps Nyanja (in Malawi) and Bambara (in Mali). In most African nations, either French, English, or Portuguese (depending on the colonial heritage) is the main or sole official language and therefore the officially promoted lingua franca. Nations which do not have an international main official language are Tanzania (Swahili); Ethiopia (Amharic); and Somalia (Somali). Yet although they are official languages, English, French, or Portuguese are known by still small percentages of the population more than ten years after independence. In some nations (with the exceptions of Tanzania, Ethiopia, Somalia), perhaps 10 percent or less of the people know their official language, although in some urban areas the numbers reach 30 and 40 percent.[3]

THE INTEREST OF GOVERNMENT
IN INTEGRATION

It is clearly in any government's interest to foster the spread of a lingua franca in the multiethnic nation if maximum national integration is a goal. That will-o'-the-wisp, modernization, is also associated with the existence of a transethnic language. In order to communicate with large pools of workers, a language intelligible to all is desirable. Dankwart Rustow recognized language's power as a resource:

> Unlike geography, language is a human phenomenon. Unlike history, which is continuous and can mean many things to many men, language divides human beings into distinct groups. There is also a close connection between language and modernization. Traditional communities survive best in isolation; but the principle of modernity is interdependence. More people in modern society talk and write to more others than ever before. *Language is therefore to a modern society what money is to its economy: a universal currency of exchange.* [italics added] . . . linguistic unity can be a modern nation's most precious possession. (1967:47)

Without social-communication channels to foster a sense of shared identity (i.e., political integration) and to offer the potential for some measure of socioeconomic integration, no government is very secure. This is not to say, however, that governments cannot rule successfully without integration at either level. I have argued elsewhere (Scotton 1979a and 1979b) that the modern African elite may place integration low on its priority list. The elite may well decide it serves its best socioeconomic interest *not* to foster the spread of the official language unduly, even at the cost of limiting national integration. (This argument applies only, of course, to those nations where the official language is not now widely known and therefore does not apply to Tanzania, Ethiopia, or Somalia.) This attitude could develop if the official language is also the main vehicle of socioeconomic mobility—as it is in all of Africa. The elite's main aim may be to restrict socioeconomic integration by restricting political and economic opportunity to its own ranks, assuming its members already know the specified language. Pragmatically, the elite needs to maintain an interest in either national or socioeconomic integration only to the degree necessary to maintain the status quo.

Thus, it is problematic whether or not, in fact, governments in multiethnic nations will attempt to step up the spread of alien, official languages or will accord status to widely known, locally based lingua francas. Witness Senegal's failure to replace French with Wolof as the official language (Sylla 1978), or Kenya's continuance with English as official in all contexts even though Swahili is much more widely known. Or consider the apparent lack of priority placed on making English or French (whichever is official) available to broader segments of the population in nations where no indigenous lingua franca has a likely potential national scope.

THE ROLE OF THE INDIVIDUAL: LANGUAGE AS A RESOURCE

History shows, however, that if governments cannot be counted on to spread lingua francas, private citizens can. Informal spread of a lingua franca occurs, provided socioeconomic benefits accrue to those who learn it. Members of a community are linked to sources of socioeconomic opportunity by communication facilities. It is here that language's role as a social symbol is most obvious. As community symbolizes contact, language can symbolize contact, and with it, *advantage*. In this way, language is a societal resource. As Lieberson noted:

> Language . . . enters into . . . forms of competition as a potential asset in the market place, the political order, or the social realm. In the same way that trading stamps are used by merchants to obtain a competitive edge, so too will language play a role in these normal forms of competition in multilingual communities. (1970:10)

As in normal economic competition, life in the multilingual nation is a buyer's market. The "buyer," in the instances with the most far-reaching consequences for the urban job-seeker, is the mobilized population which controls most of the nation's other resources—the higher-status jobs, land, education, political power, etc.—along with the official language. ("Buyer," then, is used metaphorically.)

To enter the market as a member of the mobilized, the aspirant must learn the language of the mobilized. But it is not quite as simple as that, it seems, to gain equal entry. If it were, it is argued here, the number of people who learn the official languages (where English, French or Portuguese are official) in Africa would be much larger. Opportunities clearly exist to learn the official language informally, just as other languages—sometimes from different genetic stocks—are learned. At least in urban areas, there are always some relatives, friends or co-workers who know enough of the official language to teach aspirants. Newspapers are readily available in towns, and radio broadcasts, as accessible in rural areas as in the towns, are mainly in the main official language.

But many urban job-seekers opt to learn a secondary major lingua franca which is not the official language, or is a secondary official language. Such is the case with Dyula in Ivory Coast (Partmann 1975), or pidgin English in Nigeria (Scotton 1975), or Swahili in Kampala and Nairobi (Scotton 1972 and Parkin 1974a). Along the line-of-rail in Zambia certain languages have emerged as urban lingua francas, for example, Bemba on the Copperbelt and in Kabwe, Nyanja in Lusaka, and Lozi in Livingstone (Kashoki 1978). These languages are known and used by all segments of society, but they are primarily associated with urban manual workers. Thus, those who have added the lingua franca which is not the main official language are entering the market of the mobilized, it is true, but in a worker-patron relationship. They, like the elite who speak the official language, are mobilized, but an important differential in ranking exists.

Greenberg correctly observed that once a lingua franca is established as advantageous to know, it rapidly puts other languages out of business, so that few lingua francas exist in the same market. He wrote:

> The single lingua franca tends to become the dominant solution not because anyone plans it that way, but because once a language has a head start by being the language of a numerically important group, particularly the locally dominant one, others discover the advantage or even the necessity of learning it. Once it becomes at all widespread, it has the advantage over other lingua francas so that its expansion continues. Thus is there a dynamic quality to the spread of a lingua franca. (1972:201)

The dual ranking of lingua francas indicates that Greenberg's observation needs to be amplified. Where social stratification exists, it follows that more than one lingua franca will always remain viable. Further, as this paper argues, limited entry to the elite stratum alongside need for intergroup communication will promote the spread of a nonelite language as a lingua franca of the lower strata.

Most African interethnic situations are marked by sharp differentiations in the position of participants on the socioeconomic slope. Differences in education, for example, within the same urban work unit from office supervisor to messenger or manual laborer can be as great as twelve or more years of schooling (if the supervisor reached only 'A' level secondary schooling and if the lower status employees have little or no primary schooling). Evidence supports the arguments that more than one lingua franca exists in such a milieu, one primarily the vehicle of the educated and upper-echelon workers and the other that of the lesser educated.[4]

Further, evidence also supports the hypothesis that people's perceptions of themselves in relation to the economic marketplace are crucial in language adding. For example, in comparing Nairobi neighborhood and workplace associations as reasons for language adding, Parkin concluded that the alliances which benefit individuals economically form the "market" they will seek to meet. He wrote:

> The hard economic and political facts of life in the city seem to place a much greater premium on learning languages informally for a number of purposes than do neighborhood ties: for successful, efficient or simply friendly workplace interaction; for establishing tolerable and mutually beneficial cross-ethnic short-term relationships; and even, in very rare cases, for establishing more committed cross-ethnic relationships of a patron-client nature or as in marriage. (1974a:179)

An urban syndrome of extralinguistic factors including urbanism, salaried work experience, and the exchange of goods or money causes people to add lingua francas, evidence indicates. (See Heine 1970 on Africa in general, Richardson 1962 on Zambia's Copperbelt, Abdulaziz 1972 on Tanzania, for example.) The following studies detail language adding in urban settings: A study in a Lagos suburb (Scotton 1975) showed that *all* respondents in the sample (N=187) equally including men and women, knew at least one of the three major lingua francas of Lagos: English, Yoruba, or pidgin English. Almost all respondents were salaried or engaged in trade. Only 5 percent—all of them speakers of the main indigenous language of Lagos, Yoruba—were monolingual. But 45 percent spoke two other languages *in addition to* their own first language, 29 percent spoke three other languages, and 4 percent spoke four other languages. Only 17 percent spoke only one other language. Johnson (1975) found that only 2 percent of the sample (N=286) were monolingual in Larteh, a town 35 miles north of Accra. Thirty-three percent knew one other language (Twi), 41 percent knew two other languages, and 23 percent knew three other languages. In a Zambia survey, Serpell (1978a) found that on the average nearly three other Zambian languages were claimed in addition to their home language and English by a group of 79 civil servants. (Serpell said that fluency was not tested and could have ranged considerably, but he estimated middle-level fluency in most cases.)

SYMBOLIC ATTRIBUTES OF LINGUA FRANCAS THAT SPREAD

The allocation of different linguistic varieties in a speech community to different functions is well studied (Ferguson 1959, Fishman 1972).

Ferguson distinguished varieties as either High or Low in terms of the functions for which they are allocated. High varieties are used in formal education, most written materials, and formal public contacts, whereas Low varieties are used among the family and for generally informal contacts. Fishman grouped varieties in terms of the domain for which they are appropriate, distinguishing such domains as home, work, or school. Neither of these taxonomies seems satisfactory because it tends to force binary decisions about varieties. What is valued as the High (=prestige) variety in one context is not necessarily High in all contexts, nor is one variety used exclusively even in certain "High" situations or domains.

A construct which recognizes the possibility of relating linguistic varieties to diverse situations might be more useful than constructs which attempt to find a common denominator in the situations. The more satisfactory construct may be a set of abstract attribute values for each linguistic variety.

The set of values for any variety would be congruent, but all values would not be primary in the same situations; therefore, both the unity and the varying saliency of the values associated with varieties could be captured in such a taxonomy. For example, Swahili in urban Uganda has the feature 'plus East African/national' as well as other features including 'plus informal acquisition' and 'plus or minus education'. These features are congruent since a language which is an East African or national symbol is appropriately a language which is accessible—via informal acquisition—to all. But when a superior addresses a new inferior employee in the workplace in Swahili, the feature 'plus East African/ national' is hardly salient. Rather, the features having to do with acquisition and education are salient. The superior's use of Swahili signals both his expectation that the employee will know Swahili and his lack of expectation about the employee's educational attainments.

Any value may be related to one or two or many varieties, and no variety is necessarily related exclusively to any one domain, or vice versa. Each variety emerges, then, with its own set of values. Few value sets contain only values related to a single domain. For example, as will be shown, in Africa where it is the official language, English's value 'plus authority' can relate it to both the domains of 'home' and 'work' in specific contexts. English's value as 'plus educated' hardly relates it to the 'home' domain, however, since education is not normally a salient value in African home interactions.

This construct of a set of multiple values for describing a language's allocation shows its virtues most clearly when one realizes one of the major characteristics of symbolic formations—such as language—is their multiplicity of meanings. As Abner Cohen stated:

It is indeed in the very essence of the symbolic process to perform a multiplicity of functions with economy of symbolic formation. The more
meanings a symbol signifies, the more ambiguous and flexible it becomes,
the more intense the feelings it evokes, the greater its potency, and the
more functions it achieves. (1974:32)

What follows are the major generalizations which may hold about
value sets for lingua francas in much of Africa.

Official Languages as Lingua Francas

The official language is the variety of highest prestige in the contexts
of education, government, and urban workplace. It has the attribute
value 'plus education' because it is normally acquired only in school so
that its knowledge is a sign of education. These remarks apply mainly to
the alien official languages. The indigenous official languages, Swahili in
Tanzania, Amharic in Ethiopia, and Somali in Somalia are all acquired
informally as well as taught in the schools, and therefore are exceptions
regarding this attribute. However, higher education in both Tanzania
and Ethiopia is still in English.

Because the official language is linked with unequal power relationships, it has the attribute value 'plus authority'. This link arose historically for much of Africa with the colonizing Europeans (or with local
conquerors in the case of Ethiopia), and is preserved today by language-usage patterns of superiors and officialdom in general.

The other main attribute value associated with the official language is
'plus formal' because it is most used in structured situations—at school,
and for interethnic contacts, especially in the upper socioeconomic
strata. It is also the major language of written materials, even personal
letters, an attribute which gives it special potency in relation to all three
values, education, authority and formality.[5]

Secondary Official Languages or Nonofficial Lingua Francas

Most other lingua francas which exist in African nations are regional
rather than national in spread. Some examples are Hausa in northern
Nigeria, Galla in parts of Ethiopia, Lingala along the Congo River and
in the Zairoise capital of Kinshasha, and Krio in the Freetown area of
Sierra Leone. There are, however, a few exceptions that are national in
spread, which are noted above.

Some of these languages have limited official standing. They may be
taught in the schools at the lower levels in designated regions, and they
are often used in a limited way in the mass media. (This is hardly true at
all of the pidginized forms of English, though.) Swahili in Kenya is
something of an exception in the extent of official status it enjoys. It is

the co-official language (with English) of parliamentary debate; it is a school subject at all levels and compulsory in primary schools; and it shares radio broadcast-time about equally with English, Kenya's main official language.

All of these languages have the attribute value 'secondarily official'. For example, in Lusaka when a public meeting is addressed in English, the interpreter by convention translates into Nyanja, or occasionally Bemba (Serpell 1978a:148). Swahili is used for administrative meetings all over Kenya whenever nonlocal officials are present and a lingua franca is needed, largely because of Swahili's status as the national language of Kenya and the fact that it is better known across socioeconomic strata than English, the main official language.

In contrast to the official languages, these locally based lingua francas are all marked 'neutral' to varying degrees with regard to education. Most of them are learned in informal contexts—from friends, traders, coworkers, and less frequently brothers or sisters. The extent to which these lingua francas are acquired informally rather than through schooling is dramatically revealed by a Kenya study. In Nairobi, where children can anticipate studying Swahili as a compulsory primary school subject, 46 percent of the children surveyed by Gorman claimed to have learned Swahili first outside of school (1974:360). In Kenyan rural areas, more children learn Swahili first at school; but the percent who reported learning Swahili first in school varied from 17 to 78 percent, depending on the regional ethnic group surveyed. Zambian university students surveyed reported learning indigenous lingua francas mainly from friends. For example, 58 percent said they learned Nyanja from friends and 40 percent claimed to learn Bemba in this way (Musonda 1978:233). Johnson (1975) reported that children in Larteh, Ghana, begin to acquire Twi before entering school; other indigenous lingua francas are learned by Larteh residents primarily as a result of having lived in areas where the languages are widely spoken. Many of today's adults in rural areas learned lingua francas from coworkers when they entered an interethnic urban work situation (for example, Kashoki 1978 on Zambia or Scotton forthcoming 1979a on western Kenya).

Some locally based lingua francas are studied in school, as noted above. But relative to the international language, which is always the language of higher education, these languages are not symbols of educational attainment. For example, in Kampala, persons at all levels of education reported knowing some Swahili to the extent that 97 percent of the sample (N=233) knew some Swahili. Persons at only the upper educational levels (primary-school leavers) claimed to know much English (Scotton 1972:51–99).

Because of how they are acquired, knowledge of these locally based lingua francas carries few special socioeconomic connotations in most cases. The relationship between adding these languages and age, for example, is not clear cut; however, because informal acquisition seems to be a function of length of exposure, the locally based lingua francas may be better known by older persons as opposed to official languages which are taught in the schools and are often better known by younger persons. In Zambia, for example, overall degree of multilingualism did not vary much between any age groups up to forty-five years of age. But younger people are more likely to speak English there, while older people are more likely to speak the locally based lingua francas (Kashoki 1978:43).

In Ethiopia, younger persons were more likely to know Amharic among Galla mother-tongue speakers in the Jimma-Aggaro area, whereas older persons there among Amharic mother-tongue speakers were more likely to have learned Galla (Amharic is the school language. Cooper, Singh, and Abraha 1976:236).

In general, a "travel syndrome" (including urban residence) characterizes all speakers of locally based lingua francas in Africa. They therefore are marked 'plus spatial mobility'. Many Yorubas in Lagos who report knowing Hausa beyond the greetings had served in northern Nigeria at some point (Scotton unpublished research 1971–73). Kikuyus in one Nairobi housing estate who reported knowing Kamba had lived in a proportionately larger number of other towns and in the longer established areas of Nairobi than had other Kikuyus in the sample (Parkin 1974a:160–63). Persons in a Zambian survey who had moved at least once in their lives and who have lived for at least six months in an urban area showed greater multilingualism than did others (Kashoki 1978:43–44).

Since they are acquired largely informally, locally based lingua francas have the attribute value 'minus socioeconomic status evaluation'. Scotton (1972, 1977a, and 1977b) reports on a study in Kampala which showed that male respondents associated type of employment a male speaker might have with his "goodness" of English. No such association appeared between their evaluations of a speaker's Swahili and his possible occupation. It was suggested that possession of this 'minus' attribute makes an informally acquired lingua franca more attractive in at least one way to a potential language-learner than formally acquired lingua francas, such as English or French: speakers need not feel they constantly are being judged in terms of socioeconomic background.

Locally based lingua francas also have the attribute values 'minus formal' and 'minus authority' in relation to the official language. These values derive from the manner of acquisition of the locally based lingua francas and their position in the workplace and officialdom relative to the official languages. However, it is important to stress that in situations where the official language is seldom used, a locally based lingua franca can connote authority *relative* to local languages. Reporting on rural language use, Whiteley gave the following example:

> . . . in a number of different [tea] estates, I noticed that the pickers clustered in language groups, and I could distinguish Gusii, Luo, and Luyia; the overseer, however, who moved behind the pickers to see any bad picking, used Swahili. Not only was its use here essential as the only common language, but, along with his demeanour, dress and equipment served to distinguish the overseer as the man with authority. (1974b:343–44)

The fact that these languages are not used in many formal situations, that they are associated with the masses in general without regard to educational status, and that they are indigenous gives them all the attribute value 'plus national', at least relative to the official language if the latter is an imported language. Some of them, however, have more the value 'plus regional'; some examples would be Chiluba in Zaire, Tigrinya in Ethiopia, and even Hausa in Nigeria, with accompanying negative connotations outside their regional base.

Both the official language and major locally based lingua francas generally possess the attribute value 'neutral ethnicity'. (This value only exists, however, when a large group of mother-tongue speakers of the language in question is not a significant power source in the larger society. Thus, while Yoruba, Ibo, and Hausa are lingua francas in Nigeria, none of them has the value 'neutral ethnicity'.) Possession of this value makes a language especially attractive in multiethnic contexts. The use of anyone's own language in such contexts is seen by many as a symbol of excessive accommodation to one group and, as such, is a key source of hostility, open or not, especially at workplaces. (See Scotton 1975 for several testimonials.) Scotton (1976b) argues that the wide currency of English and Swahili in East African urban centers and of English and pidgin English in Lagos arises partly because these languages are marked 'neutral ethnicity' in these urban contexts.

Fishman (1978:119) commented on English's "de-ethnicized image" in the world as a whole. He said its valuation "may be related much more to . . . process variables (modernization, urbanization, technological know-how, consumerism and a higher standard of living in general). . . ." than anything else.[6]

Minor Locally Based Lingua Francas

Many African languages whose primary identification is with specific ethnic groups serve at times as lingua francas. Their main attribute value always remains 'plus ethnicity', however. Therefore, they may serve as lingua francas where they are the dominant mother tongues, but rarely outside those areas. This differentiates them from the major lingua francas whose other attributes (discounting 'plus or minus ethnicity') seem to give them currency even outside their home areas. Limited evidence in Zambia suggests this picture, with the officially designated regional languages in use as lingua francas to some degree in non-mother-tongue areas. Minor Zambian lingua francas are confined to their home areas, such as Tumbuka in the Lundazi, Chama, and Isoka districts (Kashoki 1978:35).

In towns, most often something of a patron-client or teacher-disciple relationship is the impetus to learn a minor lingua franca. These languages then have the attribute value 'plus dominance/authority', but only for the special context in which they arise (Parkin 1974a, 1974b).

Interethnic marriages, especially in rural contexts, promote the adding of such a minor lingua franca if it is the mother tongue of one of the partners and the dominant local language (Whiteley 1974b:329). In towns, interethnic couples may speak to each other in a major lingua franca, such as Swahili in Nairobi, or Amharic in Addis Ababa, or even English if they are members of the elite.

THE PRESENT SPREAD OF
LINGUA FRANCAS

With the battery of positive attribute values they have, the official languages of African nations are the lingua francas most Africans would like to learn. Certainly, a major argument of this essay has been that the language which is seen as the best resource in the marketplace is the language most attractive to add.

In the Home Domain

As potent, transethnic symbols, it is not surprising that official languages are those which seem to be the most "in conflict" with mother tongues. For example, in 80 percent of the schools surveyed in 1968 by Gorman, teachers discouraged any other language but English in the school setting. The pupils, however, reported that English is discouraged in many homes in the rural areas, and to a lesser extent in the urban areas.

Further, Gorman stressed that only a few of the children surveyed had a repertoire exactly matching that of grandparents, parents, or even teachers. Gorman (1974:365) commented that "the relative uniformity . . . in the general configurations of language use within . . . both rural and urban samples was striking" in regard to decreasing use of mother tongue. The most usage of mother tongue was with the grandparents, its usage decreasing with parents and then decreasing again with young siblings to the most decrease with older siblings. Still, even for these children, mother tongues remain distinctly the major medium in the home. A similar pattern seems to hold in Zambia. In a survey of university students, Musonda reported:

> . . . it was apparent that in the majority of homes both parents spoke a single Zambian language and used it practically always when speaking to their children. In about 8.6% of the cases (N=93), English was used with some Zambian language in a conversation between a parent and a child, and in about 5.4% of the cases, there were two Zambian languages used side by side, i.e. the mother speaking one and the father using the other, perhaps a probable indication of an intertribal marriage. (1978:235)

For older persons for whom the possibility of acquiring the official language—if it is an alien, international language—remains at best remote, such a language is rarely even heard in homestead contexts. When it is used, it is an ambiguous symbol, standing for "progress" and class divisions at the same time. No wonder many Africans are ambivalent in their perceptions of the official language. A report by a University of Nairobi student shows the psychological conflict the competition of mother tongue and official language engenders. He reported that his brother (in their home area) had been arrested by the police for making beer without a license. His relatives' pleas for his release, couched in the local language, were ignored. But when the university student sought entrance to the police station in English, he was allowed in. "It was, I strongly believe, my English that gave me the honor to be allowed in. And it was my English, during my talk with the chief, that secured the release of my brother," he said. The same student, in another home-area context, reported resentment against use of English:

> At a beer party near my home, two boys broke into talk in English. The reaction from the old men was bitter and they said, "Who are those speaking English? Are they backbiting us? They are proud. Push them out!" Although the boys had not been addressing the beer party as such but had been talking only to each other, this use of English was regarded as an insult. (Scotten, personal communication, 1973)

The clear association of the official language—above all other languages—with the value 'plus authority', as shown in the above examples, has meant the official language is spreading into even home contexts in which authority is salient. These contexts were previously covered by the mother tongue. Educated fathers in rural areas, for example, might not practice the official language with their children in order to help them in school—as many urban fathers do—but they will discipline their children in that language (personal reports from University of Nairobi students, 1973). Swahili is used in Tanzanian homes in the same way (personal reports from University of Dar es Salaam students, 1977). Thus, even the attribute value 'plus ethnicity', which the mother tongue certainly has, does not seem as potent as 'plus authority' in all home contexts.

Even in those cities where the official language and probably a secondary lingua franca are widely known and used, the working classes do not use them at home. For example, in Nairobi, Swahili (and possibly some English) is the order of the day for the working classes in the workplace, and Swahili alone is used on the bus and in the market. But once people reach home or once they are chatting with ethnic brethren in neighborhood gathering places, the mother tongue is used almost exclusively (Scotten, unpublished research, 1977). Considering the amount of lingua franca use in public, the sharpness of the dichotomy is striking. But there is little or no spill-over of lingua francas into private life except among the educated elite.

One such reason for the split between private and public usage may be that a large part of the ferocious, though covert, socioeconomic competition in much of Africa is ethnically based. Being able to speak one's language is something of an escape valve after the pressures of the workplace. Using one's mother tongue at home is removed from but relevant to the on-going public competition because it is a symbol of self-assertion; it is in clear defiance of the norms which require using certain lingua francas in public and of the socioeconomic order which they symbolize.

The Public/Workplace Domain

There is also a conflict, but mainly at an instrumental rather than a sentimental level, between the official language and locally based lingua francas in public contexts, especially in nations where an alien, international language is official. The conflict depends on the link of the official language to education and on the advantages which will go with its use. While urban workers who have completed secondary school know and use both the official language and one or more secondary lingua francas as well, the lesser educated workers do not have the same options in their repertoire. They rarely know the official language well enough to use it in crucial negotiations of status-identification where the educated can use it to their advantage.

Thus, Calvet (this volume) spoke of the potential for the spread of

Bambara (Mandingo) in Mali in terms of its coexistence with French as a confrontation revolving around the power and privilege which go with the ability to speak French. He wrote:

> But it [Mandingo] remains in confrontation with French, and this coexistence sets a sociological problem which obstructs every kind of evolution today. The Malian middle class, mainly civil servants, has obtained a kind of social promotion thanks to French, language of the school, language for studies, language of administration (p. 192)

The same type of competition in public situations, with English gaining favor over Swahili, is also reported in Kenya by both Parkin (1974a) and Gorman (1974). They report for such situations a decrease in the frequency of Swahili use, when there is a rise in education, and an increase in the use of English. And, even while noting how Swahili is increasingly meeting the need of the low status groups in Nairobi for a lingua franca, Parkin said:

> Yet English is potentially a long-term threat to Swahili because of the flood into Nairobi from rural districts of young, educated and English-speaking but unemployable migrants. (1974c:214)

The official language and other lingua francas are for the most part very unevenly matched in their conflict. The configuration of attribute values of the secondary of nonofficial lingua francas makes them a much less attractive resource in comparison. In specific contexts, use of locally based lingua francas is even a distinct insult or at the very least a slight. In his novel *No Longer at Ease,* Chinua Achebe has his protagonist, a young, educated Nigerian, relate an incident to his cousin in which the switch from Standard to pidgin English carries an insult. The hero had been parked at the beach with his girl friend when they were approached by a policeman. The hero related to his cousin what happened:

> He the policeman said: "Good evening, sir,"
> I said: "Good evening."
> Then he said: "Is she your wife?"
> I remained very cool and said: "No."
> Then he said: "Where you pick am?"
> I couldn't stand that, so I blew up. . . . Just think of that,
> *"Where you pick am?"* (1961:74)

In Nairobi, a sales manager for a large corporation (an African) normally addressed his salesmen in English, but he switched to Swahili to chastise one for his work on a certain sales exhibit (personal communication 1977).

The lesser educated are regularly addressed by the educated in unofficial languages, a practice which inevitably draws attention to their low educational status. At the same time they are just as regularly bystanders at scenes of the educated speaking the official language among themselves. For example, at several local meetings in western Kenya, Swahili was the medium employed by agricultural officers and other governmental officials in speeches to the gathered farmers. Swahili was referred to as the *lugha ya taifa,* 'language of the nation', as it often is. At the same time, the speakers chatted in English to each other in front of the audience (personal observation 1977).

Still, in many public contexts the locally based lingua franca is definitely preferred to the official language. This is especially so in transactional situations where neither power nor ethnic identity is salient, such as in passenger-bus driver conversations. For example, the passenger on a Nairobi bus who told the conductor in English that it was the conductor's job and not his to open the window was immediately upbraided by the conductor as well as other passengers (in both English and Swahili) for the pretension to power which his use of English carried (personal communication 1977).

In certain public contexts, the educated prefer the use of the official language with members of their own ethnic group as a means of social distancing. A nurse at the Kakamega hospital in Kenya reported to me that some Luyia doctors prefer *not* to address a patient directly in the Luyia variety which they both share. Instead, these doctors have a Luyia nurse present who listens to the patient's Luyia and then "interprets" for the doctor into English. Doctors do this to disallow the establishment of an ethnic relationship between themselves and patients in favor of the preferred doctor-patient relationship.

A newspaper reporter in the same locale gave me this account of why he uses English extensively with ethnic brethren when he is on business:

> Recently I was covering drama festivals at the provincial level, and there were schools from Bungoma. And you know Bungoma speaks just one language [that is, the reporter's own first language, Lubukusu]. So these fellows, when they discovered I'm speaking Lubukusu, they go telling they want a picture. They speak in Lubukusu. So now what do you do? You have just a few snaps—you have to take the leading teams—so now they want a special favor. So now I start speaking English only—even with those Bukusu—I pretend I have never heard of such a language as theirs! (personal communication 1977)

The official language and, at a lower economic level, a locally based lingua franca, are both heavily used in the workplace to neutralize ethnic ties as well. Surveying I did in Kenya among the Luyia in both a provincial city and the capital showed that even if the boss was a Luyia, a Luyia employee would expect to address him mainly or entirely in English or Swahili, depending on their educational levels. As already noted, lingua francas are also used to neutralize ethnicity with non-ethnic brethren as well. (See Scotton 1976b on strategies of neutrality.)

Educated persons in a public bar may switch to the official language in a gathering of their own ethnic group when they wish to call attention to their authority or experience. The uneducated and to a lesser extent the educated use a locally based lingua franca in the same way. Such remarks as, "I tell you, I know this Nairobi town. I know the ups and downs; I know how to survive" (personal communication 1977) are typically made in English or Swahili in Nairobi, for example, and interspersed in a conversation mainly conducted in the ethnic language.

PRESENT DETERRENTS TO THE SPREAD OF LINGUA FRANCAS

There are times when accommodation to the "market" militates *against* the spread of a major lingua franca. Cooper and Carpenter (1976) report that multilingualism, with the seller trying to speak the buyer's language, is more the norm in Ethiopian market transactions than the use of the major Ethiopian lingua franca. Parkin (1974c) also makes a good deal of the "exploitation" by Nairobi market sellers of their knowledge of various vernaculars when addressing customers. Duran (1975) reports the same phenomenon in rural Kenya. (Of course, in these instances there is still spread of a lingua franca since the seller is using a second language; it is just that a single, major lingua franca does not dominate these contexts.)

Further, in many rural areas, especially if they are nearly homogeneous, adding a lingua franca involves few perceivable advantages. Cooper concluded that "the benefits of a knowledge of Amharic are still confined principally to the urban population and to that part of the rural population with relatively easy access to towns" (1976:293). Further, a lingua franca is a *negative* resource in many rural settings. In a rural gathering of people of the same ethnic group, there is only *one* linguistic choice which will *never* meet with censure: the shared mother tongue. In western Kenya, for instance, the local person who uses Swahili— especially fluent Swahili—in rural areas is suspected for having traveled *too* much. Use of English in the same setting could be censured as pretentious, as noted above.

The crucial deterrent to the official language's spread, however, has been the maintenance of horizontal as opposed to vertical communication patterns in Africa. (Both Mazrui and Zirimu [1974] and Heine [1977] discuss language use in these terms, although their distinctions are different.) This brings us back to the previous discussion of communication vehicles and socioeconomic integration. So long as horizontal communication patterns are maintained in Africa, with boundaries depending on socioeconomic status, only a small minority can establish links with centers of political and economic power. Horizontal patterns mean that certain language and other societal elements are accessible only to persons within a single horizontal stratum of society rather than to persons in a vertical pathway which takes in geographic and ethnic segments from the society as a whole. At present, access to the official language via formal schooling is restricted by the horizontal communication network make up mainly of the elite.

The result has already been noted: small percentages of people in sub-Saharan Africa are presently able to make use of their main official language if it is English, French, or Portuguese. Few individuals acquire these official languages in any way that does not include formal education. (Scotton 1972, for example, shows that only those Kampala respondents who had been to school sufficiently long to learn more than a smattering of English even claimed they knew it at all; yet some of these same persons informally acquired other languages. Johnson [1975:95] concluded, "The locus of acquisition of English is essentially restricted to the schools" in his study of Larteh, Ghana. Kashoki [1978: 41] reports on a nationwide Zambian sample with statistics which show that 50.9 percent of those respondents who had been through grades 5 to 7 claimed some knowledge of English, but only 4.6 percent of those with lesser education made any such claim. Clearly, school is perceived as the place to learn English.) Opportunities to enter or continue school are limited in most of Africa and too much of the schooling available is inadequate for a number of reasons ranging from lack of adequate or suitable materials to poorly prepared or motivated teachers.[7]

Neville Grant, a writer of English textbooks for African schools, who has extensive experience in both West and East Africa, made these remarks about English in the schools:

> Few pick English up outside the schools. It is worth adding that many who learn it in the schools forget it. They even forget it while at secondary school. I know of many instances, and many teachers have confirmed this,

of students who do quite well in Form 1 and seem thereafter to go down-hill in English. It gets unlearnt. I have often asked why this was so. The two most common explanations were (1) that the students "gave up" be-cause they felt they had little hope either of passing their exams or of getting a job thereafter; (2) that the students were going through the traumas of adolescence; (3) there is a good deal of poor teaching by un-trained teachers; (4) many teachers are unmotivated; (5) there is some-times even a lack of teachers—for a period, an entire term or an entire year; (6) finally there also has been a widespread belief that materials have to be difficult to be any good, and unsuitably difficult materials often put off the students. (personal communication 1978)

Given this situation—with limited schooling available and informal acquisition relatively nonexistent, it is not surprising that Heine pre-dicted that "by the year 2,000 about sixty percent of the African popu-lation will still be ignorant of the language which is used to govern, administer, and to educate them" (1977:9).

It is important at this point to remind ourselves that Africans do learn nonofficial lingua francas in great numbers, even languages from genetic groups as different from their own as are those of English or French. This language adding supports the hypothesis that people will learn a language when they feel it is in their socioeconomic interest to do so. Why, then, do they not add the main official language, for which there is certainly a far greater set of incentives?

CONDITIONS FOR ADDING A
LINGUA FRANCA

In order for individuals to want to add a lingua franca, they must be (a) dissatisfied with their present socioeconomic status *and* (b) confident that the configuration of their lives will change, triggered off by the adding of the lingua franca. (It is beyond the scope of this paper to consider whether or not the desire to add a language is conscious or even need be conscious for results to be obtained.)

Karl Deutsch's discussion of the reception of information and the analogies he used are relevant to any discussion of language adding. He said the effectiveness of information directed at the receiver (let 're-ceiver' equal 'individual language learner' here) depends on two classes of conditions. "First of all," Deutsch said, "*at least some parts of the receiv-ing system must be in highly unstable equilibrium,* so that the very small amount of energy carrying the signal will be sufficient to start off a much larger process of change." The second class of conditions is more important in the interpretation proposed in this paper and concerns the patterns already stored in the receiver. Deutsch used the analogy of a key opening a lock: "Clearly, the effectiveness of any key in turning a particular lock depends only slightly on the energy with which it is turned . . . and *far more on the correspondence of the configuration of its notches with the configuration of the tumblers in the lock*" [italics added] (1963:147–48).

To continue this analogy, in societies in which there is disequilibrium, evidenced by a good deal of migration to towns, and where migrants can see the addition of a lingua franca as a potential resource to them personally, a good deal of language spread would be expected. But there are two different kinds of in-migrants in Africa, just as there are two (or more) lingua francas in town which symbolize two different types of entry into the market of the mobilized, as noted above. There are those migrants who move to town because they *already* have added the most resourceful language, and there are in-migrants who pick up what they can *in town*. Mazrui and Zirimu refer to these two different types, using Uganda as a setting:

> . . . we think of the educated class speakers of English as *rural misfits* forced by their very qualifications at times to migrate to the cities; whereas the less educated with a smattering of Kiswahili begin by being *urban misfits,* and improve their Kiswahili as part of the process of adjustment. (1974:19)

Those in-migrants who do not *already* know the official language, through earlier formal schooling, do *not* learn that language in town. (Their rural brothers whom they left behind are even less likely to learn it, of course.) Why? The point of Deutch's analogy should make this clear. Simply placing a key (the main official language) in the lock will not open that lock unless the key complements the configuration *already present in the lock* (other societal elements, such as a schooling degree, the "right" urban contacts based on family and ethnic group ties, possibly some special expertise gained in school, etc.). The poorly educated in-migrants are simply ill-prepared to join the ranks of the mobile for more reasons than lack of language skills alone. Learning the main official language will not alleviate their situation to any significant extent. This is because receiving the education which goes with a diploma symbolizes more than acquisition of a new language. It symbolizes membership in the strata which have the wherewithal of wealth and power to survive a highly restrictive school system (in addition to having intellectual ability). Urban in-migrants recognize that there is a necessary configuration of societal elements—the right certificates, the right contacts—which they must have in order for them to be benefited by learning the main official language. Part of the power of knowing the language of authority derives from the interrelationship of this language with other societal elements. Recognizing this, in-migrants make no great effort to add that language to their repertoire in any real sense.

CONCLUSION

This essay has addressed the general question: what determines whether or not a person will learn a lingua franca? Specifically, this question has been posed: why haven't more people in Africa learned the lingua franca which is their nation's official language?

The general hypotheses suggested to answer the issues these questions raise have centered around the premise that people will learn a language if they think it will benefit them. First, it was suggested that linguistic varieties are societal elements which interlock in their spread with other societal elements such as educational attainment, special group membership, etc. Arguments have been presented to show that languages have attribute values which derive from the relation of languages to other societal elements.

Second, it was suggested that not all languages are equally resources for all people, even within the same society. Whether or not acquiring a language will be a resource for individuals depends on the configuration of societal elements they already control. Evidence has been presented to show that lingua francas with different sets of attribute values (linking them to other societal elements) have been acquired by different types of people.

Moore (1974:64–65), in reference to general social change, stated that three scarcities restrain social participation. "We may identify these scarcities as *time, treasure* (or material resources) and *troth* (loyalty or affective energy)," he wrote. In the framework developed here, it is predicted investments of time, treasure, and troth are not undertaken, because they *are* scarcities, unless individuals can see a benefit.

Third, it was suggested that changes in the power and content of languages as societal elements can occur. If such changes happen, there will be a change in the components of the attribute value set of the lingua francas discussed here. Some lingua francas would then become more attractive to learn and others less attractive.

Two specific hypotheses regarding the present and possible spread of lingua francas in Africa were suggested, both related to the above hypotheses:

1. That official languages as lingua francas will spread slowly and only then through formal acquisition as long as a limited degree of socioeco-

nomic integration exists, as it does in most of Africa. Those without the other credentials for upward mobility have found that simply acquiring the main official language does them little good.[8] Evidence has been presented to show that official languages have not spread, to date, much beyond the ranks of the educated, at least in those nations where English, French, or Portuguese are official languages.[9]

2. Locally based lingua francas will continue to spread rapidly in Africa with or without the government encouragement of making them the official mediums of specific domains. The existing diglossic situation in reference to lingua francas may then become more polarized and may petrify, with the official language mainly the medium of the upper strata and one or more other languages mainly used by the lower strata. Locally based lingua francas will spread in the lower strata for two reasons: (a) Individuals see these lingua francas as the only real vehicles available to them for upward mobility. These languages offer learners entry into the worker-patron relationships of urban areas—even if they do not offer entry into the ranks of the mobilized who know the official language and who are the supervisors. (b) Further, just as it is the norm to acquire many of these lingua francas informally, it is also the norm to acquire informally many of the skills necessary for the lower level jobs. (Schools, which have curricula geared to prepare university entrants more than any other group, offer few practical subjects.) That is, the configuration of societal elements which unlocks these jobs and which includes these locally based lingua francas is easier to come by informally than other elements in the society. Entrepreneurship characterizes the occupational syndrome in which these languages flourish.[10]

Secondary official or nonofficial lingua francas are immediately useful to the population of various socioeconomic strata, but especially the nonelite, and they can be learned well enough for efficient use across ethnic boundaries in the city. Without a change in the political-economic systems of Africa, however, these languages will receive little or no additional official recognition and therefore are not equipped to serve as symbols of national unification. They appear to be useful languages for the socioeconomic integration of African societies, but only in the lower socioeconomic strata.

Main official languages which are lingua francas, however, will not spread rapidly. Given lack of content-rich (good education) or powerful ("right" ethnic group membership and contacts) societal elements in their control, the vast majority of Africans see no reason to make the effort needed to learn the official language.[11]

The spread of a lingua franca, or indeed any language, depends on the interrelation of the power of the individual's linguistic repertoire with the power of these other societal elements. The number of contexts in which a language is used, the type of contexts, the number of speakers a language has—such "facts" about a language are relatively useless in explaining language spread unless they are considered dynamically.[12] What counts is how a language is related to other elements, for these relationships make up the system which most significantly influences language spread.

With most African societies marked by minimal socioeconomic integration, learning the official languages as a lingua franca—the language of the upper strata of those societies—seems like a futile task. For those African political societies depending on such official languages as a vehicle for true political integration, the prospect seems remote.

It is misleading to study the spread of any language out of the context of change in the entire social system. Social change is dependent on the accessibility of a configuration of societal elements of which language is only a part. The availability of resources and the ability *or* inclination of the societal structure to distribute these resources equitably may be a key factor in language spread. People will add a language which is part of a "mobility configuration" that promotes their socioeconomic advantage.

NOTES

1. The original draft of this paper was written while I was on assignment to the Michigan State University Humanities Research Center, Summer 1978. Field work in 1977 in Kenya was conducted under a grant from the Joint Committee on African Studies of the American Council of Learned Societies and the Social Science Research Council. I wish to thank Leonard Doob, Neville Grant, Jane Hill, Gayle Partmann, and James Scotton for comments on an earlier draft. I am especially grateful to Robert L. Cooper for his extensive comments.

2. Huntington (1971) is the source for some of these ideas about types of change involving societal elements and their interrelations.

3. See Scotton (manuscript 1979b) for a more detailed discussion of percentages of speakers of English and French in Africa. There are no known statistics on the knowledge of French in any Francophone country. Anglophone Africa is better studied, but reports are not always comparable since some studies only report percentages of speakers without reference to degree of proficiency. Kashoki (1978:31) reported that 26 percent of persons surveyed in a nationwide study in Zambia claimed to speak some English. Urban studies report more ability. For example, Parkin (1974a:148) found that 42 percent of household heads in a Nairobi lower-class housing estate claimed to know some English.

4. For example, Scotton (unpublished research 1971–73, but see Scotton 1975 and 1976a) found in Lagos a vast difference between reported use of the various lingua francas according to education. Those respondents (N=96) who had coworkers of another ethnic group were asked what languages they used in interethnic contacts at work. Of those with education to secondary school certificate level, 60 percent (24 out of 40) reported they used English alone. A total of 75 percent used some English, either alone or in combination with other languages and 32 percent used some pidgin. In comparison, among those respondents with primary school only, just 5.5 percent reported using English alone. Pidgin English in some combination or alone was their main choice, with 78 percent reporting using some pidgin. Half of them did report using English in some combination at times, however. Respondents with a middle-level education (above primary, but less than secondary school completion) reported using either English alone or English in combination with pidgin English about equally, with 34 percent reporting English alone and 32 percent English/pidgin English. Another 24 percent reported using English in combination with other languages, such as Yoruba. Scotton (1972) found a similar division between users of English and Swahili in Kampala, with Swahili as the main lingua franca of the lesser educated. Parkin (1974a) reported similar findings for Nairobi.

Cooper and Singh (1976:270–71) conclude that even in a Galla mother-tongue area, the dominant language in the industrial work sphere was Amharic. This was so especially in exchanges with superiors. They noted that while Galla might be used in speaking to Galla mother-tongue workers, either by speakers from other mother-tongue groups or by Galla mother-tongue speakers themselves, much less Galla was used with supervisors. Even among Galla-mother-tongue speakers, "the percentage . . . claiming to use Galla with fellow workers (67 percent) was about three times as great as with supervisors (23 percent)."

5. Whiteley (1969) concluded his study of the spread of Swahili and its use as a potential unifying force in Tanzania with the observation that Swahili's success in this role depends heavily on "capturing and holding the allegiance of the educated minority," particularly *the writers* of the nation. The people "must receive encouragement from those who, fortunate enough to control a supranational language, yet choose to write in Swahili" (p. 126).

Mazrui (1975) also commented about the idea of power being associated with the use of writing, also quoting Georges Balandier to that effect (p. 100).

6. Neville Grant pointed out, however, that at least in Anglophone Africa English is seen as something of a symbol of transnational cultural unity. (Grant cited a 1974 Kenyan report, *Recommendations of the Working Committee on Teaching of Literature in Kenyan Secondary Schools* [Inspectorate, Ministry of Education, mimeo which makes this argument.] Further, Grant noted that discussions are being held in Mozambique about changing to English as the language of education (personal communication 1978).

7. For a discussion of language in education in Eastern Africa, see Ladefoged et al. (1971) on Uganda, Whiteley (1974) on Kenya, Bender et al. (1976) on Ethiopia, and Ohannessian and Kashoki (1978) on Zambia. One of the major problems in education in many parts of West Africa, as pointed out by Neville Grant, is the policy of requiring students to buy their own books. "Thus in Sierra Leone recently teachers told me that in a class of 40 to 50, there might be only one or two English text books" (personal communication 1978).

8. This is especially so in the present social climate in Africa for two addi-

tional reasons. First, there are few entrepreneurs in the upper socioeconomic strata; the elite are, for the most part, "organization men" who got where they are by orthodox means, i.e., having a full set of the right credentials. Entrepreneurship, of course, is very common in the lower economic strata in Africa. Second, there are now in the cities masses of youth who already speak the main official language and have their diplomas and other complementary trappings as well, but who are unemployed (Parkin 1974c:213–14).

9. The growing acquisition of French in Ivory Coast, where it is the sole official language, is an exception, but an exception which supports the argument of this essay. Economic incentives for learning French and widening availability of schooling, especially post-school courses, have been important factors in the spread of French in Ivory Coast. Partmann made this point:

> The economic factors which are so far proving useful in Ivory Coast are the widening access to regular education and to special adult courses, accompanied by rewards at various levels furnished by the rapidly growing economy, so that an individual's progress is tangibly marked. (1978 ms. 13–14)

In line with the argument of this paper, it is hypothesized that the socialist states of Angola and Mozambique will take rapid steps to make Portuguese widely accessible (especially to adults through nonformal means), or that they will award official status for key functions to regional lingua francas. Unfortunately, no single language is widely known in either state.

10. It is, of course, possible that the main official languages may become prerequisites for even lower-level jobs as more and more educated job-seekers find they must take such jobs. Parkin (1974a) comments on the probable "percolating" downwards of English in Nairobi, if official language policy does not change. If the main official languages do spread to lower economic strata, this will probably restrict the spread of secondary lingua francas, since two types of lingua francas will then be in direct competition. If a diglossic situation is maintained, no such competition will occur.

11. It is obvious that the attitude of Tanzanians toward the acquisition of their official language, Swahili, should be quite different. Socioeconomic integration is occurring in Tanzania, giving individuals every reason to expect that mobility is possible and that Swahili is an accessible element in the process. (See Scotton 1978.)

12. This is not, of course, a totally new argument. Fishman (1968:50–51), for example, in calling for more attention to the analysis of social processes, said, "Categories such as urban-rural, older-younger, male-female, etc., do not explain the dynamics of culture change which carry language shift along with them."

REFERENCES

Abdulaziz, Mkilifi, M. H. 1972. "Triglossia and Swahili-English bilingualism in Tanzania." *Language in Society* 1,1:197–213.

Achebe, Chinua. 1961. *No longer at ease*. New York: Ivan Obolensky.

Barth, Frederick. 1969. *Ethnic groups and boundaries*. Boston: Little, Brown.

Bender, Marvin L., J. D. Bowen, R. L. Cooper and C. A. Ferguson (eds.). 1976. *Language in Ethiopia*. London: Oxford University Press.

Blau, Peter. 1964. *Exchange and power in social life*. New York: Wiley.

Calvet, Louis-Jean. 1979. "The Spread of Mandingo: Military, Commercial, and Colonial influence on a Linguistic Datum." This volume.

Cohen, Abner. 1974. *Two-dimensional man*. Berkeley: University of California Press.

Cooper, Robert L. 1976. "The spread of Amharic." In Bender, M. L. et al. (eds.), 244–55.

Cooper, Robert L. and Susan Carpenter. 1976. "Language in the market." In Bender, M. L. et al. (eds.), 244–55.

Cooper, Robert L. and B. N. Singh. 1976. "Language and factory workers." In Bender, M. L. et al. (eds.), 264–72.

Cooper, Robert L., B. N. Singh and Abraha Ghermazion. 1976. "Mother tongue and other tongue in Kefa and Arusi." In Bender, M. L. et al. (eds.), 213–43.

Deutsch, Karl. 1963. *The nerves of government*. New York: The Free Press.

Deutsch, Karl. 1966 (2nd ed.). *Nationalism and social communication*. Cambridge: M.I.T. Press.

Duran, James J. 1975. "The role of Swahili in a multilingual rural community in Kenya." Doctoral dissertation, Stanford University.

Ferguson, Charles A. 1959. "Diglossia." *Word*. 325–40. Also in Ferguson, C. A. 1972. *Language structure and use*. Stanford: Stanford University Press. 1–26.

Fishman, Joshua A. 1968. "Nationality-Nationalism and nation-nationism." In Fishman, J. A., C. A. Ferguson and J. Das Gupta (eds.), *Language problems of developing nations*. New York: Wiley. 39–51.

Fishman, J. A. 1972. *The sociology of language*. Rowley, Mass.: Newbury House.

Fishman, J. A. 1978. "The spread of English: a new perspective on 'language maintenance and language shift'." In Fishman, J. A., R. L. Cooper and A. W. Conrad, *The spread of English: the sociology of English as an additional language*. Rowley, Mass.: Newbury House. 108–33.

Gorman, Thomas P. 1974. "Patterns of language use among school children and their parents." In Whiteley, W. H. 1974a. 351–96.

Greenberg, Joseph H. 1972. "Urbanism, migration, and language." In Greenberg, *Language, culture, and communication*. Stanford: Stanford University Press. 198–211. Originally 1965 in H. Kuper (ed.), *Urbanization and migration in West Africa*. Berkeley: University of California Press, 50–9, 189.

Heine, Bernd. 1970. *Status and use of African lingua francas*. Munchen: Weltforum Verlag.

Heine, Bernd. 1977. "Vertical and horizontal communication in Africa." University of Nairobi. Mimeo.

Huntington, Samuel P. 1971. "The change to change." *Comparative Politics*, 4:283–322.

Johnson, Bruce. 1975. "Stable triglossia at Larteh, Ghana." In Herbert, Robert K. (ed.) *Patterns in language, culture and society: sub-Saharan Africa*. Ohio State University Working Papers in Linguistics, 19:93–102.

Kashoki, Mubanga E. 1978. "The language situation in Zambia." In Ohannessian and Kashoki (eds.), 1978. 9–46.

Ladefoged, Peter, Ruth Glick, Clive Criper. 1971. *Language in Uganda*. Nairobi: Oxford University Press.

Lieberson, Stanley. 1970. *Language and ethnic relations in Canada*. New York: Wiley.

Mazrui, Ali. 1975. *The political sociology of the English language.* The Hague: Mouton.

Mazrui, Ali and Pio Zirimu. 1974. "Church, state, and marketplace in the spread of Kiswahili: comparative educational implications." Mimeo. Paper presented World Congress of Sociology, 1974, Toronto. Also in B. Spolsky and R. L. Cooper (eds.), 1978. *Case studies in bilingual education.* 427–543. Rowley, Mass.: Newbury House.

Moore, Wilbert E. 1974 (2nd ed.). *Social change.* Englewood Cliffs, N.J.: Prentice-Hall.

Musonda, Moses. 1978. "A study of language use among local students at the University of Zambia." In Ohannessian and Kashoki (eds.), 228–43.

Ohannessian, Sirarpi and Mubanga E. Kashoki (eds.). 1978. *Language in Zambia.* London: International African Institute.

Parkin, David J. 1974a. "Status and language adding in Bahati." In Whiteley, W. H. 1974a. 147–65.

Parkin, David J. 1974b. "Language shift and ethnicity in Kaloleni." In Whiteley, W. H. 1974a. 167–87.

Parkin, David J. 1974c. "Language switching in Nairobi." In Whiteley, W. H. 1974a. 189–215.

Partmann, Gayle. 1975. "Quelques remarques sur le Dioula Vehiculaire en Cote Invoire." In *Annales de Universite d'Abijan: Linguistique.* Vol. 8: 241–59.

Partmann, Gayle. 1978. "Socioeconomic rivalry and national language competence in Ivory Coast." Manuscript.

Richardson, Irvine. 1962. "Linguistic change in Africa with special reference to the Bemba-speaking area of Northern Rhodesia." In *Symposium on multilingualism, Brazzaville.* Commission for Technical Co-operation in Africa (CCTA), 19.189–96.

Rustow, Dankwart A. 1967. *A world of nations.* Washington: The Brookings Institute.

Scotton, Carol Myers. 1972. *Choosing a lingua franca in an African capital.* Edmonton: Linguistic Research, Inc.

Scotton, C. M. 1975. "Multilingualism in Lagos—what it means to the social scientist." In Herbert, Robert K. (ed.), *Patterns in language, culture and society: sub-Saharan Africa.* Ohio State University Working Papers in Linguistics 19:78–90.

Scotton, C. M. 1976a. "The role of norms and other factors in language choice in work situations in three African cities (Lagos, Kampala, Nairobi)." In Rolf Kjolseth and A. Verdoodt (eds.), *Language in Sociology.* Louvain: Editions Peeters. 201–32.

Scotton, C. M. 1976b. "Strategies of neutrality: language choice in uncertain situations." *Language* 52,4:919–41.

Scotton, C. M. 1977a. "Linguistic performance as a socioeconomic indicator." *Journal of Social Psychology* 102:35–45.

Scotton, C. M. 1977b. "Linguistic performances as subjective measures—some findings and implications." *Studies in African Linguistics* 8, supplement. 199–210.

Scotton, C. M. 1978. "Language in East Africa: linguistic patterns and political ideologies." In Joshua A. Fishman (ed.), *Advances in the study of societal multilingualism.* The Hague: Mouton. 719–60.

Scotton, C. M. 1979a. "Language use in Kenya: an urban-rural comparison of

Luyia." To appear in special issue on urban-rural differences, Edgar Polomé (ed.), *International Journal of the Sociology of Language.* Forthcoming.

Scotton, C. M. 1979b. "Elite closures as boundary maintenance: the case of Africa." Manuscript.

Serpell, Robert. 1978a. "Comprehension of Nyanja in Lusaka." In Ohannessian and Kashoki (eds.), 1978. 144–81.

Serpell, Robert. 1978b. "Some developments in Zambia since 1971." In Ohannessian and Kashoki (eds.), 424–47.

Smock, David R. 1975. "Language policy in Ghana." In Smock, David R. and Kwamena Bentsi-Enchill (eds.) *The Search for National Integration in Africa.* New York: Free Press.

Sylla, Yero. 1978. "Some quandaries of language policy in Senegal: Negritude and Francophonie." Paper presented at 9th Annual African Linguistics Conference, Michigan State University.

Whiteley, W. H. 1969. *Swahili, the rise of a national language.* London: Methuen.

Whiteley, W. H. 1971. "Some factors influencing language policies in East Africa." In Joan Rubin, and Bjorn Jernudd (eds.), *Can language be planned?* Honolulu: University of Hawaii Press. 141–58.

Whiteley, W. H. (ed.). 1974a. *Language in Kenya.* Nairobi: Oxford University Press.

Whiteley, W. H. 1974b. "Some patterns of language use in the rural areas of Kenya." In Whiteley, W. H. 1974a. 319–50.

Young, Crawford. 1976. *The politics of cultural pluralism.* Madison: University of Wisconsin Press.

Religious Factors in Language Spread

Charles A. Ferguson

1 The distribution of major types of writing systems in the world correlates more closely with the distribution of the world's major religions than with genetic or typological classifications of language, a fact which has often been noted by sociolinguists and others interested in the spread of writing systems. This correlation between religions and writing systems does not result from any inherent relationship between religious practices or beliefs and the processes of reading and writing. Rather, the present distribution of writing systems is largely a result of the fact that in many instances the spread of a major religion has simultaneously introduced the use of writing into a nonliterate speech community. So it has happened that wherever Western Christianity has spread in nonliterate communities, it has introduced a variety of the Latin script for writing local, previously unwritten languages; and wherever Islam has spread to nonliterate communities, it has introduced a variety of the Arabic script for writing previously unwritten languages. Sometimes, when a major religion has spread to a literate community, the effect of the new religion has been to replace a local writing system without replacing the languages spoken in the community, as when the Arabic alphabet replaced the other ways of writing Persian or Malay, or when the Latin alphabet replaced other ways of writing Old Norse or Philippine languages. One of the most impressive associations of a writing system with a religion is the use of the Hebrew alphabet by the Jews. For nearly two millenia Jews have used the so-called square Hebrew letters (derived from the earlier Aramaic alphabet) to represent their mother tongues and other languages used in Jewish communities, so that Hebrew script has been used by Jews to write varieties of Arabic, Persian, Spanish, and other languages, and is regularly used for

both Hebrew and Yiddish today. In this case, the principal reason for the correlation between religion and writing system is the historical fact that Jews have traditionally become literate first in Hebrew, and then as they find it appropriate to make written use of other languages with their communities, the writing system of Hebrew is extended to them (Gold 1980).

This indirect relation between religions and the spread of writing systems gives some indication of the indirect relation between religion and the spread of languages in general. In this paper we can only explore a few common types of language spread in which religious factors play an important role. Such exploration may help us to understand better the processes of language spread as well as the role of religious factors in human social behavior. For the purposes of this paper we define language spread as the increase over time in the number of users or the amount of use of a given language or language variety, such increase being typically—although not necessarily—at the expense of the use of other languages, or language variety(ies). Religion will be understood in its general sense of beliefs or practices related to ultimate concerns, comprehensive integrative value systems, or supernatural phenomena.

LANGUAGE VARIATION

2.1 *Register.* One place to begin the exploration is with an examination of religious uses of language. Every speech community may be assumed to have special characteristics of language structure and language use which are appropriate for religious purposes, in religious settings, or on religious occasions. Such characteristics may involve differences in register, e.g., a special variety used in public religious ceremonies which is different from ordinary conversational language or nonreligious formal language. A religious register in a given speech community may even be a totally different language from the ordinary language of the community. The distribution of religious registers at a given time in a community must be the result of the spread (or receding) of language varieties during earlier periods. Let us examine one particular type—the spread of the language of sacred texts.

When a Japanese Buddhist priest in a California Buddhist church recites a *sutra* in Pali with his English-speaking congregation, this is a fine example of the spread of a particular language variety over enormous distances in space and time. When accounts of the Buddha and his sayings were collected and came to be accepted as the canon of Buddhist scripture, they were in a Middle Indo-Aryan language, Pali, whose exact provenience is not clear. When the Pali scriptures were used in worship

in India and Ceylon, the language functioned as a special religious register in many speech communities where related Indo-Aryan languages
were the worshipers' mother tongues. When Buddhism spread to areas
such as Burma, Thailand, China, and Japan, the sacred scriptures went
along. Buddhist missionaries and scholars translated Pali and Sanskrit
texts into other languages, but just about everywhere at least some uses
of Pali were kept. In these new areas, the Pali language, still functioning
as a religious register, was no longer related at all to the language of the
worshipers, but retained its aura of sacredness. This sequence of events,
with minor variations, has occurred again and again in the spread of
religions with sacred texts.

Stage I   The language of the texts is close to the spoken language of
           the religious community.
Stage II   As the spoken language changes, the language of the sacred
           texts remains more or less intact and has a special religious
           aura.
Stage III As the religion spreads to other areas, the language of the
           sacred texts functions as a sacred language in speech com-
           munities linguistically unrelated.

An Islamic counterpart to the Japanese Buddhist priest's use of Pali
would be a Pakistani *mullah,* native speaker of—let us say—Panjabi,
who recites from the Holy Koran in Classical Arabic.

It sometimes happens that a translation of the sacred text into another language achieves a status which creates a new sacred language
which in turn spreads as a religious register in the same way. Thus the
Vulgate translation of the Bible into Latin and the general preservation
of Latin as the language of learning and religion gave Latin a sacred
status in public worship in communities where it represented an archaic
but related variety (e.g., Italy) and in places where it was distantly related or not related at all to the mother tongue of the people (e.g.,
Germany, Hungary), and the use of Latin in public worship continued
to the 1960s.

The Japanese Buddhist priest in California who provided the original
example can also provide an example of a second sacred language translated from an earlier one. In current practice most of the ceremonial
language—including the chanting of sutras—when it is not in modern
Japanese or English translation, is in Classical Chinese, in the Japanese
pronunciation, and the original Pali passages are very limited in number
(Hanayama 1969, 45). This "layering" effect of successive sacred languages in the same ceremonial context is actually widespread among the

world's major religions, reflecting successive periods in the spread of the respective religions.

The extensive literature on the religious use of Latin is a mine of valuable material for the sociolinguist. It is, however, generally necessary to apply comparative dimensions, both with other sacred languages and with other types of register variation and functional allocation of different languages within speech communities. (Lentner 1964 offers an historical survey up to 1563; Kowlevsky 1957 discusses languages other than Latin in Catholic worship; many publications related to the Second Vatican Council reexamine the issues.)

2.2 *Dialect*. Another topic to explore is dialect or language differentiation that depends on the religion of the language users. Every speech community in which there are significant religious cleavages may be assumed to have linguistic reflection of those cleavages in ordinary conversational language. The most familiar case is that in which the dialect variation based on religion is the result of earlier geographical variation which has been displaced by the movement of religious groups and subsequently identified with religious differences.

The distribution of dialect differences in Konkani, an Indo-Aryan language spoken by a million and a half people in several areas of Western India, is a good example. Miranda's study of the situation asserts: "Generally, Hindus and Christians living in a given area speak considerably different dialects" (Miranda 1978, 87). A few of these differences are related to religious terminology, differences in customs for eating, dress, etc., and a few are due to the greater influence of Portuguese or Christian Konkani. The major differences, however, including several striking phonological isoglosses, reflect patterns of migration from different places at different times. In fact the patterns of migration have been such that in some instances the Hindu varieties in one locality may be closer to the Christian varieties in another locality than to the Hindu varieties there. Miranda concludes " . . . what was originally a regional differentiation has been transformed into a social differentiation . . . with an interesting complication that the distinctive characteristics associated with Hindu and Christian dialects in one area are the reverse of those in the other area" (89).

The Konkani case is of special interest also because it illustrates with unusual clarity the perennial problem of deciding what constitutes a separate language for discussion of language spread. The need for extralinguistic, sociological criteria in defining languages has been recognized for a long time (cf. Kloss 1952, Ferguson & Gumperz 1960), but the fluidity of users' identification of language status depending on changes in their perception of economic, political, religious or other values is not so often noted (but cf. Das Gupta 1974 and Duran 1974). Some varieties of Konkani shade off into varieties of Marathi, and linguistic arguments can be made that Konkani and Marathi should be regarded as two separate languages or that they should be regarded as varieties of a single language. This has been a controversial issue, with political implications, ever since the incorporation of Goa into the Indian Union in 1961, and religion is an important factor. Probably the majority of mother-tongue speakers of Konkani at the present time regard Konkani as an independent language, but the proportion is doubtless much higher among Christians. If it had not been for the spread of Christianity which resulted from the Portuguese colonial operation in Goa, the issue of the independent linguistic status of Konkani would probably not have arisen.

A perfect counterpart to the dialect variation by religion in Konkani—although not to the question of one language or two—is the Christian-Jewish-Muslim dialect variation in Baghdadi Arabic described in Blanc 1964. Here again the present-day striking phonological and morphological differences among the three varieties can be shown to have originated in geographical variation which subsequently, as a result of the movement of people, acquired social significance in the same locale.

Before leaving the topic of language varieties correlated with religious identification, we must note the obvious corollary to our introductory observation about writing systems. Since the spread of writing systems tends to reflect spread of religious systems, it would follow that the use of two writing systems of the same language would tend to reflect religious cleavages in the community, and this is indeed the case. Many (most?) instances of "multigraphism" of a language represent either synchronic religious differences or vestiges of earlier religious differences. In addition to pointing to such traditional examples of Serbo-Croatian, or Hindi-Urdu, we can refer to the written use of Konkani. In Goa proper, where nearly half of all the Konkani speakers are located, Christian writers use Latin letters and Hindu writers use the Nagari alphabet, although outside Goa the writing system employed for Konkani usually is that of the surrounding language, regardless of religion.

LANGUAGE MAINTENANCE AND SHIFT

3.1 *Immigration.* From exploration of the religious use of language in societies and its implications for language spread, we may move to the topic of religious influence on the maintenance and shift of languages in

ALLEN D. GRIMSHAW
SOCIOLOGY DEPT

addition to or apart from their religious use. Whenever the use of a language or language variety is spreading, it may be assumed that religious beliefs and practices will in some measure affect the rate and extent of the spread. Let us examine one particular type of language spread—that resulting from voluntary immigration of individuals and groups into a different speech community, the intent of the immigrants being to locate new homes and remain indefinitely. In such cases of immigration, various patterns of language maintenance and shift are possible, depending on a wide range of economic and social factors including attitudes and expectations on the part of both the immigrants and the host population.

A fine example is the substantial immigration of Germans and Japanese to Brazil. Both groups have been gradually shifting to Portuguese as a mother tongue, but the point to be made here is that their religious organizations, Christian and Buddhist respectively, have not only maintained German and Japanese in connection with religious activities but have established special schools and other activities for maintaining knowledge of the original homeland language. This pattern of linguistic conservation on the part of immigrant churches is a widespread phenomenon, very familiar to us in the American experience (cf. Fishman et al. 1966). One is tempted to claim that this is a universal phenomenon, i.e., that the reverse pattern will occur rarely or not at all. One does not expect an immigrant church to take leadership in facilitating a shift of language. Yet any such "universal" hypothesis fails to match the complexities of possible patterns of language shift in immigrant communities.

Among the South Asian communities which immigrated into East Africa in the early years of the twentieth century, very complex patterns of language shift occurred. First of all, the Asians brought with them the regional, religious, and linguistic diversity of their homelands. Then, in their immigrant adaptation, they dropped relatively little of their linguistic diversity but added to their repertoires various African languages, particularly Swahili. All the groups tended to retain religious registers (including several classical languages), to retain such South Asian lingua francas as "Hindustani" and English as Asian community lingua francas in the new setting, and to add the use of African lingua francas such as Swahili and, again, English for use with Africans and Europeans. In all this complex set of changes in language use, it is difficult to discern an overall effect of language conservation on the part of institutional religion. The Sikh religion among the Panjabi speakers acted as a preserver of the use of the distinctive Gurmukhi writing system for Panjabi, which was not learned by Hindu and Muslim Panjabis.

This preservation was, however, primarily for the reading of Sikh religious literature, not to maintain the use of Panjabi as a written language in the community. On the other hand, the Christian religion among the Konkani speakers acted to accelerate the shift from Konkani to English as mother tongue. This kind of shift had precedents in those Goans who had shifted to Portuguese or English in Goa, but it was speeded up in East Africa, and the religious identification was a strong factor.

It may still be safe to assume that in voluntary migration for socio-economic reasons, religious affiliation or commitment will tend to be language-conservative (i.e., maintenance-oriented), to the greatest extent for the language of sacred texts, next greatest for the language of public ritual and explanation of the texts, and also for the mother-tongue language of ordinary conversation. This conservation may be considerably modified by such factors as the presence/absence of coreligionists in the host population, the existence of shared lingua francas, and the ideological stance of the religion with regard to language (see 4 below). In the case of the Christian Goans in East Africa all these factors were at work. The Goans found European and African Roman Catholics in East Africa. Many of them already had some knowledge of English as a lingua franca in India, and their religion did not ascribe sacredness to Konkani for sacred texts or public ceremonies. In fact a worldwide shift in ideological stance in the Catholic church contributed to the shift to English by Goans in East Africa, namely the changeover to vernacular services in the 1960s. The shift in East Africa was from Latin to Swahili and English, and for the Goans this meant one more extension of the use of English. (Konkani is now used in churches only as a supplementary language for the non-English speakers.)

3.2 *Colonization.* Another topic to explore in the study of religious factors in language maintenance and shift is the type of spread which is associated with intentional colonization, i.e., the sending of groups of people to new areas for the purpose of maintaining outlying units of the parent community, assuring access to resources or lines of communication required by the parent community, or simply extending the political, economic, or religious power of the parent community to other societies.

Intentional colonization is an old phenomenon in human history, and probably took place also in prehistory. Two early examples in Western history were the planting of Phoenician and Greek colonies around the Mediterranean. As in many colonizations before and after them, those colonizers transplanted both language and religion to the new localities. Although the primary motivations were apparently economic, the colonizers were effective spreaders of their language and religion, tending to impose them on the "less developed" peoples with whom they came in contact. In the case of the Phoenician colonization, the language and religion survived in the biggest colony, Carthage, for centuries after both had died out in the homeland. In the case of the Greeks, it was a major characteristic of the Hellenistic period that Greek language and religion (along with other aspects of Greek culture) spread largely from Greek colonies. We can compare this phenomenon to colonizations of other times and places, including, of course, the spread of European languages and religions to the Western Hemisphere, Asia, Africa, and Oceania from the fifteenth to the twentieth centuries. The question we are concerned with here, however, is the relatively narrow one of the way language and religion are tied together in colonization.

The relation between spread of religion and spread of language in the process of colonization is not simple and direct, since there are well-documented, roughly comparable instances of colonization in which religion has spread but not language (Spanish colonization of the Philippines), and others in which language has spread but not religion (French colonization of Algeria). Yet the two are often tied together. Important explanatory factors in the spread of religion and language in colonization include: the number of colonists in proportion to local population included in the colony, the colonists' attitude toward incorporation of the local population into their society, the position of religion in the colonizing society, and the ideological stance of the religion with regard to language (see 4 below).

One very common pattern of language use in colonial religious activities, typical of British colonization in Asia and Africa in the late eighteenth and early nineteenth century, was the three-fold use of local vernaculars, local lingua francas, and English (the colonial language) in missionary schools whose primary purpose was the spreading of the Christian religion. This pattern, in which religious activities directly affected the spread of lingua francas and English in the colonies, had important consequences for language use which are still evident in the independent nations that replaced the colonies. The establishment of this pattern resulted from a unique constellation of factors in British colonization: a missionary enterprise separate from the civil authorities, the religious ideology of propagating religion through the mother tongue, a commitment to lingua francas and English based on "practical" considerations not ideology, the availability of English-speaking missionary personnel prepared to learn local languages.

This pattern of language use in colonial religious activities, typical of British colonizations in Asia and Africa, is only one among many. In order to understand its origin and its results in a general theoretical framework it would be necessary to have comparative studies of colonization in many times and places, under many policies and with different consequences, and among different kinds of religions and different kinds of languages. At this point we can only note that, in contrast to the fairly general, conservative, language-maintaining, intercommunity orientation of religion in voluntary immigration, the role of religion in colonization is often extracommunity-oriented and aimed at changing the language repertoires of speech communities. See Heath and Laprade (this volume) for a case study of religion and language spread in colonization.

4. *Religious ideology of language.* Many factors extraneous to religion may influence or even be determinative in the effect of religion on language spread. Religion as such may be secondary or even marginal in comparison with economic, political, demographic, or other factors accounting for language spread. But in at least one respect the religious factor has a certain primacy: the total religious system includes a set of beliefs and attitudes about language. Thus if a particular proselytizing religion has as part of its articles of faith that its adherents must pray in a certain sacred language, this will tend to have a different language-spread effect from that of another proselytizing religion which insists its adherents must pray in their mother tongue. We will put aside here the historical question of how a particular set of beliefs about language becomes part of a religious system, and explore several of the principal types of such beliefs.

We may safely assume that all religious belief systems include some beliefs about language. At the very least a religious system specifies that some ways of talking are better than others: it is hard to imagine any set of religious beliefs which includes no "shoulds" about verbal behavior. Religions may have myths about the origin of human language, the diversity of human language, or one particular sacred language; they may specify characteristics of the language of inspiration or possession; they may prescribe the language of ritual interaction and private meditation—the possibilities of religious beliefs about language seem endless. Here let us explore only attitudes toward mother tongue, sacred texts, and the language of religious practice (including formal teaching of religion).

It is not unusual for a religious community to have great respect for the language of the (real or presumed) founder of the religion or the mother tongue of the group in which the religion emerged (historically or mythically). Thus in the Sikh community the respect for Panjabi is great. It is noticeably greater than the respect which non-Sikh Panjabis have for their language. Hindu and Muslim Panjabis often report their mother tongue as Hindi or Urdu respectively, and these other languages traditionally function as the H varieties of diglossic situations, with Panjabi as L. Yet this religion, which started as a universal, proselytizing religion which would reconcile Hindus, Muslims, and others, does not insist on converts learning Panjabi as a language of conversation. English-speaking American converts or Swahili-speaking African converts may be encouraged to study some Panjabi in order to appreciate the Granth Saheb, their holy book, but they are not expected to acquire Panjabi as an everyday language. Religious factors alone are rarely decisive in bringing about a shift in mother tongue; but they may be strong secondary factors associated with other aspects of culture change.

The attitude toward the language of sacred texts, for those religious systems which have sacred texts, varies considerably. Thus Islam, and Hinduism—speaking broadly—attach sacredness and significance to the very language of the scriptures so that translations of the Holy Koran, or the Vedas have traditionally been disapproved or viewed with alarm. Judaism tends to share this view of the language of the sacred text, but translation/commentary helps in Aramaic were produced to aid in understanding the texts, and in the second or third century B.C.E. a Greek version of the Scriptures was produced for the large Greek-speaking Jewish community in Egypt.

On the other hand Christianity and Buddhism have from their very beginnings encouraged the translation of their sacred texts into other languages, and even though both religions have exhibited strong attachments to particular sacred languages (cf. the Latin and Chinese examples in 2.1 above), their theology and their practice have not shown the same concern for exactness of text and inherent holiness of language which Islam and Hinduism, and to a lesser extent Judaism, have shown. These differences in religious ideology about language have had their expected effects on the spread of religious languages. Wherever Islam has gone, some knowledge of Arabic has gone with it, and the Koran in Arabic is recited. Wherever Buddhism has gone, knowledge of the Eight-fold Path has gone, but no one sacred language has gone: sutras for the scriptures may be recited in Pali, Tibetan, Chinese, or some other language. Thus, all Brahman priests, no matter what their sect or mother tongue, can make use of *some* Sanskrit if they meet together in Benares, and all Muslim pilgrims to Mecca make some use of Arabic, but there is no common language for Buddhist or Christian clergy to recite the Three Treasures or the Our Father.

Many religious systems have no sacred texts in the sense of a holy book, but presumably all religions prescribe certain public uses of language as an aspect of religious practice. (Samarin 1976 offers a stimulating array of studies of language in religious practice.) This aspect of religious ideology may have more direct implications for language spread than the other two. When a religion spreads, for whatever reasons, this ideological stance is likely to be a strong determinant of an accompanying spread of language. Traditional language preferences for corporate worship, religious teaching, or public interaction (e.g., greetings), and the like must have an effect on language maintenance and shift. The use of Yiddish as the language of religious teaching in Hasidic communities and the use of German in corporate worship in Hutterite communities have helped to maintain these languages against the encroachment of other languages, to take two, often-cited examples. Yet in this no-man's-land between mother tongues and the language of sacred texts there are few studies relating religion and the spread of language. It is typical that none of the studies in the Samarin book attempts to relate the patterns of language use to the spreading or receding of the languages or varieties described.

5. This brief exploratory paper suggests the following conclusions:
a. Religious factors may be highly significant in processes of language spread (almost every paper in this volume mentions religion), but there is no simple, direct relationship between religion and language.
b. The role of religious factors in language spread may be largely dependent on the place of religion with respect to more powerful factors of language spread: economic, political, demographic, geographical.
c. When the spread of religion is tied to the use of a holy book and a traditional writing system, this complex is likely to be a strong factor in the spread of written forms of language.
d. The effect on language spread of religious ideology about language is a promising—and little investigated—topic for research.

REFERENCES

Blanc, Haim. 1964. *Communal dialects in Baghdad.* Cambridge: Harvard University Press.
Das Gupta, Jyotindra. 1974. Ethnicity, Language Demands, and National Development. *Ethnicity,* Vol. 1, no. 1, pp. 65–72. New York: Academic Press, Inc.

Duran, James. 1974. The Ecology of Ethnic Groups from a Kenyan Perspective. *Ethnicity,* Vol. 1, no. 1, pp. 43–64. New York: Academic Press, Inc.

Ferguson, Charles A. & John J. Gumperz (eds.). 1960. *Linguistic diversity in South Asia.* Bloomington, Ind.: Indiana University Research Center in Anthropology, Folklore, and Linguistics.

Fishman, Joshua A., et al. 1966. *Language Loyalty in the United States.* The Hague: Mouton.

Gold, David L. 1980. The speech and writing of Jews in the U.S.A. In Charles A. Ferguson and Shirley Heath (eds.), *Language in the U.S.A.* Pp. 462–93. Cambridge: Cambridge University Press.

Hanayama, Shoyu. 1969. *Buddhist handbook for Shin-shu followers.* Tokyo: Hokuseido Press.

Kloss, Heinz. 1952. *Die Entwicklung neuer germanischer Kultursprachen von 1800 zu 1950.* Munich: Pohl & Co.

Kowlevsky, Cyril. 1957. *Living languages in Catholic worship.* London: Longmans, Green.

Lentner, Leopold. 1964. *Volksprache und Sakralsprache.* Vienna: Herder.

Miranda, Rocky V. 1978. Caste, religion and dialect differentiation in the Konkani area. *International Journal of the Sociology of Language,* 16: 77–91.

Neale, Barbara, 1974. Language use among the Asian communities. In W. H. Whiteley (ed.) *Language in Kenya.* Pp. 263–317. Nairobi: Oxford University Press.

Samarin, William J. 1976. *Language in religious practice.* Rowley, Mass.: Newbury House.

Language Spread: The Ancient Near Eastern World

Herbert H. Paper

I. Thanks to the successful decipherments in the early and mid-nineteenth century of the writing systems known as Egyptian hieroglyphics and Sumero-Akkadian cuneiform, plus the cuneiform of Old Persian, our view of the linguistic map of the ancient Near Eastern world as early as the third millennium B.C. was remarkably enhanced. Prior to these extraordinary scholarly achievements, our linguistic horizons for that time and era—both as to the specific details of many languages as well as who spoke what and where—were limited to the known Biblical and Greco-Roman sources. Here and there certain hints and an occasional word or phrase from some languages other than Hebrew, Aramaic, Greek, and Latin could be culled from the texts. But essentially all that was known were the names of a large number of peoples who presumably spoke a variety of languages, and there was no specific information about these languages. For example, the works of Herodotus, Xenophon, and other Greeks who traveled in the Near East provided a number of words from various languages of peoples with whom they came into contact, but these were recorded rather more as curiosities or as incidental data. Many ethnic names also appear in the Bible—for example, Jebusites, Girgashites, and the like, along with the Hittites, Assyrians, Babylonians—but there was no way of knowing anything about these peoples other than their bare names or an occasional name or word identified with one of these ethnic terms. Of course, as a result of the decipherments and many subsequent discoveries and later decipherments, we now have a great deal of information about each of these peoples. Though, to be sure, for many others no new information exists.

As a result of the wealth of information gained by these superb intellectual achievements in the field of decipherment—continuing almost to our own day—we now have grammars, linguistic maps, social dialect information, literary style differentiation data, and similar matters the totality of which is nothing short of encyclopedic. Our knowledge of the language situation in the ancient Near East as of today is complex, enormous, and most instructive.[1]

Of course, the kind of topic examined by the papers in this volume is not one on which we have specific information consciously discussed by the ancients themselves. On this and many other subjects, we must rely on making inferences from hints in the extant textual evidence. There are no ancient treatises that deal in a conscious and direct manner with "language" in any theoretical way. Unlike the case of ancient India, where a tradition of grammatical analysis developed that treated phonetics, morphology, syntax, and meaning in exquisitely detailed and heuristically conscious forms, the ancient Near East has not provided us with similar treatments of either grammar or of sociolinguistic topics. (The Sumerian-Akkadian bilingual grammatical texts are more in the nature of equivalence lists from which the modern scholar can make inferences and judgments, rather than systematic treatises.) Similarly, the Biblical text includes much important ethical and philosophical material, but unlike the Greek tradition, does not present us with an essay or treatise that deals with ethics, for example, in an overall theoretical framework.

Given what we now know about the broad outline of ancient Near Eastern history (in many cases even down to the minutest details) and the demographic composition of populations over several millennia, we do have a considerable body of data that enables us to draw a linguistic map of some accuracy for each successive half millennium. Yet despite the wealth of textual material in sheer number of texts, variety of text types and subject matter, and diversity of languages, we are still left with a considerable task of analysis and deduction. Each successive decipherment and each discovery of texts in a newly excavated area have given us solutions to old problems, raised significant and enticing new ones, and have often provided us with information about a situation whose existence had been totally unsuspected before the discovery. I am thinking here of the decipherments of both cuneiform and hieroglyphic Hittite, of Ugaritic, and of the recent discoveries at Ebla in Syria, and others.

The major clue to "language spread" that we have for the ancient Near East lies, it seems to me, in the map of "writing system spread." Now it is a major thesis of modern linguistics that one must carefully distinguish and never confuse a language with its writing system. The two dimensions, so to speak, are quite distinct entities. Each has its own forebears, origins, and dynamics. The origin or filiation of a particular language is to be determined by the methodology of "historical-comparative linguistics"—a technique that applies equally and validly to both written and unwritten languages.[2] The filiation of writing systems, on the other hand, is determinable by the process of cultural diffusion. To give some obvious examples:

The use of the Roman alphabet all over Western and parts of Eastern Europe is to be explained as a datum reflecting the spread of the Latin language, Roman culture, and the mechanism of a Latin-and-Rome based religious culture—Christianity. Thus, English, French, Lithuanian, Polish, Czech, Hungarian, and Finnish—to name but a few—in their traditional use and adaptations of the Roman alphabet reflect a long-standing tradition of cultural origin in Roman imperial influence extended by the overlay and later expansion of Roman Christianity and its derivatives.

Similarly, the use of the Arabic script almost universally in the entire Islamic world clearly reflects the spread of the Islamic religion, the centrality of its holy book, the Koran, and the primacy of the original language of that book: Arabic. The script in which that language was written takes on virtual identity with and inseparability from the language itself. In this manner, languages as genetically distinct as Persian, Turkish, and Malay (among others) are and have been regularly written in a form of the Arabic script.[3]

It is thus in the realm of language and culture where the two distinct entities—"language" and "writing"—are intimately interwoven in every cultural and historical context. So much so that quite commonly—I was about to write the word "universally"—for the usual naive speaker in many parts of the world, languages are primarily thought of in their written garb; it took conscious reexamination by linguists to separate the two as distinct and independent factors.

The written form of a particular language, however, does provide us with a primary source of direct data as to otherwise undocumented details of diffusion. Were we to have no information on the specific reasons for the Turkish adoption of the Roman alphabet in 1928, but only texts in Turkish written in that script in contrast to the earlier ones in the Arabic script, we could draw certain conclusions about the degree of Western European influence. We would be wrong were we to conclude that the alphabet change reflected a specific religious change in the population. But we would be quite correct in drawing an inference about the waning of orthodox Islamic thought in the governing circles that decreed the change in script.

II. The first writing system which developed in the ancient world—for that matter, in the entire history of the world—was the system of symbols which ultimately emerged as the cuneiform system from which we can read the Sumerian language.[4] This writing system was then borrowed from the Mesopotamian cultural center and adapted for a number of languages in the ancient Near East. And this Sumero-Akkadian writing system was operative from the early third millennium B.C. down to the fourth century B.C.—with actual use occurring in a quite restricted fashion even as late as the first century B.C. Thus, if I may be permitted an incidental remark, the time span for the use of cuneiform writing is longer than that for the Greek alphabet by easily half a millennium—and under "Greek" I am subsuming everything that stems from it including the Roman, Cyrillic, Gothic, and Armenian scripts.

The earliest adaptation of Sumerian writing to another language was to Akkadian in the third millennium B.C.[5] Here some further definitions are required. Sumerian is a language whose genetic affiliation is still unknown. No attempt to show a genetic connection to any other language family has yet been successful. Akkadian—also known by the cumbersome term "Assyro-Babylonian"—is, on the other hand, a Semitic language that is quite clearly related to Arabic, Hebrew, and Aramaic. The Mesopotamian cultural domain, the major features of which were formed in the Sumerian period, was always heavily indebted to the practices and categories that had been established by the Sumerians. There is abundant evidence that the whole system of scribal training and of the ancillary handbook reference works such as glossaries and sign-lists—all on clay tablets—was established early on and remained traditional, constant, and consistent for many, many centuries (see note 4).

The adaptation of Sumerian cuneiform first to Akkadian represented also the increased domination of this new ethnic and linguistic factor in Mesopotamia, so much so that we can reasonably conclude that the primary first language of the region had become Akkadian. Yet it is also clear that Sumerian remained *the* learned, prestigious, literary language par excellence. The curriculum of scribal training long retained a very firm allegiance to Sumerian—to the language, to the written form of many words, and to its literary genres. The clearest parallel I can point to is the position of Latin in European culture for so many centuries, so that to this day many substantial bits and pieces of Latin are imbedded in the written (and spoken) English of many speakers who are quite conscious of their use and knowledge of Latin, as well as in the language of many who are totally innocent of any formal training in the language of the Romans.

Subsequently, the writing system that we should now call Sumero-Akkadian cuneiform was adapted to still other tongues: Hittite (an Indo-European language), Elamite (filiation unknown, but recently rather convincingly suggested as ultimately Dravidian), Hurrian and Urartean (filiation unknown), Hattic (filiation unknown), and occasional texts in still other languages. The network of languages spoken in a single area and their diversity is well illustrated by the discoveries at Boghaz-köi in central Turkey from which the major Hittite text finds were made. Seven languages are represented in these texts: Hittite, Akkadian, Sumerian, Luvian, Hattic, Hurrian, Palaic.[6] And yet it seems to be agreed that Hittite was probably the major language of the population or at least of the ruling elite of the society.

Let us now examine the situation of language diversity in the late second and early first millennium B.C. Akkadian in its various regional and chronological forms continues to be abundantly attested. With the discovery and decipherment of the clay tablets from Ras Shamra on the Syrian coast, a totally new Semitic language, Ugaritic, was revealed as recently as 1929. The textual parallels in Ugaritic literature to the Biblical Hebrew text have given great impetus to an extensive scholarly literature.[7] The writing system used for Ugaritic was also something of a surprise: cuneiform signs bearing little relation to those of the Sumero-Akkadian system were used in a fashion long predating but systematically identical with the consonantal writing well known from the West Semitic system of Aramaic, Hebrew, and Phoenician—that is, the bare consonantal skeleton of each word being all that was normally written. It is the West Semitic consonantal script which in the first millennium B.C. becomes quite generally used and overshadows and ultimately replaces the much more cumbersome cuneiform of the Sumero-Akkadian world. Surely the relative simplicity of the West Semitic system—two dozen or so symbols as opposed to the many dozen more, plus word-signs, of the cuneiform system—and its easy adaptability to brush and ink were important factors in the spread and popularity of the West Semitic script. Incidentally, it was from a form of this latter consonantal script that the Greek adaptation was made, involving the unique development that we know as the "alphabet"—where both consonant and vowel are indicated unequivocally in every word.[8]

There is in all of this one basic conundrum—the position of the Aramaic language.[9] It was spoken by groups who seem to have had no particular political dominance of any sort. The data force us to conclude that Aramaic was spoken quite widely throughout the Fertile Crescent. This must have been the case even for those centuries prior to the appearance of Aramaic texts, given the widespread distribution of the language in the time for which we do have textual evidence. There is probably no question of a sudden bursting forth of population from a relatively restricted geographic area as a result of or in connection with some important cultural, political, or historical event. Something of the sort has been suggested for the spread of Arabic out of the Arabian Peninsula in conjunction with a combined religious-cultural-political conquest that took place in the seventh century A.D. with the birth and spread of Islam. But there is no evidence of any kind of Aramaic empire or renaissance or conquest at any time in the first millennium B.C. It may be simply the case that a particular widespread language and its script were in the right place at the right time.

Closely related to the spread of the Aramaic script, we find the interesting phenomenon that the Aramaic language itself became a lingua franca (essentially, an international common second official language) in the Neo-Babylonian and Persian Empires.[10] Now surely this must be related to the influence of scribes and their importance in the administrative wings of governmental offices in capital cities and in provincial centers. But in addition to examples of administrative and personal correspondence and official inscriptions in Aramaic, there is also abundant textual evidence for the use of Aramaic in private documents—letters, contracts, and the like—and of course for a wide variety of literary purposes. The fact of the spread of Aramaic at least in one instance as a replacement language of one population group is attested in the Biblical account in Nehemiah 13:23–24: "In those days I saw that some Jews had married women from Ashdod, Ammon, and Moab. Half their children spoke the language of Ashdod or of the other peoples and could not speak the language of the Jews."

Further attestation to the widespread use of Aramaic in official correspondence is to be found in the accounts in the books of Daniel (2:4–7:28) and Ezra (4:8–6:8; 7:12–26) which are written in Aramaic and not in Hebrew, reflecting actual linguistic usage at the time. In addition, the later widespread use of Aramaic and its place in Jewish usage in Bible translation and in official ritual documents (the marriage document—*ketuba*—the bill of divorce, various prayers, the texts of much of postbiblical literature and of most of the Talmud, etc) attest to the virtual replacement of Hebrew and indeed the elevation of Aramaic to a position of prestige and sanctification. The relatively short sojourn in the Babylonian Exile (sixth century B.C.) is generally taken to be the source of this language shift among Jews. This alone tells us something of the linguistic map of the Babylonian Empire, alongside the known attestation of the Neo-Babylonian dialect of Akkadian at the same time. Indeed, other evidence from inscriptions shows the influence of

Aramaic vocabulary on this late southern form of Akkadian (as well as on Old Persian), and of the reciprocal influence of Akkadian on Aramaic (see note 9).

It is also important to note that the Aramaic script or its derivatives had a most unusual fate in ultimately penetrating as far as India, Chinese Turkestan, and Mongolia[11] to the east and northeast, as well as southward to Ethiopia. The Aramaic writing system served as the basis for that form of Middle Persian known as Pehlevi: a very interesting example, not by any means unique in the history of languages, of a simultaneously heterolingual scribal practice whereby the same text written in one language—Aramaic—was read out in another—Pehlevi (Middle Iranian). Ultimately, the Aramaic portions were replaced almost completely by the Iranian translation, so that finally the text is entirely in Pehlevi. The Aramaic script spread further north and east at the end of the first millennium A.D. to serve as the written vehicle for Sogdian (another Middle Iranian language) and for Mongolian and Uighur (Turkic). In the former case, there was an additional interesting graphic adaptation whereby the traditional Mongolian script, which is a modification of Aramaic-Syriac, was written in the Chinese fashion, vertically.

In the Persian Empire—that is, from the middle of the sixth century B.C. to the fourth century B.C. and the conquest by Alexander the Great—it is clear that Aramaic was widely used as the official administrative and diplomatic language. But there was still another aspect highlighting the linguistic diversity of the Empire for which another Biblical reference is instructive. In the Book of Esther, we read (3:12): ". . . a writ was issued to the king's satraps and the governor of each province, and to the officers over each separate people: for each province in its own script and for each people in their own language." And again in Esther 8:9: ". . . and a writ was issued to the Jews, exactly as Mordecai directed, and to the satraps, the governors, and the officers in the provinces from India to Ethiopia, a hundred and twenty-seven provinces, for each province in its own script and for each people in their own language, and also for the Jews in their own script and language."[12]

Interestingly enough, while there is no extra-Biblical evidence confirming any of the events described in the Book of Esther, the administrative practice mentioned in these passages is strikingly confirmed. Thus, the inscription of Darius the Great at Bisitun (in northwestern Iran), which dates from 520 B.C., is carved high on a mountainside in three languages and three scripts: Old Persian, Elamite, and Babylonian.[13] Almost all of the inscriptions of the later Achaemenian rulers of the Persian Empire are similarly multilingual. A partial copy of the Babylonian version of Bisitun has been found in the excavations in the city of Babylon itself. And an Aramaic version of the same text (with important additional details) was found in Upper Egypt at Elephantine—an outpost of the Persian Empire where a considerable body of Aramaic documents, notably letters to and from Persian administrators, has been found. From this same period, we also have Aramaic-Lydian bilingual texts (from Anatolia), and short texts also in Egyptian hieroglyphics. There is no doubt in my mind that someday we may be fortunate enough to uncover additional copies of the Bisitun inscription and of others in various languages of the Persian Empire. But here we can only hope for the good fortune that may accompany future excavations in many as yet untouched sites.

The conquest of the Persian Empire by Alexander (331 B.C.) and the extension of the Greek military and administrative representation as far as Afghanistan and Northwest India (present-day Pakistan) mark the next stage where Greek begins to appear along with Aramaic and other local languages in our textual evidence.[14] But what do these Greek inscriptions tell us about the extent of knowledge and use of Greek among the local populations? Even where larger numbers of texts have been found—e.g., Hellenistic Syro-Palestine—it is still an open question about what the actual extent of Greek was among the native population.[15]

III. At this point, it seems to me the right time to raise an issue explicitly, one with which I have been dealing in my paper all along. Those who study "language spread," which is the overall theme of this volume, ought to take cognizance of certain ancillary aspects. One of them is indeed the phenomenon of "writing." Necessarily, in treating the ancient Near Eastern world I have had to pay attention to this factor, for "written" material is all we can operate with. And it is from the written texts that we have to assemble the direct and indirect hints about the linguistic or sociolinguistic map in the absence of direct demographic or sociological data. Surely, even in modern instances where we have access to informants and to opportunities to investigate the language profile of an area directly, one important dimension is the nature of the writing system that is in use. The nationalistic passions aroused by the deep attachment to a particular writing system are almost identical with those involving the language itself. I remember reading that one of the specific immediate causes for the outbreak of hostilities in the Bangladesh conflict some years ago was a directive from West Pakistan that Bengali was henceforth to be written in the Perso-Arabic script used for Urdu. Another example: Some years ago, the large dictionary project for Serbo-Croatian that was sponsored by the Yugoslav Academy was supposed to include both forms of the language—Roman letters for Croatian, and Cyrillic for Serbian. The project foundered precisely on the rocks of the alphabet question; and plans had to be altered to provide for two separate dictionaries in the two separate scripts for what is essentially the same language.

It is surely not unimportant to consider the particular regional "script" varieties in devising new writing systems. For example, it has always struck me as having made eminent good sense when the Indigenous Language Project in Mexico in the forties planned new alphabets for many Amerindian languages of Mexico based on Spanish orthography. The ultimate goal was to produce literacy in the native language as a transition to literacy in Spanish. Similarly, the Soviet experience with developing new scripts for previously unwritten languages began in the early twenties with the use of the Roman alphabet. The later changeover to a Cyrillic script would have made better sense at the very beginning.[16] Coming as it did twenty years after the initial introduction of the Roman alphabet even for some languages as replacement for their traditional scripts, the second reform (here I quote an Iranist friend who emigrated from the USSR in 1971) "immediately made two generations of Tajik speakers illiterate." Tajik is the form of Persian spoken in the provinces of Uzbekistan and Tajikistan, which has traditionally been written in the Perso-Arabic script before the Russian Revolution; the language was then called *fārsi* "Persian" and not Tajik. To analyze the whole political side of these matters in the Soviet experience both with respect to the replacement of scripts and the manner in which they were designed is beyond the scope of the present discussion. But it would be instructive to see how the political factors can affect such matters both positively and negatively.

The writing system and the historico-cultural matrix in which a speech community exists are the essential factors that give us a picture of an actual linguistic situation. Genetic affiliation of a language is of important scholarly interest, but of little consequence for the normal speaker. (I am aware that this etymological fallacy and all sorts of mystical bonds relating to language origins still affect the linguistic attitudes of speakers in many communities. This too needs to be taken into consideration in a detailed profile of a speech community and its attitudes to its own language and history.) There are numerous examples in which languages and writing systems have spread or been imposed through conquest and political domination; but there are also significant instances where the conqueror has himself become assimilated linguistically and graphically to the culture he has come to dominate. And still other instances where loyalty to a language and a script has made for stubborn persistence of a particular tradition.

In conclusion, it is perhaps worthwhile to make the following distinction in our discussion of writing systems. On the one hand, the spread of writing systems is a phenomenon to be studied in its own right, as a cultural artifact borrowable and transmittable in line with the cultures-in-contact concept. On the other hand, writing systems also serve as an indicator of language spread. The Dutch-based orthography of Indonesian which has been revised somewhat in more recent years in favor of English practice (e.g., Soekarno > Sukarno) is one modern example. Another is to be found in the map of Roman versus Cyrillic in the history of Christian Europe. Similar examples have been given above for the ancient world. And there still remains the conundrum inherent in the spread of both Aramaic language and writing—a language representing no major power source, but which has nonetheless left its impact far and wide.

NOTES

1. Johannes Friedrich, *Entzifferung verschollener Schriften und Sprachen.* (Verständliche Wissenschaft, Vol. 51). Berlin, Göttingen, Heidelberg: Springer-Verlag, 1954. An excellent survey with bibliographies covering many ancient Near Eastern languages is I. M. D'jakonoff, *Jazyki drevnej perednej azii* ["the languages of the ancient Near East"]. Moscow: Izdatel'stvo "Nauka", 1967.

2. One of the best discussions of the comparative method in linguistics is still, in my opinion, Leonard Bloomfield, *Language,* chapter 18, pp. 297–320. New York: Henry Holt and Co., 1933.

3. For a discussion of the impact of religion on language spread, see Charles A. Ferguson, "Religious factors in language spread." This volume.

4. Samuel N. Kramer, *The Sumerians: Their History, Culture, and Character.* Chicago: The University of Chicago Press, 1963.

5. Stephen Lieberman, *The Sumerian Loanwords in Old-Babylonian Akkadian.* Harvard Semitic Series, No. 22, 1977; René Labat, *Manuel d'épigraphie akkadienne.* Paris: Imprimerie Nationale, 1952 [as well as later editions].

6. Johannes Friedrich, "Hethitisch und 'Kleinasiatische' Sprachen," Vol. 5, Pt. 1, *Die Erforschung der indogermanischen Sprachen.* Berlin, Leipzig: Walter de Gruyter and Co., 1931; Edgar H. Sturtevant, *A Comparative Grammar of the Hittite Language.* 2nd Edition. Philadelphia: Linguistic Society of America, University of Pennsylvania, 1951.

7. Cf., for example, Loren Fisher (ed.), *Ras Shamra Parallels: The Texts from Ugarit and the Hebrew Bible.* Rome: Pontificium Institutum Biblicum, I. 1972, II. 1975.

8. I. J. Gelb, *A Study of Writing.* Chicago: The University of Chicago Press, 1952 [as well as later editions].

9. Stephen A. Kaufman, *The Akkadian Influences on Aramaic.* Assyriological

Studies, No. 19. Chicago: The University of Chicago Press, 1974; Jonas C. Greenfield, "Aramaic and Its Dialects," pp. 29–43 in Herbert H. Paper (ed.), *Jewish Languages: Theme and Variations.* Boston: Association for Jewish Studies, 1978; Jonas C. Greenfield, "The Dialects of Early Aramaic," *Journal of Near Eastern Studies* 37:93–99 (1978); and especially, Franz Rosenthal, "Aramaic Studies During the Past Thirty Years," *Journal of Near Eastern Studies* 37:81–91 (1978).

10. Franz Altheim and Ruth Stiehl, *Die aramäische Sprache unter den Achaimeniden.* Frankfurt am Main: V. Klostermann, 1963; for an overall view of Aramaic texts from various localities, periods, and styles, plus a survey of grammatical details, cf. *Encylopaedia Judaica* (Jerusalem: Keter, 1972): Abraham Malamat, "Aram, Arameans," 3.252–55 and Eduard Yecheskel Kutscher, "Aramaic," 3.259–87.

11. Walter B. Henning, "Mitteliranisch," Iranistik, from *Handbuch der Orientalistik,* Vol. 4. Leiden: E. J. Brill, 1958. The entire article, which is a masterful survey from the point of view of the spread of the Aramaic writing system, is on pp. 20–130; but note especially the following on p. 21:

> Dass die Kulturellen Wechselbeziehungen auf die Sprachentwicklung eine bedeutende Wirkung ausübten, versteht sich von selbst; sie wird vielleicht am klarsten an der äusseren Form fassbar, in welche die Sprachen gekleidet erscheinen: an der Schrift. Nicht nur haben die für das Soghdische, Chwarezmische, Parthische und Mittelpersische verwendeten Schriften einen gemeinsamen Ursprung, ihre Entwicklung ist auch in vielen wichtigen Zügen zueinander parallel verlaufen, sodass es das Gegebene erscheint, die Schrift und alles, was zu ihr gehört, als das verbindende Element in den Vordergrund unserer Betrachtungen zu stellen.

12. All translations from the Hebrew Bible are from *The New English Bible with the Apocrypha* (Oxford-Cambridge, 1970).

13. Roland G. Kent, *Old Persian: Grammar, Texts, Lexicon.* 2nd Revised Edition. American Oriental Series, Vol. 33. New Haven: American Oriental Society, 1951; F. H. Weissbach, *Die Keilinschriften der Achämeniden.* Vorderasiatische Bibliothek 3. Leipzig: J. C. Hinrichs'sche Buchhandlung, 1911.

14. W. W. Tarn, *The Greeks in Bactria and India.* Cambridge: Cambridge University Press, 1951.

15. Jonas C. Greenfield, "The Languages of Palestine, 200 B.C.E.–200 C.E.," pp. 143–54, together with the responses by Herbert C. Youtie, pp. 155–57, and Francis E. Peters, pp. 159–64, in Herbert H. Paper.

16. Paul Henze, "Politics and Alphabets in Inner Asia," pp. 371–420 in Joshua A. Fishman (ed.), *Advances in the Creation and Revision of Writing Systems.* The Hague-Paris: Mouton, 1977. Also, E. Glyn Lewis, *Multilingualism in the Soviet Union: Language Policy and Its Implementation.* The Hague: Mouton, 1972.

Castilian Colonization and Indigenous Languages: The Cases of Quechua and Aymara

Shirley Brice Heath and Richard Laprade

In the late eighteenth century, when some New World colonies of the Castilian empire were beginning to prepare for their independence, there appeared in Mexico City, Lima, La Paz, and Quito an edict issued by Charles III of Spain. Attached to the edict was a long and painfully detailed letter on the language situation in Mexico, written by the Archbishop of Mexico City. Convinced that Castilian had to become the language of the colonies if the colonies were to remain under the power of the Spanish empire, the archbishop appealed to Charles III to initiate a forceful plan for its spread. A detailed historical account of repeated efforts of the Crown to establish Castilian as the language of Mexico was designed to convince the King that the empire's colonies should not continue to be an exception to what seemed to be successful processes of language spread elsewhere.

> The most learned and intelligent authors who deal with the customs of the Indies and royal decisions defend with very solid arguments not only the idea that the Indians ought to be taught to learn Castilian but also that they can be obliged to do so. They substantiate this judgment with the example of the Hebrew people, who in the space of the seventy years of their Babylonian Captivity lost their native language and learned the Chaldean tongue of the Egyptians, with the result that, in order to understand the original texts of the sacred books of the Old Testament, a knowledge of Hebrew was needed for the books written before the Captivity, of Chaldean and Syrian for the writings during or after the Captivity, and of Greek for some of the New Testament and for the Septuagint version of the Old Testament. (Lorenzana y Buitrón 1770, translation cited from Heath 1972)

Though one may argue with the archbishop's knowledge of the facts (see Paper, this volume) and his use of history to promote a current policy, his lengthy recitation gives evidence of an understanding of the increase in language functions, expansion of social roles, and cultural changes which might be expected to accompany imposed language spread.

Castilian colonies of the New World included speakers of numerous diverse languages. In some areas, such as central Mexico, one indigenous tongue, Nahuatl, had established itself as a lingua franca and was widely used in written form, first in an indigenous writing system and then in Roman letters. In other areas, such as the Andean highlands, there was no long-established lingua franca; the Inca had only relatively recently imposed Quechua as a lingua franca for the diverse Indian groups under their control when the Spanish conquerors arrived. No writing system is known to have existed during the Incan Empire; however, the knotted *quipu* was used extensively for calculations and record-keeping in the administration of the huge domain.

For most of the colonial period, the Crown espoused a policy of Castilianization, a program to spread the Castilian language to the Indians in order to Christianize them. However, by the end of the eighteenth century, the archbishop was able to remind the King that there had been great divergence between policy and practice. The policy had not been effectively or consistently imposed, and there had been too few inducements to lead the Indians to acquire Castilian. Early conquerors had depended on interpreters, and as they spread to new areas where there were more and more new languages, they had continued using interpreters. Over the centuries, some members of Spanish religious orders and creole prelates (those born in the New World) learned some Indian tongues and used this knowledge to reinforce their own positions of power. The secular clergy (regular parish priests and bishops) and the *peninsulares* (those born in Spain) were placed in unfair competition because they knew no Indian languages. The royal order to isolate the Indians in fortified villages administered by members of religious orders had allowed the friars to neglect the instruction and use of Spanish and to promote retention of indigenous languages. The archbishop called for a forceful language policy that would bring about results needed to remedy the impending dissolution of the empire. His proposal contained points similar to those today's policy makers consider when they include language in their plans to modernize developing nations or to enhance the status of minority groups within developed nations.

1. A well-ordered plan imposed by a superordinate power to spread a language will lead ultimately to the demise of indigenous tongues and/or diverse dialects.
2. The acquisition of literacy for use in educational and economic

institutions will become a major goal of those replacing their native tongue with the chosen language of power.
3. Acquiring the standard language will bring socioeconomic, intellectual, and cultural benefits to the individual.
4. The accrual of socioeconomic benefits to those learning the standard linguistic norm will motivate others to seek linguistic and cultural assimilation to the majority-language group.

Corollaries frequently associated with these views are:

1. Language spread under this imposed policy must be replacive; i.e., the power language must replace others rather than supplement them.
2. Literacy promotes the economic, social, and intellectual advancement of both individuals and social groups.
3. If replacing one's native tongue with the power language will bring individual socioeconomic *benefits*, and also *risks* to maintenance of identity with one's primary social group, the benefits will be seen as outweighing the risks.

Easily recognizable as characteristic of a colonialist mentality, these views and their corollaries are also associated with a neoevolutionary, diffusionist perspective which views minority-language speakers as backward, insular, and uninitiated in the benefits of learning the majority language. The belief often expressed is that once institutions can be established to diffuse the majority language and its culture to the minority-language group, the latter will acquire the frame of reference necessary to lead them to replace their native tongue with a chosen standard language.

These views are often assumed to be characteristic of colonial powers throughout history. However, critical analysis of historical evidence reveals there were decision makers who rejected these views. It is important to note that the eighteenth-century archbishop of Mexico City regretted the *failure* of past Castilian rulers and representatives of the Church *to adhere* to a colonialist attitude toward spreading Castilian among the subjects of the New World. The archbishop decried the alternative views concerning language spread promoted by both political and religious administrators before him. It is important when studying a language policy of the past to look at alternatives to the espoused general policy which emerged and to be aware of the extent to which knowledge of the local situation informed policy making. It is also valuable to know of ways in which local situations both altered implementation and enforcement of colonial policies and helped establish patterns of response to current national language policies.

This paper presents an in-depth analysis of one series of events in the seventeenth-century Castilianization program of the Crown and the Church to illustrate that even within this program there were decisions made which were contrary to those expected from a colonial power. The colonialist model of language policy assumes that the colonizing power will spread its own language as an instrument of empire and over the long run will subordinate or eliminate the languages of the colonized. The independence or modernization model assumes that the power elite of a developing country will foster its language or a former colonial language as a means of national integration and access to the elite. This paper points out that some assessments of the language situation and views on language spread held by these statesmen and churchmen of the seventeenth century foreshadow points made today by those who oppose a colonialist or modernization approach to language policy for minority-language groups. The paper also summarizes the contrasting responses of Quechua and Aymara Indians to national language policies of today, in an effort to demonstrate that neither a colonialist nor a modernization paradigm is adequate to account for patterns of language spread among these minority-language populations in their colonial and independent settings.

CASTILIANIZATION AND INDIGENOUS LANGUAGES IN THE VICEROYALTY OF PERU

Castilian soldiers entered the central Andean area in the fourth decade of the sixteenth century. Behind the arrival of the soldiers and treasure hunters stood the Castilian policies of religious, political, and economic extension in the New World. A papal bull of Alexander VI had conveyed to Ferdinand and Isabella the right to administer authority in the Indies, and the "Catholic Kings" executed this charge through a complex of laws designed to transform the indigenous societies of the New World. Central to this program was a belief in "language as the perfect instrument of empire" (Heath 1972). The spread of Castilian culture and Christianity was to be achieved in and through the Castilian tongue. Supportive administrative units carried out laws designed to guide Castilianization. In Spain, the Council of the Indies served as legislative, judicial, and executive director of New World affairs. Immediate administration of New World holdings was entrusted to the viceroy, the central official within each of the viceroyalties (only Peru and New Spain for most of the colonial period).

Each viceroy acted under the authority of the Council, which appointed a *visitador* for periodic evaluations of administrative affairs in each viceroyalty. *Audiencias*, second in power to the viceroys, served as advisory and judicial bodies which heard legal cases and watched over the social and economic development of the colonies. The Viceroyalty of New Spain included primarily what is known as Mexico today. The Viceroyalty of Peru included all of South America except Portuguese Brazil and was administered by the audiencias of Quito, Lima, and Charcas. Under the Castilian Crown, religious agents and colonists assumed broad cultural roles. Members of religious orders gathered the Indians into villages. In Peru, beset by civil wars throughout the colonial period, these villages became armed fortresses in which the friars held control over the daily affairs of the Indians. Many of the colonists held grants of land which included service from the Indians. As patrons over groups of Indians, they kept them in relative isolation from other groups of Indians. Priests, secular or religious, and colonists, estate-owners or city-dwellers, exploited Indian labor and offered no inducements for Indians to adopt Castilian ways of living.

Cruelties of the economic system and exploitation of the Indians by the colonists and prelates are well attested. The phenomenon of language spread, however, provides one case in which rulings and special mechanisms designed to alleviate the abuse of power over Indians were given special attention. The Council of Trent (1563) and specific papal bulls and decrees had charged the Castilian Crown with the conversion of the natives and had provided for explanation of the sacraments to them in the vernacular tongues (Schroeder 1950:197–98). With respect to all rulings, local authorities were to evaluate the injustices or conflicts which implementation of such rulings might create. The Council of the Indies was to be informed of these. Consequently, local authorities had the power to accept rulings but not to execute them, if they could claim that to do so would bring an injustice on the Indians (Haring 1947:123). The edict to which the archbishop's discussion of language spread was attached contained the familiar final statement: "with the proviso that in those places where these measures are found inconvenient in practice they will inform me of it, forwarding all pertinent documents so that in light of these it may be decided what might be my Royal pleasure in the matter. . . ." Thus, the Council of Trent's ruling and the frequent proviso against "inconvenient" practices allowed the priests to ignore rulings favoring the spread of Castilian and, instead, to promote the indigenous languages.

Relatively little is known about the pre-Hispanic spread of languages in the central and southern Andes. Torero (1972) provides the most thorough coverage of the topic, using documentary evidence and glottochronology to establish the relative time depth and extent of influence of the three major *lenguas generales* of the highlands: Puquina, Quechua, and Aru (a group which contains Aymara and is referred to as Jaqi by Hardman 1972, 1978).[1] By the sixteenth century, only Quechua and Aymara remained as lingua francas within an area populated by numerous small political units. Priests, seemingly forgetful of Castilian as the instrument of empire, recognized Quechua and Aymara as convenient tools in their task of spreading Christianity in an area reported by some priests to contain as many as seven hundred different languages.

Aru speakers inhabited the central Andes as early as the third century B.C. and probably reached the height of their development as a military power in the seventh century A.D. Between approximately A. D. 700 and the twelfth century, the Aru held imperial control in the central Andes and extended their influence into the southern Andes, where Puquina had formerly been the major language (Torero 1972). The Inca, originally established in the northern Andes, had by the twelfth century begun to move south and to divide the Aru. By the fifteenth century, the Inca had overthrown the major centers of Aru strength. Following their conquest, the Inca initiated their policy of erasing memories of past tribes. When divided by the penetration of Quechua, the Aymara branch in the south was cut off from Jaqaru and Kawki in the north. Many Aymara speakers were relocated along the coast, and subjugated tribes from other regions were settled in former strongholds of the Aymara. In particular, the Inca forbade recounting tribal histories, and they initiated the replacement of other histories with their own relatively recently formulated history. They exercised fierce control over topics of public discussion and enforced a program to spread their language, Quechua, and to prohibit use of the languages of subjugated tribes.

Thus Spanish arrival in the mid-sixteenth century came at a point when Quechua had only recently begun to spread in the central and southern Andes. Chronicles of early priests indicate that Quechua was in many areas used only for administrative functions, and that immediately after the Spanish arrived, some tribes quickly dropped Quechua and began using their native tongues across all functions in the society. To facilitate the control and conversion of the Indians, the Spaniards uprooted them from their villages and resettled them in *reducciones*, large communities made up of residents of several villages. From these fortified towns, first the Dominican friars and later the Jesuits attempted to control the Indians' life and language. The young, especially children of Indian leaders, were grouped in *conventos*, used as schools. Here the young Indians taught the priests their language, and the priests tried in turn to convert these future Indian leaders to the Church.

In general, conversion of large numbers of individuals other than those chosen as cultural and linguistic brokers was not a realistic goal. The *mita* system, which required adult male Indians to spend a portion of their time engaged in labor for the welfare of the Spanish administration, dispersed the Indians in a variety of industries throughout Peru. Many worked and perished in silver mines located at great distances from their homes. Civil wars in which the Indians attempted to wrest power from the Spaniards frequently disrupted normal patterns of activity in the *reducciones* (for a discussion, from the Hispanic point of view, of life in La Paz during this period, see Crespo 1972). The harsh climate and difficult terrain of the Andes discouraged many clergy from venturing outside the cities and fortressed communities. Consequently, prelates focused their efforts on establishing what has been termed "a visible church": buildings and the institutional apparatus to carry out rituals, celebrate holy days, and offer sacraments (Ricard 1932, 1966). The Church was a thoroughly Spanish institution which intruded into the lives of the vast majority of the Indians in only relatively superficial ways. The Indians sometimes received the sacraments, listened to and performed in religious plays and festival events, learned to recite the Catechism, and incorporated their own culture into the artwork of Churches built by their forced labor. Cherubim with Indian features and color, and the Virgin painted with jewelry typical of wealthy Indian women decorated doorways, altars, and ceilings. However, a native clergy was not permitted; the Indians had no way of gaining a meaningful role in the Church.

Castilianization in speech and customs was sometimes discussed as a program which would allow some measure of incorporation of the Indians into the life of the Church. But more often, the program's goals were to provide efficient control of the Indians by the priests and to end the need for interpreters. However, many clergy, particularly those of religious orders, argued that more meaningful conversion could take place if the Indians were taught in their own languages. Otherwise, the language and the religion they learned in Spanish would not be meaningful, but only a temporary graft. Indians would gain no receptive or productive competency in Spanish; they would only be able to parrot phrases_and responses to Catechism questions.

With these thoughts in mind, local agents in Peru and decision makers in Castile debated the choice of a language or languages to be spread, and together they established institutions and selected change agents to promote the spread of a new and different communicative network. Spanish-speaking Indians, acting as scribes and official "rememberers" for the Indian town councils established by the Spaniards, kept their traditional name of *quipo camayos* (Harth-Terre 1964:17–19). Bilingual natives were preferred for leadership posts, such as members of town councils, over Indians who could not read and write Spanish (Garces G. 1935:179, lxviii). Bilingual Indians served also as interpreters for Spanish officials, and in 1552, Viceroy Antonio de Mendoza introduced ordinances providing for the employment of translators by the Audiencia in matters affecting Indians (e.g., Murra 1967:289, an account of a 1549 *visita* in Huanuco during which a *ladino*—an Indian who knew Castilian—served as official interpreter). Ultimately, the Crown wanted Castilian to spread, but because of religious rulings regarding delivery of the sacraments in the vernacular, the royal leaders and the Council of the Indies allowed indigenous languages to be used as an initial communicative tool in religious matters. Both Aymara and Quechua were designated for this use, and in the late sixteenth century, both these languages obtained an increased number of speakers and extension of functions to include written materials, religious rituals, and sermons.

By the beginning of the seventeenth century, however, it became clear that forces other than the Castilian religious community were affecting the spread of Aymara. Fewer and fewer priests used Aymara; they preferred instead Quechua, the language which had gained a quasi-official role in the Spanish takeover of the Incan Empire. In spite of the relatively recent introduction of Quechua to many of the Indian groups, the former *lengua general* of the Inca empire was becoming established over all other indigenous tongues and, for many functions, over Castilian as well. Spanish officials' use of Quechua in political, economic, and religious affairs had continued the spread of Quechua which the Inca had begun. Aymara had not been able to hold its own as a lingua franca. Quechua had the advantage of being established in regional and local administrative units controlling distribution of labor and agricultural goods. Ethnic chieftains or *kurakas* (who were paid for their services in the collection of tributes, and received a pension from the state) saw to it that, in spite of crop failure or general bad times, the Indians maintained their fixed amount of tribute. Many of these kurakas owed their position to Incan antecedents. Thus, retention of large portions of the Incan administrative structure and personnel helped spread Quechua in commercial and political affairs, as Spanish dominion spread far beyond the area of original Incan influence.

Priests were also partially responsible for the expansion of Quechua to new groups of speakers and to functions different from those it had served for the Incas. Friars translated catechisms and sermons and prepared grammars for the language (lists of surviving grammars are in Middendorf 1959, ca. 1890; Dahlmann 1892). By 1547, the Emperor Charles V (King Charles I of Spain) requested that the Pope consider bestowing special recognition on those who learned to teach and preach in Indian tongues (Carta . . . del Emperador, Oct. 30, 1547, in Levillier 1919:II,66–67.

However, the very proficiency of the friars in preparing written materials for spreading the Christian Faith in Quechua aroused some uneasiness over the possibility that errors in doctrine might appear in Quechua translations of the catechism. By 1545 the first Archbishop of Lima, Jerónimo de Loaysa, prohibited the use of catechisms written in Quechua pending the preparation of an official version or versions. Loaysa was not so concerned over the clergy's sermons in the native tongues on the subject of the Creation and other less serious matters as he was by the widespread use of unapproved (nonstandardized) catechisms. The archbishop wished to provide some control over missionary friars who were extending their mission fields beyond the Spanish towns and spreading the use of the Quechua catechisms (Vargas 1947:xii). Such concern for the interpretations of the Faith in Indian languages probably influenced the Crown to review the random pattern of language policy in the Indies in 1550. Conflicting reports from religious and lay leaders in the colonies had supported both the Indian tongues and Castilian as the language of instruction for the Indians. However, a majority of the reports admitted the difficulties of translating matters of the Faith into indigenous tongues. Therefore, in July of 1550, Charles V wrote to his representatives in the New World that he had determined that since "even the most perfect language of the Indians" could not satisfactorily be used to explain the mysteries of the Catholic Faith without imperfections, he felt it necessary to introduce Castilian to the Indians. His proposal revealed a grave lack of understanding of the Indian situation on the part of Peninsular planners. Charles V recommended that the Indians' involvement in instruction of Castilian be voluntary; teachers and schools would be provided, and if the Indians so desired, they should attend these schools to learn Castilian (*Recopilación de leyes de los reynos de las indias* [hereafter RLI] II, 193, Lib. VI, tit.I, ley 18). By this date, the Dominicans were operating sixty primary schools for the Indians of the Andean highlands, and to encourage their efforts, the King provided them with three thousand gold pesos in May, 1551 (Vargas Ugarte 1953:I.328).

However, the 1550 decree was mildly worded and made no mention of eliminating the Indian tongues as the basic instrument of Christianization. Religious leaders, therefore, continued to recognize the stable position of the indigenous tongues in their contacts with Indians; they turned their attention not to teaching Spanish, but to systematizing evangelical methods established during the first two decades of colonization and to standardizing uses of the Indian tongues in the teaching of Catholic doctrine. In 1552, the First Liman Council, called by Archbishop Loaysa, charged both regular and secular clergy to insure that the priests who ministered to the Indians would know the native tongues and question individuals presenting themselves for baptism in their native language. The Council also approved translations of the Catechism and other religious works into various Indian tongues (Armas Medina 1953:297).

The Second Liman Council convened in 1567 and attempted to strengthen the rulings of the First Council. Priests were instructed that those who served the Indians should carefully learn their language, and the bishops should rigorously induce them to do so. Clergy negligent in this task were to be deprived of one-third of their salary, and if they persisted in not learning the Indian tongues, other punishments would follow. Ecclesiastics attending the Second Council of Lima promulgated 122 acts relating to the Indians and the organization of teachings for them. In addition to being charged to learn the language of their parishioners, priests serving Indians were asked to teach all men, women, and children to recite the Lord's Prayer, Ave Maria, Creed, and Ten Commandments in both their native tongue and Spanish. At baptism the Indians were to repeat these in Spanish, but to answer questions in their native tongue, and the priests were to make certain they understood them "according to their capacity" (Levillier 1921:I.286, II.438–39, III.79). Churchmen recognized the problem of merely grafting religious phrases in Spanish onto their native language.

Rumblings from civil and religious officials alike during the period after the Second Liman Council made it clear that the initial enthusiasm of early friars for learning the Indian tongues was not shared by those who followed them to Peru. Many priests apparently were reluctant to leave the comforts of the Spanish settlements and their environs for missionary work in the countryside or in the *reducciones*.

During this period, however, some friars defended the Indians and their languages. Fray Domingo de Santo Tomás, a dedicated Dominican friar and bishop in the mold of Bartolomé de Las Cases, an early champion of the Indians, took an active part in the deliberations of the Second Liman Council. Earlier, in 1551, he had cited as the principal task of his grammar a defense of the Indians and the Quechua tongue. He found Quechua completely adequate in vocabulary for workaday technical communication, elaborate in expression, pleasing to the ear, capable of expressing mood, time, and person in its verb system, and in every sense a complete language. True, the Indians lacked an alphabetic writing system, but the Indian students had proved extremely adept at learning to write Quechua in the Roman alphabet. Fray Santo Tomás reasoned that "as this language is so civilized, the people who use it must not be barbarians but civilized themselves" (Santo Tomás 1947, ca. 1551:8–9. His Jesuit contemporary Blas Valdera confirmed his opinion and went so far as to suggest that the learning of Quechua had a calming effect on such rude and savage groups as the Puquinas, Collas, Urus, and Yuncas (Blas Valdera 1945, ca. 1560:126).

However, the urgings of dedicated individuals and the Liman Councils could not persuade newly arrived clerics to study the Indian languages. The zeal of the early missionaries was diluted in those who arrived as the highlands continued to be torn apart by battles between the Indians and the Spaniards. During the interval between the second and third Liman Councils, the King received numerous bleak reports on the spread of Christianity. Viceroy Francisco de Toledo consistently accused many priests of laziness, greed, and obstinacy, and argued that old methods were of little use. In 1570, he discouragingly noted that many priests were ignorant of the Indian tongues, and used as translators *yanaconas*, urbanized, partially Hispanicized Indians who lived in hovels outside the towns, and who were, in his judgment, incapable of faithfully rendering the Holy Word. In some areas, Toledo noted, "priests teach in pidgin Spanish, and the Indians learn to repeat the Creed and rituals with no more understanding of them than that of a parrot who learns to talk" (Levillier 1921:III.382, *Colección de documentos inéditos para la Historia de España* 1842–1895 [hereafter CDIHE] XCIV:257–58). Toledo accused the Dominicans of offering confession only to Spanish speakers and of telling the rest of their parishioners to go into church and confess to God. Toledo estimated that in the province of Chucuito, with a population of seventy thousand Indians, no more than forty-five confessed in a single year (Levillier 1921: V.112–13; general summaries of Toledo's assessment of the state of Christianity between 1570 and 1586 are found in Levillier 1921:VIII.304–82, III.380–83, 495–97).

A Franciscan friar, Fray Antonio de Zúñiga, who served among the Indians eighteen years, argued that the slight importance given language study for the Indians was a direct cause of the sad state of Christianization. Zúñiga pleaded for a forceful Castilianization policy ordering Indians to learn Spanish within one to two years. Rewards should be given to those Indians who learned Castilian; for those who did not, only food should be provided. By showing Indians the benefits of learning the Castilian tongue, conquerors could insure that most of them would learn to value Castilian within a short time, whereas "now they put no value on speaking Spanish, and often, they speak it only when they are drunk" (CDIHE XXVI.88–94).

However, Philip II was not convinced that such a drastic change in language policy was the surest method for success. In his view, if the priests had failed to learn the Indian tongues, they had done so because of a lack of dedication, training opportunities, and incentive. Moreover, current prelates must be forced by law to return to the morality and devotion of early friars. In 1580, "believing knowledge of the *lengua general* of the Indians the most crucial means for explaining and teaching the Christian doctrine," (RLI,I.204, Lib.I, tit. xxii, ley 46), Philip II ordered the bishops of Lima, Charcas, Cuzco, and Quito to oversee the establishment of special professorships in Quechua at the University of San Marcos. As incentive, Philip decreed that ecclesiastical offices would not be open to those who did not know the major language of Indians under their charge. Diocesan prelates were to examine all candidates on their knowledge of the Indian languages (RLI,I.45, Lib.I, tit.vi, leyes 19–20; I.132, Lib.I, tit.xv, ley 6).

The Third Liman Council took note of both the King's current interest in education and conversion through the Indian tongues and the rapidly disintegrating conversion program among Indians outside the cities. The Council, presided over by Archbishop Toribio Mogrovejo, confirmed the recommendations of the Second Council and provided further reforms. The archbishop wrote the King asking that he confirm the Council's decisions and that they be allowed to print the catechism in Spanish, Aymara, and Quechua as quickly as possible. He urged that the maximum number of Indians under the care of each priest be limited to four hundred, and that a *colegio* be established for the sons of Indian nobles so that they might learn to preach to their own people (Levillier 1919:II.154–216). Ramifications of the Council's work caused other leaders to prevail on the King to provide the institutions for carrying out reform of the linguistic habits of the priests. In 1588, the Viceroy of Peru urged that a professorship also be provided in Quito for the support of an outstanding teacher of Quechua, as had been done earlier at the University of San Marcos. Only in this way could priests be adequately trained in Quechua, and, moreover, the priests who now claimed they knew Quechua could be fairly examined by this teacher. In effect, the Viceroy recommended a return to the

Incan language policy of rigorously spreading Quechua and of demanding a knowledge of Quechua as a prerequisite to any position of control over the Indians. In 1586 and again in 1591, the King sent out an edict supporting the recommendations of the Third Council and asking the support of all lay leaders in the maintenance of the new reform programs. Aimed at the abuses of power and position many priests had committed, the recommendations were not popular, and controversies surrounding the amount and direction of efforts to Christianize and Hispanicize the Indians continued through the Fourth and Fifth Councils in 1591 and 1601 (Levillier 1919:I. 419–28, II.154–259, 312–13). Philip issued another decree in 1588 to the prelates of the Indies in which he prohibited ordaining any ordinary parish clergy or members of religious orders who did not know Quechua. Philip wanted no misunderstanding of his view of the importance of the clergy's learning of Quechua.

But the succession of decrees that Philip made in support of the Indian tongues failed to persuade all of Peru's clergy that the earliest friars had set the right course for language policy. Ecclesiastics apparently continued to harass the Council of Indies with their arguments for a review of language policy. Early in 1596, the Council sent a proposed *real cédula* to Philip II in which they suggested that a forceful Castilianization language program be initiated for Peru's Indians. The Council's order asserted that under the flexible system which had hitherto prevailed in the New World, the Indians were not learning Castilian nor were they being confirmed in the Catholic Faith. The Indian tongues, even those held in highest esteem by the religious leaders themselves, could not satisfactorily be used for the translation of the Christian doctrine. Since the Indians were to become citizens of the Spanish empire, they should learn "good customs" and the Castilian tongue, so that they might more easily be governed. As inducement to the Indians, the Council suggested that after a two-year learning period, no Indian should be allowed to hold office without knowledge of Castilian. Philip received the order and returned it to the Council, asking for more information on the language situation in the New World.

The Council, drawing together information received from the various New World colonies, placed great emphasis on two points. First, the variety of tongues throughout the New World colonies necessitated a standard idiom which might be used to teach the Indians Christianity and Hispanic customs. Second, the use of the indigenous tongues in the Christianization program had favored creole prelates at the expense of priests newly arrived from Spain. More often than not, creole priests were not as rigorously trained in dogma as were graduates of Peninsular institutions. Moreover, the Council believed *peninsulares* were more likely to teach the Indians "better customs" than were creoles who had lived among the indigenous. The Council concluded that close association with the Indians had led far too many creoles to accept not only the tongue of the New World citizens but to develop a sympathetic tolerance for some of their customs. The tables had turned with a vengeance. What the Spanish had wanted to accomplish with the Indians (i.e., to convert them to their values and habits), the Indians were doing to some New World descendants of the Spaniards.

A strange thing in colonial language policy making occurred upon receipt of the Council's survey of the language situation in the New World. Philip was not persuaded by the Council's arguments. In July of 1596, he sent a milder version of the order than the one suggested by the Council to Luis de Velasco, Viceroy of Peru. Though admitting both the divine purpose and the political rationale of the Council's recommendations, Philip refused to make the learning of Spanish compulsory for the Indians. Instead, he chose to relay a personal appeal to the provincials of the Dominican, Franciscan, and Augustinian orders and to ask the cooperation of civil officials and secular clergy. Admitting that Indians might be more easily and better instructed in the Christian Faith if they knew Castilian from a young age, Philip turned his attention to the education of Indian children. If, in the primary schools, the prelates would teach Castilian as they taught the Christian doctrine, young children would grow up knowing Castilian (Zavala 1946; the *real cédula* is in Encinas 1946:IV.339–40).

Philip III continued his father's policy (Garces G. 1946:20–21,83). A change in policy came only with Philip IV, who in 1634 issued an order to archbishops and bishops commanding priests and *doctrineros* of the Indians to use "the gentlest possible means" to teach all Indians Spanish. Moreover, henceforth, they should teach the Christian doctrine in the Spanish tongue. The teaching of Spanish would not only improve the chances of the Indians' learning and understanding the Christian faith, but it would also prove beneficial in governing the Indians and altering other cultural habits (RLI:I.96, Lib. I, tit. xiii, ley 5). From this point on, the Castilian Crown gave no official sanction to Quechua or any of the former *lenguas generales* of Peru; decrees throughout the seventeenth and eighteenth centuries favored Spanish for the Indians. However, institutional support for the teaching of Spanish generally did not exist, and a series of summary decrees on language policy in the 1680s were to conclude that the early religious leaders had been too successful in convincing the Castilian Crown to hold a lenient and flexible language policy (Muro Obrejón 1956:

262–65). Though sometimes admitting the ultimate desirability of a Castilian-speaking citizenry in the New World, the Crown and its religious representatives had not implemented a strong assimilationist language policy.

LEGACY OF COLONIAL CASTILIANIZATION: LANGUAGE IN THE NATIONAL CONTEXT

The Archbishop of Mexico City first wrote Charles III in 1768 of the failure of the program for the spread of Castilian. Between 1680, when the last decree on language policy was issued, and 1768, mechanisms for the spread of Quechua established in the sixteenth century continued to exist, and further edicts favoring Quechua had not been necessary. The process initiated by external forces in the early colonial period had been taken over by internal societal forces. Throughout the colonial period, continued isolation of the Indians from the major forces for change in Peruvian society had helped insure maintenance of the indigenous languages. After the initial decimation of their numbers, some Indian groups achieved a stable population and then gradually began to increase in population. For example, disease, civil wars, and relocation efforts of the Inca and early Spaniards had sharply decreased the Aymara population. Not until the late eighteenth century did the population stabilize, and since that time it has increased to nearly two million. Early population figures taken from tribute lists of the late sixteenth century (Romero 1928:169) indicate only thirty-five thousand Aymara in the central Andes. However, the geographic region referred to in these lists cannot always be accurately determined, and this figure is, no doubt, much too low, since the Lake Titicaca region is known to have been one of the most densely populated rural areas in the world. By the nineteenth century, the Aymara were great enough in number that the government felt it worthwhile to publish some political speeches and religious materials in Aymara (Briggs 1979a).

Well before the end of the colonial period, dispersal of the Aymara had ended, and they were located primarily in the *altiplano* of the Andes. In the nineteenth and early twentieth centuries, they worked in regional markets; some located permanently in the larger population centers such as La Paz, where they lived in areas segregated from the Spanish, areas known today as *villas miseria*. Travelers' accounts of daily life in La Paz in the nineteenth century are shadowy and contradictory. However, there is little doubt that there were many Aymara Indians living in segregated areas of the city. Moreover, it is likely that most inhabitants of the city could use Aymara as a lingua franca in some situations, especially in the marketplace. However, the segregated life and the restricted functions of Aymara were not obvious to all visitors. Ernst Middendorf, a German philologist who reported his observations of various areas of Peru, Bolivia, and Ecuador (e.g., 1974, ca. 1890) apparently neither saw the segregated sections of La Paz nor heard the Aymara language used to any great extent. In his study of the aboriginal languages of Peru, he reported that he could find no speakers of Aymara in La Paz who had any competence in the language other than for addressing servants or market vendors (Middendorf 1910, cited in Briggs 1979a). Other travelers, such as Alcides D'Orbigny, a French naturalist who visited South America in the first half of the nineteenth century, gave a very different account of the role of Aymara in La Paz. His description suggests the use of Aymara beyond the segregated sections of La Paz.

> All the world speaks Aymara. The Indians know no other language and the mestizos struggle with their Spanish which is barely comprehensible and mixed with Aymara. Everywhere—in social life and in private—the inhabitants [of La Paz] speak Aymara among themselves, using Spanish only with strangers and in formal get togethers (D'Orbigny, cited in Crespo et al. 1975:191–92).

Crespo et al. (1975), drawing from numerous other primary sources, describes a highly segregated La Paz in the nineteenth century, one in which Indians were, at best, marginal to any activities which might have influenced their language and culture to shift to that of the Spaniards. Aymara was therefore primarily an in-group language of this urban population of Indians as well as of the large group of rural speakers, located in the altiplano, especially around Lake Titicaca. Opportunities for outsiders to learn and use Aymara in wide-ranging functions were restricted; *patrones*[2] and their families and regular participants in the marketplace activities learned Aymara only for particular purposes, such as bargaining, etc.

However, by the end of the nineteenth century, even these uses by non-Indians were declining. During the Chaco War of the 1930s, when Aymara and Quechua Indians filled the ranks of the Bolivian army in its border fight with Paraguay, the Indians remained separate, both from each other and from other high-ranking white and *mestizo* soldiers. After the war, they moved back into their former places in society, the traditional order of which had been gravely disrupted (Klein 1969:187). Maintenance of the *patrón* system and the influence of missionaries (Briggs, 1979b) have, since then, continued to exert certain influences on the language, but none of these has substantially contributed to the

spread of Aymara outside its own native speakers' group. In the highland commercial centers, some Indians are trilingual in Aymara,
Quechua, and Spanish. In other such centers, some are bilingual in
Aymara and Spanish; the proportion of monolingual Aymara speakers
varies greatly from center to center and among villages of the countryside.[3] There is extensive bilingualism among native Aymara speakers
in La Paz. Aymara can be heard among market women, masons, maids,
and security guards, but it is not uncommon that as soon as a native
Spanish speaker comes on the scene, they switch to Spanish, often spoken imperfectly and with an accent, but Spanish nonetheless (McGourn
1971). Using Spanish with outsiders has become the norm for many
Indians: in an interview conducted in the altiplano town of Ilave, Peru,
in 1969, 84 percent of the town's Indians were capable of handling the
interview in Spanish (Bertholet et al. 1969). In a sense, the tables have
turned. Some upper- and middle-class "Hispanic" women, who years
back had the advantage of being bilingual—at least for practical purposes of bargaining in the marketplace—today lament the fact that they
have little opportunity to use their Aymara. Relatively few middle-aged
or young native Spanish-speakers in La Paz are able to communicate at
all in Aymara, though their Spanish may be spotted with Aymara vocabulary and examples of influence from Aymara grammatical
categories. How stable this linguistic situation is remains to be seen
(Laprade 1979), and it is not clear how widespread this pattern is in
other population centers.

Quechua, on the other hand, having been given the role of lingua
franca by the Inca and Spaniards, spread over a geographic area wider
than that in which it was used when the Spaniards arrived. It is spoken
today throughout the highland areas of Peru and Bolivia, and it is spoken by individuals across a range of social and economic classes. To be
sure, it is primarily used by the Indians, but it is receiving increased
attention in the preparation of bilingual teaching materials and publications of folk literature, and it is being given greater visibility and legiti-
macy by the active Institute of Peruvian Studies in Lima. There are
several dialects of Quechua, and linguists have in the recent past been
attempting to determine a supradialectal norm for use in grammars and
other educational materials (Wölck 1972).

In Peru and Bolivia, both Aymara and Quechua (as well as all other
indigenous tongues) have recently been recognized as "national languages," a ceremonial gesture which acknowledges the existence of the
minority languages in these nations (Heath 1979). Of these minority
tongues, Aymara and Quechua are receiving the greatest amount of attention in recent efforts to increase use of Indian languages in educa-

tional programs (Albó 1977; Miracle 1975). But purposes and populations differ greatly for the two. Preparation of materials in Quechua is the responsibility of numerous institutions, both governmental and religious. The major goal of education is to spread the supradialectal norm of Quechua, especially its written form, to groups speaking widely different dialects and to speakers of other languages. Quechua is gaining in ideological acceptance and in some practical uses as a language capable of performing many of the same functions as Spanish.

The recognition of Aymara as a national language has not resulted in its spread beyond its native speakers, but rather in its expansion to new functions, primarily those associated with writing, among those for whom Aymara is the mother tongue. The Aymara Language Materials Project, directed by M.J. Hardman-de-Bautista at the University of Florida has contributed grammars, a newsletter, and numerous publications for use in the preparation of materials and the training of teachers and is continuing a long-term dictionary project. Among the organizations formed by native Aymara-speakers in Bolivia to promote Aymara language and culture are: ILCA (Instituto de Lengua y Cultura Aymara), INEL (Instituto Nacional de Estudios Lingüísticos), and *Mink'a* (the Aymara word for 'help' or 'communal task'). Despite the shortage of funds, these groups have been active in the dissemination of printed matter in Aymara. *Cursillos* (mini-courses) are offered by linguistically trained members to spark interest in the Aymara language and to encourage the teaching of literacy skills in Aymara, both for adults and for children in elementary school programs. A course in the Aymara language is offered at the Universidad Mayor de San Andrés in La Paz. There has even recently been a series of local productions for television of Aymara folktales, presented in Aymara and Spanish. These are the product of what seem to be a growing organized appreciation of Aymara by outsiders and an interest in its spread to other functions among its own speakers.

GENERAL CONSIDERATIONS

Since the colonial period, policies of language spread (though not necessarily practices) for the Indians of the Andean highlands have generally reflected a Castilianization ideology which would support *replacing* the Indian languages with Spanish.[4] In an effort to transmit some aspects of religious behavior, some practices of the clergy promoted a temporary *grafting* of Spanish onto the linguistic performance of the Indians. In parroting Catechism responses, the Ave Maria, and other formalized performances, the Indians gained no receptive or real productive knowledge of Spanish. This type of language spread was much less likely to influence indigenous language structures than either replacive or additive spread.

However, in spite of a Castilianization ideology which sometimes led to replacement or grafting, local friars and other religious and civil leaders intermittently argued the merits of an *additive* policy for Quechua as a lingua franca. The Crown responded with support—financial and ideological—on several occasions. Twice during the colonial period, in spite of great local pressure from anti-Quechua forces, the Crown, in partial recognition of the language situation among the indigenous, argued for adding Castilian to the linguistic repertoire of the Indians and not subtracting their native tongues. In this plan, Spanish priests and civil authorities would learn Quechua. In schools, Indian children would become literate in Quechua and learn to speak Spanish as well. Thus, the Crown promoted an additive language program, in which some Indians, primarily the privileged, would maintain Quechua and learn Spanish (Wachtel 1977:150–51). Thus they could better be tested on their actual understanding of Christianity, and they could better serve within the Spanish colony. They too could be better served in some ways, for they would no longer be dependent on translators, many of whom used their position to exploit the Indians (Solano 1975).

Many of the policies of the colonial power related to language spread contained provisions for limitations on imposed change. Numerous policies were considered on the basis of information regarding local language situations, and subsequent policies were determined in part in response to periodic summaries of the relative spread of Castilian and Quechua. The spread of Castilian which did occur took place primarily through the Church, and in situations in which the Spaniards were directing orders to the Indians; thus, the functions of the Castilian learned by Indians were highly restricted (Avila Echazu 1974:68–69). The school, a major agency of imposed language spread, never achieved stability in the Andean countryside, because of the frequent disruptions of civil wars and changes in leadership between creole priests and peninsulares, and between religious and secular clergy. Crespo (1975:191) reports that even in La Paz in the early nineteenth century, there was no formal instruction for the mestizo or Indian children. Repeated changes in policy on schools seems to be a characteristic of Spanish colonial administration (on the successive changes in gubernatorial education policies in Mexican California, cf. Sapiens 1979; for a more general discussion of the school as a contemporary agent of change, see Paulston 1972).

Castilian did not spread into workaday technical uses for a majority of the Indians. It became the sometime language of administrative and judicial affairs, and the tongue of those who were able to gain access to the creole class. Its use was primarily restricted to urban areas, where it was the primary language of daily interactions outside the segregated Indian areas; in the countryside it remained limited to uses in churches and governmental units. For the majority of rural Indians, it was grafted onto religious rituals, sacred texts, and polite associations with their oppressors. In some cases, this high-prestige language was adopted by the Indians in low-prestige functions, and the language was debunked even by those who learned it (e.g., its use by Indian males when they were drunk).[5] From the colonial policy perspective, there was a great disparity between the potential and actual spread of Castilian.

The present case study forces considerable rethinking about the processes of determining language spread policies in a colonial empire. Specific patterns of interaction between local conditions and empire-level plans for social or linguistic change are identified. The repetitive nature of the questions language planners ask is revealed in such a detailed look at planned language spread as the Liman conferences of the sixteenth century provide. The widely diverse causes and results of language spread under a single policy—colonization—alert modern language planners to the possibility of similar diversities in nations achieving independence today. Moreover, the legacy of the colonial period reveals itself in the differences which currently exist between the spread of Quechua and that of Aymara. Differences exist not only in the number of speakers of each language today relative to those of the sixteenth century, but, more importantly, in the current functions the two languages serve for their respective speech communities. The specific conclusions from this case study with respect to Quechua and Aymara may be summarized as follows:

1. The formalized process of language spread initiated by the colonial power served to spread Quechua (Figure 1). This language, only relatively recently introduced in the central and southern Andean highlands, was legitimated for the numerous small and linguistically diverse political units of Indians through the Castilianization program, carried out primarily by the priests. The spread of Quechua instead of Castilian illustrates that a recently imposed indigenous language is not necessarily the weaker language in competition with a European tongue. Quechua not only spread as a spoken language, but also in written functions. The administrative and economic interactions it had served in the Inca empire were supplemented over the years of Spanish rule by workaday technical functions and uses in formal rituals of worship. Today, histori-

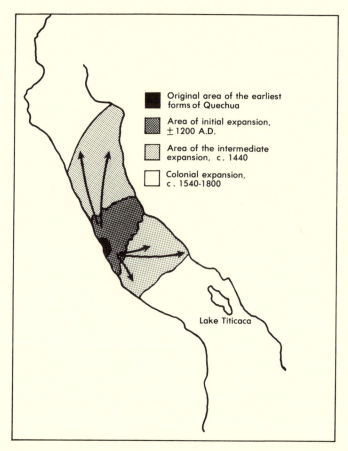

FIGURE 1. Phases of Expansion of Quechua
(adapted from Torero 1972:104).

cal accounts, folk literature, and teaching materials are prepared in
Quechua. (For a general account of the problems of establishing
Quechua as the Indian *lengua franca* in the multilingual school-age
population of Peru, see Escobar 1972). As Quechua has gained a large
pool of speakers and wider geographical dispersion, it has become advantageous for more and more speakers of other Indian languages to
learn it. It is particularly important that Quechua has been retained in
urban centers as well as rural areas.

  2. Aymara, a language which had held high prestige and a precolonial
role as a *lengua general,* lost its power as a language across groups, but
gained speakers through the population growth of its own group.

Through the years, the focus of Aymara speakers on internal-group language functions has helped create a strong linguistic awareness. The homogeneity of Aymara (Briggs 1976) and its limited geographical extension were conducive to its strong linkage with group identity, whereas Quechua, spread over a wide geographic area and with a variety of dialects (many mutually unintelligible), did not have the same potential of identification with group unity. The Aymara place a very high value on correct and proper use of Aymara and reward those who use it creatively with high prestige. (See Hardman 1972 and Hardman, Vásquez, and Yapita 1971 for a discussion of the intricacies of the Aymara language and the ability of the Aymara to give reasons for these intricacies; Hardman 1979 discusses the social context of uses of Aymara.) Many Aymara, in ways similar to those of the Otomí of Mexico (Wallis, cited in Heath 1972), recognize their language has low prestige in the nation at large, but they maintain the essence and uniqueness of their language as a matter of pride, just as they do their culture and group character. Often characterized by outsiders as rude, arrogant, and difficult to know, many Aymara are coming to accept as positive what might well be viewed as a negative history, because this characterization has contributed to their isolation and thus to the maintenance of their language and culture. In the words of one Aymara Indian: "The Incas came and conquered us, and then the Spaniards came and conquered us, but we aren't conquered yet" (cited in Hardman, Vásquez, and Yapita 1971).

In terms of ways in which modern planners view the variables associated with cultural diffusion, the cases of Aymara and Quechua provide particular cautions. *Language spread does not correlate with demographic categories, such as status, socioeconomic factors, and geographic units in predictable ways in all settings. The interrelatedness of language spread with factors such as group identity, historical verification of the role of language in group identity, and the specific preference of some groups for a language which does not have high status or correlate with socioeconomic mobility are conditions of language maintenance and spread which planners rarely acknowledge. Therefore, an effective program of language spread should make use of detailed knowledge of the groups involved.*

> Hasta cuando durará la dualidad trágica de lo indio y lo occidental en estos países descendientes del Tahuantisuyo y de España? Que profundidad tiene ahora la corriente que los separa? Una angustia oprime a quien desde lo interno del drama contempla el provenir. Este pueblo empecinado—el indio—que transforma todo lo ajeno antes de incorporarlo a su mundo, que no se deja ni destruir, ha demostrado que no cedará sino ante una solución total. (Arguedas 1974:167) [How long will

the tragic duality of Indian and Western last in these countries, descended both from the Tahuantisuyo and from Spain? How deep is the current which still separates them? A sense of anguish must oppress anyone from inside the drama who ponders its origins. This stubborn people—the Indian—that transforms everything alien before incorporating it into its own world, and does not let itself be destroyed, has shown that it will yield only to a total solution.]

In both Mexico and Peru, there are Indian groups that refuse to act as though they are oppressed or have the low status attributed them by higher socioeconomic groups. In these cases, the Indian groups have, in spite of political subjugation by other groups, maintained a strong sense of group identification and a strong commitment to some of their own institutions, oral traditions, and particular economic niches. In Mexico, the Zapotec of the Oaxaca Valley and the Otomí of the Federal District are known for their linguistic pride and maintenance of group identity in the face of political subjugation. The Aymara share a similar pride in their language and culture. To a great extent, these groups are able to maintain themselves economically with minimal dependence on or interaction with outsiders. For transactions in commercial centers, some members of the group become bilingual or trilingual depending on the market population.

Numerous explanations of assimilation programs depend upon either a colonialist/modernization paradigm or a conflict model in which the powerless struggle to gain admission to the economic infrastructure. Some few studies (e.g., Schermerhorn 1970; Fishman, Cooper, and Ma 1971) point out the factors and conditions which coincide with situations in which minority-language groups choose to maintain a large degree of cultural and linguistic independence and sometimes also to remain relatively outside the state's social and economic order. Geographic isolation, harsh physical conditions, and limited natural resources may increase a group's ability to maintain such socioeconomic independence.

For centuries, the Aymara have adapted to the harsh altiplano, and they have managed to maintain themselves in this environment. Even in the relatively recent past, if members of indigenous communities leave for permanent residence in the cities, they generally maintain close ties, for example, by sending money home, arranging jobs for relatives, or returning home to dance at holidays. The Aymara have chosen to maintain what many view as a powerless language. They have used their language for its separating function which sets its speakers apart from other Indian groups. Other markers of identity also persist, even in the urban area. The maintenance—with pride—of the *pollera,* an outer garment worn by Aymara women, parallels language maintenance to a certain extent. In La Paz, when a *chola* (an Indian seen as having given up Indianness for Hispanic traits) abandons her *pollera,* she suffers the ridicule given to *virlochas* (term of derision given to *cholas de vestido* 'chola in dress only'). On the other hand, from the Hispanic side, a great deal of ostracism accompanies use of Spanish marked by accent from one's indigenous tongue. Occasional lack of differentiation between /o/ and /u/, or the use of particular archaic words or certain syntactic constructions mark an Aymara as aspiring to a rise in class status. Unless she is able to rid herself of these sometimes very subtle interferences from Aymara, she is immediately pegged by the native Spanish-speakers as "out-group." Perhaps her children will have more success, but the benefits may be long in coming. The risks—psychological and social—of giving up Aymara are great for individuals because of the intimate association the language has with the group's identity, and the out-group status one who aspires to Hispanic membership can suffer in the transition.

The Quechua, on the other hand, have had a much more diverse geographic spread. Quechua speakers from the highlands migrate to towns and cities, seeking new ways of maintaining their families. Regional clubs, in towns such as Lima, help these new urban dwellers maintain ties with their pueblo and culture and provide support for each new influx of migrants from the rural areas (Mangin 1965, Dobyns and Doughty 1976). Their dialects are diverse, and dialect leveling, a process by which these diverse dialects lose their distinctive traits and become more like one another, occurs in some situations. In addition, literacy programs to spread the supradialectal norm are in operation.

History will allow us to reconstruct only some aspects of language spread in the Andean highlands, and we may assume that because of the absence of reliable counts, the scarcity of sources representing what happened from the Indian point of view, and the Hispanized version rendered in most colonial accounts, the picture we have is very limited. With adequate figures and descriptive accounts, for example, it would be possible to plot in-group as opposed to across-group functions, rates of spread for members of different levels of society, and the relative rate of acquisition of speaking and writing, but these figures and accounts are not available (for a discussion of problems in interpreting a recent census, see Myers 1967).

But from what little we do know of the history and current situation for Quechua and Aymara, are there factors which bear some resemblance to groups within other nations, both developed and developing? Speakers of minority languages in "old nations" (Fishman 1969) are today achieving gains in socioeconomic status and political visibility; as a result they wish to spread their languages to new functions and to majority-language speakers. Languages formerly used primarily for in-group communication are now gaining usage across groups. For example, in the United States, government representatives involved in administering and regulating minority affairs achieve credibility if they can speak Spanish, even if only in functions peripheral to actual business or legal negotiations. Thus, formerly monolingual majority-language speakers are finding it advantageous to learn a minority language to enhance their political or socioeconomic roles and to achieve communication in a larger network within their own nation.

The initial stimulation for the spread of a language may be either planned or unplanned, individual or group-initiated, derived from either within or outside the group speaking the language undergoing language spread. A change in political status may prompt a plan to promote a European language as the language of wider communication between citizens and the nationals of other countries and as a lingua franca within a nation formerly characterized by local languages. Language planning, to be effective, must include other types of social planning: altering institutions and appointing change agents—educational, religious, or political—to bring about changes in culture, material and nonmaterial, and systems of social interactions. Planned language spread, in both colonization and legitimation of newly independent nations, depends upon shifts in other areas of behavior (Heath 1976). An indigenous or immigrant group alerted to international and/or national moves for language rights may argue for both retention and extension of their native tongue, but they may themselves be unable to plan and carry out the institutional changes necessary to increase the number of speakers of their language in a given space over a period of time. Recognizing the need for political support, these groups may attempt to relate their desire for language spread to other political or social aims and thus gain institutional support from existing governmental agencies. In the United States, groups wishing to extend their language have identified their cause with social discimination, educational opportunities, and voting rights, in part to gain access to mechanisms of societal change the government provides for these areas.

In both colonization and modernization/independence movements, broker groups or individuals initiate and maintain language spread. However, even though it may be advantageous to have members of minority groups who can act as cultural and linguistic brokers in minority-majority relations, such positions may, in fact, threaten individuals' membership in their own groups. Native Americans of several tribes resist promotion of members of their group for teaching, legal, or social service positions because of the threat of membership loss to both the group and individuals.

All of these patterns and others occurred in the Castilian empire in the colonial period. Indians were promised, and many marginal individuals came to expect, monetary gain for learning Spanish and promoting Spanish within their communities. Indigenous language groups promoted their own languages for extension to Castilian leaders and manipulated Castilian institutions designed for other purposes to promote the indigenous languages. Indigenous tongues, formerly unwritten, were written and used for religious and political purposes. Castilian leaders, wishing to legitimate their goals with the indigenous, learned the Indian languages and sought to spread and maintain these, because in so doing, they helped guarantee retention of their own power. Many language planners, politicians, and social change agents involved in language spread efforts today see these patterns as new issues and find it difficult to accept the fact that they have occurred at various times and places in response to the specific histories of different languages and cultures. A greater attention to historical case studies may help overcome the tendency of modern language planners to see language spread as a type of behavior change in which the variables and interactions can be neatly predicted and controlled.

NOTES

We wish to thank Virginia Kays Creesy who, many years ago, encouraged Heath to write this article, provided numerous sources, and discussed their interpretations with her.

1. There is considerable debate over the relationship between Aymara and Quechua, the origin of Aymara, and the links between Aymara and Puquina. The major issues in these debates are summarized by Alfredo Torero, "Lingüística e historia de los Andes del Peru y Bolivia," *El Reto del Multilingüismo en el Perú,* ed. Alberto Escobar (Peru, 1972), and Martha Hardman, *Jaqaru: Outline of Phonological and Morphological Structure* (The Hague, 1966). Briggs (1979a) provides the most comprehensive survey of the literature on the Aymara language.

2. Besides the traditional meaning of 'landowner', *patron* is used with the general meaning of 'boss' in the Andean highlands. *Patrones* have often taken on extrafamilial roles (*compadres*) with the Indians of their haciendas, serving as *padrinos* for Indian children.

3. For an excellent discussion of the varying patterns of bilingualism in Aymara and either Spanish or Quechua in a town of Southern Peru, see Primov 1974.

4. Numerous prominent historians of Indo-America, such as Gibson 1966, have represented Castilianization in language as a *central* and *consistent* feature of the Castilian Crown's total policy of Hispanization. Examination of actual legislation and administrative and clerical response to this legislation in various parts of the Castilian empire indicates otherwise. Language policy in the Philippines is treated in Phelan 1959.

5. Another pattern in which the "low-prestige" language comes to dominate the "high-prestige" language in certain respects is that in which the indigenous language is acquired relatively late in the life of the individual but serves as the primary language. For an example of this pattern in an Indian language of a Spanish-speaking nation, cf. the discussion of Otomí in Waterhouse 1949.

REFERENCES

Albó, Xavier. 1977. El Futuro de los Idiomas Oprimidos en los Andes. Lima: Universidad Nacional Mayor de San Marcos, documento 33.

Arguedas, Jose Maria. 1974. Yawar Fiesta. Buenos Aires: Losada, S.A.

Armas Medina, Fernando. 1953. Cristianización del Perú. Seville: Consejo Superior de Investigaciones Científicas.

Avila Echazu, Edgar. 1974. Literatura pre-Hispanica y Colonial. La Paz, Bolivia: Libreria y Editorial Gisbert.

Bertholet, Christian J.L., et al. 1969. Puno Rural. Lima: Cisepa.

Briggs, Lucy Therina. 1976. Dialectal Variation in the Aymara Language of Bolivia and Peru. Ph.D. dissertation. University of Florida.

Briggs, Lucy Therina. 1979a. A Critical Survey of the Literature on the Aymara Language. Latin American Research Review 14.

Briggs, Lucy Therina. 1979b. Missionary, Patron, and Radio Aymara. *In* The Aymara Language in Its Social and Cultural Context. M.J. Hardman, ed. University Social Science Monographs Series. Gainesville: University of Florida Press.

Colección de documentos inéditos para la Historia de Espāna. 1842–1895. 113 vols. Madrid.

Crespo R., Alberto. 1972. El Corregimiento de La Paz: 1548–1600. La Paz: Urquizo.

Crespo R., Alberto, Rene Arze Aguirre, Florencia B. de Romero, Mary Money. 1975. La vida cotidiana en La Paz durante la Guerra de la Independencia 1800–1825. La Paz: Editorial Universitaria.

Dahlmann, Guiseppe. 1892. Lo studio delle Lingue e le missioni. Prato.

Dobyns, Henry F. and Paul L. Doughty. 1976. Peru: A Cultural History. New York: Oxford University Press.

Encinas, Diego de, ed. 1946. Cedulario Indiano. 4 vols. Madrid: Ediciones Cultura Hispanica.

Escobar, Alberto, ed. 1972. El Reto del Multilingüísmo en el Perú. Lima: Instituto de estudios peruanos.

Fishman, Joshua A. 1969. Language Problems and Types of Political and Sociocultural Integration: A Conceptual Postscript. *In* Language Problems of Developing Nations, Joshua A. Fishman, Charles A. Ferguson, and Jyotirindra Das Gupta, eds. New York: John Wiley.

Fishman, Joshua A., Robert L. Cooper, and Roxana Ma et al. 1971. Bilingualism in the Barrio. Bloomington: Indiana University Center for Language Sciences.

Garces G., Jorge A. 1935. Libro del ilustre cabildo, justicia e regimiento desta muy noble e muy leal ciudad de Sant Francisco del Quito. Quito.

Garces G., Jorge A., ed. 1946. Colección de cedulas reales dirigidas a la audiencia de Quito, 1601–1660. Quito.

Gibson, Charles. 1966. Spain in America. New York: Harper and Row.

Hardman, M.J. 1972. Postulados lingüísticos del idioma aymara. El Reto del multilingüísmo en el Perú. Alberto Escobar, ed. Lima: Instituto de Estadios Peruanos.

Hardman, M.J. 1978. Jaqi: The Linguistic Family. IJAL 44.2:146–153.

Hardman, M.J., ed. 1979. The Aymara Language in its Social and Cultural Context. University Social Science Monographs Series. Gainesville: University of Florida Press.

Hardman, M.J., Jana Vasquez, and Juan de Dios Yapita M. 1971. Aymara Grammatical Sketch. Gainesville: The Aymara Language Materials Project.

Haring, Clarence H. 1947. The Spanish Empire in America. New York: Oxford University Press.

Harth-Terre, Emilio. 1964. Cauces de Españolización en el sociedad indoperuana de Lima virreinal. Lima.

Heath, Shirley Brice. 1972. Telling Tongues: Language Policy in Mexico: Colony to Nation. New York: Teachers College Press.

Heath, Shirley Brice. 1976. Colonial Language Status Achievement: Mexico, Peru, and the United States. In Language in Sociology. Albert Verdoodt and Rolf Kjolseth, eds. Louvain: Editions Peeters.

Heath, Shirley Brice. 1979. Bilingual Education and a National Language Policy. In Georgetown University Round Table on Languages and Linguistics 1978. Washington, D.C.: Georgetown University Press.

Klein, Herbert S. 1969. Parties and Political Change in Bolivia: 1880–1952. London: Cambridge University Press.

Laprade, Richard A. 1979. Some Cases of Aymara Influence on La Paz Spanish. In The Aymara Language in its Social and Cultural Context. M.J. Hardman, ed. University Social Science Monographs Series. Gainesville: University of Florida Press.

Levillier, Roberto, ed. 1919. Organización de la Iglesia y Órdenas Religiosas en el Virreinato del Perú en el Siglo XVI. 2 vols. Madrid. Sucesores de Rivadeneyra.

Levillier, Roberto, ed. 1921. Gobernantes del Perú: Cartas y papeles, Siglo XVI. 3 vols. Madrid. Sucesores de Rivadeneyra.

Lorenzana, D. Francisco y Buitrón. 1770. Cartas pastorales, y edictos Mexico: Imprenta del Superior Gobierno del Br. D. Joseph Antonio de Hogal.

McGourn, Francis Thomas. 1971. A Study of the Pronunciation of Spanish Spoken by Three Aymara Indians of Ilave, Peru. Ph.D. dissertation. Stanford University.

Mangin, William P. 1965. The Role of Regional Associations in the Adaptation of Rural Migrants to Cities in Peru. In Contemporary Cultures and Societies of Latin America. Dwight W. Heath and Richard N. Adams, eds. New York: Random House.

Middendorf, Ernst W. 1910. Introducción a la gramática aymara. [tr. from the

German by Franz Tamayo]. Boletín de la oficina Nacional de Estadistica [La Paz] 5.517–60.

Middendorf, Ernst W. 1959. Ca. 1890. Las Lenguas aborígenes del Perú. Lima: Universidad Nacional Mayor de San Marcos.

Middendorf, Ernst W. 1974. Observaciones y estudios. Tomo III, La Sierra. Ernesto More, trans. Lima: Universidad Nacional Mayor de San Marcos.

Miracle, Andrew W. 1975. A Report on Rural Education for the Aymara of Bolivia: New Trends and Developments. Latinamericanist. 10.4:1–4.

Muro Obrejón, Antonio, ed. 1956. Cedulario Americano. Sevilla: Publicacionese de la Escuela de Estudios Hispano-Americanos de Sevilla.

Murra, John V., ed. 1967. Visita de la provincia de Leon de Huanuco en 1562; Iñigo Ortiz de Zúñiga, Visitador. Huanuco, Peru: Universidad Nacional Hermilio Valdizan.

Myers, Sarah K. 1967. The Distribution of Languages in Peru: A Critical Analysis of the Census of 1961. Ph.D. dissertation. University of Chicago.

Paulston, Rolland G. 1972. Society, Schools and Progress in Peru. Oxford, N.Y.: Pergamon Press.

Phelan, John Leddy. 1959. The Hispanization of the Philippines: Spanish Aims and Filipino Responses, 1565–1700. Madison: University of Wisconsin Press.

Primov, George. 1974. Aymara-Quechua Relations in Puno. International Journal of Comparative Sociology 15:167–181.

Recopilación de leyes de los reynos de las indias. 1943. 3 vols. Madrid: Consejo de la hispanidad.

Ricard, Robert. 1932. Les origines de l'Eglise sud-americaine. Revue d'histoire des missions.

Ricard, Robert. 1966. The Spiritual Conquest of Mexico. Lesley Byrd Simpson, trans. Berkeley: University of California Press.

Romero, Emilio. 1928. Monographía del departamento de Puno. Lima.

Santo Tomás, Fr. Domingo de. 1947. Ca. 1551. La Primera gramática quichua. Quito: Instituto Histórico Dominicano.

Sapiens, Alexander. 1979. Spanish in California: A Historical Perspective. Journal of Communication 29:72–83.

Schermerhorn, R.A. 1970. Comparative Ethnic Relations: A Framework for Theory and Research. New York: Random House.

Schroeder, J.J., ed. 1950. Canons and Decrees of the Council of Trent. St. Louis: B. Herder.

Solano, Francisco de. 1975. El interprete: uno de los eues de la aculturación. Estudios sobre Política Indigenista Española en America. Valladolid: Seminario de Historia de America.

Torero, Alfredo. 1972. Lingüística e historia de los Andes del Perú y Bolivia. El Reto del multilingüismo en el Perú. Alberto Escobar, ed. Lima: Instituto de Estudios Peruanos.

Valdera, Blas. 1945. Las costumbres antiquas del Perú. Sigo xvi. Lima.

Vargas, Jose Maria. 1947. Ca. 1551. Introduction. *In* La Primera gramática quichua. Fr. Domingo de Santo Tomás. Quito.

Vargas Ugarte, Rubén. 1953. Historia de la iglesia en el Perú 1511–1568. Lima.

Wachtel, Nathan. 1977. The Vision of the Vanquished. The Spanish Conquest of Peru through Indian Eyes 1530–1570. New York: Barnes and Noble.

Waterhouse, Viola. 1949. Learning a Second Language First. IJAL 15:106–09.
Wölck, Wolfgang. 1972. Las lenguas mayores del Perú y sus hablantes. *In* El Reto del multilingüísmo en el Perú. Albert Escobar, ed. Lima: Instituto de estudios peruanos.
Zavala, Silvio. 1946. Sobre la política lingüística del imperio español en America. Cuadernos Americanos 27:159–66.

Language Spread in a Multilingual Setting: The Spread of Hindi as a Case Study

Bal Govind Misra

The Indian subcontinent, like many other regions of the world, has witnessed movements of populations and indigenization of migrants. The linguistic prehistory of the subcontinent as unravelled by Emeneau (1954) and others gives broad but fairly reliable details of the movements and shifts of populations and of the spread and/or extinction of languages on the subcontinent in that distant past. Aryan migration (circa 2000 B.C.) to the subcontinent brought an Indo-European language, viz., old Indo-Aryan or early Vedic, which in due course spread over the entire northern part of the country. Speakers of the then-existing other languages of the subcontinent were either pushed towards the southern part of the subcontinent or to the peripheral mountainous regions in the north and northeast of the country. A large number of them gave up their languages (either willingly or otherwise) and accepted the language of the conquerors. This sequence of events, i.e., the entry of a new language and its spread and indigenization, may have occurred earlier in the case of Dravidians also, if Dravidian speakers also came to India from outside as is believed by a number of scholars on the basis of some circumstantial evidence.

The spread of the Indo-Aryan language, the language of a handful of conquerors in northern India, is a noteworthy phenomenon. The factors for its spread are not the same as those which have been suggested as contributing to the spread of Arabic, Greek and Latin in the Middle East, North Africa and Europe. Brosnahan (1963) has suggested four factors positively associated with the spread of Arabic, Greek, and Latin: military conquest, duration of military authority, linguistic diversity of the population through which the language spreads, and material advantages associated with the knowledge of the new language. The factors responsible for the spread of the Indo-Aryan in north India are not the same. Apart from its being the language of the rulers, Indo-Aryan spread because of the awareness and acceptance of the cultural and intellectual supremacy of the Aryans. The adoption of Indo-Aryan also enhanced the social status of the native populace by making them aligned, if not identified, with the higher social group of the society. All this, of course, yielded material gains apart from social, cultural and intellectual benefits. During a couple of centuries before Christ, and shortly after, many smaller groups of invaders came and settled in north India, foremost among them the Sakas, Kushans and Huns, from different parts of Asia. All of them accepted the local languages by giving up their own. The same was later true of Gurjars and Abhirs. The factors for this language replacement could not have been purely political as it was the conquerers who adopted the language of the vanquished. The factors must have been social, cultural, and intellectual. In many cases, these invading groups were predominantly male and their marrying native women and settling down may account for the eventual displacement of their languages. The small number of the invaders is also likely to have been responsible for the loss of their languages. The spread of Sanskrit and Pali in Ceylon, South East Asia and the Far East is also associated with religious and cultural factors and not with political and military reasons.

In medieval times the Muslim invasion and conquest of India resulted in the introduction of Persian into the country. Being the language of the rulers, it was accepted and used as the official language of administration and law courts. The higher echelons of the society, Muslims and Hindus alike, put a great premium on learning it as a second language and acquiring proficiency in it. Knowledge of Persian helped its learners to acquire social status, government positions, and material benefits, and to have themselves counted among the ruling bureaucracy. However, the language of culture, knowledge, and thought was still the Indian classical language, namely Sanskrit. Literature was written in Indian languages of the various regions. The languages of Hindu princely courts were also regional Indian languages. During this period a supraregional language developed and became accepted at the popular level for interlingual communication. The religious movements of this period (Sufism, devotional cults, etc.), which influenced almost the entire country and created a great mass consciousness at the religious and cultural levels, helped in the spread of the language to various parts of the country. A variety of Hindi extended its frontiers as the language of intercommunication at religious centers and places of pilgrimage in and outside the Hindi region. This accounted for the development of what some scholars have termed a "grassroots multilingualism" in Indian society (Pandit 1979). The awareness of and faith in the religious and cultural unity of the Indian society, in spite of its regional differences, contributed towards the spread of a Hindi variety of that time outside the Hindi region; and this language spread, in turn, became an instrument for furthering the awareness and convinction of unity. Thus while religious-cultural factors promoted the spread of a Hindi variety in non-Hindi regions on the one hand, military, administrative, and political factors spread Persian on the other. It may, however, be noted that, although both the languages spread as second languages, the spread of Persian was confined only to that section of the elite which was involved in the military and administrative life of the country, but Hindi spread more at the nonelite or mass level and as a kind of interlingual communication medium.

The advent of English in India marks the beginning of the modern age. The East India Company inherited the existence and use of a variety of languages for different communicative functions. The British decided to introduce the Western system of education in India, whose primary purpose, according to Macaulay who recommended it in 1835, was to prepare a class of people who, though Indian by birth, would be Western in their ideals, thoughts, preferences, likes and dislikes, and behavior and who would owe complete allegiance to the British Empire and would always further the interests of the Empire.

The British not only established and promoted English education, they also established an administrative and judicial system, which on the one hand promoted their colonial interests and on the other put a very high premium on the learning of English. With the increased mobility of a larger number of people, English became the sole medium of education, administration, trade, and commerce, in short of all formal domains of a society's functioning. Proficiency in English became the gateway to all social and material benefits. If one looked for a job in the government, in educational institutions, in trade, commerce, or industry, knowledge of English was found to be essential. English also became the hallmark of an educated, cultured, and modern man and hence a marker of social position and prestige. Thus, the assigning of all formal and even many semiformal communicative functions to English, together with the political patronage that the language enjoyed, contributed positively to its spread. English became the language of the elite class, language of privilege. With increased mobility of larger numbers of persons, and with the social and national consciousness created by exposure to Western thought and sociopolitical philosophy, English also fulfilled the function of interlingual communication for the educated elite from various parts of the country. It is really surprising that with all the powerful factors contributing to the spread of English in India, only a very small minority of the population gained access to and acquired proficiency in it.

The position of Hindi and other Indian languages at the turn of the present century was definitely unenviable. They were used in informal settings. They were not media of education at the high school level; they were taught as vernaculars, a subject of study at school. They did not find any place in higher education. All communicative functions in formal domains were performed by English and not by Indian languages. Indian languages were, however, the vehicles for literary expression. Thus, they did fulfill the affective function but not the instrumental one. They were used in personal interactions but not in transactional interactions. Because of limited interactional roles, these languages were neither developed (in the sense of being vehicles of knowledge) nor fully standardized. Many of them showed a high degree of linguistic diversity. Some speech communities like Tamil, Telugu, and Bengali, etc., were also characterized by a high degree of diglossia.

The educated elite was indifferent towards the status and role of these languages. They neither favored nor promoted them. Their attitude towards them was at best neutral, if not downright negative. However, even towards the latter part of the nineteenth century, there were some thoughtful, nationalistic-minded persons like Kesav Chandra Sen, who realized the importance of developing a national language as an interlingual communication medium for the entire country and who recognized also the potential of such a language as a binding force in the Freedom Movement. Even at this time Hindi (or Hindustani) was fairly widely understood and used in the north in general and in religious centers and other interactional locales in the south where common people from various parts of the country congregated. It was realized that while the English-educated elite had a pan-Indian communication medium in the form of English, the common people communicated in the form of Hindi/Hindustani (or a variety thereof).

During the latter decades of the nineteenth century, reform movements like Brahmo Samaj and Arya Samaj were started and became quite popular in north India. The ushering in of the twentieth century saw a wave of cultural revivalism on the one hand and the freedom movement on the other. Both these movements not only gave a positive fillip to the Indian languages in general, they also emphasized the need for developing a national language (*rāshtra-bhāshā*). B. G. Tilak, one of the first national leaders in the Indian National Congress, suggested that Hindi in Devanagari script be accepted as the national language. In a conference organized by the Nagari Pracharini Sabha in 1905, he forcefully argued for the acceptance of Hindi in Devanagari script as the most potent force for drawing a nation together (Gopal 1956: 240–42). Mahatma Gandhi brought a singular persistence and organizational involvement to the cause of the national promotion of Hindi. He pointed out five requirements for a language to be accepted as a national language: (1) it should be easy for Government officials to learn; (2) it should have the capability to function as a medium of religious, economic, and political interaction throughout the country; (3) it should be the speech of the majority of Indians; (4) it should be easy for the common people in the entire country to learn; (5) it should be chosen not on the basis of temporary or passing interests but on a longterm basis. Gandhi declared that English did not meet any of these requirements and asserted that Hindi fulfilled all the conditions (Gandhi 1956:3–4).

Gandhi not only supported the national language movement, he was also responsible for establishing the Rashtra Bhasha Prachar Samiti in Wardha for the promotion and propagation of Hindi. By this time a sizable number of voluntary organizations had already been established and were engaged in promotion and propagation work. The foremost among them were Nagari Pracharini Sabha, Varanasi; Hindi Sahitya Sammelan, Prayag; Dakshin Bharat Hindi Prachar Sabha, Madras; and the Rashtra Bhasha Prachar Samiti, Wardha. Some of these voluntary agencies had their branches or affiliates in various states in the country by this time. Thus the cause of the spread of the Hindi language was positively accelerated by the Freedom Movement.

After the Indian Independence in 1947, the constituent Assembly voted for accepting Hindi in Devanagari script as the language of the Centre, setting a time limit of fifteen years for completion of the switchover to Hindi.

Once Hindi was accepted as the official language for the Union Government, its promotion, development and spread became the constitutional responsibility of the central government. Thus three kinds of agencies have become actively engaged in the spread of Hindi— governmental agencies, semigovernmental agencies, and voluntary organizations. Individual efforts on the part of dedicated and enthusiastic nationalists still continue unabated.

As the selection of the variety of language to be developed and promoted was made, the codification and elaboration of its stylistic and registerial forms for newly created communicative functions became the main task of persons connected with the development and spread of the language, and of the language-policy-and-planning implementors within the government and outside. The constitution of the country clearly lays down the direction for the language's development and states guidelines for it.

The government undertook various programs for the implementation of the constitutional directives. The form of the standard variety was explicitly and clearly enunciated and its structural properties and details stated. Two organizations—Central Hindi Directorate and Council of Scientific and Technical Terminology—were set up. The Council (CSTT) undertook the task of preparing technical terms in various fields of knowledge—social sciences, physical and biological sciences, commerce, technology, medicine, and law and jurisprudence. On the basis of explicitly stated guidelines, committees of experts (subject-matter experts as well as language experts) engaged themselves in creating technical terms. The task, being gigantic, took a fairly long time to complete. By the latter part of the sixties, over 200,000 terms had been prepared, revised, and finalized. These glossaries are now being used in the production of scientific and technical literature in Hindi. To facilitate the conversion of the language of administration, the preparation of glossaries of administrative terms has also been undertaken. Six states and one union territory of the Hindi-speaking region were also involved in this task, and their participation has made available a wealth of competing terms and terminologies, thus affording the compilers the chance to select the most appropriate terms and gradually to discard others. This certainly created a state of confusion initially, but the situation has clarified and stabilized itself by now.

An organized program has been underway for more than twelve years now for the production of textbooks and reference materials that facilitate the use of Hindi as the medium of education at the college and university levels in different fields of study. Although translations have been done, the emphasis has all along been, and rightly so, on the production of original materials in Hindi. It must be admitted that the actual switchover of the medium of instruction has not been coordinated adequately with the production of this literature, and the priorities have also not been properly worked out. Consequently, the production of such literature has not kept pace with the need. As the work has been undertaken in haste, the quality of material has not been satisfactory. Registers of Hindi for specific fields of study have not yet been fully worked out, nor have they obtained the stability they should in terms of the form of language (the structures as well as items of use).

In the field of education, the conversion from English to Hindi as the medium of instruction at the college and university level has been gradual and cautious, so that standards of educational content and quality do not suffer. The universities and institutions of higher learning, being autonomous, have been conservative and have tended to cling to the status quo. However, Hindi now is being utilized as a medium of instruction in arts, social sciences, and to a certain extent in the physical and biological sciences. Medical and technical education still continues to be imparted through English. Many institutions now provide Hindi as well as English as optional media. This is true not only of Hindi areas, but also of some institutions in non-Hindi-speaking areas.

In school education, Hindi has been made a compulsory language under the three-language formula for the non-Hindi-speaking states. In such states Hindi is a compulsory subject for three or four years starting in the fifth grade. Provisions for its study in higher grades are also made in many states. It is possible to decline to adhere to central government policies and guidelines on the parts of the states in India. However, all the states except Tamilnadu follow and implement the three-language formula, which means that Hindi is spreading among all the school-going children and is learned by them as one of the non-native compulsory languages. Thus, the formal educational system is acting as an important agent in the spread of Hindi.

The spread of Hindi as the language of administration has been promoted by a series of governmental orders enjoining government employees to learn it, by the establishment of facilities for learning the language with a special emphasis on learning the administrative register of the language, and by a series of financial incentives and rewards. Although these measures have helped in the spread of the language for purposes of formal transactions, the results have not been satisfactory. Since acquiring proficiency in Hindi has been viewed as a voluntary, individual attainment, there has been a lack of organized effort among the hierarchies of administration. This has resulted in the creation of an atmosphere of indifference, and consequently, training has been wasted.

One of the powerful and effective agents of the spread of Hindi has been the mass media, the radio, television (wherever it is available), and the newspapers. Not only has the number of Hindi newspapers (dailies, weeklies), magazines, and journals increased, the readership has also increased. This is a function not only of increased literacy, but also of the spread of the language into areas and contexts in which it was not used earlier.

Some other steps for the spread of Hindi have also been taken by the government. Standardization of the script and of spelling and related steps have facilitated the development of technological aids like typewriters, teleprinters, printing materials, and other printing and reproducing devices which have directly and indirectly helped the spread. The role of Hindi cinema as one of the most powerful agents, if not the most powerful one, in the spread of Hindi in non-Hindi-speaking regions of the country is very well known and established.

The Hindi-speaking community is a very large one. About 30 percent of the population speaks Hindi natively, and another 5 percent are mother-tongue speakers of Urdu, which is closely related to Hindi and which, together with Hindi, was formerly referred to as "Hindustani." When we add the second-language users of Hindi, the language becomes a major force in the trade, commerce, banking, and industrial activities of the country. Knowledge of Hindi is now becoming either an essential or desirable requirement for getting jobs or promotions in many business houses, banks, advertising agencies, and the like. It may be noted here that figures recorded by the Census for the use of Hindi as a subsidiary language err very much toward underreporting. Sample studies have shown that the incidence of the knowledge and use of Hindi as a second language is much higher than reported.

Hindi has spread and continues to spread as a language of wider communication in India due to a multiplicity of factors. The forms of the language that have spread and are in the process of spreading, the functions for which they are spreading, and the degree to which the locale favors the spread—all are interrelated.

It is necessary to distinguish the spread of the standard form in the Hindi region itself from its spread in non-Hindi regions. In the region where it spreads as a superstructure, strict adherence is kept to learning the prescribed/accepted norm as far as its written form is concerned. The standard spoken form shows dialectal influences in pronunciation as well as grammar. Lack of concern as well as lack of adherence to the use of the *ne* construction (a highly marked feature of standard Hindi) in spoken standard in Eastern Uttar Pradesh and Bihar is well known. As a matter of fact, such deviations from the norms are considered to be a matter of the native user's freedom of use. These features further mark the regional affiliation of the users.

A second and important form of the language which is spreading is that which is being diffused by agencies of language spread in non-Hindi regions. The pleas for the simplification of some aspects of Hindi structures and grammatical characteristics on the part of Suniti Kumar Chatterjee and many so-called advocates of Hindi are well known. There is no great need to go into the details of this controversy. It is sufficient to state that in spite of such appeals, sometimes impassioned ones, there has been no deliberate and planned attempt on the part of Hindi or non-Hindi users to simplify the grammar of the language.

However, it is well known that standard Hindi as used, spoken as well as written, in various parts of non-Hindi regions, has developed and/or is developing distinct patterns of deviations. Studies made on Kannada-Hindi, Telugu-Hindi, Tamil-Hindi, and Malayalam-Hindi reveal these patterns (Misra 1975). A study of various other varieties will help us in determining the form of pan-Indian Hindi.

The third and the most important form of the language that has spread and is spreading further is the lingua franca form, which is highly contextualized, shows pidginized features, and has more or less exclusively a spoken form. It is learned informally in interpersonal interaction settings, serves the purpose of intercommunication between speakers and users of different languages in metropolitan centers outside the Hindi region, places of pilgrimage, religious centers, bazaars, and also in the industrial centers which draw pan-Indian populations. Quite often both the parties involved in such interactional settings are nonnative speakers of Hindi. In such locales, even in the Hindi regions, the pidginized varieties are in common vogue. It must be noted here that different varieties of pidgins have developed in different parts in the country. Studies of Bombay-Hindi, Calcutta Bazaru-Hindi, Nagpuri-Hindi, etc., have revealed differences in these varieties, as well as pan-Indian commonalities, with respect to the linguistic details of pidginization of marked linguistic features. Related to this development in the process of the spread of Hindi is also the development of specific regional lingua francas like Halbi, Sadri, etc., in specific regions, mainly regions where tribal dialects are in use as mother tongues. While the pidginized varieties show more fluidity and serve restricted communicative needs, the lingua francas have over a period of time become more stabilized and are by now showing features of creolization.

Hindi has spread and is further spreading for transactional interactions more than for personal interactions. It serves instrumental functions rather than integrative functions. The domains in which it is used are the more semiformal ones, and it is used more for between-group communication than for within-group communication functions. It has, up to this time, spread more for horizontal integration than for vertical. These functions predominantly require only speaking skills, but recently writing as well as translating skills are gaining more importance, as the formal channels of spread are being utilized more and more.

The spread of Hindi has been most rapid in urban and semiurban areas, religious, industrial, and mercantile centers up to this time. However, the exploitation of the formal educational channels is now helping the language's spread in the rural areas. Increased and more effective means of transport and communication are playing a positive role in the spread of the language by making a greater number of people mobile. Access and availability of inexpensive radios and transistors, increase in the number of movie houses, and the more frequent showing of Hindi films (due to their popularity) are also accelerating the spread of Hindi. Thus, educational facilities and mass media are now playing a positive role in the spread of Hindi in non-Hindi regions.

Formal as well as informal channels of spread are providing facilities for the creation of a greater number of adopters and conveyers of the spread of Hindi in India. Factors contributing towards its spread are social, economic, political, and cultural. In spite of a certain amount of opposition to Hindi as the language of the Union government on the part of persons and organizations in some parts of the country, the language has been gradually spreading due to the societal need for the development of a pan-Indian communication medium. Such a role, it has been realized, has not been fulfilled by English and cannot be fulfilled by any language other than Hindi, not because it is the mother tongue of one-third of the population, but because of the role it has played in the society up to this time and is fit to play in future. Nationalism, democratization, the spread of educational facilities, and economic, political, and social developments have all congregated in its favor.

REFERENCES

Brosnahan, L.F. (1963). "Some Historical Cases of Language Imposition." *In* J. Spencer (ed.) *Language in Africa*. Cambridge: Cambridge University Press. pp. 7–24.

Emeneau, Murray B. (1954). "Linguistic Prehistory of India." *In* Proceedings of the American Philosophical Society 9 S: 282–92.

Gandhi, M.K. (1956). *Thoughts on National Language*. Ahnedabab: Navajivau.

Gopal, Ram (1956). *Lokamanya Talak, A Biography*. Bombay: Asia Publishing House.

Misra, B.G. (ed.) (1975). *Studies in Bilingualism*. Mysore: Central Institute for Indian Languages.

Pandit, P.B. (1979). *India as a Sociolinguistic Area*. Poona.

Language Spread as a Wavelike Diffusion Process: Arabic in the Southern Sudan

Ushari Mahmud

> God has forbidden me to speak Arabic. I asked God, "Why don't I speak Arabic?" and He said, "If you speak Arabic, you will turn into a bad man." I said, "There is something good in Arabic!" And He said, "No, there is nothing good in it!"
>
> Chief Makuei Bilkuei (1973)*

INTRODUCTION

I use as an epigraph this reasoning by one of the Dinka chiefs in the Southern Sudan in order to highlight the bitterness that lingers there over the massive social and cultural changes and upheavals inflicted on the south by northern hegemony. Arabic was the result of such changes; for some people, like Chief Makuei, it is a reminder.

Historically, the Arabic language of the Southern Sudan emerged about the mid-nineteenth century and began a continual process of diffusion in the "settlements" established by the Khartoum ivory and slave traders throughout most of the present-day Southern Sudan. These settlements acted as satellites for the then flourishing long-distance trade; and they radically transformed several southern communities and engulfed them into a new socioeconomic system with new modes of production based mainly on slavery, forced labor, and long-distance trade. Southern men and women entered into new social relations and relations of production among themselves and with the newcomers

---

*Makuei Bilkuei is Chief of the Paan Aruw Dinka of Upper Nile Province. This part of his interview is quoted from Deng (1978).

from the north. In the process, a new language evolved in the form of several varieties of pidgin Arabic which emerged independently and simultaneously in the different settlements. As the new social and economic structural changes progressed over time, more and more southerners were brought under their influence. With the intermarriages across language and class barriers, the Arabic pidgins creolized within a short period of time. The new language started to spread as a lingua franca, as a variety for within-group communication, and as a creole native tongue. It acquired a life of its own and continued to evolve in a process of diffusion that was, at different points in its historical development, accelerated, slowed down, or momentarily reversed. But it maintained its directionality. Today, its use as a lingua franca is pervasive. And it is gradually making inroads into the home contexts for several groups, mainly in urban areas. An emergent culture that uses it as a creative medium of expression for folktales, songs, and jokes is quite prominent.

This study attempts to describe and analyze the changing language-behavior patterns of the families of some 2894 students enrolled in the different primary, junior secondary, and senior secondary schools in Juba—capital of the Southern Region of the Democratic Republic of Sudan. The study is based on questionnaires administered to the students in all the twenty-two schools of Juba—except one—and on intensive interviews with parents in two residential areas of the town: Malakiya and Hay Mayu. The students answered questions on their own language knowledge and use and on that of both their very young (five years and less) and their teenage brothers and sisters, their parents, and their grandparents. In addition, they provided demographic information on age, sex, place of birth, residential area, father's occupation, literacy of parents, tribe, and religion. The interviews with the parents involved mainly questions on the patterns of language acquisition of children, but also included questions on the linguistic repertoires of parents and grandparents and their functional allocation in different communicative contexts. The answers to the questionnaires filled in by the students were processed and tabulated using a computer program, SPSS (Statistical Package for the Social Sciences).

Access to education in Juba (and in the region as a whole) is characterized by obvious inequalities which derive mainly from social class. The children of top civil servants, salaried politicians, military and police officers, and professionals make up 26 percent of the total number of students under study, compared to 18 percent for workers and 16 percent for peasants. Given that all preuniversity levels of education—in fact all schools but one—are represented in our sample, we expect this distribution to approximate that of the total school population in Juba. However, these students exhibit a marked heterogeneity of demographic characteristics. They reported 70 different ethnic or tribal affiliations: almost every known southern tribe is represented. They come from *all* the residential areas of Juba, distinguished by some 40 different names. About 60 different occupations—ranging from unemployed to state minister—are represented. They are almost equally divided by sex (45 percent males to 55 percent females). Eighty-six percent of them are Christian, 14 percent are Moslem, and 1 percent represent other tribal religions.

Such a study is beset by problems on two accounts. First, there are the questions of how representative the sample is and to what degree the results may be generalized to the whole community. Second, the reliability of frequency returns is doubtful due to the "fluidity" of language claims, and the problems of over- and under-reporting (Khubchandani 1976).

However, the methods and strategies of analysis adopted in this study would tend to minimize both problems. What is of concern to us here are not the *actual frequencies* of knowledge or use of this or that language. Nor is any claim made to the automatic generalizability of the frequency results to the whole community of Juba. What we want to establish is the *variability* of language proficiency and use among a particular population sector of the community (i.e., students and their families). The existence of *variability* in the language behavior of this sector is indicative of a processual language change involving the diffusion of a "lingua franca" Arabic in all communicative contexts, including the home. The difference between the sector of students and their families *and* other sectors of the community would be one of *degree* of variability, and it would concern mainly at what stage these other sectors are in the evolutionary process of language diffusion and spread. Whether the students are over- or under-reporting becomes a relevant question only if we take their quantitatively specific reports as coinciding with actual behavior.

The contribution of the analytical frameworks and concepts of linguistic variation and change (linguistic variables, the continuum, the wave-theory) to describing and explaining variability in language behavior will be explored.

MOTHER-TONGUE DISTRIBUTION

The acquisition of a lingua franca as a mother tongue is only one step or one phase in the directional diffusionary process whereby that lan-

guage spreads. The acquisition takes place at different times for different sectors of a speech community. Before a lingua franca is acquired as
a mother tongue, it has to be introduced and spoken fairly frequently
by members of the same household—this being itself a relatively earlier stage in the process of the language spread.

Within the same household, different children with four or five years
age difference could have dissimilar linguistic repertoires and mother
tongues. A vernacular-Arabic bilingual couple may have their first two
children acquire the vernacular as a native language, with Arabic
learned fairly early as a second language. Their third child might have
Arabic as his first language and pick up the vernacular later. The fourth
child, on the other hand, might speak only Arabic with or without a
passive knowledge (high or minimal) of the vernacular. Such cases do
exist within some of the families interviewed in Juba. In some cases,
Arabic is introduced into the home and spoken by the children themselves, who have picked it up in the neighborhood. The parents, who
speak it but did not use it in the home, now do. In the words of one of
the interviewees, a forests inspector in Juba: "They are forcing us to
speak Arabic." In fact, the introduction of Arabic into the home domain
could be initiated at any one time by the children, their parents, or the
teenage brothers and sisters. From the time it is introduced into use
within the home, Arabic is spoken at different rates of frequency by the
different age groups. But more of this later when we discuss language
use.

The students were asked to report "the first language or dialect which
they spoke when they were very young." The 2894 students reported
50 different languages. Of these, 10 are foreign to the Southern Sudan,
being originally spoken in the Northern Sudan (Nubian, Nuba), in East
Africa (Swahili, Kongolese, Buganda, Bangala, and Tesu), in West Africa (Borgu), or in Europe (English, French). With the exception of
Swahili, which is reported by 12 students, none of the other languages
mentioned above numbers more than 5 students. Indeed, 5 of them are
claimed by 1 speaker each. This leaves us with 40 southern languages—including Arabic. Thirty-one of them are reported by less than
50 students each. This again leaves us with only 9 languages which
claim between 75 and 905 speakers each. This can be seen in Table 1.
However, in the following analysis of mother-tongue distribution, *all*
southern languages will be included together under the cover term of
"vernacular," and then opposed to "Arabic" as the language which is
making inroads and spreading by variable degrees of displacement of
the vernacular as the traditional mother tongue. This division will give
us the mother-tongue distribution, as seen in Table 2.

TABLE 1: Mother-Tongue Distribution of Sample

	Language	Number	Percentage
1.	Arabic	905	31
2.	Bari	589	20
3.	Dinka	262	9
4.	Moru	238	8
5.	Madi	137	5
6.	Kakwa	119	4
7.	Acholi	102	4
8.	Latuka	93	3
9.	Fajulu	75	3
	Other languages	374	13
	Total	2894	100

TABLE 2: Distribution of Southern Vernaculars and
Arabic as Mother Tongue

Mother tongue	Number	Percentage
Vernacular	1968	69
Arabic	905	31
	2873	100

The percentages in Table 2 should be treated with reservation. Some people who grow up speaking two or more languages in a multilingual speech community and in homes where both Arabic and the vernacular are frequently spoken might not be quite sure of the sequence in which they started speaking either the vernacular or Arabic. Sometimes both languages are picked up and spoken simultaneously. But the question was posed to the students in such a way that they had to give one language as the one learned *first*. However, another related question was incorporated in the questionnaire, and the students were requested to specify the age at which they started speaking Arabic. And while, surprisingly, almost the same number (910) claimed that they spoke Arabic within the first year after they were born as claimed Arabic as mother tongue (905), we find that these numbers do *not* refer to the *very same students.* That is, 84 percent (762) of the students who earlier reported Arabic as their mother tongue corroborated their answers by reporting a very early age (one, two, three years old) at which they started to speak Arabic. Twelve percent (109) reported four, five, and six years as the ages at which they started speaking Arabic. Three percent (27) of the students claiming Arabic as their mother tongue gave much later ages for their picking up the language—seven to thirteen years. Conversely, 27 percent (534) of the 1968 students reporting the vernacular as the mother tongue gave very early ages (one, two, three) at which they started speaking Arabic.

These apparent discrepancies point to the fluidity of such categories as mother tongue and first language in a multilingual speech community; and they indicate that in many cases two languages are spoken simultaneously as "mother tongue," thus rendering inoperative the criterion that sequence of acquisition indicates which is the mother tongue or first language. Indeed the continual change in the linguistic repertoire of a single child within a very short period of time casts doubt on the sequence criterion. For some children might start speaking the vernacular as a mother tongue and, within a very short span of time, come to lose it and to acquire Arabic as their dominant and most frequently spoken language. Such cases have considerable implications for attempts to define the terms "mother tongue," "pidgin," and "creole," and to language in education issues generally. The fluidity of the respondents' answers to questions about the mother tongue or first language is also indicative of the constantly changing linguistic situation within the home domain.

DEMOGRAPHIC CONSTRAINTS ON MOTHER-TONGUE CHANGE

The replacement of the vernacular by the spreading language is a time-governed gradual process which is susceptible to acceleration, stagnation, or reversal according to the internal constraints at play in a particular situation.

Younger students reported more Arabic than did older ones as can be seen in Table 3. Thus while only 25 percent of students of ages between 17 and 19 years reported Arabic as their mother tongue, 45 percent of the youngest group (i.e., 10–13) reported the same. What Table 3 indicates is a language change in progress, shown in apparent time.

While the trend for progressively more Arabic reported by increasingly younger students is quite clear in the above cross-tabulation of mother tongue by age for the whole sample, some indications to the contrary appear as we control for more influencing variables and look closely at the behavior of more specifically defined populations: children of peasants as compared to children of wage laborers or government salariats and those who were born in Juba compared to those born in semiurban small towns or in rural areas. In addition, these same groups are divided into children whose parents are from the same or

TABLE 3: Mother-Tongue Percentages by Age

	20+ Years	17–19 Years	14–16 Years	10–13 Years
Arabic	10	25	31	45
Vernacular	90	75	69	55
	100	100	100	100
	(52)	(800)	(1441)	(582)

different ethnolinguistic backgrounds. When examining such specifically defined subgroups, we find that the overall frequencies for the whole sample mask some differences of degree or rate of change toward Arabic, as well as a lack of an expected unilinear progression of Arabic according to age. Both these phenomena need explanation beyond what is offered by the demographic parameters of place of birth, father's job, and parental tribal background—all of which separately or jointly have an influence on mother-tongue distribution.

In some cases, the age group of 14–16 years shows more Arabic as a mother tongue than a younger subgroup—all other factors (available for quantification) being equal. On the other hand, different subgroups, while all separately adhering to the pattern of more Arabic in progressively younger ages, show different *rates* of change toward Arabic as a mother tongue. Both phenomena could be explained in various ways. First, more Arabic in some older age groups would be the result of some confounding variable that happens to be working on a particular group; e.g., early immigration and longer stay of family in Juba compared to possible late immigration of the younger group's parents into Juba. Such information is not available in the returned questionnaires. Or the phenomena could be due to the historical circumstances of the constant displacement of populations during the war which forced some families into the rural areas (vernacular-dominated) and others into urban centers (Arabic-dominated). On the other hand, there is the possibility that these differences are indicative of a reversal in the trend toward more Arabic or a slowing down in its rate of diffusion. At this point in the analysis, the question remains without satisfactory resolution.

Now we shall turn to considering the effect of demographic factors such as place of birth, father's job, and parental tribal background on the acquisition of either Arabic or the vernacular as a mother tongue. Table 4 gives us the distribution of mother tongues (Arabic, vernacular) by place of birth (Juba, semiurban towns, rural villages) while controlling for parental tribal background (parents of different tribes, parents of same tribe) and father's job (clerical and high government salariats,

TABLE 4: Mother-Tongue Percentages by Place of Birth, Parents' Tribes, and Father's Job

Language	Parents from same tribe			Parents from different tribes		
	Juba	Semiurban	Rural	Juba	Semiurban	Rural
High, Mid- and Low Salariats						
Arabic	41	19	14	66	46	54
Vernacular	59	81	86	34	54	46
Total	100	100	100	100	100	100
	(328)	(399)	(1,092)	(108)	(105)	(40)
Workers						
Arabic	48	15	2	56	42	60
Vernacular	52	85	98	44	58	40
Total	100	100	100	100	100	100
	(152)	(119)	(56)	(41)	(34)	(8)
Peasants						
Arabic	18	2	1	77	47	0
Vernacular	82	98	99	23	53	100
Total	100	100	100	100	100	100
	(50)	(138)	(164)	(9)	(15)	(15)

workers, peasants). The assumptions behind the choice of these variables and behind the way they are divided are the following: students born in Juba are expected to report more Arabic as mother tongue than those born in semiurban or rural areas respectively; students born to parents from different tribes would also report more Arabic as mother tongue than those born to parents of the same tribes; students whose parents are clerical or senior government salariats and workers are expected to show more Arabic than students whose parents are peasants.

THE VERNACULAR AS SECOND LANGUAGE

At one stage in the diffusionary process of Arabic spread, the vernacular is learned as a second language after Arabic has been acquired as first language. The data at hand do not tell us how fluently the students who report the vernacular as their second language can use that language. But they all report that they *speak* it.

Of the 905 students who reported Arabic as their mother tongue, 65 percent (592) reported the ability to speak the vernacular as a second language. The other 35 percent (313) don't speak any vernacular. Some of them, however, reported English as their second language (i.e., 69 students who have learned it in school).

So the data show that adoption of Arabic as the mother tongue does not automatically entail the abandonment of the vernacular. The process is rather a gradual one whereby the vernacular is acquired after Arabic because it is still used by other members of the household or in the neighborhood.

The acquisition of the vernacular as a second language could be viewed as an integral part of the language-spread process or as a continual attempt at maintenance. The language-spread mechanism should not be viewed with reference to the spreading language only. Nor should it be looked at totally as a displacement mechanism. Indeed one can view the vernacular in the context of language spread as having a life of its own, related to but still independent from the spreading language. For by being acquired as a second language, it is also *spreading,* except that, contrary to Arabic in this case, its future and directionality of spread are difficult to predict. After it is acquired, it could either gather momentum in a language-maintenance effort; or its spread might slacken, and it might fall into disuse.

How we view the mechanics of the language-change situation determines the model or framework of language spread that we want to build. Diffusion-of-innovation models tend to focus on the innovation only by virtue of the fact that, in most cases, the innovation is not displacing any material item. It is a mere addition of something new. The spreading language, on the other hand, makes advancement by virtue of its existence in a contradictory relationship with the traditionally used language.

VARIABILITY IN LANGUAGE USE

While language knowledge or proficiency could tell us a great deal about a linguistic situation and the qualitative changes which are taking place in it—namely, addition to the linguistic repertoires of new languages and the disappearance of others—language use, on the other hand, provides information on the quantitative distribution or allocation of the different languages in everyday usage, a distribution which precedes the qualitative changes.

The data at hand display extreme variability in the use of Arabic and the vernacular languages by different groups within the home and outside of it. People who speak both their tribal vernacular and Arabic (i.e., are bilingual) are reported to use the two languages at different frequencies in different contexts. The students were asked to report on their language use with their families at home, with friends in the neighborhood, other students in school, children and old people in the street. They also reported the language behavior of their very young (five years or less) as well as teenage brothers and sisters, their parents, and grandparents—all in the home domain. The following major language-use patterns emerge from the answers given:

I. The vernacular only.
II. The vernacular as the most frequently used language, with Arabic used sometimes.
III. Arabic as the most frequently used language, with the vernacular used sometimes.
IV. Arabic only.

English can sometimes be added to any of the above language-use patterns. But very few students report it in the home domain—which will be our main area of analysis here.

A household whose members are proficient in both Arabic and the vernacular and who are differentiated by age (children, teenagers and students, parents, and grandparents) could display one, more, or all of the above language use patterns.

What is of interest to us here is that different households use these language-usage patterns at different frequencies according to whatever social, economic, cultural, etc., factors prevail which influence language behavior. But more of the conditioning factors later. First, I would like to establish that the language-use situation is characterized by considerable variability at both the inter- and intra-personal, household, or group levels. I shall also entertain and discuss the hypothesis that this variability in language use indicates change in progress, and indeed shows that a language spreads by a progressive quantitative increase in its use in different communicative functions. The diffusion of Arabic as an integral part of the language-change process can be described by using the concepts, tools, and models which were devised to handle linguistic variation and change: namely the "continuum" (DeCamp 1971, Bickerton 1973, 1975), the "wave theory" (Bailey 1974), and the "linguistic variable" (Labov 1966). The different language-use patterns referred to above could be seen as different variants, hierarchically arranged, of a language-spread construct or variable. These different variants are propagated through a language-use continuum in a manner similar to that predicted by the wave theory for the diffusion of linguistic innovations (Bailey 1974). The application of these analytical methods and concepts will be elaborated in the following sections.

VARIABLE LANGUAGE USE IN THE HOME

Language use has often been described in terms of categorical allocation of discrete functions to individual languages. We hear often of "the
language of the home" as opposed to "the language of the street" or of
"work," the underlying assumption being that the first is always the indigenous vernacular, while the latter two are the ones newly introduced. In discussing this problem, Fishman (1976) considers such concepts as "language of religion" a "misnomer or an oversimplification."
He argues that "the societal macro-allocation of functions to codes is
particularly likely to be dimensionally and functionally complex and
overlapping," and that, as suggested by Weinrich, we should view it as a
gradient phenomenon.

Table 5 shows the frequency distribution of language use patterns as
reported for four age groups—children, teenagers, parents, and grandparents. Table 5 clearly shows that within each age group, language use
is variable. The only difference is in the relative frequencies of the
language-use patterns within and between the four age groups. The exclusive use of the vernacular is highest among grandparents (70 percent
of their reported language use); and it decreases progressively as we
move to the younger age groups (only 15 percent of the children's reported use). Conversely, the use of Arabic as either the most frequently
spoken language (pattern III) or the one exclusively spoken (pattern
IV) is reported much more frequently for children and teenagers (52
percent and 44 percent respectively) than for parents or grandparents
(24 percent and 13 percent respectively).

The quantitative increase in the usage frequency of Arabic, coupled
with a simultaneous decrease in the frequencies of vernacular usage, is
an indication of the trend whereby Arabic is making inroads and spreading across age groups. The variable frequencies of the four language-use
patterns recapitulate language spread in progress over time. For these
four usage patterns represent different stages hierarchically arranged in
a diachronic process of language change. The "vernacular" (I) is the
earliest historical stage before Arabic started its diffusion in the mid-
nineteenth century. "Arabic" (IV) represents the "later stage" in the
direction of which the change process is evolving. Between these two
stages we have a "transitional" period in which both vernacular and
Arabic are used. Different people would be at different stages in their
language behavior during this period. Their positions in one stage or
the other are constrained by demographic factors which are themselves
to be explained by chains of social, economic, cultural, and ideological
practices in the social structure of which they form a part.

TABLE 5: Language Use in the Home by Age Groups

Pattern	Percentage			
	Children	Teenagers	Parents	Grandparents
I. Vernacular only	15	19	41	70
II. Vernacular and Arabic	33	37	35	16
III. Arabic and vernacular	31	23	11	3
IV. Arabic only	21	21	13	10
Total	100	100	100	100
	(2751)	(2721)	(2752)	(1974)

What is presented above as a model for understanding a linguistic situation undergoing change is the same as that presented by Derek Bickerton in describing the creole continuum (1971, 1975). But since we are dealing with whole linguistic codes as units of analysis in the change process, we probably cannot push very far the analogy with the structural linguistic data used in the continuum studies. In his 1971 study of the Guyanese Creole continuum, Bickerton looks at the variable distribution of the complementizers FU and TO in the creole. Some speakers use only FU, others use only TO, and a third group alternates between the two. Bickerton sees this synchronic variation as indicating linguistic evolution in progress and reflecting diachronic changes. The frequency of occurrence of TO increases and becomes categorical to the replacement of the historically old FU as the creole becomes more similar to standard English. In his 1975 study of the Guyanese Tense Aspectual System, Bickerton uses the same strategy and divides the Guyanese speech community into three ranges. The "basilect" is the oldest and most extreme creole; the "accrolect" is the closest to standard English and is historically the latest stage; the "mesolect" represents all intermediate varieties and is historically transitional. Thus we can use the same method and adapt it to the description of language spread as a phenomenon of change.

THE VARIABLE PROCESS OF
WAVELIKE DIFFUSION

We have so far presented the synchronic variation of different linguistic patterns across the different age groups. Now we shall combine each set of age groups (i.e., children, teenagers *and* students, parents, grandparents) into a unit to represent a "household." For each household, the distribution of each language-use pattern will be determined as a score from zero to five. For a particular language-use pattern, zero means none of the five age groups uses that pattern; the score of five means *all* five age groups use it. Thus, taking each language-use pattern separately, we shall compute the number of households reported to use that particular language-use pattern at the index scores of zero, one, two, three, four, and five. Table 6 illustrates this distribution for language use within the home context.

Table 6 can be read from top to bottom taking each language-use pattern at a time since percentages are computed for each pattern separately. If we consider the "vernacular" (I) as an exclusively used pattern, we find that 23 percent of the 1764 households do not report it at all by itself. This 23 percent would, naturally, have their use distributed across the other language-use patterns. As we move down the column we find that the exclusive use of the vernacular has a score of 1 for 33 percent (577) of all households. What this means is that *one* of the five age groups in every one of those 577 households uses the vernacular exclusively. This single age group would most likely be either the grandparents or the children. For although Arabic would be used to some extent by some members of a household, it happens sometimes that its within-household diffusion has not yet reached the other members. Going further down the column of vernacular exclusive usage, we see that only 5 percent (85 households) has this pattern for *all age groups* within the household. We know that at least the students in these households are bilingual with some proficiency in Arabic; but they just do not use it within the home domain. What this indicates is that the *categorical* and *exclusive* dominance of the vernacular in the homes of this sector of the population under study is quite minimal; and the overwhelming majority (95 percent) is at some stage—early or late—in the language shift process.

Conversely, the table shows us that while Arabic is used to *some* degree by *some* age groups within different households, it is still far from having reached an advanced stage of categorical and exclusive use by *all* the age groups in the different households. Only 7 percent (121) of all households are reported to have Arabic as the language used exclusively in the home by *all* age groups. The majority of the households are at different points in the transitional stages of bilingual usage at home. This is where the language spread process approximates the "continuum" concept. The exclusive use of the vernacular and that of Arabic by *all* age groups represents the two extremes of the language-spread continuum. Bilingual usage, in all its quantitatively specifiable frequencies, falls in between the two extremes.

TABLE 6: The Diffusion of Language-Use Patterns
within Households

	I Vernacular	II Vernacular and Arabic	III Arabic and Vernacular	IV Arabic
Score		Percentage		
0	23	31	49	63
1	33	23	24	17
2	22	19	14	7
3	12	15	9	4
4	6	9	3	3
5	5	3	1	7
Total	100 (1764)	100 (1764)	100 (1764)	100 (1764)

And if the four different language-use patterns represent hierarchically arranged stages in the language-shift process, we will see that these different stages are articulated in a dynamic and processual relationship of constant change within each one of the families using more than one language-use pattern. More specifically, a family might have the exclusive use of the vernacular as the standard language behavior of grandparents, the exclusive use of Arabic being that of the children, and the transitional patterns of bilingual use would be the behavior of the age groups in between—i.e., the teenagers and parents. A family that is less advanced in the change process might have the vernacular spoken exclusively by *both* grandparents and parents; then the teenagers and children would speak Arabic in addition to the vernacular (transitional stage). No member in this family has yet arrived at the categorical use of Arabic within the home. On the other hand, a family in which only the grandparents report the *occasional* use of the vernacular, while everybody else uses Arabic only, is a family well advanced in the process of language spread. It has been reported and observed that two different people can communicate through the simultaneous use of two different languages.

Thus the language-spread process should be seen and analyzed at two levels: first, at the level of the individual family in which the spreading language advances on the age and time dimensions both conceived of together in a dialectical relationship. For while the older generations might have adopted the use of the spreading language earlier in *real* time, the younger generations are using it *more* frequently than the older. So even within the family level, different generations are at different stages in the language-shift process. The second level is one in which different families—as units of language spread—are at different stages in the overall process of language spread.

Thus while the processual pattern remains constant in its hierarchical stages (different language-use patterns), it will be more or less advanced in the quantitative distribution of the articulated language-use patterns according to demographic and socioeconomic structural constraints. Those families that are well advanced in the process in the direction of more Arabic would tend to be statistically more related to town than to country life, will have more mixed marriages, etc.

As a descriptive and analytical method for language diffusion, the above framework is no more than the "wave theory" proposed by C.-J. Bailey (1974) to handle the dynamics of linguistic variation in space and time. In a nutshell, the basic arguments of Bailey's wave theory are the following:

1. Linguistic change results from the introduction of some new innovation at a low relative frequency in some point in time and space. The innovation spreads to a larger social space at the same low relative frequencies, but in the process it increases its frequency of occurrence progressively in the locations it has occupied longest. The frequencies of the innovation would form an implicational scale on the temporal and spatial dimensions.

2. Synchronic variation is the result of differences in the rate of linguistic change—differences resulting from the demographic and linguistic constraints on change.

3. Time is a fundamental dimension of the dynamic framework proposed.

Now I will show more specifically how language-spread data could be seen as compatible with the mechanics of the wave model as devised by C.-J. Bailey to handle linguistic data. This is only one initial step—an exploratory one—in an attempt currently underway to see how the wave model can predict variable language data at the individual language level rather than at the level of structural linguistic items.

In the case of our language spread data, the innovation which is undergoing diffusion would be the "use of Arabic." But since the "use of Arabic" should be viewed as part of a gradient construct including the "vernacular," we shall segment it into our four categories of language-use patterns previously explained (patterns I, II, III, and IV). If we exclude the first pattern of the exclusive vernacular usage, since it does not involve any innovation, we shall have three *variants* of the "diffusion variable" that are differentiated by their increasing generality: (a) low frequency use of Arabic; (b) high frequency use of Arabic (relative to vernacular use); and (c) categorical use of Arabic to the exclusion of the vernacular. As such, our three variants of the "use of Arabic" correspond to the successively more general features or rules of the wave theory and which work as follows:*

1. Given a relative time *o* at some focal point in social or geographical space, a feature *a* may enter variably at time (i) and spread to a larger social space. (This corresponds to the most restricted use of Arabic as used together with the vernacular—pattern II. It could be introduced by one of the family age groups—e.g., teenagers—and used at a lower frequency second to the vernacular; then it becomes potentially amenable to diffusion at low frequencies among the other age groups with the family.)

2. At time (ii), a more general version *b* of rule (or feature) *a* will enter variably at the same focal point and spread, but not as far as *a*. (This would correspond to the next language-use pattern of Arabic as used together with the vernacular at a quantitatively higher frequency—pattern III. It is also started by the same teenager of rule *a* who, at this more advanced time of his life, has progressively increased his frequency of Arabic use at home until it became his most frequently used language. His language-use pattern is also theoretically and potentially subject to spread to other family members of different ages. It is possible that within a particular real family, the teenager's language-use pattern might never spread to the other age groups, due to particular constraints inhibiting the spread.)

3. At time (iii), a new, even more general form of the rule will enter at the focal point, and so forth. (This stage corresponds to the categorical use of Arabic by the same hypothetical teenager who does not use the vernacular any more and uses only Arabic. His pattern of language use could, theoretically, spread to the other age members of the family.)

The wave can be shown schematically as follows:

Time o: o   Time i: (a) o   Time ii: ((b) a) o   Time iii: (((c) b) a) o

---

*This summary of how the innovations radiate in space and time is taken from Traugott's review (1976) of Bailey (1974).

The wave model is naturally an abstract framework, and we have grafted to it an abstract teenager who, within the span of teenage years, acts as the point of origin for the "spatial diffusion of ratios"* of Arabic usage. The time parameter of the wave theory is independent of the concept of real time; it is considered in a relative sense, hence the concept "relative time." The wave model conceives of diffusion patterns as forming implicational arrays hinged on the dimensions of time and space. We shall see in the next section how language spread increases quantitatively along demographic variables as instances of dimensions of time and space.

EXPLANATION OF LANGUAGE SPREAD

Explanation of language variation and change has relied heavily on the search for correlations between ready-made demographic categories (status, sex, ethnicity, etc.) and language behavior. And while generally committed to correlations, variationists are divided on the issue of where one begins: with *language* or *geography and society*. Within sociolinguistics, the issue was raised by DeCamp (1971) when he objected to the "pigeonhole technique" of "correlating linguistic data to preconceived categories of age, income, education, etc., instead of correlating these nonlinguistic variables to the linguistic data." DeCamp views the conventional method as one that does not provide for continuous variation in the socioeconomic characteristics. Peter Trudgill (1974) rejects DeCamp's objections and argues that dialectologists should begin to consider the possibility of correlating their data, as geographers have done, with "preconceived geographical units"; and he goes on to demonstrate the superiority of such a strategy and its results in description as well as explanation of linguistic change and diffusion. C.-J. Bailey criticizes such an approach in the analysis of variation as practiced by Labov, Cedergren, and Sankoff as suffering from a homogeneity myth: it assumes that the members of a particular group are homogenous. The attack on correlative analyses and explanation also comes from an embryonic Marxist sociolinguistics. Dittmar (1975) argues that "correlations yield only restricted insight into the mechanism of sociolinguistic differentiation"; and that demographic categories of social class (defined by occupation, education, and income), ethnic group membership, etc., are too crude a basis for the analysis of group

---

*This term "spatial diffusion of ratios" is quoted from Trudgill who ascribes it to the diffusion studies of Hägerstrand. It is not clear from Trudgill's article whether it could have the same sense used here. But we are also dealing in the case of language spread here with the *diffusion of ratios* in space and time.

behavior. Explanations should be sought by a more scrutinizing analysis of the social structure as a whole and of the practical social actions influenced by this structure. We shall see the relevance of the above critiques as we discuss the demographic factors which seem to constrain and exert limitations on language behavior in the home situations.

ETHNIC GROUP MEMBERSHIP

About sixty different ethnic groups are represented by the homes reported on. Only six southern tribes are represented by more than a hundred students each. In Table 7 we give the distribution of the southern tribes with those represented by fewer than a hundred students all included in one category "Other southern tribes." It should be noted here that the numerical distribution of the students does not exactly reflect the actual distribution of the ethnic groups in Juba. The Bari and Bari-speaking groups might be more numerous in Juba than the table suggests; on the other hand, the Dinka are not as numerous as the 10 percent in the table suggests.

Ethnic-group membership as a category can be found to correlate with language behavior only insofar as different tribal groups have historically experienced different rates of evolutionary change or are significantly larger in size than others in a contact situation. And while we do find differences in language behavior across some tribal groups even when we control for such confounding demographic influences as occupation, sex, and level of education, these differences cannot be related to any *inherently* different characteristics that distinguish any one tribe from the other. To explain such differences, we will have to extend the analysis beyond the quantifiable demographic factors. It becomes imperative then to look deeper into the historically specific socioeconomic conditions that these different tribes were subject to at different points in their evolution.

Table 8 shows the language behavior of chidren in four different tribes: The Acholi and Madi, Dinka, Bari, and Moro. The table shows that the Acholi-Madi group and the Dinka show more dominance by the vernacular than do either the Bari or the Moro, which latter two are differentiated by the fact that the Moro show more Arabic dominance than do the Bari. Historically, the Bari and Moro were subject to more sustained contact with Arabic-speaking influence during the mid- and late nineteenth century than were either the Dinka or the Acholi-Madi group. The Khartoum merchants "settlements" had a greater influence on the sedentary and agriculturalist

TABLE 7: Ethnic (Tribe) Group Distribution

Tribe	Percentage	Number
Bari	21	611
Bari-speaking*	20	566
Moro	12	343
Dinka	10	293
Madi-Acholi	10	285
Latuka	4	101
Other southern tribes	17	480
Northern	6	162
Total	100	2841

TABLE 8: Children's Patterns of Language Use in the Home by Tribe

Tribe	Percentage				
	Vernacular	Vernacular and Arabic	Arabic and Vernacular	Arabic	Total
Acholi-Madi	32	40	19	9	100 (259)
Dinka	21	55	14	5	100 (278)
Bari	15	34	38	13	100 (577)
Moro	8	37	41	14	100 (327)

economies of the Bari and Moro than on the seminomadic Dinka, whose military and numerical strength enabled them to resist and challenge northern hegemony by sheer force or by migrating to inaccessible geographic areas. Moreover, most of the administrations which ruled the southern Sudan (whether colonial or indigenous) had their capitals in the middle of Bari land with the Moro at close proximity to the west.

When deeper levels of causation are analyzed to explain differential language behavior across tribal lines, the demographic category of tribe would have no analytical value for explaining language diffusion.

INTERTRIBAL MARRIAGE

Intertribal marriages are very common in the urban centers of Southern Sudan. Twenty percent (566) of the students reported that their parents were from different tribes. This does not include intertribal marriages among the six so-called Bari-speaking tribes. The languages

---

*This group speaks languages that are said to be mutually intelligible and similar to Bari. They include the Fajulu (167), Kakwa (191), Kuku (70), Nyambara (111), Mundari (27).

of these tribes are reported to be similar and showing only minimal linguistic differences. And since we are dealing with the *linguistic* effect of intertribal marriage, insofar as it brings about constraints on the children's language behavior (due to the parents' different languages), we have decided not to consider marriages among the Bari, Fajulu, Kuku, Kakwa, Nyambara, and Mundari as mixed.

Cross-marriages between the other southern tribes which speak significantly different languages show a marked difference in the linguistic behavior of children and teenagers. Table 9 shows the language behavior of children cross-tabulated with the tribal affiliation of the parents. It can be seen that children whose parents come from different ethnolinguistic backgrounds use far more Arabic at home than children whose parents come from the same background.

Parents who come from different ethnolinguistic backgrounds are reported to communicate with each other in Arabic, in their respective vernaculars, or in a combination thereof, the two parties speaking different languages simultaneously. And while the vernacular is still dominant among them, their use of Arabic is significantly higher than that of parents coming from similar ethnolinguistic backgrounds. Parents' language use at home is shown in Table 10.

While intertribal marriage as a demographic category can effectively help in predicting language behavior, it can explain language spread only superficially. In our attempt to understand how and why languages spread we should look into the hidden links and chains of causation of which intertribal marriage itself is only a result.

OCCUPATION

The students reported more than fifty different occupations for their fathers. We have grouped these into seven different categories based on a vague assessment of income and position in the work process:

1. *The Merchants:* While the number of southern shopkeepers is making a slow increase, the merchants in Juba are predominantly Arabic-speaking Moslems from the northern part of the Sudan. They are small in number, but they still exercise an almost total control of the commercial sector in all urban and semiurban (e.g., Yei) centers of the southern region. Many of them have stayed in the south for decades, and a number are married to southern women. The dominant relation between this group and the overwhelming majority of southerners has historically been commercial and mostly exploitative.

TABLE 9: Patterns of Children's Language Use at Home by Similarity of Parents' Ethnolinguistic Background

Parents' tribes	Vernacular	*Percentage*		Arabic	Total
		Vernacular and Arabic	Arabic and Vernacular		
Same	18	36	31	15	100 (2137)
Different	7	21	32	40	100 (532)

TABLE 10: Language Use among Parents by Similarity of Ethnolinguistic Background, in Percent

Parents' tribes	Vernacular	Vernacular and Arabic	Arabic and Vernacular	Arabic	Total
Same	44	37	9	10	100 (2131)
Different	30	28	18	24	100 (541)

2. *The High Salariats:* This includes the state ministers, higher civil servants, salaried politicians, professionals, and military and police officers. With the exception of two or three doctors, they are all southerners, mostly Christian, and frequently use English in their work. And while they form a relatively very small—but conspicuous—minority of the Juba population, their children rank highest numerically in school enrollment: 24 percent compared to 16 percent for peasants and 18 percent for workers.

3. *Middle and Low Salariats:* These are the teachers, nurses, and those holding clerical jobs. Their children make up 17 percent of the students under study.

4. *Policemen and Soldiers:* While all policemen are southerners, the army is integrated. But fewer soldiers from the north have their children in Juba schools.

5. *Workers:* These include those who work for the government or for private business, as well as self-employed craftsmen: drivers, guards, construction workers, carpenters, etc.

6. *Peasants:* Some own land; others work for wages on government or private lands.

7. *Unemployed:* Those without jobs, or reported by students as "poor."

The following table gives the distribution of language use by the children in the home domain cross-tabulated by father's occupation. We notice here that the only significant differences associated with father's occupation are: first, the difference which sets off "peasants" as the

TABLE 11: Children's Patterns of Language Use at Home by Father's Occupation, in Percent

Pattern	Mer-chants	High salariat	Mid-Low salariat	Police-men, soldiers	Workers	Peasants	Unem-ployed
I. Vernacular	7	10	10	11	10	35	16
II. Vernacular and Arabic	17	33	34	31	30	44	30
III. Arabic and vernacular	24	36	38	32	34	13	38
IV. Arabic	52	20	18	26	25	8	15
	100	100	100	100	100	100	100
	(152)	(638)	(421)	(205)	(443)	(395)	(221)

group with more dominance by the vernacular than any other occupational group; and second, the category of "merchants," which shows more Arabic than any other group. All the other groups (high salariat, mid-low salariat, policemen and soldiers, workers, and unemployed) show minimal differences in terms of vernacular or Arabic dominance (i.e., when we combine patterns I and II to represent vernacular dominance and then patterns III and IV to represent Arabic dominance). However, it is of interest to note that there are some fine differences in the rate of change from one pattern to another in the last two diachronically sequenced stages (Arabic dominance of III and IV). Here we notice that with the policemen and workers the quantitative evolution to more Arabic usage is accelerated and results in a slightly higher frequency of categorical language use than the high-, mid- and low-salariats and the unemployed. This "crossover" seems to be similar to that reported by Labov of the hypercorrect speech behavior of the lower middle class in his New York study (1966). But this is only tentatively so, since we are dealing here with "reported" and not "observed" data.

PLACE OF BIRTH

It is probably very rare today to find any rural locale in the Southern Sudan where Arabic is not spoken to some degree by at least one or two persons. The use of the language in urban and semiurban areas is very common. But in the rural areas, the vernaculars are dominant, and Arabic is known and spoken by fewer people mostly in out-of-the-home situations. So we cannot claim a dichotomy between town and country in relation to the diffusion of Arabic. The spread is gradual; it reaches the rural areas relatively late, and its rate is much slower here than in the town which is more dynamic and has concentrated networks of exchange transactions in the market, work and neighborhood situations—all of which necessitate the use of a lingua franca. The rural-urban dichotomy, which finds its expression in the Dualistic Model which claims a disjunction between "natural" (read rural) and "exchange" (read urban) economies as two economic orders that cannot mix, has been rejected as based on faulty assumptions and divorced from actual realities. The rural, urban, social, and economic differences in the Southern Sudan are constantly undergoing change (not all necessarily positive) due to the increasing speculations of city merchants, the establishment of extensive coffee plantations, and also the mushrooming agricultural and livestock government projects which are causing radical changes in the villages' economies and demographic compositions. These changes are bringing the village into a closer and dependent relationship to the town. This turn of events will certainly have an effect on the linguistic map of the rural areas.

And while less Arabic is reported by students born in rural areas compared to that reported by students born in Juba and semiurban centers, it is evident that the diffusionary process is underway. Table 12 shows the distribution of language use by students with their families cross-tabulated with place of birth. We notice that the majority of the students in Juba schools (67 percent) were born outside the city. And if we allow for a small number which live in "boarding houses," we get an idea of the increasing number of families leaving their villages and hometowns to come to work in Juba. These families spoke Arabic either before or after their migration into the city; and so they are at an earlier stage in the wavelike diffusion process.

CONCLUSION

Language spread as an evolutionary process can be described and analyzed by applying the concepts and analytical frameworks of linguistic variation and change—namely the wave model, as developed by C.-J. Bailey. But the success of such applications depends greatly on the kind and scope of data used to understand language spread. Data on language knowledge or proficiency alone (i.e., linguistic repertoires) are not enough. To say that all the students in the Juba schools are bilingual in Arabic and the vernacular does not say a great deal about the *process*

TABLE 12: Students' Language Use with Family by
Place of Birth, in Percent

Pattern	North	Juba	Other smaller towns	Rural
Vernacular	8	14	23	34
Vernacular and Arabic	13	24	37	40
Arabic and vernacular	22	34	24	16
Arabic	57	28	16	10
	100	100	100	100
	(191)	(938)	(1045)	(674)

of language spread. To describe this process in its dynamism we must have data on the distribution of the different codes of the linguistic repertoires across *all* communicative functions. And here, too, we should ascertain in quantitative terms the relative dominance of one language over the other within a specific communicative function or domain. For it seems that language diffuses through the different functions in a gradual time-governed process in a manner similar to the process of "lexical diffusion," whereby a linguistic change propagates itself gradually across the lexicon, from morpheme to morpheme (Chen and Wang 1975). Likewise, a language code as an innovation propagates itself across the various communicative functions, its use increasing progressively within each function *at different rates.* The question of rate of diffusion highlights the importance of collecting data that can be quantified at considerably more detailed levels than have hitherto been used in language censuses and surveys. For we can only infer rates of diffusion over time by comparing diffusion ratios in different contexts at the same time.

In the design and administrations of our questionnaires and interviews, we have attempted to approximate toward such a goal in data collection. We asked the students to hierarchize the names of languages used in a particular context according to frequency of use, for there is a difference between two bilingual use patterns of which one has Arabic as the most frequently used language, and the other has the vernacular as the most frequently used one. Even this is too crude a method to tap dominance relationships. We should be able to know by *how much of a margin* a language dominates over another for a particular person in a particular context. A bilingual use pattern in which the vernacular is used 90 percent of the time with Arabic used 10 percent of the time only is evidently an earlier stage in the Arabic-diffusion process than another stage where the ratio is 60 percent to 40 percent, for example. Such data are crucial if we are interested in more than showing that diffusion exists. Such data also become necessary if we attempt the application of the wave model or the other mathematical models of innovation diffusion used in geography and sociology (Hägerstrand 1965; Trudgill 1974).

Other than the question of "quantification of language use," there seems to be also the problem of quantifying or accurately assessing the *degree of proficiency* in the spreading language—a problem not encountered in material-innovation diffusion or diffusion of phonological, lexical, or syntactic items. The spreading language as "unit of diffusion" is itself a gradient unit (i.e., pidgin, creole, decreolized variety, dialect, standard); and proficiency in it varies from one innovator to another. However, this is a problem only in an apparent sense. First, the linguistically differentiated varieties of the spreading language are evidently taken care of by their being governed by the socioeconomic and demographic characteristics of the speakers. The variable levels of proficiency, on the other hand, are a function of the language's pervasiveness of use. And so while these aspects can be pursued in their own right, they do not constitute real problems for the description and analysis of language spread as a diffusionary process susceptible to quantitative measurement.

REFERENCES

Bailey, C.-J. N. (1974) *Variation and Linguistic Theory.* Washington: Center for Applied Linguistics.
Bickerton, D. (1971) Inherent Variability and Variable Rules. *Foundations of Language* 7: 457–92.
——— (1973) The Nature of a Creole Continuum. *Language* 49: 640–69.
——— (1975) *Dynamics of a Creole System.* Cambridge: Cambridge University Press.
Chen, M. Y. and W. S-Y. Wang (1975) Sound Change: Actuation and Implementation. *Language* 51: 255–81.
DeCamp, D. (1971) Toward a Generative Analysis of a Post-Creole Speech Community. In Hymes, D. (ed.), *The Pidginization and Creolization of Languages.* Cambridge: Cambridge University Press.
Deng, Francis M. (1978) *Africans of Two Worlds: The Dinka in Afro-Arab Sudan.* New Haven and London: Yale University Press.
Dittmar, N. (1975) Sociolinguistics: a Neutral or a Politically Engaged Discipline? *Foundations of Language* 13: 251–65.
Fishman, Joshua A. (1976) Yiddish and Loshn Koydesh in Traditional

Ashkenaz: The Problem of Societal Allocation of Macro Functions. In Verdoodt, A. and Kjolseth, R. (eds.), *Language in Sociology*. Louvain: Editions Peeters.

Hägerstrand, T. (1965) Quantitative Techniques for Analysis of the Spread of Information and Technology. In Anderson, C. A. and Bowman, M. J. (eds.), *Education and Economic Development*. Chicago: Aldine.

Khubchandani, L.M. (1976) Language Factor in Census. In Verdoodt, A. and Kjolseth, R. (eds.), *Language in Sociology*. Louvain: Editions Peeters.

Labov, W. (1966) *The Social Stratification of English in New York City*. Washington: Center for Applied Linguistics.

Traugott, E. C. (1976) Review of C.-J. N. Bailey, *Variation and Linguistic Theory*. *Language* 52: 502–506.

Trudgill, P. (1974) Linguistic Change and Diffusion: Description and Explanation in Sociolinguistic Dialect Geography. *Language in Society* 2: 215–46.

The Spread of Mandingo: Military, Commercial, and Colonial Influence on a Linguistic Datum

Louis-Jean Calvet

The linguistic group which we will treat here, *Mandingo*, covers an area in West Africa that includes Senegal, Gambia, Mali, Upper Volta, Ivory Coast, Guinea, Sierra Leone, and Ghana. It is composed of three main dialects, *Malinke, Bambara*, and *Dyula*, with mutual comprehension existing between them in every case, in spite of (mainly phonological) differences.

Mandingo is the first language of several million people but, and it is the main topic of this paper, Mandingo is also the second language, "langue véhiculaire,"* of several million other people. In fact, it is difficult to appreciate exactly the number of Mandingo-speaking people. In 1912, Maurice Delafosse gave for the colonial territory called "Haut Sénégal Niger" the following figures: 538,450 Bambara, 145,733 Malinke (Mandingo), 218,820 Dyula. And, in 1929, he stated there were 2,800,000 people "whose Mandingo is mother tongue" and 2,000,000 more "who speak and understand this dialect as well as their own language" (Delafosse 1929:19). Bernard Dumont noted about Mali, without giving figures:

> Mande, including its dialectal variants Bambara, Malinke and Diula, . . . [is] spoken throughout Southern Mali by half the country's population and used by many Senufo and Bobo, even beyond the national boundaries. (Dumont 1973:19)

Pierre Alexandre counted 6,000,000 Mandingo speakers, and Bokar N'Diaye (1970) announced for Mali: 66,700 Dyula, 300,000 Malinke and 1,665,000 Bambara.

---

*The French expression "langue véhiculaire" has been retained instead of English *lingua franca*, which is too vague in the author's opinion.

It is not easy to draw a clear conclusion from all of these figures but, once again, what is important here is that Mandingo is spoken by people for whom it is not the mother tongue: in this part of Africa, one's first reflex when one doesn't know the other's language is to try Mandingo.

"Langue véhiculaire", then, Mandingo sets the sociolinguist a lot of problems: How does a language attain such a function? And what type of domination of one community by another does this function imply?

SOME HISTORICAL STEPPING STONES

As far as Arabic chronicles allow us to go back—to the eleventh century—we find traces of two antagonist empires of which we have every reason to think that one spoke Soninke (Ghana empire) and the other Mandingo (Mali empire). It was Abu Ubaid El Bekri (1028–1094) who first mentioned the Mali empire, under a Fulani form (*Melel*): "Behind this country there is another called Melel, and its king carries the title of El Moslemani" (El Bekri 1911–13:333).

But, apart from this indication, we know nothing more about the Mali of this period. All during the nine centuries that separate us from this chronicle, the Mali empire remained concentrated around its initial area, Upper Niger, between the present Mali and the present Guinea. And, from this base, it extended or diminished according to military successes and failures. Thus, in the thirteenth century, Sundiata Keita greatly enlarged his holdings, defeating particularly the Ghana empire, and in the fourteenth century—the Mali empire's peak—it expanded northeast as far as Timbuctu and Gao, covering regions where Fulani and Songhai are spoken (Map I).

The empire began to decline at the beginning of the fifteenth century, particularly in the east and the north. In the first years of the sixteenth century, the Songhai or Gao empire, which, led by Askia Mohammed, had become a considerable power, had cut down the Mali empire on the east side (up to Segu?). And the Fulani kingdom of Macina (fifteenth and sixteenth centuries) also limited the Mali empire's development toward the east. It is likely that the fifteenth and sixteenth centuries saw Mandingo's spread both west and south. But two Mandingo kingdoms, Segu (1660–1861) and Kaarta (1670–1854), opened again the way to the east and the north.

Then, more recently, Samory Roure created at the end of the nineteenth century in the north of the Ivory Coast a kind of Dyula bastion of resistance against French colonization. All of the region that concerns us then, was the site of a succession of empires ousting one another, reciprocally limiting each other's zones of influence. These moving boundaries were, of course, political and administrative, but they had also a linguistic aspect: all we know about conquests in world history shows us that conquerors always administer in their own language. So Mandingo presence should have left linguistic traces, and we can read today's linguistic situation in the light of this past. For instance, Maurice Houis notes that:

> . . . today's importance of certain Mandingo dialects (Bambara, Dyula, Malinke) can be explained by Mali's historical importance; today's fragmentation of Malinke dialects must be put in correlation with the destruction of Mali (end of the fifteenth century) by the State of Gao and with the following dispersion of Malinke people. As for today's spread of Bambara and Dyula, it becomes clear if we attribute it to the State of Segu (1660–1861) and to the development of the commercial network towards the coast (contacts with the Portuguese factory of El Mina since the fifteenth century), the main agents of which were Dyula. (Houis 1970: 109–110)

But this commercial and military presence was not the only one. It seems in fact that the Bambara were famous warriors and that they readily became mercenaries. Thus, *Tarikh es Soudan*, a chronicle written in Arabic in the seventeenth century, described them very often as pagans in revolt:

> Prince of Macina, who had with him a large number of pagans from Bambara . . . The Châ'a-makaï, leading a troop of pagans from Bambara . . . The Fondoko Hammedi-Amina had appointed to his troops a large number of pagans of Bambara . . . Fetishists of Bambara revolted against Sanakoï and Karkokoï, etc. (1964:272, 276, 280, 411, 480)

Another chronicle, *Tarikh el Fettach*, always described the Mandingo as pagans (and employed in that case the word Bambara), and also used the words "Mallinke" and "Wangara":

> If you wish to know the difference between Mallinke and Wangara, one must know that Wangara and Mallinke are of the same origin, but that we employ Mallinke in order to specify warriors, whereas Wangara is used to specify traders peddling from country to country. (1964:65)

In fact, as far as we can go back, two peoples appear as commercial links between Blacks and Arabs: the Soninke (Sarakole) and the Dyula (Wangara). From south to north, Dyula carried gold and, from north to south, they brought salt back from Taghaza, on the northern edge of the

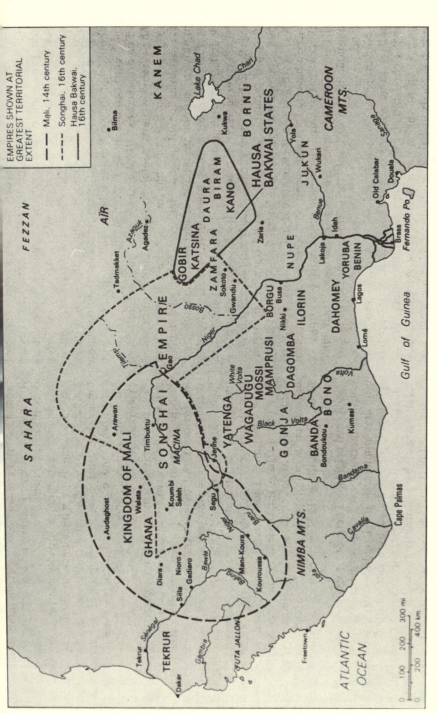

MAP 1. Principal Kingdoms and Peoples of West Africa, 11th to 16th Century. *Source*: J. Fage, *An Atlas of African History* (New York: Africana Publishing Co., 1978).

Sahara (Map 2). So the Mali empire was crossed by a gold-salt axis. Later, in the eighteenth century, when Fulani hegemony spread Muslim religion again, the same Dyula traders became the vectors of diffusion of this religion towards the south. So war, religion, and trade are the three bases of Mandingo presence throughout the centuries in this part of Africa. War, as we have noticed, led toward an imperial policy (or was led by it), a policy which certainly manifested itself in the imposition of a language, the language of the ruler, on some castes: the urban population keeping up political, commercial, and domestic relations with the invader. The imposition of the ruler's language on a subject nation sometimes leads to the disappearance of the dominated language when colonization is achieved, when it has "succeeded" and has destroyed beneath it the other's civilization. In the case of Mandingo, the empires were too unstable to lead to such an end, but commercial presence, increasing and extending military and political presence, secured a linguistic presence in the form of a "langue véhiculaire." Maurice Delafosse noted in 1929:

> Wherever the authority of a Malinke emperor or Bambara king was felt sufficiently and for long enough, wherever Dyula's commercial and religious activity was established too, the Mandingo language took root and, without having made local dialects disappear, it took their place in political and commercial domains. (Delafosse 1929:17–18)

As early as 1830, we find a confirmation of this "véhiculaire" function of Mandingo in *Journal d'un voyage à Tombouctou et à Jenné dans l'Afrique centrale*, by René Caillé. It is well known that Caillé, pretending to be an Egyptian, wanted to reach Timbuctu, a forbidden town in those times, and he had for this purpose learned Arabic. But, throughout the journey from the coast to Timbuctu, he encountered linguistic problems which he solved, if we can trust his book, with the help of two languages: Mandingo and Kisouri (i.e., Songhai). Thus, he writes: "I did not speak Mandingo well enough to carry out the sale myself." And: "A man from Kankan, knowing a little bit of Arabic, was my interpreter; I had asked him because I did not know Mandingo well enough to make myself understood" (Caillé 1830:387–404).

Later, he notes sentences in Mandingo, sentences which, though badly segmented, are perfectly understandable today. And he published, in an annex to the three volumes of his book, two lexicons, one "francais-mandingue" and the other "francais-kissour." So we have to conclude that, after he left Segu, a Bambara town, and while he was going through regions where they spoke various languages, Caillé used mainly two of them, Mandingo and Songhai, which had a "véhiculaire"

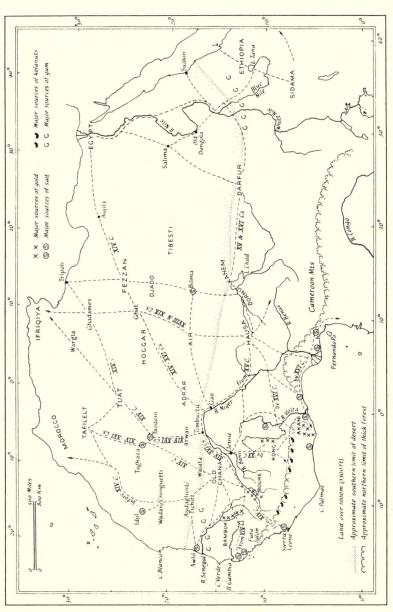

MAP 2. Trade Routes of Northern Africa, 10th to 18th Century. *Source*: J. Fage, *An Atlas of African History* (New York: Africana Publishing Co., 1978).

function: linguistic result of the history of the Mandingo peoples which we have roughly sketched above.

THE COLONIAL PERIOD AND INDEPENDENCE

These few historical facts show us that Mandingo experienced an important spread *before* the colonial period, that is to say that Mandingo-speaking people experienced a political and territorial spread, and that non-Mandingo-speaking people have thus been led to speak it. But this spread was affected by colonization in two, somewhat contradictory ways, which aided in determining the present status of the language: First, like all the other languages colonized by the French empire, Mandingo was denied, refused and faced with French in hierarchical relations. But, at the same time, on a subordinate level, its "véhiculaire" status was recognized by the colonial administration, and this recognition acted as a reinforcement.

I have brought up these problems elsewhere (Calvet 1974) and I do not intend to linger on them now. But we have to remember that the linguistic side of colonial politics has always consisted, in the French possessions of Africa, in imposing French as the only language for school and administration. Local languages, baptized "dialects" for the occasion, were nowhere taken into account, and some people consecrated themselves to demonstrating the inferiority of these tongues. Besides, if we exclude the disordered and scattered efforts of missionaries (who often taught religion in local languages), those languages were not even written: nobody was concerned with giving them an adequate alphabet. From that point of view, then, the colonial language worked as a dominating language, although it was largely in the minority if we consider the number of its speakers; and, to come back to our topic, Mandingo was on the side of the dominated languages, although it was largely in the majority.

Colonial commissioners, in the meantime, who use interpreters in their relations with the population, realized very quickly that Mandingo was, in that part of Africa, the most useful language. And a clear enough tendency appeared to make it the intermediate language between French and local languages, that is to say to reinforce its "véhiculaire" status. We have to recognize here the presence of an important element of diffusion: the colonial army. As Delafosse noted it:

> The kernel of our black troops before the 1914–1918 war was in a large majority composed by Malinke and Bambara . . . , the Mandingo language had become in some way the official language for our native military for-

mations in western Africa, the one in which orders were transmitted by native non-commissioned officers . . . , that established situation remained when one called up levies from every country, and if we think about the importance in a new large country of the factor of diffusion of a language supported by the army, we will realize that a new force of diffusion results, although indirectly, from European intervention in western Africa. (Delafosse 1929:18–19)

What does matter here is that Mandingo, mainly in the form of Bambara (because it was the form used in Bamako, colonial administrative capital), has been favored as well as disserved by colonization. The paradox, as we have seen, is apparent. Quite the opposite of Swahili for instance, Mandingo has not been transcribed, and there did not exist, at the time of independence, newspapers or literature written in Bambara or in Malinke. But, at the same time, it has been promoted to a quasiofficial status. That is to say, the language has been inserted into a bidimensional structure that opposed it simultaneously to French, the dominating language, and to the other dominated languages.

Independence introduced to this situation a supplementary factor— the divergent linguistic planning of the new states—but that bidimensional structure survived. Senegal and the Ivory Coast for instance chose to keep French as the national language, to impose it in school and administration; Guinea on the contrary favored African languages for the national languages of that young republic. Mali, for its part, organized a policy of promoting literacy in national languages and, at the same time, kept French to the official role it has in Senegal. We will develop more lengthily this last case because it is exemplary.

In 1966, following the UNESCO Congress held in Tehran (1965), Mali adopted a policy of *functional literacy*: imparting literacy to the people in their mother tongue and, parallel to this, giving them technical training in that language within the framework of a national development campaign. For that purpose, four languages were selected: Bambara, Fulani, Tamashek (Tuareg) and Songhai. Twelve years after the beginning of that policy, the balance speaks for itself: nothing has been done for Songhai and Tamashek, nearly nothing for Fulani, and only in Bambara has there been a system of large-scale literacy training. Thus, for Bambara, pedagogical material now exists for training in four different areas (rice, cotton, peanuts, and women's education). A Bambara lexicon and a grammar of Bambara sentences have been produced, and a monthly newspaper is edited, but nothing similar exists for the three other languages. We therefore risk seeing the development of a new form of cultural colonialism which would lead to the disappearance of "little languages" and would institute in Mali situations similar to those we know in France, in places like Brittany, Occitania or Alsace, in Spain, in places like Catalonia and Euskadi (Pays Basque), etc.

The status of Mandingo evolves, thus, in diversified ways in the different countries. In the Ivory Coast, as in Upper Volta, the language is always "véhiculaire"; in Mali it is potentially a national language. But it remains in confrontation with French, and this coexistence sets a sociological problem which obstructs every kind of evolution today. The Malian middle class, mainly civil servants, has obtained a kind of social promotion thanks to French, language of the school, language for studies, language of administration. On the other hand, some people have learned how to read and write their mother tongue. They do not understand why they have to use the services of interpreters or public writers in their relations with the administration when they already know how to read and write. They do not understand either why their children still study French and *in* French in school. There is, therefore, a potential demand for an official recognition of the local languages, to which the administration opposes a kind of passive resistance: to preserve the status quo for French is to preserve the acquired benefits for a minority.

Ten centuries of history have thus led to the establishment of a widespread language, the status of which is very ambiguous. A "véhiculaire" language in western Africa, Mandingo is in Mali a dominating *and* a dominated language. It is a potential national language in the meantime, but it is also a potential colonial language, since its future would consist in taking the French position. And, if this hypothesis should prove itself to be sound, the "véhiculaire" status of the language would be transformed: Mandingo would not only be, in the Ivory Coast for instance, a useful means of communication in the markets, but it would also be the national language of Mali and, for that reason, it would risk being perceived as an imperial language.

SOME THEORETICAL QUESTIONS

The case of Mandingo we have presented here is interesting only if it can allow us to set more general questions on the conditions of language spread. We will therefore set some such questions, taking as a starting point Robert Cooper's paper (this volume). The problem could be approached for instance from his idea of there being three converging points of view: form, function, and pervasiveness of spread considered as behavior. We will take those three points of view in that order.

Form

In our introduction, we have defined Mandingo as composed of three main dialects, Bambara, Malinke, and Dyula. Things are, in fact, more complex or simpler, depending on our point of view. Maurice Delafosse (1929) offered seven dialectal variants: Bambara, Dyula, Malinke in general, East Malinke, North Malinke (or Khasonke), West Malinke, South Malinke. Those variants are incontestable and could even be added to. But, at the same time, there exists a kind of common Mandingo, medium of the spread, which is baptized *Kanjè*. *Kanjè* is understood by all the speakers of the above dialects, for it constitutes something like the neutralization of the differences, and it is the form which is understood and spoken by the speakers who do not have Mandingo as their mother tongue. What we have to remember here, besides the fact underlined by Cooper that "language change, found in all language varieties, is probably accelerated by the process of spread," is that Mandingo-speaking populations demonstrate that they are conscious of the "véhiculaire" nature of the language by the name they give it. (In the same way, they make a distinction, in Central Africa, between *Sango*, mother tongue for a part of the population, and *Sango Véhiculaire*, national language). And the form of the name itself is interesting: *Kanjè* is composed of *kan*, "language," and *jè*, "white, light," and is often translated (and then analyzed) as "white language," i.e., "easy language." This analysis is plausible for it corresponds to the structure of the language, which forms some words with a noun and an adjective:

muru + *ba* = large knife
kulu + *ba* = large hill
kan + *jè* = white (easy) language

But perhaps there is also a joke in this name. *Jè* meaning white has a high tone, but there exists a verb *jè*, with the low tone, meaning "to bring together." And there is in Bambara a tradition of riddles playing with homophonies, distinctive features and sometimes tonal oppositions. So it is possible to imagine that *kanjè*, which effectively denotes "easy language," could at the same time connote, by a play on the tone, "the language which brings together." And that fact would simply mean that the spread of Mandingo goes back far enough to be impressed in the population's consciousness and to be reflected in that name.

Function

Why this spread of Mandingo? We have seen that at least three functions were present in the historical period considered: the linguistic spread is evidence of a military expansion since the time of the Mali empire; it is evidence of a commercial expansion (by the intermediary of Dyula traders in the markets of Kankan, Korhogo, Bobo Dioulasso, Abidjan, and so on, and along the gold-salt route); and it is evidence of a religious expansion (since Dyula traders were Islamized).

But there is a recent factor which seems important from a general point of view: the link between a "véhiculaire" language and national unification. The French language for instance has been *in France* a "véhiculaire" language for a long time, and the linguistic diversity could have led to a kind of federalism. The political choices made at the end of the eighteenth century imposed another evolution, but the appearance of French as a national language is isomorphic to other phenomena: centralization ("jacobinism"), denial of the right to cultural differences, etc., phenomena that France has imposed in its colonies, precisely.

This means that the *"véhiculaire" function* can assume a *unifying function* (in France, Mali, Maghreb, etc.). But three conditions must be fulfilled for a "véhiculaire" language to become a national language: a part of the population must be in power, and that power's politics must be centralizing. And this leads us to the third point of discussion, concerning pervasiveness.

Pervasiveness

The point here seems to me fundamental: the history of a language is first of all the history of populations who speak the language, and the problem of linguistic spread cannot be tackled only in terms of internal linguistics. A language which spreads is a population which spreads (not necessarily native speakers, though native speakers in our example) and most often subdues other people to its law. Which law? Its linguistic law, of course, but also its law in the general meaning.

The problem of pervasiveness is therefore a problem of power relationships and, correlatively, a problem of resistance. When a language disappears to be replaced by another language (Gaulish by Latin, in France), a population is definitely colonized; but when one language resists another (Saxon resisting French in medieval England), a population resists an invasion. That notion of resistance is important because it allows us to understand more easily the phenomenon of linguistic spread. The amount of time involved, for instance, largely depends on the type of spread, on the *function*: a "véhiculaire" language does not spread at the same speed if it corresponds, also, to an imperial function. Besides, resistance can be of another kind: the imperial spread of a language can run into the spread of another language (phenomena

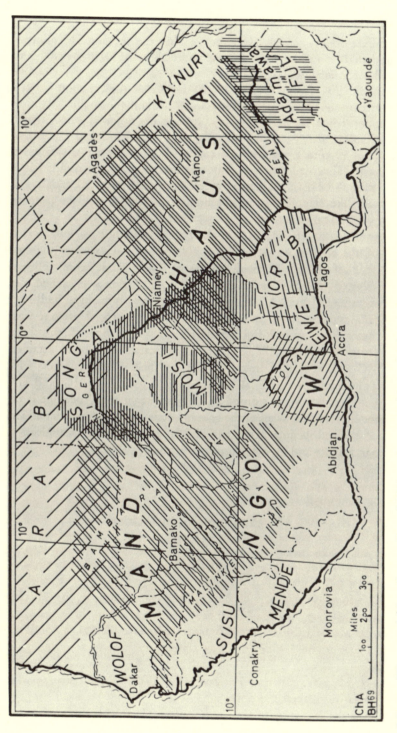

MAP 3. Western Africa. *Source:* Bernd Heine, *Status and Use of African Lingua Francas* (Munich: Weltforum Verlag, 1970).

noted by Cooper, quoting Greenberg). Thus the spread of Mandingo is limited in the north by the spread of Arabic and in the east by the spread of Songhai and Hausa (Map 3).

But, and this will be my last point, there is at the junction between power relations and linguistic relations a phenomenon which seems to me underestimated in Cooper's text: the phenomenon of *linguistic ideology* and of the *linguistic policy* translating this ideology. The case of Mandingo is here exemplary. We know nothing about the linguistic ideology of the Mali empire's conquerors but, in recent history, Mandingo met the French linguistic ideology. And the different future of languages like Bambara and Swahili can be explained by the different linguistic policies of colonial powers like France and Great Britain. Those two languages have had, sometimes for different reasons, a comparable spread. But Swahili is today the national language in Tanzania and could be tomorrow the national language in Kenya; meanwhile Mandingo is far from being able to accede to such a status, although it has the potential for such accession, in Mali, for instance. Swahili was taught in schools during the colonial period, Bambara was not; newspapers and books existed in Swahili, neither existed in Bambara. And that historical parenthesis, colonization, has thus been able to mark in an important way the future of a language. That tends to prove that the problem of linguistic spread is, of course, not only a sociolinguistic problem, but also a political problem.

REFERENCES

Alexandre, Pierre. *Langues et Language en Afrique Noire*. Paris: Payot, 1967.

El Bekri, Abdallah ibn Abdalaziz Abu Ubaid. *Description de l'Afrique Septentrionale*. French translation. Paris: Librairie d'Amérique et d'Orient, 1911–1913.

Caillé, René. *Journal d'un Voyage à Tombouctou et à Jenné dans l'Afrique Centrale*. Volume 1. 1830.

Calvet, Louis-Jean. *Linguistique et Colonialisme*. Paris: Payot, 1974. Second edition, 1979.

Delafosse, Maurice. *Haut-Senegal Niger*. Volume 1. Paris: Maisonneuve et Larose, 1912.

Delafosse, Maurice. *La Langue Mandingue et Ses Dialectes*. Paris: Librairie Orientaliste Paul Geuthner, 1929.

Dumont, Bernard. *Functional Literacy in Mali: Training for Development*. Paris: UNESCO, 1973.

Houis, Maurice. *Anthropologie Linguistique de l'Afrique Noire*. Paris: Presses Universitaires de France, 1971.

N'Diaye, Bokar. *Groupes Ethniques au Mali*. Bamako: Editions Populaires, 1970.

Tarikh el Fettach. French translation. Paris: Librairie d'Amérique et d'Orient, 1964.

Tarikh es-Soudan. French translation. Paris: Librairie d'Amérique et d'Orient, 1964.

Language Spread and Recession in Malaysia and the Malay Archipelago

Asmah Haji Omar

1. SPREAD OF MALAY IN THE ARCHIPELAGO

What is generally referred to as the Malay archipelago is an area that covers Malaysia (inclusive of Peninsular Malaysia), Indonesia, the Philippines, Singapore, and Brunei. This area encompasses a total of 700 to 800 islands plus a peninsula and is populated by some 172,146,635 speakers: 122,864,000 in Indonesia; 10,433,635 in Malaysia; and 38,849,000 in the Philippines.[1] The languages spoken in these countries are of many types: indigenous, immigrant, languages of wider communication, and creoles. Of the indigenous languages, there are some 200 to 400 in Indonesia,[2] about 100 in the Philippines, and about 30 in Malaysia.[3]

On the basis of number of speakers, the predominant language is Javanese with more than 70 million native speakers, more than a third of the total population of the archipelago. One would think that such widespread use, coupled with a long and very rich history of Javanese civilization and culture, would have made Javanese the language of the archipelago either in the capacity of a medium of intergroup communication (a lingua franca of some sort), as a language of cultural prestige, or as the national language of Indonesia. However, Javanese was not destined to hold any of these functions. Rather these functions belong to the Malay language, which has been the lingua franca and a language of cultural prestige of the archipelago—specifically in Malaysia, Indonesia and Southern Philippines—besides being the national language of Malaysia, Indonesia, Singapore, and Brunei.

That Malay has served as a lingua franca in the Southeast Asian islands ever since the early centuries of the Christian era is a well-known fact. No one knows when its use began, but foreign travelers visiting the Malay peninsula and the islands as early as the seventh century A.D. recorded that the language used by the people as a common medium of communication was Malay. Native speakers of the language even in those days were the Malays of the peninsula, eastern and central Sumatra, and Brunei on Borneo Island. Numerically, the native speakers of Malay had never dominated even the Javanese, let alone the sum total of all the western Austronesian ethnic groups in Indonesia.

The population of Javanese speakers has always exceeded that of the Malays. At present the population of Javanese speakers in Indonesia is more than 70 million, while that of native Malays is about 10 million (inclusive of those in Brunei and Sumatra).

The culture of the Javanese is far superior to that of Malay. In classical and modern literature, art, dancing, and music the Javanese culture is about the richest and the most advanced in the whole Malay archipelago. The Javanese system of writing and written literature date back to the seventh century A.D., and there has never been a hiatus in their existence, though this continuity was punctuated by changes and innovations which are natural to any living language. Although the Malay writing system also dates back to the seventh century, as evidenced by three stone inscriptions found in Sumatra and Bangka, the history of the Malay language and literature has followed a path quite different from that of Javanese.

The Javanese language has made use of a single writing system (that originating from the Indian Devanagari script) for many centuries. In the nineteenth century Javanese adopted the Latin script as well. The Islamization of Indonesia did not affect the writing system of the language. Even with the adoption of the Latin script, the Javanese script appeared to be the more dominant of the two. There were individual efforts to write the Javanese language in the Arabic script, but they did not really receive a response worth noting. The current official scripts are the Javanese and the Latin scripts. There is no implication of a religious or cultural cleavage here, because Javanese language users, if they ever write at all, are free to choose either of the two systems, although more and more publications in Javanese have resorted to the Latin script.

With the Malay language, there appears to have been a greater degree of flexibility and adaptability as to the choice of writing systems. The first writing system ever given to the language was that used for the inscriptions on the stone monuments found in Sumatra and Bangka, mentioned above, a system adapted from the Indian Pali script. With

Islamization, the Malays totally abandoned the script of Indian origin and adopted the Arabic system of writing, inserting modifications to suit the Malay phonological system. After almost five centuries of using only this script to write their language, the Malays found it feasible to adopt the Latin script from the West. Up to the first half of this century the Arabic script, better known as the Jawi script, had always been the preferred one. After the Second World War and the increase of secular education via the Malay language, the Latin script began to advance in popularity. Today the Latin script is still the more popular of the two. This situation has been reinforced by the Language Act of 1963, which clearly stated that "the script of the national language shall be the Rumi script," Rumi (from Rome) being the Malaysized nomenclature for the Latin.

Adoption of the Rumi script has of course facilitated the learning of Malay by ethnic groups other than the Malays, and in a way has been one of the factors which helped to spread Malay, or rather the sophisticated written variety of Malay, across ethnic boundaries. However, the Jawi script is still very much in use today. Malay native speakers are, for the most part, proficient in reading both the Rumi and the Jawi scripts. The older generation, those who had undergone the Malay vernacular system of education prior to Independence (1957), still show a predilection for the Jawi script. This predilection is even more pronounced with the people in the rural areas where published materials in the Jawi script are still preferred over the ones in Rumi. Hence, it is no surprise that the most popular Malay language newspaper is the *Utusan Melayu* printed in the Jawi script.

The fact that it was Malay and not Javanese that became the lingua franca of the entire Malay archipelago was due to linguistic, sociolinguistic, as well as extralinguistic factors. Malay is indeed an easier language than Javanese for nonnative speakers to acquire. The Malay consonants are easier to pronounce than the "heavy" ones of Javanese, while the vowels are primary cardinals, except in a few dialects, for example, the Kelantan dialect of the peninsula, where they are secondary cardinals.[4]

It is not only the simplicity of the phonological system that makes Malay easy to master by nonnative Malay speakers within and without the archipelago; the grammatical system devoid of inflexions and categories of tense, case, gender, and number has also simplified the learning of the language a great deal. Word order is rigid, particularly at the phrasal level where the nucleus precedes the modifiers. It is quite usual for foreign speakers like the Chinese, the Europeans, and so on, to gain a proficiency in the language within three months that enables them to hold day-to-day communication and to be relatively fluent within a year. A seventy-five-hour course of two to three months for real beginners, conducted by the University of Malaya Language Centre, enables the student to converse with ease in the language in the conduct of his day-to-day affairs. For a nonnative Malay speaker of Austronesian background, mastering the language is naturally a much easier task than it would be for his non-Austronesian counterpart.

William Marsden, writing in the very early part of the nineteenth century, about life on the island of Sumatra, had this to say about the spread and characteristics of the Malay language:

> The Malay language which has commonly been supposed original in the peninsula of Malayo, and from thence to have extended itself throughout the eastern Islands, so as to become the *lingua franca* of that part of the globe, is spoken everywhere along the coasts of Sumatra, prevails without the mixture of any other, in the Island country of Manangkabau and its immediate dependencies, and is understood in almost every part of the Island. It has been much celebrated, and justly, for the smoothness and sweetness of its sound, which have gained it the appellation of the *Italian of the East*. This is owing to the prevalence of vowels and liquids in the words (with many nasals which may be thought an objection) and the infrequency of any harsh combination of mute consonants. These qualities render it well adapted to poetry, which the Malays are passionately addicted to.[5]

Simplicity of grammar is also a characteristic of Javanese. Nevertheless, the latter language offers the learner great difficulties, not in its structural patterns as such, but rather in the variety of items, grammatical or lexical, which must be chosen among to fill in those patterns. These difficulties derive from the sociolinguistic levels or strata existing in Javanese. There are four main levels—Kromo Inggil, Kromo, Maydo and Ngoko in that descending order—and in certain cases each has its own set of grammatical and lexical items. A beginner in Javanese is faced with the problem of memorizing the sociolinguistic sets of affixes and lexis. He may not be required to know all, but at least he has to know the *ngoko* and the *kromo* to enable him to interact in day-to-day life with his peers and superiors.

In addition, the speaker may at the moment of speaking be placed in a dilemma with respect to the choice of the variety most appropriate to the situation. The speaker's assessment of the situation and of the degree of intimacy holding between him and the other participants in a particular speech event may not be compatible with the assessments of his listeners. It is this factor that prevented the spread of the language to the other islands of the archipelago and to people other than native Javanese. On this special feature of the Javanese language, Sir Stamford Raffles, the British Governor-General of Java in the first decade of the nineteenth century, had this to say:

> But there is no feature in the language more deserving of notice, than the difference of dialect, or the distinction between the common language and what may be termed the polite language or language of honour . . . so clearly is the line drawn on Java, between the higher and the lower classes of society, that on no account is anyone, of whatever rank allowed to address his superior in the common or vernacular language of the country. This language is exclusively applied when addressing an inferior, or among the lower order or uneducated, when distinction of rank may not be acknowledged. Persons of high and equal rank, when discoursing among themselves, sometimes use the polite language but in general they adopt a medium, by introducing words belonging to both branches of the language; and this is generally adopted by them in epistolary correspondence.[6]

Raffles's comments on the grammar in relation to the sociolinguistic stratification of the Javanese language are also quite relevant to the point in question concerning the factors that impeded the spread of Javanese as a common language in the archipelago.

> . . . and although the general construction of the language, and its grammatical principles are not altered, so effectually is the language of inferiority contrasted with that of superiority, that it is possible to suppose a case in which a person might well be acquainted with one dialect, without being able to understand one sentence of the other.[7]

There is no doubt that Javanese is spoken in certain parts of the Malay Peninsula and Sumatra, but in these foreign lands it is not the first language of the people of those lands but rather the first language of first and second generation Javanese immigrants. The third generation of Javanese immigrants generally do not speak the language any more. Instead, they adopt the language of the place or the national language. Living testimonies to this process can be found in various Javanese settlements on the Malay Peninsula.

Another factor which had been responsible for the spread of Malay since ancient times is the geographical situation of the areas considered to be inhabited by originally Malay-speaking people. The Malay Peninsula and Sumatra face the straits of Malacca, a very important maritime route which linked the Far East to India, the Middle East and Europe. Hence, traders, migrants, and even pirates who plied up and down the

Straits of Malacca could not escape contact with the Malay-speaking people. The Malays themselves have been said to be sea-faring people, who roamed the seas for the purpose of trade and conquest, and as such had spread their language to the people of the other islands.

The rise, from time to time, of Malay empires in Sumatra and the peninsula could have given great impetus to the spread of Malay. In the early years of the Christian era, the great Srivijaya empire dominated the greater part of Southeast Asia. This was a Malay empire with its headquarters in Palembang in Sumatra and Kedah on the peninsula, as evidenced by archaeological remains in these two places. It is not surprising that stone Malay inscriptions, like the Gandasuli inscriptions dated A.D. 827 and A.D. 832, have been found in Gandasuli, Central Java.[8]

About a century after the decline of the Srivijaya empire at the end of the thirteenth century, another Malay empire came into being. This was the Malacca empire, which lasted until 1511 when Malacca fell into Portuguese hands. As the center for entrepôt trade for over a hundred years, Malacca became the meeting place for people from all over the archipelago. Communication among the natives of the islands and between natives and foreigners to the region was via Malay.

2. SPREAD AND RECESSION OF ENGLISH

The immigrant languages in the archipelago are the Chinese languages, the Indian languages, Arabic, Thai, and some other minor ones. All these languages are spoken in Malaysia more than in the Philippines or Indonesia, mainly due to the high percentage of immigrants in the population there. The number of immigrants adds to the high degree of diversity already in existence in Southeast Asia, a diversity such that lingua francas were needed for intergroup communication; hence there emerged pidgins and languages of wider communication which were once colonial languages. These are English (in Malaysia, Indonesia, and the Philippines) and Spanish (only in the Philippines).

All three of these countries, being members of the Educational Pact known as SEAMEO (Southeast Asian Ministers of Education Organization, which was established in the 1960s) have chosen English as their principal foreign language for two main purposes: one, as a language for international communication; and two, as a language which gives access to the latest developments in science and technology. Knowledge of English gives the individual added prestige as well as a means of personal advancement in professional and academic fields.[9]

For Malaysia and the Philippines, the choice of English as second or foreign language was a continuation of their acceptance of a former colonial language. This is not to say that there was no antagonism towards the colonialists in Malaysia or the Philippines. But in these countries antagonism toward the colonial rulers did not include antagonism toward their language. Malaysia and the Philippines have been very pragmatic in their treatment of the language of their colonial masters. They have always realized that the English language was an asset to hold on to, since it could provide them with an avenue to international relations as well as a means to their advancement in science and technology.

For Indonesia, the choice of English was totally without precedent. The colonial language of Indonesia had been Dutch, but this language, predominant for three centuries, began to recede after 1945, when Indonesia achieved independence from Dutch colonial rule. Dutch receded both because of antagonism toward the Dutch colonial government and because the Dutch language was not a language of wider communication.

The change in status of English in Malaysia from a colonial to a principal foreign language has resulted in the recession and spread of this language at one and the same time. English was a language of government administration during the colonial period and ten years after independence. Its position as the language of prestige education, which had its beginning in the colonial days, would have continued indefinitely had there not been the enactment and enforcement of a National Education Policy (beginning in 1957), which required ultimately a uniform system of education for all using Malay as medium of instruction. This policy as well as the official language policy, which required that the government administration use Malay, have of course been responsible for the recession of English from the two important positions it had for long occupied as medium of instruction and as language of government administration.

However, the adoption of English as a principal foreign language has had another effect, and that is the geographical spread of English. The National Education Policy requires that English is taught in every government-sponsored school, be it fully or partially assisted, and no matter what its location. The situation was quite different in colonial times, when English was confined to the English-medium school and to the urban areas. In those days, English was an optional language in schools other than English schools, which latter were found only in the towns. Other factors, such as the lack of opportunity given to rural schools to teach the language, had made English a language accessible only to urban people and those with means. The spread of the English language during the colonial period was one determined by town boundaries.

One point needs to be made about the wide geographical spread of English, or rather the spread of ELT (English Language Teaching), in Malaysia today, and that point concerns the relationship of the spread to the level of language proficiency acquired by the learners. When the language was confined to a smaller geographical area and was limited to being the medium of education in selected schools, the level of proficiency was very high. Now, when it is spread over a wider area and is just a language that must be acquired, divested of its role as medium of education, the level of proficiency is very low.

These two phenomena, recession and spread, affecting English, are balanced by two similar phenomena affecting Malay. In the colonial period, Malay, as a medium of instruction, was confined to the Malay schools, the great majority of which were located in the rural areas. It was only an optional subject in other schools, namely the English-medium school, the Chinese vernacular school using Mandarin as medium, and the Tamil vernacular school using Tamil as medium. With the implementation of recommendations in the Education Ordinance (1971) Malay has become, or is in the process of becoming, the main medium of education in all government and government-aided schools. This means that the level of proficiency in Malay, particularly among non-Malays, is on the rise. This will be discussed in greater detail in section 4.

3. LEVELS OF SPREAD

Historically speaking, the spread of Malay on the archipelago occurred at three different levels which reflect three different types of language use: (i) the lingua franca level; (ii) the cultural level; and (iii) the educational-scientific level.

At the lingua franca level, the type of Malay that spread far and wide was the "low" or "bazaar" Malay. Van der Tuuk, a well-known Dutch scholar of Malay, classical Javanese, and Balinese, noted in 1856 that the lingua franca was "not even a real language," and was not used by true Malays.[10] This bazaar Malay still exists today in market places, spoken by people of different linguistic backgrounds. It was this pidgin or bazaar Malay that later developed into Ambonese Malay of the Ambon islands[11] and the Baba Malay of Malacca.

The spread of Malay at the cultural level accompanied the use of the language as a tool for the dissemination of religion and literature. The variety of Malay used for this purpose is what is generally known as

High Malay. This has been the variety used by Malay speakers when they speak among themselves. Within this variety there are subvarieties: the royal and nonroyal varieties, the standard and nonstandard varieties, and so on.[12] It was in the High (nonroyal) variety that Islam and Christianity were spread to the people of the archipelago. It was also in this variety that the Malay classics were written and into which Javanese, Indian, and Arabic literary works were translated.

Islam, which came to the archipelago long before Christianity, brought with it not only religious works but also Arabic tales and poetry. The most notable of the Arabic literary genres brought into the Malay world was a type of verse known as the *shair*. This form became very much favored by the Malays. Later *shair* verses were created by local people with local themes, and these were taken from island to island.

Having the Malay language as its working tool and probably the "true" Malays as its earliest converts, Islam over the centuries has been closely associated with Malay, with both the Malay people and their language. Hence, the term *Melayu* (for "Malay") among the ethnic groups in Malaysia and Indonesia is generally taken to mean one professing the religion of Islam. The Muslim Indonesians generally refer to themselves as Melayu. In Borneo Malaysia (Sabah and Sarawak), the Muslim groups (inclusive of the Malays) consisting of the Melanau of Sarawak, and the Bajau, Suluk, and Illanun of Sabah, are also known as Malays although they do not speak Malay as a first language. Where Peninsular Malaysia is concerned, Malay and Islam are inseparable; the Malaysian Constitution defines a Malay as one who habitually leads the Malay way of life, speaks the Malay language, and is a Muslim.

In the dissemination of Christianity on the Malay archipelago, the Christian missionaries, like their Muslim counterparts, chose High Malay as their linguistic tool. As a rule the propagation of the Christian religion was directed toward those groups who had not been visited by Islam. Such groups were those whose first language was not Malay, but who spoke the Malay language as a form of intergroup communication. Nevertheless, the missionaries, like the Dutch colonial government, were not in favor of stooping to use Low Malay.[13] The Dutch, for instance, did their best to introduce High Malay, the usage current in the Malay Peninsula and the Riau islands, to the people of the Netherland Indies.[14]

It was the conversion of the Ambonese people to Christianity via the medium of the Malay language that was responsible for the ultimate emergence of Ambonese Malay, the variety of Malay used by the Christians of Ambon island. This language has since become their first language, although in a creolized form.[15] Curiously enough, the Muslims of this island speak a language totally different from Malay.[16] Hence, it can be deduced that the Ambonese had been in possession of a language, the Ambonese language, and that this language receded from use among the Christians. This would not have happened if Christianity had been introduced to them in their own language. The fact that the Christian community of Ambon could discard their original language in favor of Malay could have been due to the intensity of the use of the latter in their religious life. On the other hand, Muslims anywhere in the world pray only in Arabic without necessarily abandoning their mother tongue.

At the educational-scientific level, the spread of Malay emerged only after independence from colonial rule, both in Indonesia and Malaysia, promoted the use of Malay in government administration, official functions and educational institutions.

In the development of a Malaysian nation, two linguistic phenomena have been in operation, one being the converse of the other. These are the spread of Malay and the recession of English, both caused by the implementation of the language and education policies of the country. The Language Policy had established Malay as the national language of the country at the time of independence from British rule in 1957. It was only ten years later that this language became the sole official language of the country. For the first ten years after independence, Malay was one of two official languages, the other being English. During those ten years the exalted function of Malay as national language and as one of the official languages was manifested mainly in its being the language of the national anthem, of the King's Parliamentary speech, and that in which interviews for jobs took place in certain government departments. Otherwise, the language that mattered in government administration, firms (local and foreign), and educational institutions was English.

The official language situation changed in 1967 in Peninsular Malaysia when English had to be phased out from the function it held in officialdom in favor of Malay. This process of phasing English out of the administration of the country took almost three years to complete. Implementation of Malay as official language could be carried out instantaneously in government administration, but elsewhere, namely in the private sectors, a slower pace for withdrawal of English seemed to be more desirable. This is of course due to the nature of private enterprises themselves. Private business enterprises, be they local or foreign, had always preferred people with an English-language educational background. These firms were not owned by Malays, and firms with foreign dealings felt that engaging a managerial staff who did not know English would be a great liability.

The Malaysian Education Policy aims at providing a system of education to all Malaysian children through a common language medium and common core syllabuses. This policy began its slow yet steady process of implementation in 1957 and is still in process, though nearing the end of the period scheduled for implementation.

According to Malaysian education planning, students of the arts and the social sciences entering the universities in 1981 to do their first year of study will all have experienced only Malay as the linguistic medium of their education. By 1983, the sciences too will be admitting only students who have been educated in Malay.

The phasing out of English from the Malaysian schools has indeed taken a long time, but the gradualness of the process was deliberate and sprang from the planners' desire not to jeopardize academic excellence. This was the planners' main concern, as the maintaining of an academic standard is a delicate affair which calls for a number of preparations — obtaining textbooks in the relevant fields of study, and training lecturers to be proficient in Malay.[17]

The replacement of English by Malay did not proceed at the same rate for all subjects in the curriculum. Those subjects that could without difficulty adopt the Malay language as medium of instruction were the first to be affected by the conversion process. This meant that history and geography were ahead of mathematics and science in their adoption of Malay. Whether a subject could convert easily or not from English to Malay as the language for its instruction was of course based on the existence of Malay technical terms and the availability of textbooks in the fields of study concerned. These factors were contributive to the two-year delay in the full implementation of the National Education Policy in the sciences compared to the more rapid conversion of arts from English to Malay at the school level.

As was said earlier, the learning of Malay by every Malaysian citizen regardless of race or creed, specifically after independence, was a goal given impetus by the enforcement of the Language Act and the National Education Policy.[18] The latter, which promotes a uniform type of education for all Malaysians, is very much linked to the New Economic Policy of Malaysia which aims at giving equal opportunity to everyone in acquiring the nation's wealth. By this, the policy hopes to correct the inequitable economic situation of today which identifies economic wealth with one ethnic group and poverty with another.[19] This imbalanced state of affairs had partly been caused by ethnic-based systems of education which were directed toward the three main groups of

Malaysia, namely Malays, Chinese, and Indians. Differences holding between these systems did not lie in the language media alone but also in the school curricula.

Besides these ethnic-based systems, there was an elite group, prior to independence, that used English as medium of instruction. While the majority of the pupils from the different ethnic groups chose the system of education identified with their ethnicity, those with financial means and who lived in the urban areas chose the English schools instead. Although by the nature of their curriculum and language medium, the English schools were not to be identified with any ethnic group, in practice the English schools were mostly populated by the Chinese. Thus, it is not surprising that until today professionals and educators are, in the majority, Chinese, not to mention the Chinese businessmen and the industrialists who operate in clans and to whom language does not form an important factor for success.

The New Economic Policy, which operates partly through the National Education Policy, has acted to remedy this imbalanced situation. Homogeneity of language medium for education and official interaction is an instrument for achieving an equal distribution of wealth.[20] With the same type of education, all graduates can apply for any type of job and compete for the same career opportunities. Posts in government institutions, especially in the middle and top rungs of the ladder, were designed for the English-educated people only.

4. GEOGRAPHICAL CONTINUITY OF LANGUAGE SPREAD

At present, Malay is the national language of four countries which are geographically contiguous with one another. These are Malaysia, Indonesia, Brunei, and Singapore. In the first three, this language is also the official language and medium of instruction in the educational institutions. Singapore, a predominantly Chinese country, has chosen Malay to be its national language (with four official languages: Malay, Chinese, English, and Tamil), and has thus assisted in maintaining the spatial continuity of language spread. Indeed the decision made by Singapore to choose Malay (although only 20 percent of her population were Malays and although knowledge of the language among the rest of the population was limited to a very few) and not Chinese as national language, was purely based on political and regional considerations rather than on linguistic ones. However Malay, as national language in Singapore, serves only as a symbol of nationalism and as the language of the national anthem. It is the medium of instruction in the few Malay schools, but in the far more numerous English and Chinese schools, it is an optional subject chosen mostly by pupils of Malay origin. Otherwise, English is still very much the language of the republic. In its geographical setting, Singapore is in a Malay world, and it is surrounded by Malay-speaking countries whose indigenous people originated from a stock quite different from the Chinese. Being only an island of about three hundred square miles and devoid of a hinterland of its own, it is imperative that it share a common identity with its neighbors, even if the identity factor is one whose function is minimal in the everyday life of the population as a whole.

Historically, Singapore was a Malay island, with a predominantly Malay population. This was before 1819, when the island was leased to the English East India Company by the Sultan of Johore. Ever since then, the Malay language has receded in importance in tempo with a decline in the Malay population. It has been displaced from its own geographical origins by Singapore (pidgin) English and an assortment of Chinese languages.

5. NATIVITY FACTOR IN LANGUAGE SPREAD

Now we come to the concept of "nativity" in the geographical distribution of a language. A language is native or indigenous to an area if it is the first language of its indigenous people. The nativity criterion applies to Malay in Peninsular Malaysia, Singapore, Brunei, a small part of Sarawak, and small parts of Indonesia: the Riau islands and the eastern part of Sumatra. Again one sees the Malay homeland forming a region surrounding the Straits of Malacca and the Riau islands.

That only a small portion of Sarawak is indigenously Malay, though it is wholly Austronesian with groups speaking languages closely related to Malay (that is, Malay synonymous to that of Peninsular Malaysia), is a situation that dates back to before the nineteenth century, when Sarawak was still part of the Brunei (Malay) Sultanate. The Austronesian ethnic groups were spread far and wide in Brunei and Sarawak, as at the present moment, but the Malay population were predominantly located in Brunei proper and in the territory that is now the First Division of Sarawak. Piracy along the coasts had induced the Sultan of Brunei to enlist the assistance of Captain Brooke, an English adventurer. For his services, Captain Brooke was successively rewarded with stretches of land, until his acquisition grew to the Sarawak of today.

A language spread in nativity is different from one that is superimposed. The former usually originates from the presence of a native population speaking that language as first language, and from the function of the language as an official language, that is, one that is used in government administration and other official functions. A language spread in nativity may also derive its strength from the existence of a literary tradition which precedes the rise of national movements and the forming of nation states. For a language with such a literary tradition, the spread of language is synonymous with the spread of culture.

Superimposed language spread can be planned or otherwise. Planned spread emerges with nationalism and the building of nation states and springs from a desire to further national unity and identity. Indonesia gives an excellent example in the planned spread of Bahasa Indonesia, a language based on Malay. Such superimposed spread is usually linked with the educational-scientific spread of a language, although this is not always the rule, as in the case of Singapore. Conversely, unplanned spread most commonly proceeds from the need for a lingua franca. In such cases, the most important factor in operation is the basic human need to communicate.

NOTES

1. *Report of the Regional Workshop on the Feasibility of a Sociolinguistic Survey of Southeast Asia*, SEAMEO Regional English Language Centre, Singapore, 1973, Appendix C.

2. See Amran Halim, "Bahasa Indonesia in Relation to the Vernaculars," in *Journal of the Siam Society*, Volume 63, Part 2, July 1975, p. 72.

3. *Report of the Regional Workshop*, ibid.

4. See Asmah Haji Omar, *The Phonological Diversity of the Malay Dialects*, Dewan Bahasa dan Pustaka, Kuala Lumpur, 1977.

5. William Marsden, *The History of Sumatra*, Oxford University Press, London, 1811, p. 197.

6. Thomas Stamford Raffles, *The History of Java*, Volume One. Oxford University Press, London, 1965, p. 66.

7. Ibid.

8. S.T. Alishahbana, *Indonesia: Social and Cultural Revolution*, Oxford University Press, London, 1966, p. 58.

9. See Asmah Haji Omar, "The Malaysian Mosaic of Languages," in Asmah Haji Omar, *Essays on Malaysian Linguistics*, Dewan Bahasa dan Pustaka, 1975, pp. 23–24. See also Amran Halim and A. Latief, "Some Sociolinguistic Problems in Indonesia," in *Report of the Regional Workshop*, p. 35.

10. J.E. Hoffman, "The Malay Language as a Force for Unity in the Indonesian Archipelago 1815–1900," *Nusantara*, no. 4, July 1973, p. 28.

11. James T. Collins, *Ambonese Malay and Creolization Theory*, mimeograph 1975.

12. See Asmah Haji Omar, "Languages of Malaysia," in Teodoro A. Llamzon

(ed.), *An Introduction to the Languages of Indonesia, Malaysia, Philippines, Singapore and Thailand*, RELC Publication, Singapore, forthcoming.

13. See J.E. Hoffman, *Malay Language as a Force for Unity*.

14. Ibid.

15. James Collins, *Ambonese Malay*.

16. James Collins, *personal communication*.

17. See Asmah Haji Omar, *The Teaching of Bahasa Malaysia In the Context of National Language Planning*, Dewan Bahasa dan Pustaka, Kuala Lumpur, 1976, chapter 8.

18. For a detailed discussion on this, see Asmah Haji Omar, *Language Planning For Unity And Efficiency*, University of Malaya Press, forthcoming.

19. See Asmah Haji Omar, "Language and National Ideology," paper presented at the Third Conference of the Asian Association on National Languages. Jakarta, 1–6th December 1975.

20. See Joshua A. Fishman, "Some Contrasts Between Linguistically Homogeneous and Linguistically Heterogeneous Polities," in Stanley Lieberson (ed.), *Explorations in Sociolinguistics*, 1966, pp. 18–30.

REFERENCES

Abdul Razak Ismail and Asmah Haji Omar, "The Sociolinguistic Situation in Malaysia," in *Report of the Regional Workshop on the Feasibility of a Sociolinguistic Survey of Southeast Asia, 1973*, SEAMEO Regional English Language Centre, Singapore, 1973, pp. 51–63.

Alisjahbana, S. Takdir, *Indonesia: Social and Cultural Revolution*, Oxford University Press, London, 1966.

Amran Halim, "Bahasa Indonesia in Relation to the Vernaculars," in *Journal of the Siam Society*, Volume 63, Part 2, July 1975, pp. 72–77.

Amran Halim and A. Latief, "Some Sociolinguistic Problems in Indonesia," in *Report of the Regional Workshop on the Feasibility of a Sociolinguistic Survey of Southeast Asia*, 1973, SEAMEO Regional English Language Centre, Singapore, 1973, pp. 29–39.

Asmah Haji Omar, *Essays on Malaysian Linguistics*, Dewan Bahasa dan Pustaka, Kuala Lumpur, 1975.

Asmah Haji Omar, "Language And National Ideology," paper presented at the Third Conference of the Asian Association on National Languages (ASNAL), Jakarta, 1–6 December 1975.

Asmah Haji Omar, *Language Planning For Unity and Efficiency*, University of Malaya Press, Kuala Lumpur (forthcoming).

Asmah Haji Omar, "Languages of Malaysia" in Teodoro A. Llamzon (ed.), *An Introduction to the Languages of Indonesia, Malaysia, Philippines, Singapore and Thailand*, RELC Publication, Singapore (forthcoming).

Asmah Haji Omar, "The Malaysian Mosaic of Languages," in Asmah Haji Omar, *Essays On Malaysian Linguistics*, Dewan Bahasa dan Pustaka, Kuala Lumpur, 1975, pp. 12–27.

Asmah Haji Omar, *The Phonological Diversity of the Malay Dialects*, Dewan Bahasa dan Pustaka, Kuala Lumpur, 1977.

Asmah Haji Omar, *The Teaching of Bahasa Malaysia In The Context of National Language Planning*, Dewan Bahasa dan Pustaka, Kuala Lumpur, 1976.

Collins, James T., *Ambonese Malay and Creolization Theory*, mimeograph 1975.

Fishman, Joshua A., "Some Contrasts Between Linguistically Homogeneous and Linguistically Heterogeneous Polities," in Stanley Lieberson (ed.), *Explorations in Sociolinguistics*, Mouton & Co., The Hague, 1966.

Hertzler, Joyce O., "Social Uniformation and Language," in Stanley Lieberson (ed.), *Explorations in Sociolinguistics*, Mouton & Co., The Hague, 1966, pp. 170–184.

Hoffman, J.E., "The Malay Language as a Force For Unity in the Indonesian Archipelago 1815–1900," *Nusantara*, no. 4, July 1973, pp. 19–36.

Marsden, William, *The History of Sumatra*, Oxford University Press, London, 1811.

Raffles, Thomas Stamford, *The History of Java*, Volume One, Oxford University Press, London, 1965.

Report of the Regional Workshop on the Feasibility of a Sociolinguistic Survey of Southeast Asia, SEAMEO Regional English Language Centre, Singapore, 1973.

Movements and Agencies of Language Spread: Wales and the Soviet Union Compared

E. Glyn Lewis

1. INTRODUCTION

a) Definitions and Explanations

It is the main contention of this paper that, in any country, movements for social change, as well as the agencies associated with them, are determined by the manner in which factors promoting social change cluster in that area. Wales and the Soviet Union are compared from this point of view because on the face of it they are about as different as two countries can be in many respects, including the movements and agencies within them which have contributed to language spread.* "Movement" and "agency" are terms with wide ranges of meaning: they are used here with strictly limited connotations, and it should be understood how we propose to use the two terms. "Movement" is taken to mean, in the first place, the particular kind of force or dynamism which characterizes the manner in which a language spreads, whether it spreads by adding to the roles it plays in the communication habits of existing speakers or (alternatively but sometimes additionally) by attracting new speakers of the language. Just as in musical analysis "movement" refers to a section, a piece or passage which has its characteristic form of development—its melodic progression—so, in our present context, "movement" may refer to the characteristics of the spread of a language at a particular time and place, for instance the speed, intensity, and consistency of spread as well as modes of interaction with other languages.

---

*In the space available it will be impossible to compare these two countries over the range of all relevant variables. It must be appreciated that the treatment is highly selective.

We also mean by "movement" a series of actions which exemplify a body of social principles or ideologies. Thus nationalism, the growth of secularism, socialism, or as is the case in Wales the development of religious nonconformity constitute movements which we are able to identify by social actions or changes which have a characteristic consistency. Whether we conceive of "movement" in terms of the characteristic mode of progression or on the other hand as a set of social principles in action, "agencies" in the present context are the personal or institutional organizations by means of which these movements are realized in action. Such agencies are those concerned with the planning of a language, are sometimes religious or antireligious organizations, or are simply militant activities directed at promoting the use of a language in competition with another, etc. Such agencies may be directly and almost exclusively concerned with language, although in other cases the linguistic interest of the agency may be only one, sometimes a subordinate, aspect of the agency. Nationalist movements are a case in point, for it is often difficult to decide whether the main motivation of the institution is political, economic, narrowly cultural, or linguistic. Sometimes an agency, like the Socialist party in Wales, may be divided in its attitude to language. But simply because the agency has divided aims is no reason to ignore its significance in having promoted the spread of English at one time, while at present it attempts to secure a wider role for the Welsh language.

There are at least four sets or categories of factors which promote social change and which tend to determine the kinds of agencies and movements which operate in language spread. The first set is composed of language attitudes. Aspects of such attitudes include the strength of efforts to maintain or to reinforce a threatened language as well as efforts to restrict the functions of an indigenous language. A second category consists of factors related to between-group interaction such as geographical contiguity and relative ease of communication, conquest, and colonization together with the attitudes which they create, and the nature of the relationship between the colonial "center" and the "periphery." A third set of factors includes those which are related to "modernization": intensity of economic development, the degree of external exploitation of indigenous resources, urbanization, and related demographic considerations such as population mobility and the age, sex, intelligence, and levels of education of the mobile population compared with that of the stable groups. A fourth category includes the political theories and religious and cultural characteristics associated with a linguistic group, especially the "distance" between the spreading language and other languages in contact with it with respect to these theories and characteristics.

Not only do the elements of any one category interact with each other, but the clusters or classes of factors do also. Movements which help to decide the characteristics of the spread of a particular language or the differences between its spread in different areas, though they are not synonymous with the factors already referred to, take their character from them, while specific agencies which give effect to the aims or the progression of "movements" of spread or restriction are created by the historical conditions of the progress of such movements. The latter are the sociolinguistic manifestations of broad patterns of social change, the extent of which is usually far wider than changes in the incidence of particular languages. For instance the "movement" we refer to as "modernization" does not differ markedly between Wales and the Soviet Union, whereas profound differences between the two countries in religion and in political philosophies ensure that the agencies which make modernization a reality have very different characteristics—for instance the degree of centralized and authoritarian control as against voluntary effort and diversity—if not conflict of immediate purpose. On the other hand agencies tend to be directed sometimes to the achievement of equally broad social changes and sometimes to limited purposes like the promotion of a language. We can regard "factors" as the *material* causes of social change including (sometimes only incidentally) language spread; "movements" as the *formal* causes determining the manner of spread; and "agencies" as the *efficient* causes giving effect to the programs representing the aims of movements.

b) Historical Considerations

The historical dimension is especially important in considering the spread of any language, and though I do not intend to introduce any quasimetaphysical notions concerning such historical considerations in the manner of Spengler, Toynbee, or the philosophers of historical determinism, it is not without interest that some languages seem to be carried forward for very long periods and over equally wide territories almost with the appearance of historical inevitability. The Aramaic language was one of these languages the spread of which few if any historians or linguists have been able to explain satisfactorily (Paper, this volume). Greek developed a momentum of its own which carried it over the Middle East and the western Mediterranean; Celtic, similarly, moved inexorably eastward to Galatia, southward to Italy, and westward to Gaul and Spain to end up in Britain, beyond which it advanced into the New World; Latin (and its Romanic derivatives), English, and Arabic exemplify the same progression which the measurement of the force of specific factors has not been able to explain (Lewis, 1978 a).

The fact that it is possible to identify some of the factors in the massive spread of these languages for such long periods cannot blind us to the possibility that a language, once it is set on a particular course, acquires a characteristic melodic progression which is *sui generis*.* It is because such a possibility exists and because it may be permissible to postulate inherent characteristics to the dynamism of a language, that one questions the proposition that "it is speakers who acquire languages" and that "languages do not acquire speakers" (Cooper, this volume). A language proves attractive to speakers of other languages for many reasons: sometimes because of their belief in its innate superiority as a language, or in its elegance, sometimes because of its linguistic history, and sometimes for more mundane utilitarian reasons. While it is obvious that new speakers have to learn a language for it to spread, it is also true that what a language is perceived to be or to stand for, irrespective of objective considerations, is what attracts the increasing clientele. In that sense a language does "acquire speakers."

c) Language Spread or Population Mobility

Another consideration needs to be clarified. In discussing "spread" are we concerned with a language as such or with the mobility of speakers of the language? Or is it impossible to make the distinction? There are some who argue that a language may spread when existing speakers use it to fulfill new functions or to recover the use of hitherto abandoned functions, as has been the case with Welsh. It is doubtful whether this is a form of "language spread" as distinct from "functional reinforcement" of the language. To my way of thinking, language spread involves at least the acquisition of new speakers to the relevant language community, though such new speakers may, additionally, extend its functions. On the other hand a language can spread without the immediate and local intervention of speakers of that language. It may be read in newspapers, periodicals, and books, or it may be heard on the radio. Nevertheless it is doubtful whether a language can long retain its dynamism at a particular place and time unless it is represented by a sufficient number of speakers. Consequently effective spread involves, almost by definition, population movement, either to inaugurate or to consolidate its presence.* At the same time, increases in the size of a

---

*Lieberson (this volume) makes a valuable point which is relevant to this issue, when he elaborates on the importance of "third party interests" in a second language (I am indebted to the editor for drawing my attention to this).

*I would wish to distinguish between the "injection" of a language into a particular area (a phenomenon which may be associated with very newcomers) and its "appreciable spread."

particular group of speakers of a language are not synonymous with its spread for any significant length of time. For instance, in the Soviet Union the degree of language maintenance among migrants is considerably lower than among the stable population speaking the same language. This difference amounted to 37% among the Ossetes, 31.4% among the Karachai, and was seldom less than 10% among the peoples of Daghestan as a whole. The migration of speakers of these languages to new areas is no guarantee of languages' survival in those areas (Lewis, 1972, 137). The same is true of migrating Welshmen, whatever their destination: the Chibut Valley of Patagonia, North America, or even neighboring English cities like Birmingham or Manchester. For all these reasons, while demographic analysis may not have been recognized as one of the research traditions of language spread, it is unlikely that our understanding of the phenomenon can be advanced very far unless we take into account aspects of such an analysis.

d) Patterns of Language Relationships

So far as Wales and the Soviet Union are concerned, it is possible to identify the following patterns of relationships between language spread and other sociolinguistic developments:

(i) A decline in the proportion of the total population speaking a particular native language coincides with an increase in the range of uses to which it is put by native speakers—either by a more extensive exploitation of existing uses or by an increase in the number of functions or a combination of both. We have already referred to this as "functional reinforcement." It is characteristic of Welsh, but not, in general, of the languages of the nationalities (national languages).

(ii) The functional reinforcement of the native language may be accompanied by an increase in the number of native or second-language speakers of the intrusive language and a corresponding increase in the functional spread of that language (increasing pluralism). This was the case of the hitherto nonalphabeticized Soviet languages in the 1930s. Or functional reinforcement of the indigenous language may be accompanied by no functional advance of the intrusive language (promoting though not actually constituting stable pluralism), as is the case in the thoroughly Welsh-speaking areas. Or again there may be functional restriction of the intrusive language (decreasing pluralism). This is exemplified mainly in former colonial territories which have become independent.

(iii) The indigenous language may be in decline demographically and/or functionally in the face of the intrusive language (demographic and/or functional substitution leading to shift). This is the case in Welsh and Soviet urban areas.

2. LANGUAGE SPREAD AND OTHER SOCIOLINGUISTIC PHENOMENA

a) General Comparisons

These considerations respecting the Soviet Union and Wales suggest that while language spread is a useful and distinguishable sociolinguistic concept, it cannot be considered in isolation from other sociolinguistic processes. One of these is "language maintenance"—either demographic or functional. A language like English can spread in certain ways without affecting the demographic stability of the native language(s). Thus, while the English language spread into Wales from the time of the Normans (twelfth century) onwards, it was restricted to strictly limited enclaves, Norman boroughs, and the immediate environs of those Norman strongholds, the castles. During five centuries the spread of English was hardly significant, especially if we take into account the increase of the total population of Wales during that time, mostly if not almost entirely native born. The same is true of the Soviet Union. Up to 1970, while the Russian language has spread increasingly into other Soviet republics, the incidence of Russian has been limited to the large towns and cities. At the same time in none of these Union Republics has the percentage claiming the native language (like Uzbek or Georgian) descended below 71.9% (in the case of Belorussia). Consequently, as in Wales, the spread of Russian and the maintenance of the nationality language coincides with a high level of bilingualism involving Russian: in Latvia 45%, in Kazakhstan 41.8%, in Belorussia 49%, in Lithuania 35.9%. The lowest percentages are found in the central Asian republics, with an average of 14%, and in Georgia with 21% (Lewis, 1972).

Generally speaking, at present Russian is an additional language in the areas to which the main Soviet languages are native. While this was true of English in Wales for many centuries it is now no longer the case. Demographically there has been a continuous substitution of English for Welsh through a transitional phase of bilingualism. Between 1891 and 1971 (Table 1) the total number of Welsh monolinguals has declined from 508,000 to 32,700, representing a decline from 29% to 1.3% of the total population. During the same period the *number* of bilinguals has increased from 402,000 to 510,000, but as a *percentage* of the total population this represents a decline from 24% to 19%. At the other extreme the total number of monolingual English speakers has increased from 759,000 to 2,060,000 representing an increase from 41% to 89%, partly because of language shift and partly because of continuous migration from across the border and the perpetuation of monolingual English speakers in the families of such migrants.

b) Planning

i) The Soviet Union

Looked at from the standpoint of "functional maintenance" of the indigenous languages, the Soviet Union and Wales differ very considerably. The spread of the Russian language constitutes an increasing restriction on the use of the national languages. It is true that for a limited period after 1926 there was considerable encouragement for the advance of the functional status of the minority languages, even the very smallest. About fifty languages like Abazin, Balkar, Cherkess, Dargun, Even, Ingush, Karakalpak, Lak, and Mansi were alphabeticized for the first time, thus ensuring the creation of native-language literacy in addition to or independently of Russian literacy. Consequently, between 1926 and 1959 the general level of Soviet literacy rose from 1.3% to 51%; among the Uygur, for instance, from 4.5% to 51%. However, while the potential for increased functional exploitation of these national languages was improved, overall the languages have been restricted, and Russian has become a substitute language. This is most apparent in the field of education, to which we shall refer later.

But education is only the most obvious of the areas of social action in which the functions of the national languages are restricted by the spread of the intrusive Russian and for which this spread of Russian is planned. Every phase of the interrelationship of Russian and other Soviet languages is calculated and planned by official agencies. Planning is as much an aspect of the development of the languages as of the economy of the USSR. "The extension of the social functions of the new written languages was carried out in a planned fashion" (Deseriev and Prochenko, 1966, p. 16). And this plan was governed by political considerations. For instance, during the early years of Soviet power, essentially political exigencies induced the fragmentation of hitherto closely related and almost identical language communities: Kirgiz and Karakalpak were separated from and developed separately from Kazakh. Similarly, changes in the alphabets of Soviet languages were dictated largely by political aims. The adoption of the Latin alphabet made it easier to emphasize differences between Central Asian Soviet

TABLE 1: English- and Welsh-speaking populations of Wales, 1891–1971

	a	b Welsh only			c English and Welsh			d Total Welsh-Speaking: b + c			e English only		
	Total population in thousands	1 Total in thousands	2 1 as % of a	3 Percentage difference from previous return	1 Total in thousands	2 1 as % of a	3 Percentage difference from previous return	1 Total in thousands	2 1 as % of a	3 Percentage difference from previous return	1 Total in thousands	2 1 as % of a	3 Percentage difference from previous return
1891	1,813	508	29	—	402	24	—	910	51	—	759	41	—
1901	2,013	281	14	−45	649	32	+61	930	46	+2	928	54	+22
1911	2,421	190	8	−36	786	32	+21	976	39	+5	1,108	46	+30
1921	2,656	153	6	−19	746	29	−5	900	36	−8	1,467	63	+33
1931	2,593	98	4	−36	820	32	+10	909	36	+1	1,552	64	+5
1951	2,472	41.1	2	−57	673	27	−18	714	28	−22	1,758	72	+13
1961	2,518	26.1	1.0	−38	629	25	−7	656	26	−8	1,862	74	+6
1971	2,602	32.7	1.3	+30	510	19.6	−20	542	21	−20	2,060	89	+20

Source: Censuses of England and Wales, reports on Welsh-speaking population.
Note: The totals of the language categories d) & e) do not, as they should, equal the totals in a) because of omissions in language-data returns. (No Census was taken in 1941.)

languages and identical languages outside the Union; one of the principal aims of the change to Cyrillic was to facilitate easier acquisition of Russian as a second language.*

On the purely structural level, planning has supported and stabilized a very large number of ethnic languages. But apart from the fact that the very principle of planning, and especially planning which is governed by a central authority, may be inimical to the spirit in which the social functions of severely localized ethnic languages are sustained, it has had specific adverse consequences as well. One of the functions of language planning in the Soviet Union, as elsewhere, is determining and "defining the objectives to be achieved" (Bernard, 1970, p. 65). This implies the delimitation of the social functions of languages in contact: "language contacts require conscious control by society," and in fact "society is entitled to regulate processes of interaction between languages" (Deseriev, 1973, pp. 9 and 17). The planning of the social interrelationship of these languages officially and the political pressure towards assimilation and integration have meant that large numbers of native speakers have shifted to another language, even in the relatively superficial roles of casual social and work contacts, but more importantly in intimate family role-relations. Furthermore, because of increasing social and cultural convergence, the stylistic innovations within each of the national languages, brought about by the speakers' need to adapt to new roles, tend to follow a uniform pattern across languages because of the omnipresence of the Russian influence. "*Common* trends and laws of development and mutual enrichment of languages [which] are clearly manifested in the formation of a special style of sociopolitical and publicistic literature of the Soviet epoch, took shape under the influence of the Russian language" (Deseriev and Prochenko, 1966, pp. 16–17). These developments are governed by the "principle of minimum discrepancy" among national languages and between them and Russian ("printsip minimal'nykh raskhozhedniy" Deseriev and Prochenko, 1966). Even where Russian is not substituted for the national languages, its influence undermines the continued existence of such languages.

The Russian language is expropriating the most prestigious and socially significant roles. More and more non-Russians claim Russian as their native language, 18% in the case of Udmurt, 12% Uygur, 33% among the peoples of the north, 17% Khakass, 13% Altai, etc. In in-

---

*This fact does not invalidate Ferguson's suggestion (this volume) that in normal circumstances in any speech community, religious cleavages are reflected in the use of different writing systems where different writing systems coexist with religious differences. So far as the Soviet Union is concerned, this rule held until the initiation of conscious and deliberate language planning together with a drive towards atheism as a uniform phenomenon embracing Christians and Muslims.

dustry the more sophisticated technical operations involve the use of Russian, the local languages functioning at the level of casual discourse unless the degree of ethnic heterogeneity makes even the low-level use of national languages inconvenient. In science and technology, as well as state administration, Russian is asserting an almost exclusive functional prerogative, although the national languages take precedence in oral communication in severely local situations. In the domain of mass communication, too, Russian predominates. National languages are used in newspapers and periodical publications, and on radio and films, but their use is localized, and more and more readers are turning to Russian publications. Similarly, the non-Russian languages have very subordinate roles in trade and other public services. The local languages play a part in face-to-face oral communication, but Russian tends to be used for the recording of transactions. In the administration of justice all languages are guaranteed a role, and this is strictly observed, but only Russian is current in all courts and at all levels of legal affairs: in a union republic the basic language has no higher claims than has Russian, and the minority languages merely supplement the use of Russian by means of translation and interpretation.

These aspects of the functional differentiation among Soviet languages may be illustrated in the case of Yakut. Although this nationality has a 96.3% level of literacy and 16.4% have received secondary education, it is only in primary schools that the language is the medium of instruction. In the administration of law, in science and technology, Russian is used. The shift to Russian as the native language is accelerating (in 1939 less than 1% claimed Russian, by 1959 the figure was nearly 3%, and by 1971 it was nearly 5%). Similarly, though the Abaz language (spoken by nearly 20,000) was alphabeticized in the early 1920s, it has not been promoted as a language of secondary education. Schoolbooks of only the most elementary sort have been produced in the language, and adult literature is restricted to political literature and ephemeras. Even when Russian and another language are used for the same purposes there is considerable difference in the intensity of their employment. For instance, both Russian and Georgian are used in the Georgian SSSR in teaching physics. But because, it is claimed, earlier Georgian writings concerning physics have not covered all aspects of the subject, whereas Russian has, the use of the latter in this domain is far more intense than that of Georgian (Deseriev, 1973, p. 22).

Planning at an official level ensures the comprehensiveness of the Russian expropriation of sociolinguistic functions. In adapting to the lexical requirements of new social functions (contrary to the case of Welsh in relation to English), it is stressed that the dependence of the national languages on their inherent resources must be modified by the availability of Russian terms and the desirability of incorporating them: "the tendency must be strongly resisted to translate artificially into the native tongue terms which are already known to the masses in their Russian form, and which thus translated would become unintelligible" (Baskakov, 1960, p. 36). It is also stressed that sometimes Russian terms have to be introduced "if the literal translation of the Russian terms does not reflect the specific meaning given to them in Russian" and even when a language possesses a suitable indigenous item (Mordvinov, 1950, p. 6). Russian, unlike English in Wales, is being promoted as the sole intermediary for introducing into non-Russian languages any new international concepts and terminology. In most Soviet languages up to 80% of the new terms have been borrowed directly from Russian or from other sources via Russian (Vyshka, 20/6/72, p. 3). Thus Russian comes to be regarded not only as the source but also as the model for the development of non-Russian languages. The use of the Cyrillic alphabet is only one, though perhaps the most patent example of this tendency. The habit of forming new compound terms on Russian lines (Sov. Kirg. 10/4/73, p. 3), as well as the use of Russian models in forming abbreviations, contractions, and other linguistic innovations (Salys, 1967, p. 47) have been documented.

The influence of Russian is so comprehensive because it is the lingua franca, not simply for communicating information, but for ensuring the international sharing of cultural achievements: "the representatives of all the nationalities . . . exchange the accomplishments of their cultures only with the aid of the Russian language" (Mordvinov, 1950, p. 7); and this is not unlike the position in Wales in respect of English. In consequence the currency of the national languages in the Soviet Union (and of Welsh) is being limited more and more to intraethnic functions. In the early years of the Soviet regime there were possibilities that contact between nationalities might be mediated by the respective national languages, by a network of "reciprocal bilingualism," two nationality languages being acquired by significant numbers of both peoples. Thus, it was conceived that "Azeri ought to serve as a bond of union between Daghestan and neighbouring countries" (Samursky, 1931, pp. 117–18). This hope has been frustrated by the operation of one of the main elements in Soviet language planning: the obligation to take account of Russian as a second language. Among the factors which determine how a language's social functions should be allowed to develop, Deseriev includes the "level of a given people's political and cultural development, its possession of statehood, the size of the population speaking a language, and *the existence of a second language that performs extensive social functions*," in this case Russian. International communication is the province of Russian, and in Wales the function of English.

The comprehensiveness of the Russian influence (as of English in Wales) is matched by its exclusiveness—it tends to preempt other influences either from within or from outside the Soviet Union (or Britain). For instance Gagauz, like many other "small group" languages still spoken in the Soviet Union, survived as a viable means of communication through many vicissitudes because it has always been able to draw on multiple resources, not only upon Slavic languages such as Bulgarian and Russian, but Greek, Rumanian, Turkish and many others as well. Similarly, Welsh drew on French and Italian, and its vocabulary, morphology, and phonetic structure reflect the characteristics of several other languages, giving Welsh a peculiar individuality it would not have possessed had it been exposed exclusively to the influence of English.

With demographic penetration of Russian into Moldavia, and the intensification of Russian mass communication and Russian-based education, the viability of Gagauz is threatened. Among speakers of Gagauz who are bilingual only 8.6% claim a non-Russian language as their second language, while over 63% claim to be able to speak Russian along with Gagauz. It is probable that the 8.6% who speak Gagauz and a non-Russian language are trilingual, able to speak Russian as well. Gagauz is being drawn ever more firmly into the Russian embrace. Again, in the early years of the regime Uzbek linguists tried to replace terms that were being introduced from European Russia by words of Persian or Arabic provenance. This tendency was opposed, and because of the constant repetition and wide dissemination of Russian lexical items in the press, over the radio, and especially in teaching, Uzbek was unable to offset the strong Russian influence by other influences, some of which were more in character with its own traditional methods of language elaboration and development (Baskakov, 1960, p. 22). (The experience of Wales during this century has been very different, and attempts are made to borrow, where necessary, from original sources and not via English.)

There are at least three ways in which Russian has spread at the cost of the other languages of the Soviet Union; English at the cost of Welsh. Both have induced structural changes in orthography, phonology, vocabulary, and syntax. Evidence of these changes can be adduced (Lewis, 1972 and 1978b).* Second, Russian and English appropriated

---

*Cooper, in commenting on this paper, has suggested that structural change resulting from language contact should not be regarded as an aspect of language spread, but of "diffusion" of structural items. However, it is a fact that where structural change is caused by the influence of one language only (English in Wales, Russian in the Soviet Union) and where such influences are directed consciously as they are in the USSR so as to ensure the "rapprochement" of Russian and other languages, diffusion of items like the changes in writing systems comes to act as an agent of spread insofar as it facilitates the acquisition of Russian (or English).

more and more of the social functions of national languages within as well as between communities. Thus the social functions of national languages are limited, especially where advances in thought and innovations in science and technology might be expected to induce the development of their own resources, together with the resources of other languages, in promoting structural change. Third, because of the encroachment of Russian and English both functionally and demographically, speakers of non-Russian languages and of Welsh tend to "shift" to Russian or English, respectively, as their native language. For many ethnic groups, their native tongue is in the process of becoming their subordinate language. The second and third of the ways in which Russian affects the national languages not only reinforce the direct structural "interference" of Russian with these languages but are, potentially and in the long term, more influential than the first.

Garvin postulates two requirements in a standard language, namely flexible stability and intellectualization. "The codification needs to be flexible enough to allow for modification in line with cultural change and should allow increasing accuracy along an ascending scale of functional dialects from conversational to scientific" (Garvin, 1959). The argument which has been advanced here is that in spite of the considerable effort that has gone into the standardization of Soviet languages, the social influence of Russian is such as to frustrate the possibility of many Soviet languages achieving "flexibility" or "intellectualization," in Garvin's terms. This was the case with Welsh from the sixteenth to the nineteenth century. Many, though far from all, of these languages are in danger of declining demographically and of becoming restricted functionally. Narrowing the functional range leads eventually to stylistic inflexibility and to code restriction, a preponderant employment of a limited range of the resources of the language. This is a phenomenon frequently attested to in other contact situations (Lewis, 1974; Hill, 1973; Samarin, 1971). A child growing up in a bilingual situation who is denied the opportunity to use his native language as a means of acquiring the higher ranges of skill and knowledge, or to use it across the whole "range of social functions from conversation to science," will know only the range of usage found in the restricted code, and in time the structure of the language will atrophy. "The inner-structural development of a language depends in considerable degree, on the volume of its social functions" (Deseriev, 1973, p. 24). In evaluating the influence of the spread of Russian and English, the proposition should be entertained that the spread of these intrusive languages has accelerated the decline of the use of national languages, including Welsh, for their traditional functions, leading to language shift; and, secondly, has frustrated the same languages from operating in domains where the speakers of those languages have not been accustomed to operate. These two propositions lead to a third, namely that the structural characteristics of the national languages may be adversely affected by such restriction, inflexibility, and limited intellectualization, and that in the long term such restrictions are likely to have greater effect than direct structural influence. The difference between the USSR and Wales is that these processes are accelerating in the former and are at least being halted if not reversed in the latter.

ii) Wales

So far as Welsh is concerned, the functional aspects of language spread are almost completely the reverse of the functional aspects of the non-Russian languages in their relation to Russian. Welsh, contrary to the Soviet nationality languages like Bashkir, or Mari and to a lesser extent some of the Baltic languages, did not start at a disadvantage, either demographically—since Wales was almost completely Welsh speaking—nor from the standpoint of its functional adequacy—since it had been used for centuries at all levels of communication including the highest levels of scholarship. The Act of Union of 1563, while doing nothing to endanger the demographic status of the language, began a process of functional attenuation and erosion in favor of English. This process continued from the middle of the sixteenth to the middle of the nineteenth centuries. At that point the demographic and functional positions of the Welsh language began to be reversed. Within half a century the language was overrun by English in the crucial areas of economic development and modernization. At the same time the national consciousness of the Welsh, threatened as it was, and fed by the romantic and ethnocentric ideas of the late eighteenth century and by the Methodist religious movement, began to insist on a recognition of the value of the native language and to seek to repair the damage which had been done to it structurally because of its functional decline.

The structural survival of the language was largely the consequence of the efforts of poets and preachers working within the mold of the existing norms and styles. Nevertheless there were may writers and scholars who set out to revive the tradition of the Welsh humanists of the sixteeth century, who had worked in close contact with Italian and French scholars at Milan and Douai respectively, and had in mind the deliberate and conscious rehabilitation of the language: its deliberate planning. It cannot be said that the attention devoted to modifying the corpus of the language, overall, has been a major contribution to Welsh language planning. The level of disarray to which the language had declined was not so great as to require any tour de force of planning.

Nevertheless during the sixteenth and early seventeenth centuries and more recently, there has been conscious *"monitoring"* of the development of the language so as to ensure its functional adequacy and its independence from English in achieving functional adequacy. The term "monitoring" is used because planning Welsh has not entailed any significant changes in the alphabet, for example, which with a few minor exceptions has remained the same for over a millennium. Its grammar has evolved naturally: coming under some English influence, but never departing from its historic character. There has always been a standard form of Welsh pronunciation, due in large part to the fact that the tradition of Welsh verse—the use of strict meter involving rigid rules concerning consonantal alliteration, assonance and stress—meant that because of their close association with the courts of Welsh princes and with the aristocracy, those who were educated as bards set the standard of pronunciation nationally, whatever the dialect of the poet might be (Jones and Williams 1928).

Until 1928, agreement on Welsh orthography was most difficult and evasive. This was to be expected in view of the comparatively late arrival of mass literacy in Welsh. Spelling was apt to be idiosyncratic. Sir John Prys in the sixteenth century refers in his introduction to the first book published in Welsh to the changes he had been forced to introduce in printing the book. Salesbury, not very long after, conceded that "many who would have otherwise praised my work complained that I have perverted the whole orthography of the tongue." It was Sir John Rhys, Professor of Celtic at Oxford, and president of Jesus College, Oxford, who laid the foundations for the understanding of the historical principles of Welsh orthography, in his lectures at the end of the last century. His work promised the hope of a fair compromise between the demands of contemporary pronunciation and those of sound etymology, but the practical results were few. It was left to a group of scholars of the University of Wales, commissioned by the Board of Celtic Studies, to set out details of an agreed scientific orthography. It was included in the report of their work in 1928, *Orgraff yr Iaith Gymraeg: Welsh Orthography* (Lewis, 1928), and has been the foundation of scholarly practice for over fifty years, although some few improvements have been introduced from time to time. So far as the corpus of the language was concerned, the main problem was maintaining the traditional vocabulary against the onslaught of English and ensuring that the language continued to be its own source of the lexical productivity required by a modernizing society, and thus be able to meet the needs of scientific and technological as well as commercial and industrial advance.

Perhaps the most obvious aspect of the planning of Welsh to meet the challenge of English intrusiveness was the enrichment and purifying of the Welsh vocabulary. In the initial absence of acknowledged academic institutions in Wales itself, work on expanding the vocabulary was undertaken by individual lexicographers and interested laymen, many of whom behaved very arbitrarily. For instance, in 1775, Lewis Morris (a civil servant) wrote to his brother in London who was preparing a list of seashells: "You must make your *cregyn* (shells) Welsh names if they have none; there is no *if* in the case. You must give them names in Welsh . . . and it is an easy matter to invent new names and I warrant they will be as well received as Latin or Greek" (quoted in T.J. Morgan, 1966). During this century the University of Wales together with the Welsh Department of the Ministry of Education and the Schools Council have taken the lead in stabilizing the linguistic characteristics of Welsh, while at the same time creating a new variant. Educated speakers tended to use native Welsh terms in formal contexts and to turn to English items on other occasions. Place names, administrative, and scientific terms were always susceptible to English influence, and though the removal of foreign terms has been advocated regularly since the sixteenth century, there is little evidence that the number of English words is declining, though the occasion of their use as well as the form in which they are borrowed and employed are being controlled more effectively.

Three methods have been used to enrich the Welsh vocabulary: where words have been borrowed from other languages via English there is tendency now to revert to the original foreign form: thus Plato and Aristotle are now written as *Platon* and *Aristoteles*. Most technical terms appear in forms which, though hardly distinguishable in pronunciation from English, are introduced in written forms which are clearly Welsh. "Astronaut" has become *astronot*. Sometimes however no attempt is made to modify the pure English form as, e.g., "safety-belt" or "steeple-jack." Attempts have been made to introduce loan translations but many have not been accepted. Instances of such failures are *oer-gell* ("deep-freeze," literal translation: "cold cell") and *rhewgell* ("refrigerator," literal translation: "frost cell"). Other translations are more in keeping with the genius of the language, for instance "multiply" has given *amlhau* (aml = often + infinitive). If a technical term is hyphenated, sometimes one part may be borrowed while the other is entirely native: for instance "sonata-form" gives *ffurf-sonata*. Increasingly a second method of elaborating the vocabulary is adopted—exploiting the capacity of the language to produce new words by using Welsh affixes (of which there is an abundance) as part of the loan word. For instance the suffix *aid* (meaning full) is used with the English words "box" or "basket" to give *bocsaid* and *bascedaid* (boxful and basketful).

The third method of extending the vocabulary is to revive forgotten or scarcely remembered native terms, usually those associated with oc-cupations and crafts which have disappeared from the contemporary scene. The editors of the "Geirfa Natur" (Nature Terms) stated their aim to be "the discovery of terms which may still survive in some place or other and to include every word that is thought to have some value." Most of the terms had several dialect variants and some of these have now reappeared after a long absence in written and spoken Welsh, for instance *Asgell Fraith* for chaffinch, and *Croeso'r Gwanwyn* (Spring Welcome) for narcissus. Schools which use Welsh as a medium of instruction are popularizing these revivals, and many of them are used in dialect areas to which they are unaccustomed.

Because of the influence of English on the Welsh lexicon, two new features have been introduced into Welsh phonology: "ch" as in English "chips" or "chain"; and "j" as in English "jam" or "jury." A third sound was already a feature of Welsh phonology but had not hitherto appeared in positions where it is now common to find it: "sh" as in English "shave" used to appear in Welsh words only when "s" preceded "i" as in *eisiau* (pronounced "eishiau"). New symbols have been introduced to distinguish these new features. The definitive University Dictionary uses "ts" for "ch" as in *tsain* or *tsips* although many teachers prefer "tsh" as in *tships*. The "j" of "jail" has been incorporated as it stands, so that a new item has been introduced to the Welsh alphabet. The third sound is handled according to past practice when it occurs in nonfinal position as in "shop" spelled in Welsh as *siop*. In final position it is spelled as "s" alone, or as "sh" giving alternatively *brws* (brush) or *brwsh*.

The next most important aspect of the planned development of Welsh in the face of the intrusive English language was the standardization of the spoken language. Although Welsh has several dialects, they have not presented serious problems to mutual intelligibility on any linguistic level. In addition there existed from the middle of the seventeenth century a standard of spoken Welsh developed by nonconformist preachers who traveled throughout the country on their evangelizing missions. This "pulpit Welsh" was based upon the standards of the literary language which had been formed by the acceptance of the norms of medieval and early modern Welsh literature exemplified in the sixteenth-century translation of the Bible. The "preacher's standard" was important partly because it illustrated the advantages of national norms of spoken Welsh, and partly because, although it was too closely allied to the formal style of the Bible translation and therefore tended to be ponderous and somewhat inflated, the standards of spoken and written Welsh were closely related.

The pressures to stabilize contemporary spoken Welsh became irresistible only within the last two or three decades, although the need had long been felt. For instance, a Committee of the Cymmriodorion, meeting at Cardiff, found it impossible to carry on their discussions concerning the Welsh language because speakers of different dialects claimed that they were mutually unintelligible (Y Beirniad, 1897:54). The demand for a uniform spoken Welsh was intensified as well as facilitated by improved transport within Wales, greater mobility of labor between north and south as well as between rural and urban areas, but especially because of the increased emphasis on the teaching and use of Welsh in schools, particularly as a second language. The demand for educational technology to support this increased teaching pressure together with the mobility of the teacher-corps and the cost of producing tapes and records, etc., made it necessary to produce a model of spoken Welsh which would be acceptable in all parts of Wales as the foundation for an oral/aural approach. The University College at Swansea had initiated a project for limited standardization of spoken Welsh, and in 1964, a group in the Ministry of Education led by the present writer convened a national conference to enable the project to proceed farther. The first result was the production of *Cymraeg Byw* (parts 1 to 3), which offered such a model. Professor Williams, who wrote the introduction, maintained that "the purpose of the model was also to bridge the gap between the written and the spoken language and to offer the schools a model of spoken Welsh acceptable throughout the country, which will help Welsh-speaking children to polish their speech and non-Welsh speakers to learn the language more easily" (*Cymraeg Byw,* 1967). Since its publication the National Language Centre near Cardiff has produced *Geirfa a Chystrawen* (Vocabulary and Syntax) for use in teaching the spoken language and in examining students at sixteen years of age and at pre-university level.

3. MOVEMENTS LEADING TO LANGUAGE SPREAD

a) Colonization

i) The Soviet Union

The present linguistic and ethnic composition of the populations of Britain (so far as concerns the Celtic countries) and the Soviet Union is in each case the product of the conquest of some territories, the more or less pacific acquisition of others, colonization, and massive immigration—all acting on primordially native groups and interacting with each other. The United States and Canada, on the one hand, the Soviet Union and the Celtic-speaking peoples of Britain, on the other, exemplify two different but complementary processes of colonization and immigration. So far as North America is concerned, where very many different peoples have been attracted to one continent from many parts of the world—an intensive process of ethnic and linguistic *convergence*—the colonial movement is *centripetal.* In the case of Britain (English) and the USSR (Russian) the process has been *centrifugal:* English diffused in order to assimilate the peripheral Celtic lands to the north and west of Britain, as well as North America, while Russian from its Kievan and Muscovite bases spread to the European west and sought out the diverse Asian nations of the south and east. To all intents the United States, in spite of the predominance of the English language, has been a nation of *induced* diversity. Diversity was an inescapable consequence whatever attempts were made to ignore it; so that the American problem has always been to ensure unity while accommodating diversity. On the other hand, Russia and now the Soviet Union has always set out to *acquire* diversity. It was always able to enforce Russian political unity and prepare for linguistic dominance by its military strength and by the cult of the Orthodox Church, and now by the promotion of a single party, a uniform ideology. From its point of view the problem has been to acknowledge (without sustaining) the inescapable linguistic diversity within a uniform political system. Britain attempted to suppress linguistic diversity, and the Soviet Union began by seeking to preserve it. The different processes of colonization have resulted in different emphases on aspects of the intractable problem of the relation of linguistic unity and diversity, which is at the root of language spread.

It was not until 1552–54, when Ivan IV conquered the Khanates of Kazan and Astrakhan, that the seal was set on the transformation of the small Russian-speaking state into a multinational polyglot empire. With the acquisition of the North Caucasus in the middle of the sixteenth century, the period of very extended colonization got under way rapidly. From then on to the time of Peter the Great in the eighteenth century, Russian pushed northward to the province of Archangel, eastward into Siberia, and southward beyond the Caucasus. It met such linguistic groups as Nenets, Komi, Permean, Vogul, and Ostiak, and later the more numerous Mordvin-speaking group. Other linguistic groups like the Karelians and Estonians in the northwest, Tatar Finnic and Chuvash to the east, Lithuanians, Jews, Germans, and others on the Baltic seaboard had to contend with Russian. The advance into Central Asia, where the Uzbeks, Kirgiz, and Kazakhs, speaking traditionally important languages, had long established themselves in the territories which they have continued to occupy, did not occur until after the death of Peter. The North Caucasus including Daghestan with its thirty-two distinct linguistic groups became an area of Russian penetration in force only in 1813. South of the Caucasus, Georgia became a protectorate in 1783, and in 1831 eastern Armenia was annexed, thus extending the intrusive role of Russian.

As a result of these colonizing activities the linguistic pattern of the Russian state changed enormously. In 1724 the number of unassimilated non-Russians in the southern districts, alone, was over 2 million. By 1859 the figure was well over 4 million. At that time the total population of the Empire was 125 million of which 30 million were non-Russians, 17.5 million in the Asiatic parts. Of this Asiatic population 7.5 million inhabited the two main administrative divisions of Central Asia. Table 2 indicates the linguistic character of Central Asia at the beginning of this century.

At the end of the last century and at the beginning of this, the "Asiatic destiny" of Russia, which motivated the early process of colonization and a great deal of later immigration, was stressed as much as was the "manifest destiny" of the United States. Dostoevski (1896) wrote "this conquest of Asia is necessary because Russia is not only in Europe but also in Asia; because Russia is not only a European but an Asiatic power. Not only that: in our coming destiny, perhaps it is precisely Asia that represents our main way out."

ii) Wales

In spite of nearly six hundred years of existence as a conquered nation, the degree of English intrusiveness in Wales was relatively small, and most of it was inevitable because of geographical contiguity and ease of demographic penetration along the northern and southern seaboards, and in central Wales along the Severn Valley. In 1840, an observer claimed that over two-thirds of the total population of Wales still spoke Welsh, and of these, more than half were monolingual. The Commissioners of 1847 spoke of South Wales exhibiting the "phenomenon of a peculiar language isolating the mass from the upper portion of society." In 1848 it was estimated (Mills, p. 64) that 400,000 were monolingual Welsh, 200,000 had a slight acquaintance with English, another 200,000 spoke English well, while 100,000 spoke only English. Two-thirds of the population were Welsh speaking. In 1858 in a representative area of North Wales with a population of 52,000, there were "probably from 44,000 to 47,000 who may be said to speak and know Welsh only, while of the remaining 5,000 a large proportion amounting to at least two-thirds though conversant to a greater or lesser extent with English use Welsh as their vernacular language." Even in South Wales the same investigator estimated that 74% to 77% spoke Welsh habitually. The schools serving these areas maintained a high level of

Welsh, though they reflected the increasing influence of English on the
older children, and a growing disparity between the incidence of the
language in North and South Wales (Table 3).

Among the children under ten years of age the level of Welsh language maintenance was high and appreciably higher in North Wales
than in the South. Among the older children the decline amounted to a
loss of 28% in North Wales and 35% in the South, due no doubt to the
influence of exclusively English instruction in the schools and the increasing contact with English outside school. Ravanstein (1879) in his
pioneering investigation of the distribution of the Celtic languages
(Journal of the Royal Statistical Society) calculated in 1879 that Welsh
was spoken by 934,500 persons, 81% of the population three years and
over. There is wide variation in the estimates arising, with the exception
of Ravenstein's, from the partial coverage of any investigation, and
partly because the estimates were intuitive. Nevertheless it is probable
that the proportion of the Welsh-speaking population at the middle of
the nineteenth century was higher even than Ravenstein's figure. In
some areas it amounted to well over 90%.

The estimation of the size of the population prior to 1801 is an
entirely hazardous enterprise. Widely differing accounts have been offered, but it is now generally accepted that about the middle of the
sixteenth century the inhabitants of Wales numbered approximately
278,000. By 1700 they had increased to 419,000 and by 1800 to
587,000. During the period 1801–31 the increase in Wales alone kept
pace with the general increase for England and Wales together, although
the counties of Monmouth and Glamorgan were beginning to forge
ahead, the former moving from 46,000 to 98,000, and the latter from
72,000 to 126,000. In just over fifty years from 1800–51, the population of Wales doubled, something it had taken two hundred and fifty
years to do prior to 1800. In the nineteenth century as a whole it increased three times over. During the first part of the present century up
to 1950, the rate of increase declined considerably, the increase being
of the order of 32%. During the first twenty years of this century the
decennial increases for Wales alone were nearly double those of England and Wales together—20.3% and 9.5%, compared with 10.9%
and 4.9%. During the next forty years the population of Wales has been
relatively stable, while that of England and Wales together rose by an
average of 4.3%. In fact Wales suffered an overall reduction of 4.8%
during 1921–31, which corresponded to approximately one-fifth of the
rate of growth of the previous decade.

TABLE 2: Central Asia in 1897: linguistic composition (in thousands)

Division	Rus-sian	Kaz-akh	Uz-bek	Tatar	Turkic	Kara-Kalpak	Ujgur	Tad-zhik	Dun-gan	Euro-pean	Others	Total
Total	690	4,050	2,038	60	249	112	102	358	15	49	24	7,747
Steppe Krzy	493	1,903	–	42	–	–	–	–	–	10	18	2,466
Akmolinsk	226	427	–	11	–	–	–	–	–	8	10	682
Semi-palatinok	68	605	–	10	–	–	–	–	–	1	2	685
Turgay	35	411	–	3	–	–	–	–	–	–	4	453
Ural	164	461	–	18	–	–	–	–	–	1	2	645
Turkestan Krzy	197	2,147	2,038	18	249	112	102	358	15	39	6	5,281
Ferghana	10	260	1,139	1	–	19	41	97	–	5	–	1,572
Samarkand	14	71	518	–	–	–	–	245	–	11	1	860
Semirechye	95	790	15	8	–	–	61	–	14	1	4	988
Syr-Darya	45	952	365	5	–	93	–	7	1	10	–	1,478
Transcaspia	33	74	1	4	249	–	–	9	–	12	1	382

Source: Census of 1897.

TABLE 3: Competence in English and Welsh among pupils of some schools in North and South Wales (1858)

| | *Children under ten years* | | | | *Children over ten years* | | | |
| | *1* | *2* | *3* | *4* | *1* | *2* | *3* | *4* |
	Total	*Good English*	*Imperfect English*	*Welsh only*	*Total*	*Good English*	*Imperfect English*	*Welsh only*
N. Wales	903	110 (12%)	437 (48%)	356 (39%)	557	239 (43%)	244 (44%)	74 (13%)
S. Wales	374	111 (30%)	160 (43%)	103 (27%)	212	133 (63%)	67 (32%)	12 (6%)

Source: Appendix D, p. 631 of Reports of the Assistant Commissioners appointed to Enquire into The State of Popular Education in England and Wales. Vol. II, London, 1861. Percentages in columns 2, 3, and 4 are based on Totals in Column 1.

b) Modernization

i) Social-Value Change

Modernization tends to produce changes which appear to move in contrary directions according to the original level of social and economic development of the countries involved. Groups which are moving from a traditional to a post-traditional phase almost invariably tend to emphasize the preservation of traditional values and the ethnic language. Many of the Soviet nationalities are in this situation. Where there is a sudden acceleration of modernization in a country like Wales, which had already experienced it on a small scale, the same stress on traditional values is apt to appear. The recognition of traditional values and of the ethnic language arises largely from the fact that only in a modernizing society, where contact with other groups and languages is fairly frequent, does an ethnic group becomes self-conscious. Consciousness is a function of contact with others. A second reason is that in a modernizing society the ethnic language becomes a convenient, though not a necessary, instrument of literacy; and, in turn, learning to read and write promotes a greater respect for a language among those who speak it. One of the first, if temporary consequences of modernization is a resumption of interest in the ethnic language, coinciding with the spread of the intrusive language—English or Russian, in the present case.

If groups moving into a post-traditional phase of development stress the traditional values and the ethnic language, groups which have already modernized tend to support changes which cut across ethnic divisions, and are willing to substitute a language which is functionally better suited to a modern age for one which symbolizes the authenticity of their cultural values and their traditional way of life. Among such groups are the western nations of the Soviet Union—the Slavic, Romanic, and Baltic. This is also the case in Wales where the growth of Welsh language militancy is as much a response to an increasing awareness of a positive evaluation of English by the Welsh, as it is to the militants' positive evaluation of the Welsh language. In a modern or modernizing society, the tendency is toward unilateral bilingualism, only the minorities—in this case, the Welsh and the Soviet nationalities—learn a second language. Few English immigrants learn Welsh and proportionately fewer Russians learn a minority language.

ii) Population Mobility

In Tsarist Russia after the Emancipation, there was a great deal of internal migration of Russians, partly a response to the economic conditions in the densely populated areas which had made Emancipation necessary in the first place. Since the downfall of the Tsarist regime, Russian penetration to the west and north but more especially into the vast Central Asian territories has been pushing forward unceasingly. Although explorers since the fifteenth century were interested in the area, which covers nearly 45% of the total territory of the USSR and is inhabited by over fifty different ethnic groups, the imperial dynasties had not been greatly interested in Asiatic Russia. But after the discovery of gold in the nineteenth century, an intense economic interest was roused, and at the end of the century the imperial administration began to promote migration to Siberia as well as to the Central Asian lands. With subsidization and the setting up of the All Union Migration Committee in 1925, movement of Russians beyond the Urals accelerated and in this the Trans-Siberian Railway helped considerably. Exiles and prisoners as well as peasants helped to increase the number of migrants from 375,000 between 1801 and 1850 to 2,310,000 by 1900. From 1900 to the end of the Revolution over 3,000,000 (mostly native speakers of Russian) are estimated to have settled in the area.

There were no Russians in the East Siberian Region at the beginning of the seventeenth century: a hundred years later they accounted for 40% of the population. This large nucleus of a Russian-speaking population subsequently attracted to the same area members of the same language group. Thus the ratios of speakers of Russian to the indigenous ethnic groups changed completely. Having been about equal at the start of the nineteenth century the Russians became the majority (62%) fifty years later, and have continued to increase. Many, like the Transbaykalian Tungus, were Russified; and some, like Aga Buryats, escaped that condition only by isolating themselves territorially and shunning contact.

Turkestan Kray had 200,000 Russians in 1897, 3% of its total population. In 1911 the number of Russians had increased to 410,000 (7%). Table 4 shows that in 1920 the Russians represented an even greater proportion of the Turkestan population.

In the same period (1897–1911) the Russian penetration of the Steppe Kray had increased from 20% of the total population to 75% (Census 1930). In 1934 the number of Russians in the territory now recognized as the Estonian SSR was 41,000. By 1959 (Table 5) they had increased sixfold and by 1970 over eightfold, to a total of 335,000 (Census 1970). The history of nearly all the other federated republics is similar:

Only in Georgia, Lithuania, and Armenia is the Russian element less than 10% of the total population. The flood of Russian immigration has been retarded in only one Republic, Georgia, where the total of Russians was reduced by 11,000 between 1959 and 1970. Elsewhere the tendency has been very much in favor of Russian immigration.

The abnormal growth of the population of Wales, especially in South

TABLE 4: Number (in thousands) and percentage of Russians in
the total population of each oblast in the Turkestan A.S.S.R.; 1920

Amu-Darya		Semirechye		Samarkand		Syr-Darya		Turkmen		Ferghana	
No.	%	No.	%	No.	%	No.	%	No.	%	No.	%
5.7	3.6	268.8	28.0	21	2.7	167	12.8	30	9	48	2.3

Source: 1930 Census

Wales, like that of the non-Russian areas of the USSR, is a reflection of
the development of industry. Before 1750, the economy of Wales was
pastoral and depressed. The extractive and metallurgical industries
which were later to change the whole economic life, the culture, and
the language of South Wales were sparse and sporadic. Coal was ex-
tracted by individual farmers and only where it outcropped on their
land. Since the beginning of the eighteenth century, furnaces and forges
using this coal had sprung up in small and scattered hamlets. Even
when, with the help of English capital, the local landowners who owned
the coal and iron deposits were able to expand, the required work force
was recruited from neighboring Welsh-speaking villages and townships.
These industrial changes were made possible by and have led to large
increases of population in a few areas, and this selective increase is
characterized in turn by considerable migration, in the first instance,
from Welsh-speaking areas and, only later, in large numbers from England. During the last one hundred years the population of Welsh-
speaking mid-Wales has fallen by over 25% and in the present century
alone by over 17% compared with a 50% increase in Wales as a whole.
The recognized pool of Welsh speech has become increasingly shallow.
In terms both of actual numbers and of proportions of the population,
the balance has shifted progressively to South Wales, though after 1911
the English midland counties have tended increasingly to attract rural
emigrants, thus accentuating even more the Welsh language losses. The
decline of rural Wales cannot be attributed exclusively to out-migration,
however. The rate of natural increase has almost invariably been unfavorable to the rural areas, and this disadvantage has tended to increase.
The rate of natural increase for England and Wales from 1951 to 1961
was 4.5% and for Wales alone 3.4%. During the same period in the
Mid-Wales rural counties it was only 0.4%. In the two most thoroughly
Welsh-speaking counties, Merioneth and Cardiganshire, deaths exceeded births. Consequently in those three counties, Caernarvon, Cardigan, and Merioneth, the decline in natural growth has been greater
than out-migration by 8.5%, 14.8%, and 6.6% respectively.

Population mobility has not been restricted to the immigration of
nonindigenous groups. On the contrary, so far as the Soviet Union is

TABLE 5: Number (in thousands) and percentage of Russians in the Federated Republics, 1959–70

Republic	Total population		Indigenous population				Russian population			
	1959	1970	1959 No.	%	1970 No.	%	1959 No.	%	1970 No.	%
RSFSR (Russian Rep.)	117,534	130,079					97,844	83.8	107,748	82.8
Ukrainian	41,869	47,126	32,158	77.0	35,284	74.9	7,091	16.9	9,126	19.4
Belorussian	8,056	9,002	6,532	81.1	7,280	81.0	660	8.2	938	10.4
Uzbekistan	8,261	11,960	5,044	61.1	7,734	64.7	1,114	13.5	1,496	12.5
Kazakhstan	9,153	12,849	2,727	29.8	4,161	32.4	3,950	43.2	5,500	42.8
Georgia	4,044	4,656	2,601	64.3	3,131	66.8	408	10.1	397	8.5
Azerbaydzhan	3,698	5,117	2,494	67.5	3,777	73.8	501	13.6	510	10.6
Lithuania	2,711	3,128	2,151	79.3	2,507	80.1	231	8.5	268	8.6
Moldavia	2,885	3,569	1,887	65.4	2,304	64.6	293	10.2	414	11.6
Latvia	2,093	2,364	1,298	62.0	1,342	56.8	556	26.6	705	29.8
Kirgizia	2,066	2,933	837	40.5	1,285	43.8	624	30.2	856	29.2
Tadzhikstan	1,981	2,900	1,051	53.1	1,630	56.2	283	13.3	344	11.9
Armenia	1,763	2,492	1,552	88.0	2,208	88.6	56	3.2	66	2.7
Turkmen	1,516	2,159	924	60.9	1,417	65.6	263	17.3	313	14.5
Estonia	1,197	1,356	893	74.6	925	68.2	240	20.1	335	24.7

Source: Soviet Census 1970 Izvestiya Apr. 1971.

concerned the attraction of rural elements to expanding or entirely new urban areas has been far greater than "long distance" migration. The depopulation of the Welsh-speaking rural counties was not a total loss to the Welsh language, any more than it has been to the local languages of the Soviet Union. In fact Pokshishevsky (1972) claims that, apart from reinforcing the already urbanized indigenous and native-speaking populations of heterogenous cities, such depopulation may serve the indigenous language by intensifying the ethnic consciousness of speakers of the languages in urban areas.

The period 1851–71 in Wales is characterized by short-distance migration, very much of it to and from adjacent Welsh-speaking counties. The condition of the language in South Wales at present would be very much poorer than it is if the migration from England had not previously as well as simultaneously been offset by the deployment of the internal human resources of Wales. During the period 1850 to 1871 about 70% of the migrants into Glamorgan came from the neighboring Welsh-speaking counties. A large proportion of these immigrants were monolingual Welsh or nearly so. It was between 1871 and 1881 that long-distance migration really set in, so that only 38% came from the five neighboring counties, while migration from the southwest counties of England rose rapidly to 37%.

One feature of very early short-distance migration from Welsh areas which census figures cannot reveal, but which was of great importance, was its occasional or seasonal character. Farm workers and owners of small holdings in Carmarthenshire and Breconshire were accustomed to move into the iron works and mines of Monmouthshire and Glamorgan during the slack farming seasons and return home when the pressure of farm work required their presence. This constant mobility had two opposite consequences. It helped regularly to reinforce the existing Welsh character of the industrial areas. At the same time it facilitated the disintegration of the settled traditional Welsh pattern of rural life, helped to promote the acceptance of novel ideas, and to prepare the way for the forces tending towards the anglicization of even remote rural areas. Such consequences are a part of seasonal migration or commuting and are characteristic of the USSR and other parts of Europe as well. This aspect of migration assumed greater importance in the short period between 1876 and 1879 in Wales, when temporary recession drove large numbers of short-distance migrants back to the farms.

The history of immigration into Wales is largely, though not entirely, the history of changes in the economic life of the South Wales coalfield. Glamorgan and Monmouth were high in the order of urbanizing counties, next after London, Durham, and Lancashire in the middle of the last century. Considering one indicator of urbanization—population growth—the urbanization of Glamorgan was faster and more intensive even than that of the Durham coalfield in the north of England. By 1871 the urbanization of the British Isles was concentrated in the north (Durham and Lancashire), the Midlands (Staffordshire and Warwickshire), London, and the two South Wales counties, Glamorgan and Monmouthshire. Furthermore, urbanization, following industrialization and migration in Wales, did not spread to other counties, although the urban population of the principality as a whole intensified because of migration into the two coal-mining counties.

Glamorgan has a "special place in the history of internal migration in Britain," and belongs to a group of English and Welsh counties which experienced a net positive gain in the first period, between 1851 and 1871, and net losses thereafter—a simple and consistent equation. Between 1801 and 1851, when the population of Glamorgan more than trebled from 71,000 to 232,000, the county was still largely agricultural and Welsh speaking, with a population density at the end of that period which was less than that of even Cornwall or Somerset, i.e., 243 compared with 259 and 289 per square mile. During the next 60 years, while the population of England and Wales as a whole rose by only 80%, there was more than a fivefold rise in Glamorgan. Over half a million of this increase was accounted for by immigration, of these 67% were recruited from neighboring English counties: Somerset, Gloucester, Devon, Wiltshire, and Hereford. There was therefore both a massive rise in the number of migrants and, equally important, a decisive shift in the area of origin. When the total number of in-migrants was held to no more than 21,000 (1861–1871), the main areas of origin were Welsh, who provided 3 of every 4 migrants. As the numbers increased to 74,000, then to 108,000, 105,000 and finally, in 1911 to 128,000, the Welsh contribution fell to 1 in every 2. Between 1861 and 1911 the number of nonnative-born inhabitants of Glamorgan increased to 390,000, which represented the residuum of nearly 430,000 migrants,* over 55% of them English monolinguals. The ratio of nonnative to native-born remained constant between 1861 and 1911, at around 35%, and this constant ratio, in view of the rapid rise in the total population, is due to the equally constant reinforcement we have described. After 1911 the ratio falls to 21% because of the cessation of in-migration. But the decline in the ratio is no consolation from the standpoint of the Welsh language, because the second and third generation migrants though native born were predominantly if not exclusively English in speech.

---

*After allowing for "reverse migration."

The resistance to English still evident in Glamorgan is due partly to the fact that industrialization began in the strongest Welsh-speaking areas—the hills—and was fed by migrants from other Welsh-speaking areas. This was the first phase, ending around 1850; and it is consideration of this phase which has led some researchers to maintain that industrialization and immigration did not affect the Welsh language adversely (Thomas, 1930). Their contention is valid for this first phase and for this first phase only. During the second phase (from 1845 to 1890) the balance of "cultural advantage" finally swung decisively to the side of anglicization and with it went the last hope of preserving a Welsh culture on the coalfield. The second phase was characterized by a predominantly English labor supply, which was massive but of a relatively short duration. The first phase gave the Welsh language an opportunity to adapt to change: the second phase was too intense and too rapid to allow the English to be assimilated. This fact was stressed by the Commission of Enquiry into Industrial Unrest. Until 1895 "the inhabitants, in many respects, showed a marked capacity for stamping their own impress on all newcomers, and communicating to them a large measure of all their own characteristics. Of more recent years the process of assimilation had been unable to keep pace with the continuing influx of the English-speaking immigrants."

iii) Age Differentials

Another aspect of population mobility which favors the intrusive language is the fact that the immigrants of whatever nationality tend to be young and better educated than the average. For instance, the percentage of those over 60 in the Central Asian in-migration areas is about half that of the Russian-speaking areas. In 1970, while the proportion of the total Soviet population under 29 years was 49%, the proportion of that age group in Central Asia was over 63%. Since 1959, the proportion of the total Soviet population in the same age group has fallen by 5.5% but the proportion in Central Asia has risen by approximately 1% (1959 Census, 1962–1963 and 1970 Census reported in Komm. Tadzh. May 6, 1971). Already more than half the youngest citizens of the Union live outside the Russian Republic, although the population of that republic represented over 54% of the total population of the Soviet Union. Sixty percent of the immigrants between 16 and 29 became urbanized in 1964. Of the age group 15 to 24 in a Novosibirsk village approximately 35% moved into large towns and cities (Vest. Stats 7:1965). Most of the parents involved in such moves had a higher or complete secondary education. Only 13% of those studied in a 1972 survey (Toplin) had not continued beyond the elementary level. About 40% were engineers, technicians, or office workers. These were highly motivated young people whose ambitions for their children were not likely to be met if those children received an education which was principally in the national language. Furthermore a willingness to speak a local language when a prestige language is also part of the child's repertoire does not usually characterize young people in bilingual countries. In fact among non-Russians, the younger the age group, the more likely its members are to claim Russian as its native language. Generally speaking, twice as many young people between the ages of 10 and 19 compared with men and women between 25 and 29 tend to shift away gradually from their native tongue. Table 6 instances four minority nationalities which may in the context of the Soviet Union be regarded as comparable to the Welsh in Britain.

The same differences in the sex and age distribution of immigrants compared with the stable population is revealed in Wales. Thus in 1921, at the end of the period of massive immigration into Wales, the only counties to show a disproportionate number of males were the industrial areas of Glamorgan (964 females per 1,000 males), Monmouthshire (940 per 1,000), and Breconshire (973). The areas of Wales which had supplied the work force in the first phase of industrialization had a considerable preponderance of females over males: Cardigan (1.187), Caernarvonshire (1.183), Merioneth (1.143) (Census 1921, p. 62). The 1921 Census does not provide the same breakdown of the age distribution by counties. But if we compare the whole of Wales to areas in England, like the southern counties, including those in the west, Wales has a population which is higher than average between the ages 5 and 49 and lower than average thereafter while the southern counties reveal the exact opposite distribution (Census 1921, p.71). These differences between the age and sex distribution of immigrants and those of the stable population are reflected in the linguistic distribution. Monolingual English-speaking persons are most numerous at ages 15–25, bilinguals at 45–65, and monolingual Welsh-speaking persons at 65 and upwards.

It would, of course, be erroneous to argue that the current linguistic composition of the Soviet Union or of Wales is entirely the result of migration. It is the product of the conquest of some territories, the more or less pacific acquisition of others, colonization, as well as massive migration. However, though English and Russian are alike in having adopted aggressively intrusive roles, the mode of that intrusion has differed in some areas of spread and is alike in other areas.

For example, if we omit the relatively small Amerindian population, so far as postcolonial United States is concerned, the main linguistic feature has been the convergence and centripetal descent of many lan-

TABLE 6: Percentage of population claiming the
Russian language as its native tongue

Ages	Chuvash	Mari	Mordvin	Udmurt
All ages	16	16	22	23
10–19 years	34	28	58	36

Source: 1959 Census.

guages on a single territory where English was already well established. In the Soviet Union, as in Wales, the main characteristics of language spread have been until comparatively recently the result of long-standing historical contact between geographically contiguous, stable ethnic groups sharing common frontiers. Furthermore while the American immigrations, for instance, brought together very many languages simultaneously to provide a potential restriction on the spread of English, contacts between different languages in the Soviet Union, until comparatively recently, have been phased: a particular ethnic group might experience contact with several other ethnic groups during its history but hardly ever would the same group face many other groups at the same time in any one place.

Traditional European language-contact also differs from postcolonial contact in the United States. In the former language interaction has been of a phased character and the present situation reflects the phasing. For instance Baskakov (1973) points to the successive layers of linguistic influence within Gagauz, spoken in parts of Moldavia. The language is close to Turkic, and, because of this basic affinity, it is in fact easier to distinguish the Greek, Romanic, and Slavonic adstrata than the original Turkic element. This is true of Welsh also, where we can identify continental and later insular Latin influence, post-Roman English, Norman French, and finally modern English influences in phased sequence affecting the fate of Welsh. Such phasing of contacts enables a language like Welsh or a Soviet nationality language to adapt to even powerful novel linguistic influences and yet maintain its inherent character. In the United States the immigrant languages, with some exceptions, tend not to change but to disappear. So far as the spread of English in Wales is concerned, its history corresponds to the European (and Soviet) rather than to the North American pattern.

c) Intermarriage

The linguistic effect of such movements on both the stable and migrant language groups is reinforced by the increase in interethnic marriages. Since the Russian Revolution, migration has offered greater opportunities for such marriages and the taboos against them have tended to be ignored. For instance, in Ashkabad between 1951 and 1965, 29% of the marriages involved men and women of different nationalities. Twenty percent of the marriages in Tashkent and Samarkand belong to the same category. In Frunze the percentage rose between 1953 and 1962 from 22.4 to 27%. In Tataria, marriage between Tatars and members of other nationalities amounts to 13.2% of the total number of marriages (Busygin and Zorin, 1973). "In zones of ethnic contacts with multinational populations (borderlines between different ethnic areas, big cities, areas interspersed with populations of different nationalities, etc.) mixed marriages produce families which prove micro-environments for the processes of integration and natural assimilation." Mixed marriages are most likely in the Baltic republics: they increased from 25% of all marriages there in 1960 to 32% in 1964. On the other hand, only 6.3% of all marriages in Armenia were ethnically mixed in 1970 (3.8% in villages). In the USSR as a whole, 13.5% of all families were of mixed nationality in 1970, of which 17.5% were urban and 7.9% rural. Linguistic trends show an increasing preference for Russian; though this is not great: 6.1% of the population indicated the language of another nationality as their native tongue in 1970—an increase of only 0.4% since 1959; 87% of this number indicated Russian. The most marked Russian trend was among Jews, Germans, Poles, Hungarians, and Romanians. Tatars giving Tatar as their native language declined from 35.2% to 29.2% (1969–70), while neighboring Bashkirs increased their native speakers from 61.9% to 66.2%. The biggest increase in native-language use was among the Gypsies: 59.3% to 70.8%.

Among the factors determining the ethnic development in such families "the leading role is played by the language and national self-consciousness" (Gantaskaya and Terentieva, 1973). The result is a long period of bilingualism tending finally to Russian, since in most cases the spouses speak different languages even though they may share knowledge of the Russian language. Where one of the parents is of European Soviet origin, though the children may continue to use the local language with their grandparents, the main language is Russian. In the two districts of Tashkent, a 1963 survey (Lewis 1972) showed that where one of the parents was a native speaker of Russian, that language became the normal means of communication in 79% and 47% of the families, respectively. In 86% and 54% of the cases in the two districts the children adopted Russian as their native language. In Latvia the number of 10th grade students who claimed Russian as their native tongue was found to be considerably greater in mixed families, whatever the nationality of the parents, than in families where both parents were of the same language group: 33% of such students were bilinguals claiming Lettish and Russian (Kholmogorov, 1970). Often Russian becomes the basic language of the families even though neither of the parents is a native speaker of the language.

However, the tendency toward Russian is not equally strong in all such families. A great deal depends on the locality and the linguistic environment. In Kazakhstan, when both parents were Slavs (Russians, Ukrainians or Belorussians), 85% to 100% of the children in most areas chose Russian. But when one of the parents was a Kazakh though the other might be Russian or Tatar, because of the local influence, 67% to 90% of the children chose Kazakh (Nauchnyi Komm, 73, 4:2834). In mixed Daghestan families, where one parent was a member of the indigenous nationality, 82% of the children chose the native language of the area, and 17% chose Russian. Where both parents were members of different nationalities though still indigenous to Daghestan, the choice tended to be evenly divided between the two nationalities. Where one parent was Russian and the other was a member of a nation indigenous to the North Caucasus, though not of the ethnic group among whom they lived, two-thirds of the children chose Russian as their native tongue (Sergeeva and Smirnova, 1971:4). Busygin and Zorin (1973) conclude from their data on the middle Volga that "Russian is the basic language in bi-national families. This is the case with 85% of all the surveyed interethnic families. The remaining 15% use both Russian and the national language."

Ethnicity as such does not possess the same significance in Wales as it does in the Soviet Union, and this hinders us from making age and sex comparisons between native Welsh speakers and English immigrants. The ethnic differences between Welsh and English have long since been eroded by intermarriage. Except in the case of immigrants to Wales, and not very often then, ethnicity is no longer a safe marker. All we can do is use the data which record the *language* of the parents. From Table 7 it is clear that at every age there are great differences in the language claimed by the child according to the linguistic composition of the home. Where both parents speak Welsh, 70% of the children claim Welsh as their first language, compared with 6.1% where the father alone speaks the language, and 10.5% where the mother alone does so. These differences are also reinforced by the linguistic character of the environment of the home. Whereas in Wales, as a whole, the figures are as we have stated, in Glamorgan which is heavily English speaking the respective percentages are 42% (both parents), 4% (father alone), and 7% (mother alone). In the most thoroughly Welsh-speaking areas of Wales (Merionethshire and Caernarvonshire), the figures are 96% and 91% (both parents), 19% and 20% (father only), and 43% and 39% (mother only).

TABLE 7: Pupils between 5 and 15 years classified according to
the relation of their first language to the language of their parents

Age group	Pupils both of whose parents speak Welsh			Pupils whose fathers alone speak Welsh			Pupils whose mothers alone speak Welsh		
1	2	3	4	5	6	7	8	9	10
	Total of pupils	No. of Pupils whose 1st language is Welsh	3 as % of 2	Total of pupils	No. of Pupils whose 1st language is Welsh	6 as % of 5	Total of pupils	No. of Pupils whose 1st language is Welsh	9 as % of 8
5– 6	6,310	4,763	75.5	2,324	183	7.9	1,951	289	14.8
6– 7	7,061	5,215	73.9	2,576	154	6.0	2,126	296	13.9
7– 8	7,104	5,140	72.4	2,707	154	5.7	2,311	244	10.6
8– 9	6,567	4,694	71.5	2,543	125	4.9	2,176	237	10.9
9–10	6,252	4,304	68.8	2,379	143	6.0	2,085	174	8.3
10–11	6,442	4,361	67.7	2,384	106	4.4	2,171	186	8.6
11–12	7,334	5,209	68.6	2,763	159	5.8	2,475	222	9.0
12–13	6,780	4,519	66.7	2,696	198	7.3	2,293	232	10.1
13–14	6,587	4,423	67.1	2,446	175	7.2	2,236	234	10.5
14–15	5,828	3,958	67.9	2,024	129	6.4	1,722	149	8.7
Totals + %s	66,265	46,406	70.0	24,842	1,528	6.1	21,546	2,263	10.5

Source: The Place of Welsh and English in the Schools of Wales (1953).

In 1961 statistics were gathered concerning the same variables as were analyzed in 1951. It was found that in the first place there had been a sharp decline of 19% in the number of homes where both parents claimed to be able to speak Welsh as first or second language. At the same time the percentage of families where only one parent made such a claim for the language had risen. In each of the three categories of family (Welsh claimed by both parents, by father only, or by mother only) there had also been a decline in the percentage of children claiming Welsh as their first language: 3% in the case of homes where both parents spoke Welsh, and 9% and 6% in each of the others. The effect of linguistically mixed marriages is not only an immediate phenomenon, but is intensified as the years go on (WJEC Language Survey, 1961). It is noteworthy in this respect that both in the Soviet Union and Wales, migrants tend to be younger than the stable population, they are predominantly males and possess a higher level of education. Consequently ethnically or, as in the case of Wales, "linguistically" mixed marriages tend to attract the younger and abler men. This generally means that the intrusive language—English or Russian—has an additional advantage since the men, involved in the more extended network of communications, favor the language of wider communication, while the women, more usually concerned with the limited environment of the home, generally favor the ethnic language. This effect is very evident with respect to the Soviet Union.

4. AGENCIES

Whereas social "movements" tend to have a comprehensive and diffused influence and are frequently difficult to define because of the many aspects of social change they represent, "agencies" are more limited in their aims and the scope of their influence. They have been defined as "action personified" (O.E.D.), and in the context of our discussion they are the immediate personal or institutional channels of language spread, maintenance, or restriction. In one sense every speaker of a particular language and every institution which makes use of it is an agent. Consequently the number and kinds of agencies are literally too numerous to describe. What we can do is categorize types of agencies and compare the Soviet Union and Wales from the standpoint of the importance they attach to such categories. It is important to distinguish between agencies which promote (or limit) the spread of a language by acting as motivators, propagandists, and pressure groups, on the one hand, and agencies which react to such pressure and use the language without necessarily being particularly concerned with its fate.

The first category of agency may propagandize the spread of Welsh, for example, without itself using the Welsh language. This was the case of the Honourable Society of Cymmrodorion and is also at present the case among many branches of the Socialist Party in Wales. Agencies in the second category might use Welsh as a matter of expediency or because they are forced to do so by governmental departments, examples being the "nationalized" corporate bodies like the Inland Revenue, the transport system, or the post and telecommunications. Policy, in all respects, is determined by the Central Authority.

The second distinction to be made is between "voluntary" and "state dependent" agencies. Such voluntary agencies may be broadly cultural, political or religious, or simply linguistic in their orientation, and there is plenty of evidence of their existence. However, generally speaking they have been attached to languages under threat, the national languages in the Soviet Union, or Welsh in Wales. The Armenian Church is a good example of a non-state-controlled agency which is able to do a little towards the maintenance of Armenian; but among such religious organizations, those of the Muslim peoples of Central Asia are undoubtedly the most powerful. In the field of political action there is virtually little scope for spreading Soviet national languages, though there are occasional short discussions concerning the linguistic disadvantages of the politically encouraged development of intermarriage. Sometimes, too, the state-encouraged concept of the "merging" of languages is vigorously attacked and as vigorously defended. The most powerful agents of the national languages in the Soviet Union are the individual artists and writers who insist, in spite of official disapproval, on working within their own native languages. Among them are Tatar novelists and playwrights, Ibragim, Amirkhan, and Burnash, as well as the Uzbek Filrat, Kadri, Cholpan, and many others, especially among the Kazakhs.

In Wales not only do individual writers similarly act as agents, but many cultural and quasiacademic organizations have been set up to promote the Welsh language. Of the more informal but prestigious agencies, perhaps the most important is the Honourable Society of the Cymmrodorion (literally translated The Honourable Fellowship). It was founded in London by expatriate Welshmen in 1751 and reconstituted in 1830 and 1873. Apart from the publications of its transactions annually (in English) during the nineteenth century, its meetings and investigations drew attention to the declining fortunes of Welsh literature. In the late nineteenth century its meetings, some of which were held in Wales, were devoted to attempting to whip up some enthusiasm for the place of Welsh in primary schools. It circulated questionnaires and, in conjunction with the old Welsh Language Society and the Movement for the Use of Welsh, it served as a pressure group on the then Privy Council Committee for Education (later the Board of Education) to have the codes which governed the school curriculum changed so as to allow for the teaching of Welsh, initially as a voluntary subject and then as a class or examinable subject.

Two other institutions have played important parts in promoting the status of the language. The National Museum of Wales, apart from being a focal point for interest in the history of Wales, has an important Folk Department (now a separate Welsh Folk Museum) in which folk studies are encouraged, rapidly dying dialects are recorded, and the results published. Perhaps its most important function, however, is to confirm a *national* status for Welsh culture and for its study, much as the National Library of Wales has done for Welsh bibliographical scholarship as well as for the collection and preservation of Welsh manuscripts. The National Library shares with the British Library, the National Library of Scotland, and the Bodleian Library (Oxford) the prestige of being a library of deposit, having the same kind of status, though less prestige, as the Library of Congress.

In the last resort, however, whether in an authoritarian country like the USSR or a democratic country like Wales, it is the attitude and the efforts of the state which are most influential in promoting or restricting the spread of a language. Under the Tsars, Russian was the official language of the empire, and what Matthew Arnold (1857) wrote of the Welsh language could equally well have been written by a Tsarist official: "There can I think be no question but that the acquirement of the English language should be more and more insisted upon by your Lordships in your relations with these schools, as the one main object for which your aid is granted. Whatever encouragement individuals may think it desirable to give to the preservation of the Welsh language . . . it must always be the desire of a government to render its dominions as far as possible homogenous. . . . Sooner or later the difference of language between England and Wales will probably be effaced" (Arnold, 1908, pp. 10–12). The state has always acted both directly, e.g., in forbidding the use of Welsh in the sixteenth century, and indirectly by financing the agencies it favors. And since so far as Wales and the Soviet Union are concerned, radio/TV and book publishing are almost entirely subsidized from state funds, directly or indirectly the state is the principal agency. Though they are not, strictly speaking, state agencies, the units of local administration, as well as nationalized industries like coal, gas, electricity, and transportation, can do very little but act in conformity with the policies laid down by the state.

Next to the system of formal education in schools and colleges, no one doubts that the state-controlled radio and TV, within the short time they have existed, have contributed most to the use of Welsh on public occasions, to the diversification of the varieties of Welsh so used, to the embellishment of the language especially so far as concerns vocabulary, as well as to improving the understanding of the place of Welsh in the life of the Welsh-speaking population. General radio and television are organized so as to provide a national coverage for Wales. Together with Independent (commercial) TV, they ensure an average of approximately three hours of "radio broadcasts" in Welsh on two or three nights or more at peak hours. Welsh programs meant for general listening and/or viewing include Welsh drama, comedy, documentary and travel programs, and political discussion, news and commentary. In addition the BBC broadcasts on sound radio *Dewch I Siarad* ("Let's Speak Welsh"), which is a well-articulated, progressive program for non-Welsh speakers. Though the broadcasting companies provide more time than the proportion of speakers of Welsh would appear to justify, the number who habitually listen to and view Welsh language programs is relatively low. For instance, the number of children between the ages of 5 and 15 registered in the schools of Wales in 1976 was 389,500. Of this number only 35,000 (9%) listened to such programs.

Even more important in many ways is the work done for Welsh by the Schools Broadcasting TV sections of the BBC and Independent Television, and by BBC radio. The BBC alone broadcasts Welsh programs for over thirty hours annually in primary grades and for ninety-six hours in secondary grades, in addition to broadcasting programs in English about Wales. The programs range from those catering to pre-school listeners to those for pre-university age groups. In addition to the programs themselves, which are received by approximately 75% of all schools (though not all schools take all or even more than a very few programs regularly), an extensive range of literature, (pupil guides, teacher guides, background material for several of the programs, film-strips, work cards and evaluations) accompany the programs. The broadcasting authorities have their own committees in Wales, on which teachers are represented, and the Welsh committees arrange training programs in teacher training colleges in which the use of broadcast programs in Welsh is explained and the teachers prepared for their use.

Considerable advances have been made in the publication of Welsh books, and the distribution and promotion of such publications have been well organized. One of the most active cultural agencies in Wales, covering all the arts, is the Welsh Arts Council (an affiliate of the Arts Council of England and Wales). They make grants to promising writers of Welsh literature, offer scholarships to enable writers to obtain sabbaticals for more intensive effort, free of their normal occupations; they run competitions and make grants to the British Broadcasting Authority in Wales to broadcast agreed programs in Welsh. The Council has its own book shop where Welsh books are displayed. There exists also the Welsh Book Council, which is associated in part with almost every other "book promotion" agency in Wales, and which, in the area of school books, tends to duplicate efforts of agencies like the WJEC, the Schools Council, and the National Language Unit. The work of the University Press Board is devoted almost exclusively to academic and scholarly works. By and large all the financial support for these activities is provided from public funds, central or local government. Even independent publishers are subsidized from central government funds, the University acting as distributing agent. The distribution of Welsh books by means of public libraries is satisfactory since the libraries themselves are in close touch with the localities they serve and possess an excellent network of mobile libraries.

Since the passing of the Welsh Act of 1967, the position of Welsh "in any legal proceedings in Wales and Monmouthshire is that the Welsh language may be spoken by any party, witness, or other person who desires to use it subject . . . to prior notice. And any necessary provision for interpretation shall be made accordingly." The same stipulation applies to the preparation of legal and administrative documents. Where the use of the language is felt to be important to a local administrative unit, like county councils, the choice of language and of how translation or interpretation is handled is left to the local authority. At the same time, in all cases, the English version of any document or statement is deemed to be the authoritative one (Welsh Language Act 1967, ch. 66). This enactment has ensured that Welsh is an official (albeit subordinate) language; most official forms are available on request in either language within Wales. The change in the status of the language was made on the recommendation of a committee presided over by an eminent Welsh-speaking academic jurist. The committee enunciated the principle of "equal validity": in all situations the use of either language was deemed to be equally acceptable officially.

The most recent committee to consider the language (The Council for the Welsh Language, 1978) argued that the principle of "equal validity" has not brought any improvement and recommended that a new principle should be substituted. The former principle placed the emphasis on the right of the individual to choose either Welsh or English, whatever his competence in either. The more recent suggestion goes beyond this and proposes that policy for the language should aim to produce in all inhabitants of Wales an equal ability in both languages. Choice of language is made to depend on being able to use either language with something like equal competence. The former principle recognized the right of any monolingual person to be ignorant of either language. The new principle seeks to postulate that no person can be free to choose unless he has something like equal competence in both. "Every individual should . . . achieve sufficient facility in both Welsh and English to *choose* which of the two languages to use on all occasions and for all purposes in Wales." The first principle is based on the existence of a bilingual society in which both languages are equal, as is the case in Switzerland, though particular individuals may choose not to be bilingual. The second principle envisages not so much a bilingual society as a society which *consists entirely of bilingual individuals,* much as is the case in the Republic of South Africa with respect to English and Afrikaans.

In spite of considerable efforts there is little evidence of the spread of Welsh. The most exhaustive analysis of the use of Welsh was made by the Council for Wales and Monmouthshire: *The Welsh Language Today* (1963). They found that the demand to use Welsh by participants in legal causes (civil and criminal) amounted to no more than one in two thousand cases. The most frequent requests occurred in the local Magistrates Courts, though there is no doubt that more would have used the language had they not thought that using it might prejudice their case. In administration, Welsh is spoken frequently in communications between citizens and officers in thoroughly Welsh-speaking areas. This is certainly the case in rural areas and more especially among the older generations. Once we move out of the thoroughly Welsh-speaking areas, the amount of Welsh used in administration falls dramatically. Furthermore where the writing of the language is concerned there is a marked disinclination to choose Welsh rather than English. Nine percent of the local authorities use only Welsh in their meetings, while another 9% use both Welsh and English. The same percentage prepare their minutes only in Welsh, while 13% use both languages. Among all local authorities, 10% consider Welsh essential to their employees, and of this 10%, 70% of the administrative employees have to do with education. Ten percent of the authorities consider Welsh to be an advantage to their officers and of this 10%, 25% have to do with education. Five percent of the authorities initiate correspondence in Welsh in a substantial proportion of cases, and an additional 9% initiate such correspondence in Welsh sometimes. Over 56% reply to Welsh correspondence in the same language, and 42% reply to Welsh correspondence in English (Council for Wales and Monmouthshire 1963).

Welsh is used very extensively in the agricultural occupations, especially in the Welsh-speaking areas of the north and northwest. This is truer of the older generations, but the younger generations make frequent use of the language as well. There is very much less use of Welsh in commerce, but this varies somewhat according to the linguistic background of the area. Welsh is still strong among certain types of industrial workers such as woolen manufacturers, weavers, and quarry men. However whether the workers tend to use Welsh or not, the management cling to the use of English. The Council's report makes it clear that the trend over the last forty years has been for the Welsh language to decline as a means of communication in industry and commerce of all kinds. The Report of the Council for Wales and Monmouthshire (*The Welsh Language Today*) concludes that "the frontiers of the Welsh language in commerce, industry and especially agriculture are receding very rapidly, and in those areas which are most thoroughly Welsh speaking, the young people are certainly more completely bilingual than they used to be in their ordinary conversation." Nevertheless there are large areas of North and West Wales where ignorance of Welsh would be a considerable disadvantage to those who are occupied in the industries we have referred to.

Finally, of all the agencies of the state, the most influential is the system of education; and in this area of social action, Wales and the Soviet Union have, over many years, succeeded in setting up almost identical systems of bilingual education directed to promote the spread of the major language (English or Russian), while seeking, ostensibly, to safeguard Welsh or the national languages if that is the wish of the parents. In both countries English/Russian is taught to all students of whatever nationality from the age of seven. There are English/Russian-medium schools for those whose native language is English or Russian, but nonnative speakers of these languages can also choose to attend such schools. Second, there are Welsh or national-language medium schools where Russian is taught as a second language. In the Soviet Union there are also schools where a nonnational minority language, like Armenian in Georgia, may be used as a medium of instruction, with Georgian and Russian also being taught. There is a third type of school, referred to as "the integrated school" in the Soviet Union, where two or more language groups, like Lettish and Russian in Latvia, are taught in their native languages, while the other is learned as a second language. Thus there is one school accommodating two language streams, or more. However, whereas the Soviet Union has created such schools in areas where the national languages are immensely stronger than Russian, and has done so as a means of promoting Russian, which is the language of school administration, in Wales the reverse is the case. The language of instruction has been predominantly English, even in the strongest Welsh-speaking areas, so that the introduction of a "Welsh-medium" stream is meant to restrict the spread of English.

This difference between Wales and the USSR is illustrated by two other educational developments which reveal the relaxation of the principle of linguistic homogeneity so confidently expressed by Matthew Arnold. The first development is the creation of special schools. Children who come from Welsh-speaking families, but are submerged in the dominantly English atmosphere of their normal English neighborhood school, are offered the opportunity to transfer to selected schools, conveniently situated to receive them. In the designated or specially selected school most of the curriculum is handled in Welsh, and these *Ysgolion Cymraeg* (Welsh Schools) function in anglicized areas exactly as a school in a thoroughly Welsh area would do. The first of these special schools was created by a group of parents in 1939, under the aegis of the *Urdd* (Welsh League of Youth). Since that time they have been organized by the local authorities. By 1977 over eighty such primary schools had been formed throughout Wales, catering to nine thousand children. In anglicized areas there are ten secondary schools which are almost exclusively Welsh medium catering to over five thousand students, some of whom take their university examinations in Welsh. The second recent educational development is the Welsh Nursery School Movement (*Mudiad Ysgolion Meithrin*). Most of these Ysgolion Meithrin are part-time, play-school organizations. In 1977 there were well over three hundred of them, and their activities were coordinated by a full time organizer grant-aided by central government. Apart from the establishment of new types of schools and the extension of the teaching and use of Welsh in existing schools, an increasing amount of research has been devoted to the subject of Welsh studies. This is organized by the Schools Council Committee for Wales, The National Language Centre, and by University Departments of Education or of Welsh.

Undoubtedly the University of Wales is the principal academic institution involved at all levels of the spread of Welsh planning, since it has played a vital role in monitoring changes in the formal characteristics of the language and has contributed also to the improvement of its status as well as the extension of its social functions. During its early days in the middle of the last century the University, through the University Press Board, was primarily concerned with editing and publishing the hitherto unavailable texts of the sixteenth century and earlier, and, by this means, it not only added to the effective corpus of the literature, but ensured that the texts on which the normalization of the Welsh language had been founded were available for the critical examination of scholars interested in justifying or modifying the language in accordance with new criteria. Associated with the University are the Board of Celtic Studies, which plays an important part in contributing to corpus planning and monitoring, the Guild of Graduates, which has initiated developments in status planning by offering evidence to important commissions concerning the future of the language and by acting as a pressure group. Branches of the Guild also publish, in Welsh, papers delivered at meetings of specialists of various descriptions, such as *Efrydian Athronyddol* (Philosophical Studies), thus maintaining the high prestige of the language among scholars and helping to enrich its vocabulary and stylistic range. Part of the University's function has been to promote extramural studies whereby faculty members have conducted extensive lecture series in remote areas of Wales and thus brought home Welsh scholarship and a knowledge and appreciation of Welsh literature to otherwise isolated communities. The University, though slow in taking up the challenge, has of recent years promoted the use of Welsh in its own teaching of subjects like geography, anthropology, history, chemistry and philosophy up to the doctoral level. Finally it has played an important function in the training of teachers of Welsh, in the first instance for secondary schools. But of recent years it has been brought into the area of primary-school teacher-training, and so is able to promote the status of Welsh at all academic levels.

5. CONCLUSION

Welsh has progressed far since the prohibition of its use in the sixteenth century. There is hardly any part of Wales where the language is not used, and in many of the thoroughly Welsh-speaking areas it is used in nearly all social, scientific, and technical contexts, though not extensively. So far as the "corpus" of the language is concerned, there is again no doubt that it is as well written as ever it was, and spoken much more fluently in some areas than it used to be. In other areas it is spoken less well, but the dialectal differences have tended to disappear, and the written and spoken language to that extent may be said to be *national*. How long the position will last is a debatable point. The number of those claiming to speak the language is less than 20% at present and the proportion able to write it much smaller (14.5%). Of these a high proportion will have learned Welsh as a second language. It is this combination of falling numbers and the loss of "naturalness" which militates most against the language. The promotion of Welsh has been successful in maintaining knowledge of the language (competence), but it can be argued that the practical aspects of language use (performance) have declined, and this latter decline can be attributed in some measure to planning which has kept alive a language that many think has been dying. In Wales a strong case can be made for the proposition that while, demographically, Welsh is continuing to decline, there is an increasing proportion of Welsh speakers who speak Welsh as a second language. At the same time the "functional" aspects of Welsh have improved. So that we are faced with fewer people, many with only a mediocre command of the language, having the option to use it for more purposes, some of them the most prestigious. It is an ominous situation, suggesting the creation of an increasingly militant, declining minority disproportionately reflecting the views of and led by ministers of religion, university and school teachers, and "intellectual" professional interests, as well as small but highly "activist" University student groups. In the Soviet Union the reverse is the case. There is little danger demographically to the main national languages, but an increasing threat to the maintenance of their functions. Soviet élitism is a function of the acquisition of Russian, though there are intellectualist leaders of groups speaking national languages. However, the latter are supported dominantly by those who belong to lower occupational strata.

REFERENCES

Arnold, Matthew. *Reports on Elementary Schools* (Collected Edition, 1908). London: HMSO, 1857.

Baskakov, N. A. *The Turkic Languages of Central Asia* (translation). Oxford: Central Asian Centre, 1960.

Baskakov, N. A. The scope of Adstrat influences on a language functioning in complicated interethnic relations. Paper to the Ninth Congress of Anthropology and Ethnology, Chicago, 1973. Pre-congress paper.

Bernard, P. J. *Planning in the Soviet Union* (translation). Oxford: Pergamon Press, 1970.

Busygin, E. P. and N. V. Zorin. Interethnic families in the national republics of the middle reaches of the Volga. Paper to the Ninth Congress of Anthropology and Ethnology, Chicago, 1973. Pre-congress paper.

Central Advisory Council for Education. *The Place of Welsh and English in the Schools of Wales,* E. G. Lewis, ed. London: HMSO, 1953.

Commission of Enquiry into the State of Education in Wales. London: HMSO, 1847.

Cooper, Robert L. A framework for the study of language spread. This volume.

Council for the Welsh Language. *A Future for the Welsh Language.* Cardiff: HMSO, 1978.

Council for Wales and Monmouthshire. *The Welsh Language Today.* London: HMSO, 1963.

Cymraeg Byw. Cardiff: Welsh Joint Education Committee, 1967.

Deseriev, Y. *The Development of the Languages of the USSR* (in Russian). Moscow: Moscow University Press, 1966.

Deseriev, Y. Social linguistics. *Language in Society* 3, 1973.

Deseriev, Y. and Prochenko, I. *Patterns in the Development and Interaction of Languages in the Soviet Union* (in Russian). Moscow: Moscow University Press, 1966.

Dostoevski, Feodor. *Selected Works* (in Russian). St. Petersburg, 1896.

Gantaskaya, C. A. and L. N. Terentieva. The ethnos and the family in the USSR. Paper to the Ninth Congress of Anthropology and Ethnology, Chicago, 1973.

Garvin, Paul. The standard language problem: concepts and methods. *Anthropological Linguistics* 2: 28–31, 1959.

Hill, Jane H. Language death, language contact, and language evolution. Paper to the Ninth Congress of Anthropology and Ethnology, Chicago, 1973.

Jones, E. J. and G. J. Williams. *Y Penceirddiaid.* Cardiff: University of Wales Press, 1928.

Kholmogorov, A. *International Character of Soviet Nations: Based on Concrete Sociological Studies in the Baltic.* Moscow: Moscow University Press, 1970.

Lewis, E. Glyn. Multilingualism in the Soviet Union. The Hague: Mouton, 1972.

Lewis, E. Glyn. The sociological bases of the inter-relationship of Soviet languages. *Forum Linguisticum* I and II, 1974.

Lewis, E. Glyn. Bilingualism and bilingual education: the ancient world to the Renaissance. In B. Spolsky and R. L. Cooper, eds., *Frontiers of Bilingual Education.* Rowley, Mass.: Newbury House, 1978 (a).

Lewis, E. Glyn. Bilingualism and social change in the USSR. In B. Spolsky and R. L. Cooper, eds., *Case Studies in Bilingual Education.* Rowley, Mass.: Newbury House, 1978(b).

Lewis, E. Glyn. Bilingualism in education in Wales. In B. Spolsky and R. L. Cooper, eds., *Case Studies in Bilingual Education.* Rowley, Mass.: Newbury House, 1978 (c).

Lewis, Henry, ed. *Orgraff yr Iaith Gymraeg.* Cardiff: University of Wales Press, 1928.

Mills, John. Y Cymry, Y Gymraeg a Gwybodaeth. *Traethodudd,* 1848. Pp. 62–71.

Mordvinov, A. E. Language development in Soviet nationalities (in Russian). *Voprosy Filosofi* 3, 1950.

Morgan, T. J. Quoted in Geiriadurwyr y Ddeunawfed Ganrif. *Llen Cymru* 10, 1966.

Paper, Herbert H. Language spread: the ancient Near Eastern world. This volume.

Pokshishevsky, V. V. Urbanization and ethnogeographical processes (in Russian). *In Problemy Urbanizatsii.* Moscow: Moscow University Press, 1971. Pp. 52–62.

Ravanstein, E. G. On the Celtic languages in the British Isles. Journal of the Royal Statistical Society 42: 579–636, 1879.

Salys, A. The Russification of the Lithuanian vocabulary under the Soviets. *Litanus* 13: 2, 1967.

Samarin, William. Salient and substantive pidginization. In Dell Hymes, ed., *Pidginization and Creolization of Languages.* London: 1971.

Samursky, E. *Dagestan* (in Russian). Leningrad-Moscow, 1931.

Sergeeva, G. A. and I. Smirnova. The question of ethnic self-identification of urban youth. *Sovetskaya Etnografiya* 4: 86–92, 1971.

Thomas, B. The migration of labour into the Glamorgan coalfield. *Economica* 10: 275–92, 1930.

Thomas, B. *The Welsh Economy: Studies in Expansion.* Cardiff: University of Wales Press, 1967.

Toplin, A. Regulation population migration in the eastern regions of the Russian republic (in Russian). *Planovye Khozavistvo,* 1972.

Watkins, A. *Ieitheg.* Cardiff: University of Wales Press, 1967.

Welsh Joint Education Committee. *Language Survey.* Cardiff, 1961.

Y Beirniad. Volume 12, 1897.

Nationalism and the Mandarin Movement: The First Half-Century

Dayle Barnes[1]

I. THE EMERGENCE OF NATIONALISM IN CHINA

A. The Historical Background

It was not until the last decade of the nineteenth century that a specific national consciousness began to emerge among Chinese intellectuals. Throughout the preceding centuries of China's long history, its domestic institutions, as well as its relationships with other countries, had developed in a way which was quite different from the growth of the nation-state in Europe.

Internally, the traditional Chinese governmental apparatus operated in accord with a body of ethical and political precepts which were viewed as universal in character. The functionaries in this government were scholars qualified by their mastery of an immense corpus of canonical literature. They in turn served an Emperor who, in his conduct of the realm and in his personal behavior, exemplified those universally valid norms upon which harmonious relations between man and man, and ultimately between man and nature, were predicated.

Externally, relationships between the Chinese Empire and other states with whom she had contact were based on a formula consistent with this world view. The unique role of the Emperor as a mediary standing between man and the natural universe implied that other civilizations were necessarily morally and culturally inferior to China's. It was only appropriate, therefore, that formal relationships between China and other states would be conducted on an unequal basis. Given the dominance of Chinese civilization throughout most of East Asian history, together with China's relative isolation from the main currents of Western civilization until the middle of the nineteenth century, there was little in the world which most Chinese encountered to challenge this historically sanctioned way of life. "Sinocentrism," according to one historian, "was deeply rooted in geography as well as culture" (Bianco 1971: 3).

Its attitudes toward other peoples shaped by this world view, China was "a world in itself, not a nation among nations" (Fairbank 1968: 12). However, during the latter half of the nineteenth century a stubborn adherence on the part of the Chinese leadership to this world view proved increasingly unrealistic. Beginning with the cession of Hong Kong to the British in 1842 and intensifying alarmingly after 1895, the Chinese government was unable to prevent foreign powers from annexing and occupying tract after tract of Chinese territory. The palpable national humiliation, together with the uncertainty of China's future as a sovereign entity, gave rise to the decidedly nationalistic feelings which have suffused Chinese history throughout our era.

The initial Chinese responses to this Western challenge were cosmetic. Military technology and Western knowledge were selectively imported as reinforcements in an attempt to preserve the traditional Chinese political structure, the Chinese scholar-bureaucracy, and the Manchu ethnic minority which had ruled the country since 1644 (Biggerstaff 1961: passim). The inadequacy of this policy was searingly exposed in 1895, when China was defeated at the hands of tiny Japan, a nation historically regarded with condescension by Chinese as a cultural vassal state. Forced at last to recognize the extent of their vulnerability, Chinese began to question their venerable political system and, eventually, even the social and cultural presuppositions which underlay it.

Thus, in the years before 1911, the dominant mood of China's educated citizenry was a nationalism committed to the eradication of political and territorial encroachments and to the organization of a modern nation-state capable of guaranteeing China's sovereignty. The Manchu Dynasty, unable either to lead or to dodge the forces of change, came under attack as an alien element and was swept away in the revolution which marked the beginning of the Republican era (Wright 1968: 3–4).

B. Writing Reform

Language was not exempted from the evaluation of social institutions which began in China in the 1890s. Both the spoken and the written language came under scrutiny, but proposals for modification of the written language have been more numerous, the reactions to them on the part of Chinese more volatile, and the analysis devoted to them by scholars more probing. This was perhaps inevitable, first because of the historical role of the written language in its classical form in the transmission of traditional learning and values and, secondly, because the script has proved thus far to be such a durable emblem of distinctively Chinese ethnicity. However, in this attempt to trace the origin and development of the national language question, there is only space to present the briefest summary of orthographic matters before turning to the Mandarin Movement itself.

Perhaps the most widely publicized change in written language habits from the traditional period was marked by the decision, reached in 1917, to write in such a way as to approximate contemporary vernacular speech, discontinuing the centuries-old practice among literate individuals of writing in the classical style, which had centuries earlier ceased to function as a medium of communication.

This important linguistic revolution, which Chinese refer to as *baihua yundong* (the Vernacular Language Movement), is an example of the elevation to prominence of a writing style long available within the society but previously unsanctioned for serious writing purposes.

In the Chinese case, vernacular writing had been employed principally in literature written for entertainment rather than for scholarship. Thus, for centuries China's literate elite had written philosophy and poetry in the classical style, surreptitiously creating and enjoying fiction and drama written in the vernacular (Hightower 1966: 102–03). In the decade before the revolution of 1911, newspaper publication in the vernacular language was attempted by a few reform-minded Chinese but, without exception, these experiments attracted little notice and few readers, and quickly disappeared (Fan 1963: passim).

In the latter half of the nineteenth century, Protestant missionaries often selected the vernacular language as the best medium for translating religious literature into Chinese (DeFrancis 1948: 20), and in so doing, the missionaries increased slightly the total amount of publication in the vernacular. But as uninvited propagators of an alien religion whose work was ultimately protected by foreign troops garrisoned in China, the missionaries' use of the vernacular contributed little to the enhancement of its prestige among most literate Chinese.

Only in 1917—fourteen years after the beginning of western education in China, twelve years after the abolition of the Confucian-oriented civil service examinations, and six years after the political revolution of 1911—did the twin traditions of classical scholarship and classical writing collapse. Already accepted by the educated public, the institutionalization of vernacular writing in the schools was first mandated in 1920 (Wang 1951: 160).

A second thrust relating to written-language reform was directed not at the style of writing but at the character orthography itself. Beginning in the 1890s, Chinese authored dozens of proposals to adapt or to alter the traditional character script in order to render it more easily accessible to an immense body of potential learners (Ni 1958: 61).

Perhaps the best known of these initiatives is the decision made by the People's Republic of China in 1955 to substitute simpler forms for a large number of the traditional and complex characters previously in general use. Some of the simplified forms have been available for centuries as variants of the complex characters, while others have only relatively recently been established. Simplified characters were in the past reserved for informal writing purposes, and so this program is really an analogue at the level of orthography to the substitution of the vernacular language for the classical: both events reflect the reallocation of functions to previously existing forms, and both were achieved with indigenous resources.

The adoption of phonetic annotation systems to facilitate acquisition of the character script has undoubtedly served a useful purpose by reducing illiteracy and improving formal education. These systems, too, have their antecedents in China's pre-modern period.

No proposal to replace the character script has yet met with acceptance, but speculation continues as to whether the romanized annotation system currently used in the People's Republic of China, known as *pinyin*, may eventually supersede the character script. This matter, however, has been treated in considerable detail elsewhere (DeFrancis 1950; 1967: passim).

II. THE DEVELOPMENT OF A NATIONAL LANGUAGE POLICY IN CHINA

A. Linguistic and Geographic Boundaries

The languages spoken by contemporary Chinese on the Chinese mainland, on Taiwan, and in overseas Chinese communities are in reality "divergent modern forms of a common original tongue of some centuries ago" (Swadesh 1952: 274). Linguistic criteria have been employed to divide these languages into eight major groups—North Chinese (Mandarin), Wu (spoken in Shanghai), Xiang, Gan, Kejia (Hakka), and Northern and Southern Min (Fukienese) (Lo and Lü 1956: 5–6). The accompanying table indicates that by far the largest number of ethnic Chinese on the China mainland speak one of the varieties of North Chinese or Mandarin, while perhaps a little less than one-third of the population uses natively another of the regional forms of speech.

Geographically, North Chinese speakers are actually distributed quite widely over the heavily populated central areas of the country in a belt running from Manchuria in the northeast to the provinces of Szechuan, Yunnan, and Kweichow in the southwest (see Fig. 1). Speakers of the other "dialect" groups are concentrated in the southeastern provinces along the South China Sea coast. The amount of difference which obtains between these speech groups has been obscured by the tradition of referring to them as "dialects," and there is compelling evidence that speakers of these groups are not as a rule capable of intercommunication. It seems more appropriate, therefore, to regard these "dialects" as regional languages insofar as speech is concerned.

Figure 1. Modern Chinese Regional Language Distribution.
Source: Paul Kratochvil, *The Chinese Language Today*
(London: Hutchinson University Library, 1968).

Modern Chinese Regional Language Distribution
(estimated, 1979)

Name	Geographic Location (approximate)	Number of Speakers*	
		in millions	percentage (to nearest %)
North Chinese (Mandarin)	North of the Yangtze River; northeastern provinces; southwestern provinces;	674.5	71.0
Wu	Kiangsu-Chekiang	76.0	8.0
Xiang	Hunan	47.5	5.0
Gan	Kiangsi	19.0	2.0
Kejia (Hakka)	Kwangtung	38.0	4.0
Yue (Cantonese)	Kwangtung	47.5	5.0
Southern Min (Fukienese)	Fukien	28.5	3.0
Northern Min (Fukienese)	Fukien	9.5	1.0
Total		940.5	99.0

Source: Lo and Lü 1956: 5–6.

*These figures are unsubstantiated estimates for 1979. It is assumed that China's total population was 950 million, and that the percentage of distribution of native speakers of its several regional languages is the same as in 1953, when the first national census was reported. The figures include the population on Taiwan, but not those living in Chinese communities abroad.

B. Functional and Status Aspects

Interestingly, the prestige of North Chinese or Mandarin was not until comparatively recent times commensurate with its dominating position geographically and demographically. *Guan hua* 'the language used by officialdom', the term by which Mandarin was known in imperial times, was "technically . . . the language of the court and its capital—Pekingese under most of the Ming and all of the Ch'ing" (Latourette 1964: 643). Successful candidates for government service who grew up speaking natively a regional language other than North Chinese eventually acquired some form of the latter for professional use in situations requiring face-to-face dealings with functionaries in the capital or with other scholar-officials whose native languages they did not use. The special significance of the dialect of the city of Peking as a linguistic norm for the North Chinese dialect area is thus largely attributable to its status as the language of state business. It has also had a certain formative influence on the other North Chinese dialects as a consequence of the assignment of imperial officials to service in the provinces (Forrest 1965: 8).

The *guan hua* of imperial days was not quite the same thing as the speech of Peking, nor was it in all respects a prototype for the national language program of current times. Rather, it was not a language at all in the ordinary sense, but, in the words of the Chinese phonologist, "une style de langue parlée, arrangé en modifiant quelques élémentes d'un dialecte afin qu'il puisse être plus facilement compris par ceux qui parlent les autres dialectes" (Liu 1925: 51).

It was this language, for example, which the Jesuit orders elected to learn in connection with their missionary activity in China beginning in the sixteenth century. The renowned Father Matteo Ricci (1552–1610) referred to it as "an official language for civil and forensic use . . . [which is] now in vogue among the cultured classes, and is used between strangers and the inhabitants of the province they may visit." Ricci added that "a province dialect would not be used in polite society, although the more cultured classes might use it in their home province as a sign of neighborliness . . ." (Ricci Journals 1953: 29). The public functions for which this early Mandarin was employed in the sixteenth century, toward the end of the Ming Dynasty, apparently remained very much the same through the nineteenth century, when British Embassy personnel learned it in preparation for official dealings with their counterparts in the imperial government (Kennedy 1964: 301).

The dominance of Mandarin in the conduct of government business was based for the most part on practical considerations rather than on the acclaimed prestige of the language itself. Its exclusive franchise within the government sphere did not extend routinely into other domains of discourse. Rather, it appears that a relationship of functional complementarity obtained between *guan hua* and the other regional languages. In this relationship, the regional languages served until early in the twentieth century as the vehicles through which a classical education was acquired. True, in education lay the key to service in the imperial government, but education began in one's home province and its substance was conveyed in the local language. Such was the prestige accruing to each of these local forms of speech as a consequence of its role in the transmission and perpetuation of classical knowledge that within China no one form of speech was generally recognized as a standard national language (Chao 1961: 171).

Excerpts drawn from the life of the Chinese linguist Chao Yuen Ren (b. 1892) are suggestive of what further research may reveal to be a general pattern. The ancestral home of the Chao family was in the city of Changchow, in the Wu-speaking portion of the province of Kiangsu in the Yangtze River basin near Shanghai. Chao himself, however, was actually born in Tientsin, and in the first eight years of his life before his family returned to Changchow, he lived in the North Chinese-speaking province of Hobei, in which the capital city of Peking is located.

It was during these years that Chao began his education, proceeding as was the custom of the time to write, pronounce, and finally to memorize whole texts of the traditional Confucian canon. Nevertheless, despite their residence in the province of Hobei, and the fact that Chao's mother spoke Pekingese, the family did not consider the selection of a local and therefore North Chinese-speaking scholar to serve as his tutor. Instead, a teacher native to the Changchow area was invited north to live with the Chao family so that in his formal education the pronunciation of the home locality would be preserved. Indeed, in this family of Changchow (Wu) speakers living in Hobei, not only was a Peking-speaking tutor considered unsuitable as a teacher but, in the opinion of one of Chao's cousins, Pekingese enjoyed a social status no higher than the language of the North Chinese-speaking servants who worked in their home (Chao 1971: 304). Additional evidence of the language component in local solidarity and identification would clearly be of great interest.

C. The Last Decade of Ch'ing Dynasty Administration, 1900–1911

It has been observed that "when no one can read or write, it makes little difference in what language they are illiterate; the introduction of universal education, however, makes the choice of language instruction imperative . . ." (Rustow 1968: 104). In China, too, the earliest steps in the direction of the national language were coincident with the imperial government's decision in 1903 to inaugurate a system of public education. The content of this policy stipulated only that existing courses on Chinese classical literature in the prescribed curriculum should include instruction in the pronunciation of *guan hua* (MOE 1934: 591). Some of the shortcomings of the educational reform as a whole were reflected in the difficulty of implementing even this modest language initiative. No provision was made in these early plans for the training of teachers, and so there could be no common instructional strategy. Neither were there any teaching materials suitable for classroom use. Reflecting a pattern which would recur frequently, the implementation of national educational policy depended heavily upon the inclination and the resources of local schools (Li 1935: 24–25). The result was a very irregular level of compliance with the policy, particularly in areas where the influence of regional languages was strongest.[2]

The events of the decade 1900–1910, during which the Ch'ing dynasty began to concede participation rights in public administration, led to a refinement of the 1903 policy. By 1910, the Ch'ing Ministry of Education had acceded in principle to a program in which *guan hua* would be taught as a subject, beginning with the fifth grade. It had also agreed that, beginning in 1916, the ability to teach *guan hua* would be included among the requirements for certification of teaching competence (Ibid.: 31).

To these plans were added a parallel set of recommendations emanating from the Central Educational Conference, a separate advisory organ reporting in 1911 to the Ch'ing Ministry of Education. Addressing one of the major defects in the 1903 plan, this conference proposed the establishment of a Mandarin training center. Graduates of the center, which was to be established in Peking, would assume responsibility for conducting in-service teacher training programs in their home districts. On the negative side, by incorporating into the definition of *guan hua* certain phonological elements found in other Chinese regional languages but not found in Mandarin (QMWJ 1958: 143–44), the conference modified the earlier sense of *guan hua* as a national language based on the speech of a well-defined geographical area.

D. The Conference on the Unification of Reading Pronunciation

The Republican revolution of 1911 nullified the work, but not the concerns, of language educators. Soon thereafter, the Ministry of Education of the new government announced the organization of a Conference on the Unification of Reading Pronunciation (*Duyin tongyi hui*; hereafter CURP), which convened in the spring of 1913. The CURP took a conservative attitude toward the need to provide education in a single Chinese language. As its very name suggested, CURP was charged with deciding upon a phonological standard which could serve the entire country as a point of reference whenever Chinese literature was read aloud in the school system. Because substantial portions of the Chinese curriculum did involve reading aloud either by teachers or by students, and because of the importance still attached to the pronunciation of characters according to often very old phonological conventions, the limited focus of the CURP's work insured that some obsolete readings of characters would live on as relics in the new national pronunciation.

The likelihood that this might occur was probably enhanced by the way in which the delegates to the CURP were selected. Earlier groups dealing with the language question generally comprised active, professional educators who were often nominated by officials at the national level. However, the spirit of the immediate post-revolutionary period dictated a larger participatory role for the provinces, and thus perhaps conduced to a relatively traditionally-minded membership. The criteria for nomination as a delegate were diverse, and could be satisfied by those accomplished in any one of four kinds of skills: an understanding of native language sounds, a knowledge of one or more regional languages, competence in one or more foreign languages, or experience in elementary education (Fang 1965: 17–18).

This meeting of relatively obscure language scholars attracted little public notice (Li 1935: 65). During this period power was already slipping away from the inexperienced Republican leadership into the hands of military leaders and particularly the president, Yuan Shi-kai. As a consequence, most of the work of this conference was simply ignored until the period of cultural and intellectual ferment of the May Fourth Movement of 1919, of which the *baihua* movement of 1917 was a precursor.

Nevertheless, two of the decisions reached by the CURP had a disproportionate impact on the early development of the national language program. The first was its creation of a National Phonetic Alphabet. This body of phonetic signs, in large part an aggregate comprising parts of previous proposals, would serve as a means of indicating the pronunciation of individual Chinese characters. It was intended that one of the alphabet's most important applications would be in school classrooms to facilitate the acquisition of the traditional script, which otherwise would have to be memorized character by character, as it had been in the past.[3]

The conferees also proposed a workable mechanism for implementing the alphabet through national and regional training centers modeled along the lines of the Mandarin training centers mentioned in the plans submitted by the Central Educational Conference in 1911 (MOE 1934: 591).

However, with respect to the matter of a national phonological standard (although one whose function was to be limited to reading), the CURP could only produce an unworkable compromise. The national pronunciation, or *guoyin,* that it adopted amounted to a linguistic amalgam. Although the North Chinese language constituted its primary component, the mixture also contained several features characteristic of, or having some historical significance in, the regional languages

(Fang 1968: 1–3). The outcome was an invented language, unspeakable and unspoken by anyone in China.[4]

In the decade and a half after the CURP, the Republican Government underwent disintegration and civil authority devolved by default on regional military commanders. In Peking the government's authority extended no further than the adjoining military satrapy. The Ministry of Education, however, continued to function as if its decisions reached a national constituency.

In 1918, the Ministry authorized for teaching purposes the National Phonetic Alphabet, based on the heterogeneous national pronunciation which had emerged from the CURP (Taga 1976, II: 497). Then in 1920, in the same year that the vernacular language was to replace the classical for school instruction, the Ministry issued a dictionary (*Guoyin zidian*) in this *guoyin* pronunciation (MOE 1972: 13–14). Because this dictionary was authorized by the Ministry of Education, the national pronunciation of the CURP was accepted by many as the authorized phonological standard for instruction in the primary school system (Wang 1951: 160–64).

The practical unworkability of this national pronunciation was not lost on supporters of the Mandarin Movement. Their involvement in the compilation of the *Guoyin zidian* may have been motivated by the hope of establishing a legal basis for an early revision reflecting Pekingese pronunciation (He 1976); preparations for just such a project were under way even as the dictionary was being printed (Wang 1951: 66). The "swift, total, and dizzying" success of the *baihua yundong* (Bianco 1971: 44) from 1917 through the Ministry of Education orders relating to the use of the vernacular language in primary schools in 1920 suggested an increasingly favorable public attitude toward realistic language reforms. But the momentum to complete a revision of the national pronunciation could not be sustained in the politically fragmented China of the 1920s. Indeed, it was not until 1932 that this revision was actually achieved.

Meanwhile, between 1920 and 1932 teachers seeking to implement the 1920 directives were forced to choose between loyalty either to the national language authorized by the Ministry of Education in Peking, or to Pekingese itself, or to the Chinese regional language spoken natively in their own areas. Some opted for compliance with the 1920 directive, and were observed in the classroom teaching forms of the language which they would never use outside it (He 1975: 3). Some called for an immediate withdrawal of the government-authorized *guoyin*, nominating Pekingese in its place (Li 1921: 24). Still others, like the staff of the *Guanhua zhuyin zimu bao* (*Guanhua* Annotated Biweekly Newspaper), a semiofficial publication with ties to the Ministry of Education, were caught in the middle; the vernacular-language newspaper they published appeared with the phonetic annotation appropriate for the *guoyin* pronunciation printed to one side of each character and a second annotation, reflecting Pekingese pronunciation, at the other (Fang 1965: 204).

E. The Adoption of a Phonological Norm in 1932

In 1932 the Nationalist Government designated Pekingese as the phonological norm for the Chinese national language. This decision took the form of a publication of a large inventory of Chinese characters together with their accepted phonological values. It was issued by the Preparatory Commission for the Unification of the National Language, an advisory group within the Ministry of Education. This document, the *Guoyin changyong zihui* (A Vocabulary of [12,219] Common Characters in the National Pronunciation),[5] adopted as normative the phonological system and most of the grammatical apparatus of Pekingese. Individual lexical decisions were not prescribed but were to be handled consensually in recognition of the fact that a certain amount of Pekingese vocabulary enjoyed only a local and not a national currency (TPMPC 1952: 73).[6]

The publication of the *zihui* clarified the technical linguistic definition of the national language, but important questions concerning the proposed functional relationship between the national language and the other Chinese regional languages on the one hand, and between Chinese languages as a group and non-Chinese national minority languages as another group on the other hand, remained unspecified.

A cursory examination of some of the relevant literature suggests that a consensus on these questions was not available in the 1930s. To cite one example, the use of Mandarin as the language of instruction in the schools was a fairly consistently articulated government policy even in the dozen years before the final decisions regarding the linguistic outlines of the national language were taken in 1932 (Cheng 1923: 29). Still, agreement was not reached regarding the scope, timing, and targets of this policy. A statement pertaining to these matters was issued in 1926 by the All-China Conference on the Mandarin Movement.[7] Reflecting a private rather than a governmental viewpoint, this statement candidly recognized the obstacles to immediate and universal implementation of Mandarin, and it accepted the fact that in some areas education in the regional language would have to continue for an indefinite period (Wang 1951: 42–44). These ambiguities in the implementation of the government's policy seem to have gone unresolved.

At the very least, this suggests a lack of unanimity among educators regarding the urgency, and perhaps even the need, for a single medium of classroom instruction.

F. Assessment

After 1900, as China moved toward political and economic reform, the potential role of Mandarin assumed increased importance.[8] By the 1920s, textbook publishers tacitly accorded its written form de facto recognition (He 1975: 6). The intervening years were marked by the growth of nationalism, but for most of this period it was a nationalism committed largely to the preservation and defense of a traditional social order, including its accepted patterns of social and linguistic behavior. Only after the May Fourth Movement of 1919, preceded by the drive to replace the classical language with the written vernacular, did the traditional cultural order finally succumb to the attack of social revolutionaries.

The evolution of a national language policy during these years was governed by cultural forces. The decision taken initially by the Ch'ing government to teach *guan hua* in schools was in the form of an imperial decree rather than a carefully conceived plan. Furthermore, in the absence of central direction and training, local results could only have been exceedingly diverse. More important, this plan bore no relationship to the predominant contemporary social valuation of languages. Thus, although Mandarin served the needs of government, other Chinese languages continued to function as before in their respective social and educational spheres. This was clearly the case in the realm of scholarship, where "not to be able to speak Mandarin continued to cast no aspersions on a scholar" (Chou 1959: 52).[9] In a day when reformers dared innovation and China's youth dreamed of great changes, "a command of Mandarin . . . was regarded rather as a convenience than a matter of prestige . . ." (Chao 1961: 171).

The difficulty of obtaining consensus for a national language based on North Chinese became apparent once responsibility for this matter passed out of the imperial bureaucracy and into the public realm. There, the 1903 plan to promote an unadulterated *guan hua* was modified to include historically prestigeful linguistic components from other regional Chinese languages.

This interpretation is consonant with the results of the CURP. Its organizing principle was to adopt a unified pronunciation for reading purposes. It was not expected, nor did the conference recommend, that the *guoyin* function as the basis for a national spoken language. Li Jin-xi, the Mandarin Movement's chief chronicler, was correct in assigning the responsibility for the adoption of *guoyin* to delegates insistent on having features of their regional languages reflected in the prestigious new reading pronunciation (Li 1921: 25). In this case the expression of sectional linguistic loyalties was made especially easy by the decision-making process adopted by the conference: each delegate voted his own pronunciation preference for each of the 6,500 characters whose pronunciation was fixed during the meeting.

Still, what purpose was served by establishing even a reading norm native to none and alien to all? If the majority of delegates could assent to a standard based for the most part on North Chinese, why not on all of it? In a modern western society a language such as Mandarin—native to three-quarters of the population and distributed throughout two-thirds of the cultivable area of the country—might be thought to have considerable credibility as a national language candidate. And even if a small group of scholars was unwilling to accord formal recognition to North Chinese, why did the Mandarin-speaking majority not demur?

It has been suggested that in pre-modern Chinese society, ultimate value to a literate individual inhered in mastery of the Confucian canon and familiarity with traditional literature.[10] In the case of some regional languages, the sounds and rhymes of those earlier days could still be heard. But North Chinese, unlike those languages which were known to have retained the linguistic characteristics of earlier historical periods, had undergone significant phonological change. As a result, elegant classical poetry no longer rhymed properly in North Chinese. Even in Peking opera the performers spoke, not in contemporary Pekingese, but in a North Chinese pronunciation of an earlier era (Chao 1961: 174–75). Historically the newest of Chinese languages, North Chinese had the weakest claim to veneration by scholars for whom the men, the lessons, and the speech of the past were held in highest regard. "Little wonder," as Chao remarked, "that Mandarin was held in low esteem by the literati" (Ibid.: 172). Accordingly, when the *Guoyin zidian* was published in 1920, the Minister of Education urged the acceptance of the *guoyin* phonological standard because it gave due recognition to important sound features of special value from several speech areas (Wang 1951: 138–40). So construed, the national language of the CURP and the *Guoyin zidian* was not a harbinger of a new age but a memorial to one that was passing away.

In 1913, traditional Chinese political institutions had given way to others, but Chinese values and behavior had not, and would not for several years. Far-seeing and impatient men like the talented Li Jin-xi reacted with understandable disappointment to the national pronunciation of the CURP, viewing it as a step backwards in the realization of a nationally serviceable and teachable form of speech (Li 1935: 107–08). But the delegates to the CURP were, in education and temperament, still committed to the past, not to the future. The CURP was an assembly composed of classically educated men meeting in the twilight of China's long traditional period, and its work was a reflection of its time.

It may be instructive to ask what relationship if any obtained between written language reforms, mentioned earlier in this section, and the advocacy for a national language. A substantial consensus was achieved rapidly with respect to writing in the vernacular, while decisions pertaining to the form and the function of the national language emerged much more slowly. Interestingly, the most vocal advocates of vernacular writing, although they were at the same time nominally associated with the national language movement, never brought to it an equivalent level of commitment.

One hypothesis is that the relative indifference to the promotion of a national language in China during this period was attributable to the comparatively peripheral role played by speech in the lives of literate individuals as against the dominant role of writing.[11] It is undeniable that the written language has enjoyed a unique place in Chinese history—in part as an art form, and in part because as a character orthography it mediated between phonologically disparate speech forms. But it is inconsistent with all that is known about peoples and their languages to ignore the fact that spoken languages also, quite apart from their written representations, are independently endowed with their own social values and that changes in the relative status of those languages have a special history of their own.

In China, in this early period of national language planning, the evidence suggests that the difficulties encountered in arriving at a national language policy cannot be clarified by reference to speculation drawn from the realm of orthography. Rather, their explication is to be found elsewhere—at one level, in the absence of a consensus about the functions to be performed by the several Chinese languages; and at another level, how and to what extent the new China would accommodate the values of the old.

III. THE IMPLEMENTATION OF THE NATIONAL LANGUAGE IN THE NATIONALIST PERIOD, 1927–1937

A. Political Stability

China in the period before 1949 was a country with an enormous population, 80 percent of which was predominantly rural, agricultural, and sedentary. Although exposed to some schooling, most Chinese were prevented from participating in a national community because of illiteracy and inadequate communications (see Appendix).

It was also, especially between 1916 and 1937, a country marked by social ferment and the disruption of established authority. In 1911, the Ch'ing Dynasty passed into history. The civil apparatus intended to replace it disintegrated after 1916, and the next ten years witnessed the reign of independent regional militarists. According to one count, 1,300 such local warlords fought 140 domestic wars in the period between 1912 and 1928 (Tien 1972: 9). The threat to internal order posed by local warlords began to recede as the Nationalist Government pressed its claim to national hegemony after 1927, only to be replaced by an intensified civil conflict between the Nationalists and the Communists throughout the 1930s until the latter's victory in 1949.[12]

These were also the years of Japanese aggression. A major transformation occurred in the relations between these two countries after the 1890s. At first, Japan was regarded as a model for Chinese modernization, a home for her restive students, and a haven for revolutionary thinkers. But by 1928, as a result of repeated diplomatic and finally military adventures, the Japanese had become "the most detested foreigners in China" (Israel 1966: 21). Occupying Manchuria outright in 1931, the Japanese Army extended its influence into North China. War erupted in 1937.

The decade of Nationalist rule prior to 1937 was tranquil only by comparison with the previous decade of warlordism. The authority of the government was firm in two coastal provinces, marginal in eight other central provinces, and nominal in the rest (Tien 1972: 5). There was hardly a year in which the nationalist government was not challenged by intrigues, military revolts, Communist insurgency, or Japanese aggression (Pye 1972: 137–38).

B. Financial Considerations

One of the legacies of the earlier warlord period was a determination to establish a national government unassailable domestically and internationally (Pye 1972: 127). However, the pursuit of this elusive goal by the Nationalist Government was not paralleled by an equal commitment to social reforms—an orientation which is evident in the government's fiscal operations.

During the 1920s, the work of the "national" government in Peking was severely limited by insufficient resources. Local taxes simply did not leave the provinces (CYB 1929–1930: 628). During those years the land tax in particular, as well as other excises, became the principal form of support for regional military governments. In 1928, the Nationalist Government accepted and institutionalized this arrangement, either because it was incapable of altering the situation or in order to avoid the inconvenience and expense of a national land survey and registration. "Nanking [the capital of Nationalist China] would draw its revenues primarily from customs duties and the salt tax; the land tax, the most lucrative source of revenue, was reserved for the provincial governments" (Tien 1972: 75).

Whether by necessity or by design, central government revenues were derived from nonagricultural sources, and these only within the limited geographic area over which it exercised control. In extending that control against the claims of rival militarists, Communists, and the Japanese, large portions of that small revenue base were siphoned away. Thus, in 1928–29, the government divided over 89 percent of its income between military expenditures (50.8 percent) and service on international debts (38.3 percent). By 1935, these figures were 34.4 percent and 24.1 percent, respectively; aggregated, they averaged 75 percent of all government expenditures throughout this period (Ibid.: 83–84).

C. Support for Education

These fiscal priorities left little margin for social-reform programs, including education. In practice, the central government devoted its meager educational resources to higher education, leaving the support of primary education to the provinces. This meant that it contributed little or nothing to primary education—the only form of education the overwhelming majority of the population ever received. As an international team of educational experts noted, the average annual expenditure for primary education for each student in China averaged $3.50–4.00 (Mexican dollars), compared with $600–800 at the university level—a ratio of approximately 1:200. Comparable ratios in European countries were on the order of one to eight or ten (Becker et al. 1932: 51).

Limitations accepted by the government regarding its power to tax explain in large measure its ineffectiveness in implementing plans for compulsory education, plans which depended almost entirely upon local revenues it did not control (Ibid.: 85). Similarly, the shortage of teachers necessary to realize national compulsory elementary education was acute; 770,000 of these would have been required, but in 1929–30 only 10,000 each year were being graduated (CYB 1929–30: 526).

Many of the difficulties encountered in the implementation of the national language program are reflected in the above data. Only a few details can be sketched here, but something of the handicap under which language promotion was attempted can be seen in the difficulties faced by the Nationalist Government's Preparatory Commission for the Unification of the National Language. Constituted in 1928, it had a standing committee of thirty members but only seven of these were salaried and principally occupied with the business of the commission (Wang 1951: 102). Between 1928 and 1930, the commission was empowered to appoint forty deputies in fifteen local areas, but in all likelihood these deputies were merely local functionaries already overburdened with routine administrative tasks. Since they were probably not compensated for this additional assignment, it is unlikely that they welcomed it or construed it as of great importance (Li 1934b: 288).

The Preparatory Commission proposed to establish an institute to train Mandarin specialists and to pursue language research, but the funding did not materialize (Ibid.: 289). Interest in spoken language and related pedagogy was therefore not advanced, leaving the ranks of Mandarin promoters thin and their state of knowledge static. At one point the Preparatory Commission appealed to the Ministry of Education to assign special Mandarin inspectors to promote compliance with the government's language policy in the schools (Wei 1934: 256). The appointment of such a corps of technically qualified language supervisors, even if it could have been assembled, would have been but a palliative in realizing a program which existed for the most part nowhere but on paper.

By abstaining from support of primary-level education, the Ministry of Education consigned the national language program to the uncertainties of local financing and staffing and the certainty of local inertia. However, even within the national-level educational administration, the coordination of Mandarin promotion activities with other areas of the curriculum was far from perfect.

Some excerpts from the history of the National Phonetic Alphabet (NPA) illustrate the problem. Although Mandarin promotion was institutionalized within the Ministry of Education, its advocates apparently had little influence among the regular circles of educational administration. As early as 1920, following the government's recognition of the NPA as a means for phonetic annotation of characters in the school system, the (Peking) Ministry of Education recommended the introduction of the NPA in the first year of primary school (Wang 1951: 161). But in the unofficial yet widely observed school curriculum promulgated in 1923, the NPA was not recommended for introduction until the *fifth* and *sixth* grades, when it would be too late either to facilitate the acquisition of the character script or to have much impact on the development of accurate phonological habits in the national language. Moreover, this document specified that, in the absence of a teacher qualified in Mandarin, education in the local language was explicitly accepted during the lower primary school years (grades one through four) and even through the higher primary school (grades five and six) (Cheng 1923: 29, 31). Subsequently, in the 1929 and 1932 curriculum revisions, schools were required to teach the NPA earlier, in the *third* and *fourth* years, although its introduction at that time was still not related in any way to the teaching of Mandarin. In practice, however, even perfunctory observation of these regulations could not be assumed (Li 1934a: 309).

Throughout these years, the impact of the NPA on Mandarin instruction was negligible, apparently because most educators continued to construe it as merely a device for facilitating dictionary searches. Accordingly, it was relegated to the periphery of educational attention, neglected first by provincial normal schools, then by the graduates of those schools who subsequently became primary school teachers, and finally by students of the next generation who had received no instruction in it.

Although much remains to be learned about the implementation of the Mandarin program, the failure of the program was conceded by the government itself. The official publication of the Ministry of Education for 1948 reported that

> . . . although elementary schools have uniformly established a national language course in their curricula, in reality the large majority of these schools did not teach Mandarin; rather, they conducted such classes in the pronunciation of the local language. Of the four principal skill categories which comprise the Mandarin course goals—speaking, reading, composition, and calligraphy—the goal for the speech skill as a rule was not attained; and the National Phonetic Alphabet, whose function was to facilitate character acquisition and the attainment of a uniform pronunciation of the script, was seldom taught (MOE 1948: 1169).[13]

The above situation, evaluating Mandarin promotion as of 1943, was identical to that described by the Ministry of Education's national language commission a decade earlier, in 1934 (Li 1934a: 309). Both of these evaluations indicated that, although most children in primary schools were reading materials printed in the vernacular rather than in the classical language, their pronunciation of these materials, as well as the customary language of classroom activity, was that of the local language. Inevitably, the Mandarin spoken by students who were exposed to this kind of training in the schools was of the "blue-green" variety, predictably and conspicuously marked by the many linguistic peculiarities of the learner's local speech (He 1946: 2). At mid-century, said the

Chinese linguist Lo Chang-pei (1899–1958), "The Mandarin Movement was trailing far behind the Vernacular Language Movement" (Lo 1956: 275).

Given these circumstances, one can more fully appreciate the discouragement in the words of Wu Zhi-hui (1864–1953), for many years the head of the Mandarin Promotion Commission of the Nationalist Government and the spiritual leader of the national language program, who in 1943 said of his thirty years' involvement in the promotion of Mandarin that "there was hardly anything about it one would want to celebrate" (TPMPC 1946: 10).

D. Assessment

How national consciousness affected the spread of Mandarin prior to 1949 is uncertain. That nationalism contributed importantly to revolution, civil war, street demonstrations, student crusades, and boycotts is well attested by the historical record. But only a relatively small number of people proved capable of equally heroic levels of dedication on behalf of an abstract and scholarly national language program.

In the period of policy formation, the Ch'ing Dynasty's decision to teach *guan hua* reflected an uncritical imitation of foreign educational systems. The designation of Mandarin for use in education actually ran counter to contemporary evaluations of language status. Resistance or indifference to the adoption of Pekingese as a norm for pronunciation continued through the 1920s.

It remains unclear to what extent the existence of this prior commitment of the imperial government to *guan hua* preempted or foreclosed the consideration of alternatives to the implementation of a national language program. Rubin (1977: 165) has remarked that premature codification of a language norm may endow it with an aura of acceptance that it does not objectively enjoy. In China, Li Jin-xi (Li 1921: 7) once asserted that a majority of educators in the early years of the Republic favored the use of local languages for education. Historically, even individuals active in the Mandarin Movement have displayed an interest in the preservation and development of minority languages which is not always found in official literature (Wang 1951: 42–43).

Once formally adopted, the national language policy faced still other obstacles. Nine out of ten targets of the national language program lived generation after generation in isolated rural areas. Most of them farmed as a livelihood. Fewer than half ever had the leisure or opportunity for formal schooling. Four-fifths could not read or write and often found the acquisition of these skills irrelevant to their daily lives (Lamson 1935: 197–98). Some of the conditions which elsewhere have facilitated the spread of languages—"industrialization of the area, development of its mass communications, and the proximity of rural aggregates to the networks" (Tabouret-Keller 1968: 113)—were absent in China.

It is significant that in the period under study civil institutions were disrupted as a result of political instability and foreign aggression. During the 1920s, resources which might have been devoted to educational programs were frequently diverted to the maintenance of regional warlord armies. Still later, the Nationalist Government was unable to assert its authority throughout the country and as a result the 60 percent of the country's gross national product generated in rural areas remained beyond the government's ability to tax. The bulk of the government's relatively small revenues went into domestic pacification efforts. The government's contribution to the support of primary-level schools, in which the national language was to have been introduced, was negligible.

Even the depth of the government's commitment to its national language program must remain open to question. In 1934, nearly half of the membership of the Nationalist Party, which alone governed the country, were natives of provinces where regional languages predominate. These include Kuangtung, where the Yue and the Kejia languages are spoken, 25 percent; Kiangsu, 8 percent, and Chekiang, 5 percent, where the Wu languages are spoken; Fukien, where both Northern and Southern Min are used, 3 percent; and Kiangsi, where the Gan language group predominates, 7 percent (Tien 1972: 29; see Fig. 1). In some of these provinces, of course, it could be argued that the authority of the Nationalist Government was weak or nonexistent. Yet it was just in these provinces of southeastern China that the lack of a common national medium of communication would have been most keenly felt. At this writing, however, the proper interpretation of these data remains problematic.

Finally, it is worth mentioning that members of the small urban professional class may have attached greater importance to the acquisition of foreign languages than to a second Chinese language like Mandarin. For recipients of higher education, for students of special or technical subjects, and for entrepreneurs whose lives and careers were oriented toward the West, the immediate utility of learning Mandarin may have been questionable (Kuo 1923: 23). It has been noted that in this period the graduates of Western-oriented schools enjoyed an economic and social advantage over their peers trained at institutions where the curriculum was not so influenced (Wang 1966: 376).

In conclusion, the Nationalist Government did little to advance the development of the national language program in China because its activities were predominantly urban rather than rural, and its demands upon the rural sector in terms of its contribution to a national culture were minimal, as were the government's own contributions to rural development. Therefore, for those who did not speak natively some form of Mandarin, and for the large majority of the population which was not mobilized, the government provided little motivation to potential learners of the national language. In short, there were few who really needed to acquire Mandarin, and the resources devoted to teaching it were correspondingly meager.

NOTES

1. An earlier draft of this paper was presented at the Conference on Language Spread and Recession at the University of Aberystwyth, Wales, September 12–14, 1978. I am grateful to the participants of the conference for their observations, and to Donald S. Sutton who also read and offered critical comments on the paper. The responsibility for its content remains my own. Financial support for the preparation of this paper was provided by the Center for Applied Linguistics, the Faculty Grants Committee and the Bowman Faculty Award of the University of Pittsburgh, and the Chinese Cultural Center of New York, Inc. Chinese terminology is romanized according to the conventions of the *pinyin* system for phonetic annotation promulgated in the People's Republic of China; exceptions to this format include certain dynastic reign names and geographical terms whose pre-1949 romanized forms are still more familiar to Western readers than the current *pinyin* variations. Translations from Chinese texts are by the writer.

2. Li Jin-xi (1935: 26) wrote that the failure to designate teaching materials made implementation of the MOE order difficult. Neither could the most suitable set of phonetic symbols then available be employed because its author had fled the country to escape execution for his political activities. And in southeastern Fukien, the only sizeable group of speakers capable of using *guan hua* were soldiers in the locally garrisoned Manchu military units.

3. Prior to 1918, when the NPA was officially recognized by the MOE, literate Chinese had for the most part indicated the pronunciation of a character, which is always a single syllable, by reference to two other characters: the first character represented the initial consonant (if any), while the second represented the vowels, the final consonant (if any), and the tone. This was called the *fanqie* 'reverse cut' system.

4. However, phonograph recordings in *guoyin* were authorized by the Ministry of Education, following the recommendations of the CURP, and prepared as a guide to teachers by Chao Yuen Ren in 1921 (Chao 1961: 175).

5. Reissued in 1947 in Taiwan under provincial auspices as the *Guoyin biaozhun huibian* (TPMPC 1947).

6. This linguistic characterization of the national language of the Nationalist Government reappeared in 1956, with only minor changes in wording, in a document issued by the State Council of the People's Republic of China (State Council 1956: 249).

7. For the full text of the 1926 statement and the program of the All-China Conference, see the 1948 edition of the Ministry of Education's Yearbook (MOE 1948: 1163).

8. The potential contribution of Mandarin as an instrument of national communication may have been recognized by some political reformers much earlier. One of them, K'ang You-wei (1858–1927), was reported to have directed that Mandarin be used in schools he established among dialect-speaking Chinese in Java around 1900 (Peake 1932: 231).

9. Chao attested to the existence of the same attitudes as late as the 1940s (Chao 1943: 66).

10. Candidates for the imperial examinations were responsible for memorizing, by one count, 431,286 characters of running text (Miyazaki 1976: 16).

11. Such was the view of Forrest (1965: 7), whose comprehensive treatment of the Chinese language first appeared in 1948. This view has also been expressed by Chinese actively involved in national language promotion in Taiwan (Wang 1963: 53).

12. The role played by the Communist Party during this period has been alluded to in Barnes (1977: 257). Although Chinese communists in Russia recorded their opposition to the national language program of the Nationalist Government as early as 1931, the party itself was outlawed until 1936, and its membership was unable to work openly in support of the strengthening of the regional languages which it ostensibly favored.

13. This state of affairs with respect to Mandarin promotion in China as of mid-century was repeated by the Chinese linguists Lo Chang-pei and Lü Xuxiang in the People's Republic of China:

> The actual use of [Mandarin], moving along the pathways created by the development of commerce and communications, is just now in the midst of expanding. However, [Mandarin] has had no impact in the small and middle size cities and in the villages of the vast agricultural sections of those regions which speak other Chinese [regional] languages. In these areas, theater conducted in [Mandarin] has little appeal to audiences, movies are produced in the [regional] language, radio broadcasts are carried in both [Mandarin] and the [regional language], and even in the schools the medium of instruction in the majority of cases is [not Mandarin but] another [regional language]. (Lo and Lü 1956: 8)

APPENDIX
Data Relating to Language Implementation

Section 2 has discussed the ways in which cultural attitudes impinged upon the planning for a national language program. Section 3 alluded to some of the factors which may have had a bearing upon the later implementation of the national language program. It has been argued that these variables may be useful in interpreting the development of social programs by revealing the extent to which a population is mobilized for intercommunication (Deutsch 1966:

126). Although the accuracy of some of the information collected here remains in question, it is nevertheless suggestive of the conditions which existed in China prior to 1949.

A. Demography

Semiofficial western-language sources placed the aggregate population of China at approximately 331 millions in 1912, the year after the Republican Revolution (CYB 1912: 2–4). These figures were estimates, based on counts of households, and were subsequently adjusted upward to 486 millions where, for lack of better estimates, the figure remained for the balance of the 1930s (CYB 1929–1930: 3–4; CYB 1935: 2).

The distribution of this immense population was heavily rural. Official sources for 1929–30 claimed that 75 percent lived or worked in farming areas. Buck's data, collected during a massive survey throughout nineteen provinces during 1929–30, showed 79 percent of all families living in farms and villages; another 11 percent lived in market towns, and 10 percent were city-dwellers (Buck 1937: 362, 365). A 1931 survey of Ding County, Hobei, made famous as a model for social experimentation, approximated Buck's higher figures indicating that well over 80 percent of all males and 80 percent of females were engaged in farming as their primary vocations (Gamble 1954: 52).

It may be useful to compare this situation with that of Japan, another Asian nation which underwent major social and economic change after 1850. By 1930, the proportion of its work force deriving its livelihood principally from agriculture was 55 percent and falling (to 25 percent in 1962). The importance of this shift in vocational distribution, according to Lockwood, was that by 1964 "most [Japanese] farmers lived within 50 miles of an industrial center with which they have easy communication" (Lockwood 1964: 138). Lockwood specifically compared this development with the case of China with its "half-million villages remote from urban influences."

A considerable amount of evidence, largely anecdotal, confirms Lockwood's inference regarding the significance of the predominantly stable character of the Chinese population for the promotion of a language program. Chao Yuen Ren, for example, writing of his family's return to Changchow after 1902, noted that relatives of his parents' age were capable of understanding Mandarin, presumably because of travel outside the province in connection with official business, but those of his generation were not (Chao 1971: 308). Changchow was located midway between Shanghai, a Wu-speaking area, and Nanking, a North Chinese-speaking area, but clearly the Wu speakers felt no compelling need to acquire Mandarin. Less than a generation later, Li Jin-xi reported indifference to national-language promotion among family heads in Shanghai, because few occasions required the use of Mandarin (Li 1921: 8). The sedentary population and accompanying pattern of local language use posed special difficulties for Buck in the conduct of agricultural field research, necessitating the selection of investigators who were native to the areas under investigation (Buck 1937: viii). The same isolation of rural areas was dramatically illustrated in the 1936 Peking students' crusade to rouse the countryside to the threat of Japanese aggression and against the government's policy of appeasement. The dialogues between the nationalistically inspired students and the incredulous village locals were, according to one observer, "a babel of dialects" (Israel 1966: 135).

B. Education and Literacy

For centuries, education in imperial China meant a thorough grounding in the essential texts of the Confucian classics—the Analects, the Mencius, the Book of Changes, the Book of Documents, the Book of Poetry, the Book of Rites, and the Tso Chuan, as well as related commentaries. Boys customarily began their tutelage at age eight and completed the curriculum at fifteen (Miyazaki 1976: 16). The content and method persisted until the Ch'ing government issued instructions for a new national school system at the turn of the century (Chao 1971: 306).

The principal object in acquiring an education was to qualify, through state-administered examinations, for an official career. The state, however, did not provide the education, which was arranged and financed privately, typically at the family or clan level. Only a small minority of the population received an education through this system (Cameron 1963: 65).

The inauguration of the public school system after 1901, including the addition of some Western subjects, was followed by increased enrollments. Lower primary school enrollments (grades one through five) were 1,148,297 for the 1909–1910 school year (CYB 1912: 323). Official figures for 1923 revealed 6,417,321 students in government elementary schools, grades one through six (CYB 1926: 408). For the 1929–1930 school year, these figures had increased to 8,839,434 (Becker et al. 1932: 76). Nevertheless, during the 1930s only about 21 percent of the lower primary school age population (ages 6–9) was attending classes (Lamson 1935: 193). Substantially the same situation was reported in Gamble's study of Ding County, Hobei Province in the early 1930s (Gamble 1954: 192).

Among the population at large, the number of people who had attended school never rose above 50 percent. Buck's earlier study in seven north and east-central provinces in 1921–25 reported that only 47.5 percent of the farm operators had ever had any formal schooling (Buck 1930: 407). In a second and geographically more comprehensive survey undertaken in sixteen provinces during 1929–30, that figure was even lower—45.6 percent (Ibid. 1937: 373).

The incidence of functional literacy was almost certainly even lower. Buck found that approximately 47 percent of his respondents had attended school, but only 30 percent of the males and about 1 percent of the females were literate (Ibid. 1937: 373). Gamble's study of Ding County, Hobei, indicated an average of 80 percent illiterate for the three groups surveyed (Gamble 1954: 187).

For linguistic reasons, even the competence of those certified literate must remain very much a question. In Ding County, for example, the criteria for literacy certification were: (1) at least two years study in a lower primary school, or (2) two months study in a [Mass Education Class] in which a [high-frequency] inventory of over 1,000 characters was taught (Gamble 1954: 186).

To evaluate these criteria it is necessary to refer to tabulations of school materials used in the 1930s. These revealed that regular elementary school students would have encountered approximately 1,200 characters in their first two years (the same number as Mass Education Class students), and 2,700 by the end of their fourth (Ai 1965: 57–58). The average number of years of schooling received by male respondents in both of Buck's field surveys was 4.1 (1930: 407; 1937: 374). Yet Gamble alluded to the widely held view that "some 5,000 characters were needed for general newspaper reading" (Gamble 1954: 185–86).

Although the following argument is guilty of oversimplification, it is never-theless possible to understand that even graduates of the four-year lower pri-mary school were at best precariously balanced between literacy and illiteracy, while Mass Education Class students could not begin to read ordinary adult literature. For the group of adults surveyed by Buck in his earlier study, whose educations had been predominantly of the old classical type, and even then limited to but a few years, the result was the same (Buck 1930: 408). Thus, as all observers agree, it is likely that students with little more than a lower pri-mary school education would eventually "forget their knowledge of reading and writing through disuse" (Lamson 1935: 194). In fact, most of these individuals would never have reached the threshold on which literacy is based.

C. Communications

The information in this section relates to newspaper circulation, railroad and road development, and postal and telegraph service, and is intended to be a suggestive rather than an exhaustive description of the situation in China.

1. Newspapers. According to the *Shun Pao Year Book* for 1933, only two daily newspapers claimed a circulation in excess of 100,000. These were the *Shun Pao* and the *Sin Wan Pao*, both published in Shanghai, each with a circula-tion estimated at 150,000. Thirteen papers were estimated to have circulations of between 10,000 and 35,000. Seventeen more claimed circulations of be-tween 5,000 and 9,000 (Lin 1968: 145–46). Historically, these data indicate a significant increase in circulation for the *Shun Pao*, which claimed a circulation of only 15,000 in 1895 (Britton 1933: 68). However, circulation figures were by no means identical with readership, especially since many newspapers in China were not received at home but were read on public bulletin boards. One estimate, by the journalist and essayist Lin Yu-tang, set newspaper readership at 5 percent of the population (Lin 1968: 149).

2. Railroads. The significance of the data regarding railroad mileage in ser-vice and the number of passengers handled annually by the system is rendered problematic by the size of the total population, which was apparently under-estimated in the early years of the Republic. A semiofficial source reported 5,297 miles of track in use, or 0.12 miles of track for every 10,000 persons, for the end of 1909; the same figures for the United States were 237,182 miles of track, or 27 miles for each 10,000 persons; and for India, 31,483 miles of track, or 1.1 mile for each 10,000 persons (CYB 1912: 184–86). Rough computa-tions for slightly different and perhaps incomplete data for 1911 suggest that on the average one out of each 23 Chinese may have been a railroad passenger (Ibid.: 171–83). For the fiscal year 1934, the upwardly-revised population esti-mate of 485,503,838 used during these years divided by 44,783,656, represent-ing the number of passengers carried during that year, indicates that one out of every eleven Chinese used rail service during that year (CYB 1935: 224–25). Absolute railroad mileage has proved difficult to calculate for this period, but at no time does it appear to have exceeded 7,000 miles of track (CYB 1929–30: 358).

3. Roads. Available sources indicate that as of 1934 there existed 52,698 miles of road open to traffic; however, there was no indication of how much of this road system was paved. More specific data are available for the seven cen-tral provinces belonging to the Interprovincial Highway System administration established by the Nationalist Government in 1932. These indicate that for the provinces of Chekiang, Kiangsu, Anhwei, Kiangsi, Hupeh, Hunan, and Honan

there existed a highway system of 10,528 miles of which 5,046 miles were
surfaced and 5,482 miles were unsurfaced, and that approximately one-third of
this mileage had been added to the system during 1934 (CYB 1935: 240–41).

4. Postal and Telegraph Service. The data regarding postal service are even
more difficult to use with confidence. It was under the control of a foreign
Inspectorate-General of customs through 1911, after which it was transferred to
the Ministry of Post and Communications. For 1910, the last year it was under
foreign administration, available information indicates that the aggregate total of
articles entrusted to the postal service, including letters, parcels, money orders,
and the like, was only slightly in excess of the figure representing the total
population. Allowing for statistical discrepancies, it appears that 1.0 items were
dispatched annually per person through the postal service (CYB 1912: 196). If
only letters were counted, the appropriate figure would be 0.09 items per person per year.

Later, following the upward revision of the population estimate to 485 millions, the number of letters and postcards sent for 1927 yielded an average user
rate of 0.86 items per year (CYB 1929–1930: 458a). The same figure for volume of service as of 1930 was 1.6. Comparative data for other countries for the
same year include: India, 3.8; Germany, 88.0; Japan, 63.8; and Great Britain,
139.5 (CYB 1935: 252).

The single figure available from the Chinese Telegraph Administration reports activity as of June, 1934. Based on the 485 million population figure, per
capita use of the telegraph system amounted to 0.008 (CYB 1935: 266).

REFERENCES

Ai Wei 1965. *Hanzi wenti* (Chinese Characters). Taipei: Guoli bianyiguan.
Barnes, Dayle 1977. "National Language Planning in China," in Rubin, Joan,
    Björn H. Jernudd, Jyotirindra Das Gupta, Joshua A. Fishman, and Charles A.
    Ferguson. *Language Planning Processes*. The Hague: Mouton Publishers,
    255–73.
Becker, C. H., M. Falski, P. Langevin, and R. H. Tawney 1932. *The Reorganisa-
    tion of Education in China*. Paris: The League of Nations' Institute of Intellec-
    tual Co-operation. Reprint. Taipei: Ch'eng Wen Publishing Company, 1974.
Bianco, Lucien 1971. *Origins of the Chinese Revolution, 1915–1949*. Stanford:
    Stanford University Press.
Biggerstaff, Knight 1961. *The Earliest Modern Government Schools in China*.
    Ithaca: Cornell University Press.
Britton, Roswell S. 1933. *The Chinese Periodical Press, 1800–1912*. Shanghai:
    Kelly & Walsh, Limited.
Buck, John Lossing 1930. *Chinese Farm Economy*. Chicago, Illinois: The Univer-
    sity of Chicago Press.
Buck, John Lossing 1937. *Land Utilization in China*. Third Printing. New
    York: Paragon Book Reprint Corporation, 1968.
Cameron, Meribeth E. 1963. *The Reform Movement in China, 1898–1912*. Re-
    printed edition. New York: Octagon Books, Inc.
Chao Yuen Ren 1943. "Languages and Dialects in China," in *The Geographical
    Journal* 102: 63–66 (July-December).
———— 1961. "What is Correct Chinese?" in *Journal of the American Oriental
    Society* LXXXI, 3: 171–77 (August-September).

———— 1971. "Wo de yuyan zizhuan" (My Linguistic Autobiography), in *Bulletin of the Institute of History and Philology* XXXXIII, Part 3: 303–17 (November). Abridged English translation in Ibid. 1976. *Aspects of Chinese Sociolinguistics: Essays by Yuen Ren Chao*. Selected and introduced by Anwar S. Dil. Stanford: Stanford University Press, 1–20.

Cheng Tsung-hai 1923. "Elementary Education in China," in the Chinese National Association for the Advancement of Education, Peking, China, *Bulletin* II, 14: 1–40.

Chou Kuo-p'ing 1959. "Red China Tackles Its Language Problem," in *Harpers* CCXIX, 1310: 49–54 (July).

CYB. Bell, H. T. Montague, and H. G. W. Woodhead (Eds.), *The China Year Book*. Nendeln Liechtenstein: Kraus-Thomson Organization Limited.

DeFrancis, John 1948. "A Missionary Contribution to Chinese Nationalism," in the *Journal of the North China Branch of the Royal Asiatic Society* LXXIII: 1–34.

DeFrancis, John 1950. *Nationalism and Language Reform in China*. Princeton: Princeton University Press.

———— 1967. "Language and Script Reform," in Thomas A. Sebeok (Ed.). *Linguistics in East Asia and South East Asia*. Vol. II of *Current Trends in Linguistics*. The Hague: Mouton and Co., 130–50.

Deutsch, Karl W. 1966. *Nationalism and Social Communication: An Inquiry into the Foundations of Nationality*. Cambridge: The M.I.T. Press.

Fairbank, John King 1968. *The United States and China*. Revised and enlarged edition. New York: The Viking Press.

Fan Fang 1963. Zhongguo guanyin baihua bao (Chinese Vernacular Newspapers in the North Chinese Dialect), in Zhongguo renmin gongheguo, zhongguo kexueyuan, jindaishi yanjiuso, jindaishi ziliao bianjizu. (China, People's Republic of, 1949, Chinese Academy of Sciences, Institute of Modern History, Department on Compilation of Modern Historical Materials.) *Jindaishi ziliao*. (Modern Historical Materials). No. 2. Peking: Zhonghua shuju, 110–13.

Fang Shi-do 1965. *Wushinian lai zhongguo guoyu yundong shi* (The History of the Chinese National Language Movement in the Past Fifty Years). Taipei: Guoyu ribaoshe.

Fang Shi-do (Ed.) 1968. *Zengbu guoyin zihui* (Revised and Expanded List of Characters in the National Pronunciation). Taipei: Taiwan kaiming shudian.

Forrest, R.A.D. 1965. *The Chinese Language*. Second Edition, Revised and Expanded. London: Faber and Faber, Ltd.

Gamble, Sidney D. 1954. *Ting Hsien: A North China Rural Community*. New York: Institute of Pacific Relations.

GYZK-II. *Guoyu zhoukan*. (Mandarin Weekly, Second Series.) Peking: Guoyu tongyi choubei weiyuanhui (The Preparatory Commission for the Unification of the National Language and the Ministry of Education, Mandarin Promotion Commission). 2 Vols. Reprinted. Taipei: Zhonghua wenwu chubanshe, 1975.

He Rong 1946. "Lun mahu zhuyi de guoyu jiaoyu" (On Indifference Toward Standard Language Education), in *Taiwan Xin Sheng Bao*, March 10, 1946: 2.

He Rong 1975. "Guoyin biaozhun de laili" (The History of the Adoption of a Standard Pronunciation for the National Language), in Ibid. *He Rong wenji* (Selected Writings of He Rong). Taipei: Guoyu ribaoshe, 1–7.

He Rong 1976. Interview with He Rong, March 1, 1976, Taipei, Taiwan.

Hightower, James Robert 1966. *Topics in Chinese Literature: Outlines and Bib-*

liographies. Revised Edition. Harvard-Yenching Institute Studies, Volume III. Cambridge: Harvard University Press.

Israel, John 1966. *Student Nationalism in China, 1927–1937*. Stanford: Stanford University Press.

Kennedy, George A. 1964. "The Butterfly Case (Part I)," in Li Tien-yi (Ed.), *Selected Works of George A. Kennedy*, New Haven: Far Eastern Publications, Yale University, 274–322.

Kuo Ping-wen 1923. "Higher Education in China," in Chinese National Association for the Advancement of Education, Peking, China, *Bulletin* II, 10: 1–24.

Lamson, Herbert Day 1935. *Social Pathology in China*. Shanghai, China: The Commercial Press, Limited.

Latourette, Kenneth Scott 1964. *The Chinese: Their History and Culture*. Fourth edition, revised. New York: The Macmillan Company.

Li Jin-xi 1921. *Li Jin-xi de guoyu jiangtan* (Li Jin-xi's Lectures on the National Language). Shanghai: Zhonghua shuju.

Li Jin-xi 1934a. "Jiaoyubu guoyu tongyi choubei weiyuanhui zuijin liu nian jilue, min shiqi (1928)–min ershisan (1934)," (A Summary of the work of the Ministry of Education's Preparatory Commission for the Unification of the National Language During the Past Six Years 1928–1934), in GYZK-II No. 138: 287–88 (May 19, 1934); No. 139: 289–90 (May 26, 1934); No. 141: 293–94 (June 9, 1934); No. 143: 297–98 (June 23, 1934); No. 144: 299–300 (June 30, 1934); No. 148: 307–308 (July 28, 1934); No. 149: 309–310 (August 4, 1934); No. 150: 311–12 (August 11, 1934); No. 152: 315–16 (August 25, 1934).

Li Jin-xi 1934b. "Dazhong yuwen de gongju-zhuyin fuhao" (An instrument [for the promotion of] the Common Language—the National Phonetic Alphabet), in GYZK-II No. 157: 327–28 (September 29, 1934); No. 158: 329 (October 6, 1934); and No. 159: 331–32 (October 13, 1934).

Li Jin-xi 1935. *Guoyu yundong shigang* (Outline History of the National Language Movement). Nanchang: Shangwu yinshuguan.

Lin Yu-tang 1968. *A History of the Press and Public Opinion in China*. New York: Greenwood Press, Publishers.

Liu Fu [Liu Ban-nong] 1925. *Les Mouvements de la Langue Nationale en Chine*. Pekin and Paris: Presses de L'universite nationale de Pekin.

Lo Chang-pei 1956. "Lue lun hanyu guifanhua" (Some Remarks on the Standardization of the Chinese Language), in SCD 1956: 274–75.

Lo and Lü 1956. Lo Chang-pei and Lü Xu-xiang. "Xiandai hanyu guifan wenti" (Problems in Standardizing Modern Chinese), in SCD 1956: 4–22.

Lockwood, William W. 1964. "Economic and Political Modernization [in Japan]," in Ward, Robert E. and Dankwart A. Rustow (Eds.), *Political Modernization in Japan and Turkey*. Princeton: Princeton University Press, 117–45.

Miyazaki, Ichisada 1976. *China's Examination Hell: The Civil Service Examinations of Imperial China*. Translated by Conrad Schirokauer. New York: John Weatherhill, Inc.

MOE 1934. Zhonghua minguo, jiaoyubu (China, Republic of, 1911–, Ministry of Education). *Di yi ci zhongguo jiaoyu nianjian* (China Education Yearbook, First Edition). Shanghai: Kaiming shuju.

MOE 1948. Zhonghua minguo, jiaoyubu, jiaoyu nianjian bianzuan weiyuanhui (China, Republic of, 1911–, Ministry of Education, Committee for the

Compilation of the China Education Yearbook). *Zhongguo jiaoyu nianjian di er ci* (China Education Yearbook, Second Edition). 4 Vols. Shanghai: Shangwu yinshuguan.

MOE 1972. Zhonghua minguo, jiaoyubu, guoyu tongyi choubeihui (China, Republic of, 1911–, Ministry of Education, Preparatory Commission for the Unification of the National Language). *Jiaogai guoyin zidian* (A Pronouncing Dictionary in the National Language). Revised edition. Taipei: Taiwan kaiming shudian.

Ni Hai-shu 1958. "Hanyu pinyin de gushi" (The Story of Phonetic Spelling Systems for Chinese), in *Yuwen huibian, diwuji* (Selections on Language, Vol. 5). [Hong Kong: Lungmen shuju], 1968.

Peake, Cyrus H. 1932. *Nationalism and Education in Modern China*. New York: Columbia University Press.

Pye, Lucian W. 1972. *China: An Introduction*. Boston: Little, Brown and Company.

QMWJ 1958. *Qingmo wenzi gaige wenji* (Documents on Language Reform in the Late Ching Dynasty). Peking: Wenzi gaige chubanshe.

Ricci Journals 1953. *China in the Sixteenth Century: The Journals of Matthew Ricci: 1583–1610*. Translated from the Latin by Louis J. Gallagher, S. J. New York: Random House.

Rubin, Joan 1977. "Language Standardization in Indonesia," in Rubin, Joan, Björn H. Jernudd, Jyotirindra Das Gupta, Joshua A. Fishman, and Charles A. Ferguson. *Language Planning Processes*. The Hague: Mouton Publishers, 157–79.

Tabouret-Keller, A. 1968. "Sociological Factors of Language Maintenance and Language Shift: A Methodological Approach Based on European and African Examples," in Fishman, Joshua A., Charles A. Ferguson, and Jyotirindra Das Gupta (Eds.), *Language Problems of Developing Nations*. New York: John Wiley & Sons, Inc., 107–18.

Rustow, Dankwart A. 1968. "Language, Modernization, and Nationhood: An Attempt at Typology," in Fishman, Joshua A., Charles A. Ferguson, and Jyotirindra Das Gupta (Eds.), *Language Problems of Developing Nations*. New York: John Wiley & Sons, Inc., 87–106.

SCD 1956. Xiandai hanyu guifan wenti xueshu huiyi mishuchu (Secretariat of the Conference on Problems of Standardization of Modern Chinese). *Xiandai hanyu guifan wenti xueshu huiyi wenjian huibian* (Collected Documents of the Conference on Problems of Standardization of Modern Chinese). Peking: Kexue chubanshe.

State Council 1956. [Zhonghua renmin gongheguo], guowuyuan ([China, People's Republic of, 1949–], State Council). "Guowuyuan guanyu tuiguang putonghua de zhishi" (The Directives of the State Council Regarding the Promotion of the Common Language), in SCD 1956: 249–51.

Swadesh, Morris 1952. A Review of John DeFrancis 1950. *Nationalism and Language Reform in China*. Princeton, New Jersey: Princeton University Press, in *Science and Society* XVI: 273–80. (Summer).

Taga, Akigorō 1976. *Kindai Chūgoku kyōikushi shiryō–Minkoku-hen, chū*. (Source Materials on the History of Education in Modern China: The Republican Period, Vol. 2.) Taipei: Wenhai chubanshe.

Tien, Hung-mao 1972. *Government and Politics in Kuomintang China, 1927–1937*. Stanford: Stanford University Press.

TPMPC 1946. [Zhonghua minguo], Taiwansheng, guoyu tuixing weiyuanhui ([China, Republic of 1911–], Taiwan Province, Mandarin Promotion Commission). *Taiwansheng guoyu jiaoyu shishi gaikuang* (An Outline of the Implementation of Mandarin Education in Taiwan Province [during 1946]). [Taipei].

TPMPC 1947. [Zhonghua minguo], Taiwansheng, guoyu tuixing weiyuanhui ([China, Republic of, 1911–], Taiwan Province, Mandarin Promotion Commission). *Guoyin biaozhun huibian* (A List of Characters in The National Pronunciation) Taipei: Taiwan kaiming shuju.

TPMPC 1952. [Zhonghua minguo], Taiwansheng, guoyu tuixing weiyuanhui. (China [Republic of, 1911–], Taiwan Province, Mandarin Promotion Commission). *Guoyin biaozhun huibian* (A List of Characters in the National Pronunciation). Taipei: Taiwan kaiming shudian.

Wang Ju 1951. *Guoyu yundong de lilun yu shiji* (Theory and Practice of the Mandarin Movement). [Taipei]: Guoyu ribaoshe.

Wang, Y. C. 1966. *Chinese Intellectuals and the West, 1872–1949.* Chapel Hill: The University of North Carolina Press.

Wang Yu-chuan 1963. "Shifan xueyuan yu guoyu" (Teachers Normal Colleges and Mandarin), in Ibid. *Wo de guoyu lunwenji* (A Collection of My Writings on Mandarin). Taipei: Guoyu ribaoshe, 49–56.

Wei Jian-gong 1934. "Minguo ershisan nian yi yue qi ri guoyu tongyi choubei weiyuanhui diershijiu ci changwu weiyuanhui de yijue'an" (The Resolutions of the 29th meeting of the Standing Committee of the Preparatory Commission for the Unification of the National Language, held January 7, 1934), in GYZK-II, No. 122: 253–54, (January 27, 1934); No. 123: 255–56 (February 3, 1934).

Wright, Mary Clabaugh (Ed.) 1968. *China in Revolution: The First Phase, 1900–1913.* New Haven: Yale University Press.

Attracting a Following to High-Culture Functions for a Language of Everyday Life

(The Role of the Tshernovits Language Conference in the "Rise of Yiddish")

Joshua A. Fishman

The "spread of language" does not always entail gaining new speakers or users—whether as a first or as a second language. Frequently it entails gaining new functions or uses, particularly "H" functions (i.e., literacy-related functions in education, religion, "high culture" in general, and, in modern times, in econo-technology and government, too) for a language that is already widely known and used in "L" functions (i.e., everyday family, neighborhood, and other informal/intimate, intragroup interaction). Wherever a speech community already has a literacy-related elite, this type of language spread inevitably involves the displacement of an old elite (the one that is functionally associated with the erstwhile "H") by a new elite that is seeking a variety of social changes which are to be functionally associated with the prior "L" and which are to be instituted and maintained under its own (the new elite's) leadership.[1] The last century has witnessed the rise and fall (but not the complete elimination) of such efforts on behalf of Yiddish.

The traditional position of Yiddish in Ashkenaz (the traditional Hebrew-Aramaic and Yiddish designation for central and eastern Europe, Jews living in or deriving from this area being known, therefore, as Ashkenazim) was—and in many relatively unmodernized Orthodox circles still *is*—somewhat more complex than the H versus L distinction usually implies. At the extreme of sanctity there was *loshn koydesh*[2] alone, realized in hallowed biblical and postbiblical *texts*. At the opposite extreme, that of workaday intragroup life, there was Yiddish alone: the vernacular of one and all, rich and poor, learned and ignorant, pious and less than pious. Although "sanctity" and "workaday"

291

existed on a single continuum and were connected by a single overarching set of cultural values and assumptions, they were, nevertheless, distinct, overt cognitive and emotional opposites. In between these two extremes were numerous situations in which (a) *loshn koydesh* and Yiddish co-occurred insofar as intragroup life was concerned, and less numerous ones in which (b) coterritorial vernaculars or written languages were employed insofar as intergroup activities involving the worksphere, government, and infrequent "socializing" required.

The traditional *intra*-group intermediate zone resulted in a Yiddish oral literature of high moral import and public recognition (sometimes published in Yiddish but, at least initially, as often as not, translated into *loshn koydesh* for the very purpose of "dignified" publication). It also included the exclusive use of Yiddish as the process language of oral study, from the most elementary to the most advanced and recondite levels. And it included the exclusive use of Yiddish as the language of countless sermons by rabbis and preachers and as the language of popular religious tracts (ostensibly for women and uneducated menfolk). Thus, Yiddish *did* enter pervasively into the pale of sanctity and even into the pale of sanctity-in-print (hallowed bilingual texts—*loshn koydesh* originals with accompanying Yiddish translations—had existed ever since the appearance of print and, before that, as incunabula), but it never existed in that domain as a fully free agent, never as the sole medium of that domain in its most hallowed and most textified realizations, never as fully independent target medium but only as process medium underlying which or superceding which a single *loshn koydesh* text or a whole sea of such texts was either known, assumed, or created (Fishman 1975).

As a result, when traditional eastern European Jewry enters significantly into the nineteenth century drama of modernization, *loshn koydesh* and Yiddish are generally conceptualized, both by most intellectuals and by rank-and-file members of Ashkenaz, in terms of their extreme and discontinuous textified versus vernacular roles, their shared zones having contributed neither to the substantial vernacularization of *loshn koydesh* nor to the phenomenological sanctification of Yiddish. As the nineteenth century progressed there were increasing efforts to liberate Yiddish from its apparent subjugation to Hebrew (the latter being metaphorically referred to as the noble daughter of heaven, Yiddish being no more than her handmaiden), particularly for more modern intragroup H pursuits. In addition, there were also increasing efforts to liberate Yiddish from its inferior position vis-à-vis coterritorial vernaculars in connection with modern learning and nontraditional life more generally. It is with the former type of language spread that this paper deals most directly (and with its implications for the role of *loshn koydesh,* which was also then being groomed for modern H roles at the intragroup and at the intergroup levels), although the spill-over from the former to the latter type of language spread was often both an objective and an achievement as well. Obviously, when one component of a traditional diglossia (here: triglossia) situation changes in its functions, the societal allocation of functions with respect to the other(s) is under stress to change as well.

THE TSHERNOVITS LANGUAGE
CONFERENCE: SUCCESS OR FAILURE?

Three different positive views concerning Yiddish were clearly evident by the first decade of the twentieth century, and a fourth was then increasingly coming into being.[3] The earliest view was a *traditional utilitarian* one, and it continues to be evinced primarily by ultra-Orthodox spokesmen to this very day. In accord with this view Yiddish was (and is) to be utilized in print for various moralistic and halahic[4] educational purposes, because it has long been used in this way, particularly in publications for women, the uneducated and children. Any departure from such use—whether on behalf of modern Hebrew or a coterritorial vernacular—was and is decried as disruptive of tradition. Another view was a *modern utilitarian* one, namely, that Yiddish must be used in political and social education if the masses were ever to be moved toward more modern attitudes and behaviors, because it was the only language that they understand. This view was and, to some extent, still is widely held by maskilic[5] and Zionist/socialist spokesmen. A third view was also evident by the turn of the century, namely that Yiddish was a distinctly indigenous and representative vehicle and, therefore, it had a *natural role to play both in expressing and in symbolizing Jewish cultural-national desiderata.* Finally, we begin to find expressed the view that for modern Jewish needs, Yiddish is the *only or major natural expressive and symbolic vehicle.*

In the nineteenth century the first two positive views (and the counterclaims related to them) were encountered most frequently, but the latter two were beginning to be expressed as well (see, particularly J.M. Lifshits's writings, e.g., 1863, 1867; note D. Fishman's discussion [1978] of Lifshits as transitional ideologist). In the twentieth century the latter two views (and their respective refutations) came into prominence and the former two receded and were ultimately almost abandoned.[6] The last public encounter of all four views was at the Tshernovits Language Conference. There the first two views were presented and strongly refuted whereas the last two remained in uneasy balance, neither of them appearing clearly victorious over the other.

PLANNING THE CONFERENCE

The father of the idea to convene an international conference on behalf of Yiddish was Dr. Nosn Birnboym (Nathan Birnbaum) (1864–1936)[7] who came to the United States in 1907 with that very purpose in mind. Birnboym, who had coined the word "Zionism" (in German: *Zionismus*) and had conceptualized much of its mission in the early 1890s, had by then already broken both with Theodore Herzl (1860–1904) and with Herzlian Zionism on the grounds that to save Jews ("to solve the Jewish Question") without aiming at fostering Jewishness ("to solve the Jewishness Question") was tantamount to fostering assimilation under Jewish auspices. In the course of his own Jewish self-discovery he came to regard Yiddish as a vehicle of genuine, rooted Jewishness and, therefore, as the preferred vehicle of a kind of modernization that would also be particularly attuned to the simultaneous need for continuity of Jewish culture, traditions, and values. He had begun to write in this vein by the beginning of the century in the German periodical *Selbst-Emancipation* (that he founded in Vienna in 1885) and continued doing so subsequently in his Yiddish weekly, *Dokter birnboyms vokhnblat,* that he founded in Tshernovits (Czernowitz, Czernowce, Chernovtsy, Cernauti),[8] to which he had moved at the invitation of university students in Vienna who hailed from Tshernovits, were sympathetic toward Yiddish, and who had come under the influence of his writings. However, Tshernovits did not give him the visibility (nor the income) that he required and he decided to visit the United States in pursuit of both and on behalf of Yiddish, "the world language of a world people."

Birnboym's initial host in the United States was the socialist-Zionist Dovid Pinski, already well known as a Yiddish novelist and dramatist, who had read Birnboym's articles in German and was eager to help him reach a wider pro-Yiddish audience. Immediately attracted to Birnboym's cause was the socialist-territorialist[9] theoretician and philosopher Khayem Zhitlovski (for extensive bibliographic details see Fishman in press). The three of them formed a curious troika (a neo-traditionalist on his way back to full-fledged orthodoxy, a labor-Zionist, and a philosophical secularist), but together they issued a resolution for a world conference concerning Yiddish, composed in Pinski's apartment on Beck Street in the South Bronx (also signed by the playwright Yankev Gordon and the publisher Alex Yevalenko), and together they brought it to a less than massive public at two "evenings" (Yiddish: *ovntn* although not necessarily transpiring in the evening) on the Lower East Side. Far more unforgettable than the arguments that they then marshalled for such a conference, and more impressive than the proposed order of business suggested in connection with it, was the fact that its chief architect, Birnboym, spoke to the audiences in German (for he could not yet speak standard or formal Yiddish, although he had begun to write Yiddish articles in 1904). His addresses, although purposely peppered with Yiddishisms, struck most commentators as impressive but funny, funny but painful. The intelligentsia was learning its mother tongue so that the latter could fulfill new functions and thereby provide new statutes to masses and intelligentsia alike.

But there *was* an intended "order of business" for Tshernovits, no matter how much it may have been overlooked at the *ovntn* or even at the conference itself. Birnboym, Zhitlovski, and Pinski agreed (primarily at the latter's insistence) to "avoid politics" and "resolutions on behalf of Yiddish" (Pinski 1948), particularly since the political and ideological context of Yiddish differed greatly in Czarist Russia, in Hapsburg Austro-Hungary and in the immigrant United States. Thus they agreed upon a "practical agenda" and a "working conference" devoted to the following ten points:

1. Yiddish spelling
2. Yiddish grammar
3. Foreign words and new words
4. A Yiddish dictionary
5. Jewish youth and the Yiddish language
6. The Yiddish press
7. The Yiddish theatre and Yiddish actors
8. The economic status of Yiddish writers
9. The economic status of Yiddish actors
10. Recognition for the Yiddish language

The agenda starts off with four items of corpus planning.[10] Yiddish was correctly seen as being in need of authoritative codification and elaboration in order to standardize its usage and systematize its future growth. Major corpus-planning efforts for Yiddish—though previously called for and attempted—were a sign of its new importance. Point five recognized the dangers that modernization represented for the ethnic identity of the younger generation, particularly if it pursued education and advancement in coterritorial vernaculars to the exclusion of Yiddish. Points six to nine stressed press and theater—their quality and their economic viability—the massive means of bringing modern Yiddish creativity to the public. Finally, the last point recognized something that was certainly on Birnboym's mind. Jews themselves—not to speak of gentiles—were unaccustomed to granting recognition to Yiddish, and, therefore, such recognition was often begrudged it even by democratic or democratizing regimes that gave some consideration to cultural autonomy or to officially recognized cultural pluralism (as did pre-World War I Austro-Hungary). As Pinski in particular feared, the entire agenda of the conference was "subverted" by the tenth point and, indeed, was dominated by what was in reality only half of that point: *Jewish* recognition for Yiddish.

WHY WAS THE CONFERENCE HELD
IN TSHERNOVITS?

Tshernovits was only a modest-sized town (21,500 Jews out of a total population of 68,400) and of no particular importance vis-à-vis Jewish cultural, political, or economic developments. It was clearly overshadowed by Warsaw, Vilna, Odessa, and several other urban centers in the Pale of Settlement within the Czarist empire. Nevertheless, the recent history of Czarist repressions may have made it undesirable (if no longer clearly impossible) to convene the conference in one of those centers. Even within the Austro-Hungarian empire, however, such Jewish centers as Kruke (Cracow), Lemberik (Lemberg), Lvov, and Brod (Brodie) were clearly of greater importance than Tshernovits. Tshernovits was, of course, easily accessible to Yiddish speakers in Austro-Hungary and Czarist Russia, but its symbolic significance far surpassed its national convenience and was twofold: (a) Not only was it in *Frants-yosefs medine* (the Austro-Hungarian empire) but many segments of its hitherto significantly Germanized Jewish intelligentsia were already struggling to revise its attitudes towards Yiddish—a struggle that was particularly crucial for that period in Austro-Hungarian cultural politics vis-à-vis Germans, Poles, Ukrainians/Ruthenians, and Jews in Bukovina and in Galicia as well—and (b) Birnboym had already decided to relocate there and had several young followers there (many of whom were students at the university in Vienna during the school year—and had there been influenced by Birnboym). These young followers could provide (on a volunteer basis and during the summer vacation period in particular) the technical/organizational underpinnings of a world conference for Yiddish. Indeed, these followers constituted, with Birnboym, the organizational committee that sent out the invitations to individual organizations and committees, secured a hall (not without difficulty), planned a banquet and literary evening, and disbursed the meager fees that the participants in the Conference paid in order to be either delegates (5 Kronen) or guests (1 Krone). Both of these factors (the convening of the Conference in Tshernovits, and Birnboym's young and inexperienced followers there in the grips of their own discovery of H-possibilities for Yiddish) influenced the course of the Conference. The delicate balance of minority relations in Galicia and Jukōvina resulted in more widespread attention being paid to the first Yiddish World Conference than its sponsors had bargained for. The census of 1910 was already being discussed, and it was apparent that the authorities again wanted Jews to claim either German (in Bukovina) or Polish (in Galicia) as mother tongue (as had been done in 1890) in order to defuse or counterbalance the growing pressure from Ukrainian/Ruthenians and Rumanians for additional language privileges and parliamentary representation. Previously, Jews had been counted upon to buttress the establishment out of fear that "unrest" would lead to anti-Jewish developments of one kind or another. It was equally apparent that young Jews were disinclined to play this role any longer and that they were threatening to claim either Yiddish or Hebrew, even though neither was on the approved list of mother tongues and even though claiming a language not on the list was a punishable offense.[11] Indeed so great was the tension concerning the Conference that the President of the Jewish Community (*kehile*) in Tshernovits refused to permit the Conference to meet in community facilities for fear of incurring official displeasure or worse. Clearly, a new within-fold status for Yiddish would have intragroup repercussions as well: upsetting the former within-group diglossia system was also related to new intergroup aspirations and these were, of necessity, political and economic (or likely to be suspected of being such), rather than merely cultural (no matter what the official agenda of the Conference might be).

Moreover, meeting in Tshernovits also determined the very nature of the guests and delegates (a distinction that was soon ignored) that could attend, discuss, propose, vote upon, and ultimately implement the Conference's deliberations and resolutions. The regional tensions in conjunction with national/cultural rights resulted in attendance by a more substantial number of students and ordinary folk, many in search of something spectacular or even explosive, than might otherwise have been the case. Similarly, because of the characteristics of Bukovinian Jewry per se there were more Zionists and fewer Bundists,[12] more traditionally-religiously oriented and fewer proletarian-politically oriented delegates and guests than would have been the case elsewhere. Birnboym's youthful admirers and assistants were quite incapable of rectifying this imbalance by such simple means as sending more invitations to more "nationally conscious" circles. Indeed, for them, as for most Jewish intellectuals in Tshernovits, the idea of a Conference *on behalf of* Yiddish and conducted *in* Yiddish was not quite believable even as it materialized. Most local Jewish intellectuals were "the mainstay of . . . daytshtum (Germanness), and of a *sui generis* daytshtum to boot, Bukovinian daytshtum. None of the socially and politically active local (Jewish) intellectuals imagined anything like speaking to the people in its language. Indeed, when Berl Loker, who belonged to the exceptions, then a young student, was about to give a lecture in Yiddish, he invited my wife to attend as follows: 'Come and you will hear how one speaks pure Yiddish at a meeting!' The best recommendation for a speaker was the accomplishment of being able to speak to a crowd in lovely and ornate German" (Vays 1937). Thus, the lingering disbelief that Yiddish was suitable for H pursuits ("Is Yiddish a language?") *surrounded* the Conference and even found its way *into* the Conference, and did so in Tshernovits more than it would have in many other, more industrialized and proletarianized centers of Jewish urban concentration and modernization. Bukovinian Jewry and its modernizing elites were then both still relatively untouched by the more sophisticated pro- and anti-Yiddish sentiments that were at a much higher pitch in Warsaw, Vilna, Lodz, or Odessa.

WHO ATTENDED THE CONFERENCE?

The invitations sent by Birnboym's "secretariat" were addressed to those organizations and communities whose addresses they happened to have. Many *unimportant* societies and clubs were invited, whereas many even more important ones were not. Personal invitations were few and far between. The writer and essayist Y. L. Perets (Warsaw, 1852–1915), perhaps the major influence upon the younger generation of Yiddish writers and a conscious ideologist of synthesis among all Jewish values and symbols, modern and traditional, *was* invited and came with his wife (with whom he spoke more Polish than Yiddish). The two other "classicists of modern Yiddish literature," Sholem Aleykhem (1859–1910) and Mendele Moyker Sforim (1836–1917), were also invited but did not come. Sholem Aleykhem at least claimed to be ill; but Mendele, in his seventies, offered no excuse at all, and, as a result, was sent no greetings by the Conference such as were sent to Sholem Aleykhem. Zhitlovski came, but Pinski was "busy writing a book" (Pinski 1948). A young linguist, Matesyohu Mizes (Mathias Mieses), was invited (as were two other linguistics-oriented students, Ayzenshtat and Sotek) to address the Conference on the linguistic issues that apparently constituted forty percent of its agenda. Other than the above individual invitations, a general invitation was issued and broadcast via the Yiddish press and by word of mouth "to all friends of Yiddish." All in all some seventy showed up and these were characterized by one participant (and later major critic) as having only one thing in common: "They could afford the fare. . . . Everyone was his own master, without any sense of responsibility to others" (E[ste]r 1908).

The geographic imbalance among the resulting participants is quite clear:

From the Czarist empire: 14. Among this delegation were found the most prestigeful participants: Perets, Sholem Asch (still young but already a rising star), Avrom Reyzin (a well known and much beloved poet), D. Nomberg (writer and journalist, later a deputy in the Polish Sejm and founder of a small political party, *yidishe folkistishe partey,* stressing Yiddish and diaspora cultural autonomy), N. Prilutski (linguist, folklorist, journalist; later a Sejm deputy), Ester (Bundist, later a Communist [Kombund and Yevsektsiya] leader). Zhitlovski (though coming from the United States) and Ayznshtat (though then studying in Bern) were also usually counted with the "Russians."

From Rumania: 1. I. Sotek of Braila (an advocate of writing Yiddish with Latin characters and a student of slavic elements in Yiddish).

From Galicia and Bukovina: 55. Among these were eight minor literary figures and forty-seven students, merchants, bookkeepers, craftsmen, etc., including one "wedding entertainer" (*badkhn*). This group was the least disciplined and, on its home territory, least impressed and convinced by attempts to keep to any agenda.

> At the most crucial votes no more than forty members participated. . . . In the vote on the resolution that Yiddish be considered a national [Jewish] language no more than 36 individuals participated. People always were arriving late to sessions. Some did not know what they were voting about. People voted and contradicted their own previous votes. In addition it was always noisy due to the booing and the applauding of "guests from Tshernovits." No one at all listened to Ayznshtat's paper on Yiddish spelling. (E[ste]r 1908)

Nor were the banquet or the literary program any more orderly or consensual. When local Jewish workers arrived to attend the banquet

> it was discovered that they lacked black jackets and they were not admitted. They began to complain. Some of the more decently clad ones were selected and admitted without jackets. Some of the "indecently" clad

workers took umbrage and protested so long that the policeman took pity on them and sent them away. As a result, the "decently" clad ones also decided to leave. After the opening remarks I called everyone's attention to what had occurred. It immediately became noisy and I was told to stop speaking. I left the banquet and a few others accompanied me. (E[ste]r 1908)

Attracting an elite to modern H functions for an erstwhile traditional L runs into problems due to the fact that prior and concurrent social issues have established allegiances and identities that are not congruent with those that further the interests of the new elite and the new functions. Reformulation of identities and regrouping of allegiances is called for and is difficult for all concerned.

THE CONFERENCE PER SE

The Conference began on Sunday, August 30, 1908, and lasted for a little under a week.

A quarter after ten in the morning there walked onto the stage Nosn Birnboym in the company of Y. L. Perets, S. Asch, Dr. Kh. Zhitlovski and other distinguished guests. . . . Dr. N. Birnboym opens the Conference reading his first speech in Yiddish fluently from his notes. . . . He reads his speech in the Galician dialect. (*Rasvet*, September 1908: quoted from *Afn shvel* 1968)

Birnboym stressed the fact that this was the first worldwide effort on behalf of Yiddish, sponsored by its greatest writers ("respected even by the opponents of Yiddish") and the beginning of a long chain of efforts yet to come. These opening remarks caused a sensation among local Tshernovitsians.

Everyone knew that he [Birnboym] doesn't speak Yiddish and that the speech would be translated from German. However, all were eager to hear how the "coarse" words would sound coming from the mouth of Dr. Birnboym who was known as an excellent German speaker. . . . However at the festive banquet in honor of the esteemed guests . . . he spoke superbly in German, the way only he could. (Vays 1937)

Indeed, a speaker's ability to speak Yiddish well and the very fact that Yiddish *could* be spoken as befitted a world conference, i.e., in a cultivated, learned, disciplined fashion in conjunction with modern concerns, never ceased to impress those who had never before heard it so spoken.

Zhitlovski made the greatest impression on all the delegates and guests, both at the Conference and at the banquet (which was a great event for Yiddish culture that was still so unknown to most of those in attendance). "That kind of Yiddish is more beautiful than French!" was a comment heard from all quarters and particularly from circles that had hitherto rejected Yiddish from a "purely esthetic" point of view. (Vays 1937)[13]

ה.ד. נ$ָ$אמבּערג, ד"ר זשיטלאָװסקי, ש.אַש, י.ל.פּרץ, אבֿרהם רייזען .

628.   אין טשערנאָװיץ .

A postcard printed soon after the Tshernovits Conference,
showing left to right, Avrom Reyzin, Yitshak L. Perets,
Sholem Asch, Khayem Zhitlovski, and Hersh D. Nomberg.

Yiddish used adeptly in an H function was itself a triumph for Tshernovits, almost regardless of what was said.

But of course a great deal *was* said substantively as well. The linguistic issues were "covered" by Azynshtat, Sotek, and Mizes. Whereas the first two were roundly ignored, the third caused a storm of protests when, in the midst of a paper on fusion languages and their hybridlike strength, creativity, and vigor, he also attacked *loshn koydesh* for being dead, stultifying, and decaying. Only Perets's intervention saved Mizes's paper for the record as "the first scientific paper in Yiddish on Yiddish" (Anon. 1931).[14] Obviously, the tenth agenda item stubbornly refused to wait its place in line and constantly came to the fore in the form of an increasingly growing antagonism between those (primarily Bundists)

who wanted to declare Yiddish as *the* national Jewish language
(Hebrew/*loshn koydesh*—being a classical tongue rather than a mother
tongue—could not, in their view, qualify as such) and those (primarily
Zionists and traditionalists) who, at best, would go no further than to
declare Yiddish as *a* national Jewish language, so that the role of
Hebrew/*loshn koydesh*—past, present and future—would remain unsul-
lied.[15] In the midst of this fundamental argument more primitive views
still surfaced as a result of the presence of so many ideologically unmodernized guests. One of the delegates recounts the following tale:

> . . . (T)here suddenly appears on the stage a man with a long, red beard,
> wearing a traditional black *kapote* (kaftan) and *yarmelke* (skull-cap). He be-
> gins speaking by saying "I will tell you a story." The hall is full of quiet
> expectancy. We all listened carefully in order to hear a good, folksy anec-
> dote. The man recounts in great detail a story about how two Jews once
> sued each other in court because of a *shoyfer* (ritual ram's horn) that had
> been stolen from the *beysmedresh* (house of study and prayer). With great
> difficulty they explained to the gentile judge what a *shoyfer* is. Finally the
> judge asked: "In one word—a trumpet?" At this point the litigants shud-
> dered and one shouted to the other: "Is a *shoyfer* a trumpet?" The assem-
> bled participants in the hall were ready to smile at this "anecdote" which
> had long been well known, when the man suddenly began to shout at the
> top of his lungs: "You keep on talking about language, but is Yiddish
> (*zhargon*) a language? (Kisman 1958)

The compromise formulation penned by Nomberg ("*a* national
Jewish language") was finally adopted, thanks only to the insistence of
Perets, Birnboym, and Zhitlovski, and over the vociferous opposition
of both left-wing and right-wing extremists who either favored an exclusive role for Yiddish ("*the* national Jewish language") or who wanted
no resolutions at all on political topics.[16]
Very little time was devoted to organizational or implementational
issues such as whether the Conference itself should sponsor "cultural
work," convene a second conference within a reasonable time, or even
establish a permanent office (secretariat) and membership organization.
Although the last two recommendations were adopted (the first was
rejected due to unified left-wing and right-wing disenchantment with
the Conference's stance re the "*the* or *a*" national language issue), and
although Birnboyn and two young assistants were elected to be the executive officers and to establish a central office, very little was actually
done along these lines. At any rate, the tasks entrusted to the secretariat were minimal and innocuous ones indeed. In addition,
Birnboym soon moved even closer to unreconstructed Orthodoxy and

to its stress on matters "above and beyond language." (He subsequently continued to defend Yiddish as a bulwark of tradition but pointed out that it was the tradition rather than the language that really counted. He therefore metaphorically translated the prayer book phrase *roymemonu mikol loshn* not, as it was usually understood, "Thou hast raised us above all other languages," but rather, "Thou hast raised us above all languages," Birnboym [1946].) At any rate, he was not an administrator/ executive but an ideologue. He was, as always, penniless, and the funds that were required for an office and for his salary never materialized. Zhitlovski returned to America and threw himself into efforts there to start Yiddish supplementary schools and to restrain Jewish socialists from sacrificing their own Jewishness and the Jewish people as a whole on the altar of Americanization disguised as proletarian brotherhood. Perets did undertake one fund-raising trip to St. Petersburg where Shimen Dubnov (1860–1941), the distinguished historian and ideologist of cultural autonomy in the diaspora and himself a recent convert to the value of Yiddish, had convened a small group of wealthy but Russified potential donors. The latter greeted Perets with such cold cynicism that he "told them off" ("our salvation will come from the poor but warm-hearted Jews of the Pale rather than from the rich but cold-hearted Jews of St. Petersburg") and "slammed the door." Thus, for various reasons, no office was ever really established in Tshernovits and even the minutes of the Conference remained unpublished. Although S. A. Birnboym helped prepare them for publication by editing out as many Germanisms as possible, they were misplaced or lost and had to be reconstructed more than two decades later from press clippings and memoirs (Anon. 1931).

Intellectuals (and even an intelligentsia) alone can rarely establish a movement. Intellectuals can reify language and react to it as a powerful symbol, as the bearer and actualizer of cultural values, behaviors, traditions, goals. However, for an L to spread into H functions, more concrete considerations (jobs, funds, influence, status, control, power) are involved. Only the Yiddishist left wing had in mind an economic, political, and cultural revolution that would have placed Yiddish on top. But that left did not even control the Tshernovits Conference, to say nothing of the hard, cruel world that surrounded it.

AMERICAN REACTIONS TO THE TSHERNOVITS CONFERENCE

The increasingly democratic, culturally pluralistic, and culturally autonomistic prewar Austro-Hungarian empire was the model toward which mankind was moving insofar as the leading figures at Tshernovits were concerned. One of the areas of Jewish concentration in which this model did not prevail was most clearly—and where the very concept of a symbolically unified, modernized, worldwide Jewish nationality with a stable, all-purpose vernacular of its own was least understood, accepted, and actualized, was the United States. No wonder then that the Tshernovits Conference was generally accorded a cool reception here and even a derisive one.[17] The idea of teaching people how to spell or write or speak Yiddish "correctly" was viewed by one journalist as being no less ridiculous than the idea of teaching people to laugh correctly, grammatically (Sambatyen, "A falsher gelekhter, gor on gramatik," *Yidishes Tageblat*,[18] Sept. 1, 1908). The *Tageblat* was an Orthodox-oriented paper, and in its editorials before and after the Conference it stressed that *loshn koydesh* alone was of value for Jewishness while English (or other coterritorial vernaculars elsewhere) met all of the general and citizenship needs that Jews might have. To elevate Yiddish to H functions was not only ridiculous but blasphemous.

> If the resolutions of the Conference declare . . . that all of Jewishness will be found in Asch's drama "God of Vengeance" and in Perets' "Shtrayml" . . . will anyone care? Our people decided long ago that we are a nationality and that our national language is none other than that in which the spirit of the Jewish people developed . . . the language in which the Bible is written, the Book that has made us immortal. (Sept. 20, 1908)

If the Orthodox-bourgeois *Tageblat* was unfriendly toward the Conference, to say the least, the secular-socialist *Forverts* (still publishing to this day) was almost every bit as much so. Its correspondent Moris Roznfeld (a famous Yiddish laborite-poet in his own right) wrote from Galicia just a few days before the Conference opened

> I know that with just a few exceptions there is not much interest in America in this Tshernovits Conference and for many reasons. First of all, most believe that nothing practical will come of it. Secondly, the American Yiddish writer, as well as the Yiddish reader, is not terribly interested in rules of grammar. What difference does it make whether one writes   , or   [all pronounced geyn/gayn depending on speaker's regional dialect],   ,   ,   or even   [the first three pronounced id/yid and the last—utilized only ironically/contrastively in Yiddish—Yahudi, and, therefore not really an orthographic variant in a continuum with the first three], as long as it can be read and understood? . . . Among the majority of even our good writers, Yiddish is regarded merely as a ferry that leads to the other side, to the language of the land, which each of us must learn in the land in which he finds himself.

But these views, objectively and impartially stated, apply only to America. Here, in Galicia, they are more than merely grammatical issues. Here it is a political issue, an issue of life itself. . . .

. . . If it were to be officially decided that *loshn koydesh* is the Jewish language, then the Jewish masses would lose their power and their vernacular would be ignored. Only the Jewish snobs, the aristocratic, "let-them-eat-cake" idealists, would gain thereby. Therefore, the eyes of the real friends of the people and of the friends of the workers in Galicia and even in Russia are turned toward Tshernovits. Therefore the Conference there has major, historical importance. I don't know from what point of view the Conference will treat the language issue . . . The Conference might even be of an academic, theoretical nature . . . Nevertheless, the Conference will have strong reverberations on Jewish politics in Galicia.

Note Roznfeld's total disinterest in either the linguistic portion or in any portion of the Tshernovits agenda as being valid for Americans. In 1908 few American Yiddish writers, few even of the secular laborites among them, aspired to H functions for Yiddish. In their eyes Jews, as workers, were destined to be part of the greater American proletariat; and English would, therefore, be its language for higher socialist purposes, and, ultimately, its brotherly interethnic vernacular as well. The Bund's 1905 Declaration, and its positing of Jewish cultural autonomy in eastern Europe, with Yiddish as the national language of the Jewish proletariat, was considered, at best, to be a politically relevant platform for eastern European Jewry alone, but one that was irrelevant for those who had immigrated to "the Golden Land." Thus, if neither the linguistic nor the political potentialities of the Conference applied here then the Conference as a whole was merely a distant echo, and either a somewhat funny one or a clearly sacrilegious one at that. If it was difficult to assign H functions to Yiddish in its very own massive heartland, where its stability was less threatened (so it seemed) and where all agreed as to its utility, how much more difficult was it to do so in immigrant-America where its transitionality was assumed by secularists and traditionalists alike?

EASTERN EUROPEAN REACTIONS
TO THE CONFERENCE

If the brunt of American commentary on the Conference was negative, that in eastern Europe was initially equally or even more so, and on three grounds. As expected, the Hebraist and extreme-Zionist reaction was unrelentingly hostile. In their eyes Yiddish was a language that demoted Jewry from its incomparable classical heights to the superficiality and vacuousness of such illiterate peasant tongues as Ukrainian, Lithuanian, Rumanian, etc. To foster Yiddish struck J. Klausner, I. Epshteyn, and many other Hebraists as being laughable, if it were not so sad, an exercise in self-impoverishment and self-debasement. A considerable number of those who shared their view urged that a massive counter-conference be convened (and, indeed, the First World Conference for the Hebrew Language *was* convened in Berlin in 1910) and that an even more massive propaganda campaign be launched to attack Tshernovits and its infamous resolution. However, the veteran Hebraist and philosopher Aḥad Ha'am (1856–1927) argued vehemently against such efforts, on the grounds that they would give Tshernovits more visibility than it could ever attain on its own. According to Aḥad Ha'am, the Jewish people had already experienced two great philosophical disasters in the diaspora: Christianity and Ḥasidism.[19] Both of these had mushroomed precisely because Jews themselves had paid too much attention to them by dignifying them with unnecessary commentary. This sad lesson should now be applied to Tshernovits and to Yiddishism as a whole. They were *muktse makhmes miyes* [mukẓa maḥamat mius], *loathsomely ugly,* and the less said about them the better.

   If the right-wing opposition generally elected to counter Tshernovits with a wall of silence, the left-wing opposition apparently decided to drown it in a sea of words. From their point of view Tshernovits had been a "sell out" on the part of those who were willing to water down, render tepid, and weaken the position vis-à-vis Yiddish of "the broad folk-masses" and "the Jewish proletariat," in order to curry favor among the bourgeoisie, by adopting an uninspired and uninspiring "all Israel are brothers" approach. The modern, secular, socialist sector of the Jewish people, "the revolutionary and nationality-building sector," had, by then, already surpassed the meager goals and the lukewarm resolutions of Tshernovits. They, therefore, refused to be compromised and whittled down by a conference that was "an episode instead of a happening" (Kazhdan 1928) and whose resolution was no more than "a harmful illusion" (Zilberfarb 1928) and "a mistake that must not be reiterated" (Khmurner 1928).

   The Tshernovits Conference was converted into the opposite of what its initiators had projected. Its isolation from the Jewish labor movement took its revenge upon the Conference. . . . The great masters of Yiddish literature did not possess the magic to convert the Jewish middle class and the bourgeois intellectuals into co-combatants and partners with the Jewish workers in the latter's great national role of limitless loyalty to the Yiddish language. Yiddish cultural life therefore far surpassed the Tshernovits Conference. . . . Neither at the Teachers Conference in Vilna, nor at the organizational Convention of the Central Yiddish School Organization (*Tsisho*), nor at the Tsisho-Convention of 1925 where the founding of the Yivo [Yiddish Scientific Institute; today: Yivo Institute for Jewish Research] was proclaimed, nor at any of the many other [Yiddish] teachers' conferences in Poland was there even a word spoken about the Tshernovits Conference. . . . Today, 60 years after Tshernovits we know: Tshernovits was not destined to have any heirs. . . . There was really nothing to inherit. (Kazhdan 1969)

Even now, over three decades after the Holocaust—when most commentators tend to wax lyrical about Jewish eastern Europe and to remember it in somewhat rosy terms—there remain Bundist leaders who remember Tshernovits only as a flubbed opportunity.

Even those who were quite satisfied with Tshernovits in symbolic terms soon realized that it was a fiasco in any practical organizational terms. As soon as the First World War was over (and, indeed, in the very midst of the War in anticipation of its conclusion), various Yiddish writers and cultural spokesmen began to call for "a world conference for Yiddish culture as a result of purely practical rather than demonstrative and declarative goals. We have outgrown the period of mere demonstrations and theoretical debates. There is much work to be done!" (Sh. N[iger] 1922). Zhitlovski himself called for "an organization to openly unfurl the flag on which it will be clearly written: Yiddish, our national language, our only unity and freedom . . . a 'Yiddishist' organization with the openly unfurled flag of our cultural liberation and national unity" (1928). Others repeatedly reinforced and repeated this view (e.g., Lehrer 1928, Mark 1968, Zelitsh 1968). As a result, most subsequent major nonpartisan or suprapartisan international efforts to organize Yiddish cultural efforts more effectively have viewed themselves as the instrumental heirs of the Tshernovits Conference (e.g., YIKUF-Yidisher kultur farband 1937; Yidisher kultur kongres 1948; Yerushelayemer velt konferents far Yiddish un Yidisher kultur 1976). Clearly, however, the realities facing Yiddish after World War I were far different from those that Tshernovits assumed. The multiethnic Austro-Hungarian empire had been split into several smaller states, each jealously protective of its particular national (state-building) language and quick to set aside the Trianon and Versailles guarantees to Yiddish (Tenenboym 1957/58). The former Czarist "pale of settlement" was either in the same situation as the foregoing (insofar as Poland and the Baltic states were concerned) or, ultimately, under even more powerful Russificatory control than before (in White Russia and in the Ukraine). Despite Bundist grievances, a good part of the spirit of Tshernovits lived for two postwar decades in the Yiddish schools, youth clubs, theaters, and cultural organizations of Poland, Lithuania, and Rumania, and, despite Communist attacks, in their regulated counterparts in the USSR. However, by just prior to the Second World War, the former were economically starved and politically battered (Eisenstein 1949, Tartakover 1946), whereas the latter were being discontinued under duress of Russification fears and pressures (Choseed 1968). After the Second World War Jewish eastern Europe was no more. It became incumbent on Yiddish devotees in the United States and in Israel, i.e., in two locales where Yiddish was originally not expected to benefit from the spirit of Tshernovits, to defend it if possible.

REEVALUATING THE
TSHERNOVITS CONFERENCE:
SHADOW OR SUBSTANCE?

Notwithstanding Kazhdan's lingering negative evaluation in 1968, distance has made the heart grow fonder insofar as the majority of commentators is concerned. Those few who initially held that the symbolism of Tshernovits had been substantial, i.e., that it had raised Yiddish to the status of an honorific co-symbol, regardless of what its practical shortcomings might have been (for example: Mayzl 1928, Prilutski 1928, Pludermakher 1928), finally carried the day. The views that are encountered today in Yiddishist circles are very much like those that began to be heard when the first commemorative celebrations in honor of Tshernovits were organized in 1928. (In September 1918 the First World War had technically not yet ended and celebrations were presumably not possible.) "Yes, Yiddishism is a young movement, but it is not all that poor in traditions. One of the loveliest traditions of Yiddishism is the memory of the Tshernovits Conference. No memoirs, pedantry or arguments can darken the glow of that bright cultural dawn's early light that is known by the name: The Tshernovits Conference of 1908" (Pludermakher 1928). Perhaps it was and perhaps it wasn't necessary to compromise in connection with the crucial resolution. In either case, no one was fooled by the compromise. "The Tshernovits Conference was recorded on the morrow immediately after the last session as the Yiddishist revolt—and that is the only way in which the opponents of the Yiddish language *could regard* it" (Prilutski 1928) for even to claim H *co*-functions *alongside* of Hebrew/*loshn koydesh* was a devastating rejection of what these opponents were aiming at. As a result, Tshernovits deserved to be viewed as "the first mobilization" (Mayzl 1928) on behalf of Yiddish.

Seventy years after Tshernovits, Yiddishist opinion with respect to it is, if anything, even mellower. Living as they do with the constant if quiet anxiety produced by the continual attrition of Yiddish, Yiddishists have come to view Tshernovits not merely as a milestone in the millennial struggle of Yiddish for symbolic recognition, but as symbolic of the best that eastern European Jewry as a whole achieved and can offer to its far-flung progeny today. Tshernovits is viewed increasingly as a byproduct of the confluence of the three organized movements in modern Jewish life: Jewish socialism, Zionism, and neo-Orthodoxy. At Tshernovits, representatives of all three recognized the significance of Yiddish. Tshernovits was the byproduct of a confluence (and, therefore, it disappointed those who wanted it to be all theirs). It was a momentary confluence of three disparate forces; it quickly passed, and from that day to this, no one has been able to "put them together again." Indeed, distance does make the heart grow fonder.

> They were three, the convenors of the Tshernovits Conference: the champion of Jewish cultural renaissance and consistent Zionist, Dovid Pinski. He came to the land (of Israel) in advanced age and died here. Khayem Zhitlovski, one of the first Jewish socialists who, after countless reincarnations in search for a solution to the Jewish question, in his old age, sought to attach himself to the "Jewish" Autonomous Region, Birobidjan. And Nosn Birnboym, the ideologist of Zionism and nationalism, who, after various geographic and ideological wanderings, after various apostasies and conversions, finally reached the shores of Jewish eternity. He waited for the Messiah all his life and suffered terribly the pangs of His delayed coming. . . . He sowed everywhere and others reaped. He gave up this world for the world to come. All three of them served the Jewish people, each in his own way, and as such they [and Tshernovits] will remain in our historical memory. (Roznak 1969)

THEORETICAL RECAPITULATIONS

The late nineteenth and early twentieth century efforts to gain and activate intellectual and mass support for Yiddish, and the Tshernovits Conference of 1908 in particular, illustrate several of the problems encountered in a particular type of language spread: the spread of a former L into H functions in High Culture (education, literature, scholarship), government, technology, and modern literacy-dependent pursuits more generally.

1. Many of those most active on behalf of advocating, rationalizing, and ideologizing this type of language spread will, themselves, have to learn how to use the erstwhile L in H functions, and, indeed, may have to learn the L per se. In this respect the spread of an L into H functions

poses similar problems for those who are already literate (and who may, indeed, be the gatekeepers or guardians of literacy), as does the spread of any new vernacular into H functions. Nationalist language-spread movements that are not derived from an intragroup diglossia context (e.g., the promotion of Czech, Slovak, etc., in pre-World War I days or of Catalan, Occitan, Irish, Nynorsk, etc., more recently) also often begin with intelligentsia that do not know or master the vernaculars that they are championing. In the Yiddish case many intellectuals of the late nineteenth century were not only *oriented* toward Hebrew/*loshn koydesh* as H for Jewish cultural affairs but *toward* either German, Russian, or Polish as H for modern purposes. Thus Ls existing within a traditional diglossia setting may face double opposition in seeking to attain H functions.

2. One set of factors hampering the spread of Ls into H functions is their own lack of codification (e.g., in orthography, grammar) and elaboration (in lexicon). However, there is a tension between such corpus planning, on the one hand, and status-planning needs, on the other hand. It is difficult to turn to serious corpus planning while status planning is still so unsettled (or opposed), and it is difficult to succeed at status planning (particularly insofar as attracting ambivalent or negative intellectuals and literacy gatekeepers is concerned) on behalf of an L that is clearly deficient in terms of corpus characteristics that might render it more suitable for H functions.

3. The vicious circle that exists between lack of corpus planning and lack of status planning is most decisively broken if a status shift can be forced (by legal reform, revolution, or disciplined social example). The Tshernovits Conference's gravitation toward the "political (status-planning) issue" was a spontaneous recognition of this fact, so often pedantically overlooked by language technicians and "experts" who are oriented toward the relatively easier corpus-planning task alone.

4. The very same intragroup and intergroup status and power reward systems that previously led intellectuals to seek and acquire literacy and position through one or more Hs subsequently hinder the spread of Ls into these H functions. Any such language spread would imply a major dislocation or a change in intellectual and econo-political elites and prerogatives. If Yiddish had achieved H intragroup functions in the cultural-intellectual realm this would have threatened rabbinic/ traditional and modern Zionist/Hebraist hegemony in that sphere. In addition, the spread of Yiddish into H functions would not only have meant the displacement of one power/status elite by another but the popularization/massification/democratization of intragroup political participation and a de-emphasis on elitism as a whole. This too is similar to

the dynamics and consequences of many modern nationalist advocacies of vernaculars, except that the cultural-political opposition faced in the case of Yiddish may have been more variegated insofar as "preferred" language is concerned, since not only Hebrew/*loshn koydesh* but Russian, German, and even Polish were its rivals for H functions throughout the Pale.

5. However, just as modern recognition of Ausbau languages (see note 20, below) derives more from their adoption for nonbelletristic than for belletristic functions, so it is the spread into econo-political functions that is particularly crucial in this century if status planning for erstwhile Ls is to succeed. In connection with Yiddish, only the Bundists seem to have glimpsed this truth before, at or soon after Tshernovits (subsequently the Jewish communists—many of them ex-Bundists—did so as well, but with quite different purposes and results), and even they spoke of Yiddish more commonly in terms of cultural autonomy. Ultimately, however, their design foresaw a socialist revolution: the complete displacement of religio-bourgeois econo-political control and the recognition of separate but, interrelated and orchestrated, culturally autonomous populations *each with control over its own immediate econo-technical apparatus.* Although the political representation of Yiddish-speaking Jews *as such* (i.e., as a nationality with its own national [mother] tongue) in the coterritorial parliaments was advocated also by some Labor Zionists, by minor Jewish parties such as the Folkists and the Sejmists, and even by (some) ultra-Orthodox spokesmen (e.g., those of Agudas Yisroel), only the Bundists had a real economic realignment in mind with educational, political, and cultural institutions deriving from and protected by firm Yiddish-speaking proletarian economic control.

6. The weak representation of Bundists at Tshernovits led to the complete neglect of a consideration of the economic basis of Yiddish as either *a* or *the* Jewish national language and to a complete preoccupation with cultural ideology, cultural symbolism, and cultural rhetoric. As a result there also arose the view that the Conference itself might be an ongoing moving force—either because it would have an executive office for "cultural work" or because it simply had convened and sent forth its resolutions into the world. However, languages are neither saved nor spread by language conferences. Ideology, symbolism, and rhetoric are of undeniable significance in language spread—they are consciously motivating, focusing, and activating—but without a tangible and considerable status-power counterpart they become, under conditions of social change, competitively inoperative in the face of languages that do provide such. They may continue to be inspirational but—

particularly in modern times — they cease to be decisive, i.e., they ultimately fail to safeguard even the intimacy of hearth and home from the turmoil of the econo-political arena. The ultimate failure of Tshernovits is that it did not even seek to foster or align itself with an econo-political reality that would seek to protect Yiddish in new H functions. The ultimate tragedy of Yiddish is that in the political reconsolidation of modern eastern Europe its speakers were either too powerless or too mobile. They were the classical expendables of twentieth century Europe and, obviously, no language conference or language movement per se could rectify their tragic dilemma. Unfortunately, few at Tshernovits were sufficiently attuned to broader econo-political realities to recognize that instead of being en route to a new dawn for Yiddish they stood more basically before the dusk of the central and eastern European order of things as it had existed till then.

7. However, it is the delicate *interplay* between econo-political and ethno-cultural factors that must be grasped in order to understand both success and failure in language spread. Any attempt to pin all on one or another factor alone is more likely to be doctrinaire than accurate. The Yiddish case, because it involves a diglossia situation and multiple possibilities for both L and H functions in the future, is particularly valuable because it makes the simultaneous presence of both sets of factors so crystal clear. Awareness of econo-political factors alone is insufficient for understanding the internal rivalry that arose from *loshn koydesh*/Hebrew or appreciating the fact that the latter was undergoing its own vernacularization and modernization at the very same time that Yiddish was being championed for H functions. On the other hand, no amount of internal ethno-cultural insight can explain the allure that German and Russian (and, to a smaller degree, Polish) had for the Jewish bourgeoisie and intelligentsia. Finally, as a capstone to what is already an insuperable burden of opposition to Yiddish, there comes the linguistic relationship between Yiddish and German — the extra burden of all weak Ausbau[20] languages — and the cruel compound of moral, esthetic, and intellectual caricature and self-hatred to which that lent itself. After being exposed to such a killing array of internal and external forces for well over a century, is it any wonder that the 1978 Nobel Prize for literature awarded to the Yiddish writer I. B. Singer often elicits only a wry smile in what remains of the world of Yiddish.[21,22]

NOTES

1. The traditional coexistence of a nonvernacular language of high culture (H) and a vernacular of everyday life (L), the former being learned through formal study and the latter in the context of familial intimacy, was dubbed *diglossia* by Charles A. Ferguson (*Word,* 1959, 15, 325–40). Such contexts and their similarity and dissimilarity vis-à-vis other multilingual and multidialectal contexts have been examined by several investigators, among them John J. Gumperz, "Linguistic and social interaction in two communities," *American Anthropologist,* 1964, 66, no. 6, part 2, 137–53, and in my "Bilingualism with and without diglossia; diglossia with and without bilingualism," *Journal of Social Issues,* 1967, 23, no. 2, 29–38.

2. Throughout this paper the distinction will be adhered to between the traditional amalgam of Hebrew and Aramaic, referred to by Yiddish speakers as *loshn koydesh* (Language of Holiness) and Modern Hebrew, as developed in Palestine/Israel during the past century as a language of all of the functions required by a modern econo-political establishment. Where the distinction between Hebrew and *loshn koydesh* is not clear or is not intended they will be referred to jointly.

3. For a full treatment of each of these four substantively distinct but also interacting views of Yiddish, see "The Sociology of Yiddish: A Foreword" in my *Never Say Die! A Thousand Years of Yiddish in Jewish Life and Letters,* The Hague, Mouton, in press.

4. Halaḥic, an adjective derived from halaḥa (Yiddish: halokhe), refers to the entire body of Jewish law (Biblical, Talmudic, and post-Talmudic) and subsequent legal codes amending, modifying, or interpreting traditional precepts under rabbinic authority.

5. Maskilic, adjective derived from *haskala* (Yiddish: haskole), an eighteenth- and nineteenth-century movement among central and eastern European Jews, associated in Germany with the leadership of Moses Mendelssohn (1729–1786), designed to make Jews and Judaism more modern and cosmopolitan in character by promoting knowledge of and contributions to the secular arts and sciences and by encouraging adoption of the dress, customs, economic practices, educational programs, political processes and languages of the dominant non-Jewish coterritorial populations. For observations as to differences between the haskole in central and eastern Europe, see Fishman (in press).

6. Both Zionists and socialists increasingly shifted from the second to the third positive view at or around the turn of the century. In 1889 the Zionist leader Sokolov defended Yiddish merely as a necessary vehicle of mass agitation and propaganda (Roznak 1969), and even Herzl, who knew no Yiddish, founded a weekly (*Di velt*) in 1900 in order to reach the eastern European masses. Similarly, socialist spokesmen such as Arkadi Kremer merely advocated the use of Yiddish in order to attain their mass educational purposes in 1893 and organized *zhargonishe komitetn* (Yiddish-speaking committees) in order to foster literacy and to spread socialist publications among Jews in the Czarist empire. Soon, however, a new (the third) tune began to be heard. In 1902 the Zionist editor Lurye (coeditor with Ravnitski of the well-known periodical *Der yid*) wrote that Yiddish must not only be considered as a means of propaganda but as "a national-cultural possession which must be developed to play the role

of our second national language (Roznhak 1969)." In 1905 the Bund adopted its declaration on behalf of Jewish national-cultural autonomy with Yiddish as the language of the Jewish proletariat and of the intellectuals that serve and lead that proletariat. Scholarly literary organizations in the field of Yiddish began to arise soon thereafter: in 1908, The Yiddish Literary Organization (St. Petersburg); in 1909, The Yiddish Historical-Ethnographic Organization (St. Petersburg); and also in 1908, The Musical-Dramatic Organization (Vilna).

7. The Yiddish advocacy of Nosn Birnboym (Birnboym being a major protagonist of this paper) deserves special mention and, indeed, further investigation in connection with the topic of re-ethnification of elites. Such re-ethnification and accompanying re-linguification is a common process in the early stages of very many modern ethnicity movements (see my *Language and Nationalism,* Rowley, Newbury House, 1972) and exemplifies both the proto-elitist return to (or selection of) roots (often after failure to transethnify "upwardly" in accord with earlier aspirations), as well as the masses' groping toward mobilization under exemplary leadership. However, modern ethnicity movements are essentially attempts to achieve modernization, utilizing "primordial" identificational metaphors and emotional attachments for this purpose. Thus, they are not really "return" movements (not really nativization or past-oriented). They exploit or mine the past rather than cleave to it. Partially transethnified elites can uniquely serve such movements because of their own double exposure. Birnboym is therefore exceptional in that he ultimately rejected his secularized, Germanized, Europeanized milieu on behalf of a "genuine return" to relatively unmodernized Orthodoxy. By the second decade of this century he had rejected Jewish modernization (in the guise of socialism, Zionism, and diaspora nationalism, all of which he had once charted) as hedonistic and as endangering Jewish (and possibly world) survival. There is about the late Birnboym a Spenglerian aura foretelling the "decline of the West" and cautioning Jews that their salvation (and the world's) would come only via complete immersion in traditional beliefs, values, and practices (Birnboym 1918; 1946). He viewed Yiddish as a sine-qua-non for that goal, rejecting its use for modern, hedonistic purposes such as those which he himself had earlier espoused both immediately before and after the Tshernovits Language Conference of 1908. This rare combination of complete Orthodoxy and uncompromising defense of Yiddish within an Orthodox framework has made Nosn Birnboym into something of a curiosity for both religious and secular commentators. Such *genuine returners* to roots also exist in the context of other modernization movements (for example, in the nineteenth and twentieth centuries Greek, Arabic, Slavophile, and Sanscrit contexts) and represent a vastly overlooked subclass within the study of ethnicity movements. Even in their case it would be mistaken to consider them as no more than "spikes in the wheels of progress" merely because they frequently represent an attempt to attain modernization without Westernization. A contrastive study of Birnboym and other such "genuine returners" would be most valuable for understanding this subclass as well as the more major group of "metaphorical returners." Note, however, that Birnboym remained a committed advocate of Yiddish (although not in any functions that would replace *loshn koydesh*) even when he embraced ultra-Orthodoxy, whereas "true returners" in other cases embraced their respective indigenized classic tongues. To revive Hebrew was long considered antitraditional and was not possible except in speech networks that were com-

pletely outside of the traditional framework—ideologically, behaviorally (in terms of daily routine), and even geographically. The dubious Jewish asset of complete dislocation and deracination was denied the unsuccessful advocates of Sanscrit and classical Greek, Arabic or Irish.

For a more detailed examination of Nosn Birnboym's life and thought see my forthcoming *Nosn Birnboym: A Study in Personality, Ideology, and Languages* (ms).

8. Tshernovits is currently located in the Moldavian SSR. Between the two World Wars it was in Rumania. At the time of the Language Conference, and ever since the Austrian occupation in 1774 (after defeating the Ottoman Turkish occupants), it was in a section of the Austro-Hungarian empire known as Bukovina (until 1948 administratively a part of Galicia with which Bukovina remained closely connected as far as "Jewish geography" was concerned).

9. Territorialism acknowledged the need for planned Jewish resettlement in an internationally recognized and protected Jewish territory, but did not consider Palestine to be the only or the most desirable location for such resettlement in view of the conflicting claims and geopolitical perils associated with it. Various territorial concentrations in eastern Europe itself, in Africa (Angola, Cirenaica, Uganda), in South America (Surinam), in North America (Kansas-Nebraska), in Australia (Kimberly Region) and elsewhere have been advocated since the latter part of the nineteenth century. At one point Herzl himself was not convinced that a homeland in Palestine and only in Palestine should be adamantly pursued and was willing to consider a "waystation" elsewhere. Most territorialists split with the Zionist movement and set up an organization of their own in 1905, when the Seventh Zionist Congress rejected an offer by the British government to create an autonomous Jewish settlement in Uganda.

10. Corpus planning is one of the two major branches of language planning: the authoritative allocation of resources (attention, funds, manpower, negative and positive sanctions) to language. Corpus planning entails modifying, enriching, or standardizing the language per se, often through publishing and implementing orthographies, nomenclatures, spellers, grammars, style manuals, etc. Its counterpart is status planning, i.e., attempts to require use of a language for particular functions: education, law, government, mass media, etc. Corpus planning is frequently engaged in by language academies, commissions, or boards. Status planning requires governmental or other power-related decision-making and sanctions-disbursing bodies: political, religious, ethnocultural or economic. The two processes must be conducted in concert if they are to succeed and take hold across a broad spectrum of uses and users. Yiddish has constantly suffered due to deficiencies in the status-planning realm and, as a result, its corpus-planning successes are also limited, although several can be cited (Shekhter 1961). For a detailed empirical and theoretical review of language planning, see Joan Rubin, et al. *Language Planning Processes,* The Hague, Mouton, 1977.

11. Vays reminisces as follows (1937, i.e., thirty years after the Conference):

As is well known, Yiddish was not recognized in Austria as a language, just as the Jewish people was not recognized as such. At the university, e.g., it was necessary to fill out a rubric "nationality" and no Jew was permitted to write in "Jew." The nationalist-oriented Jewish students, not wanting to cripple the statistical distribution in favor of the ruling nationality to the detriment of the minority nationalities, sought various ways of forcing the authorities to recognize the Jewish nationality.

Some wrote the name of a nationality that happened to occur to them. There was no lack of entries of "Hottentot" mother tongue and "Malay" nationality.

This context for the Conference led the Yiddish *Sotsyal demokrat* of Cracow to greet the Conference as follows: "The significance of the Conference is augmented by the fact that it takes place in Austria where Yiddish is closest to official recognition" (Kisman 1958). Tshernovits itself also impressed the delegates and guests from abroad (primarily from the Czarist empire) not only with its ethnic heterogeneity but with its "air of relative democracy, where at every step one could feel European culture" (Kisman 1958).

For eastern European Jewry the late nineteenth and early twentieth century Austro-Hungarian empire represented Western-style democracy plus national-cultural rights, both of which were still sadly lacking in the Czarist empire and both of which were foundational to the Conference's goals, although neither was explicitly referred to at the Conference itself.

12. The Bund (full name: Jewish Workers Bund [Alliance] of Russia, Lithuania and Poland) was organized in Vilna in 1897, the same year as the first Zionist Congress was held in Basel. Always socialist, it adopted a Jewish cultural-autonomist, Yiddish-oriented platform in 1905, as a result of which it clashed with Lenin, Trotsky, and other early Bolshevik leaders. The Bund became the mainstay of secular Yiddish educational, literary, and cultural efforts in interwar Poland. For further details and entree to a huge bibliography, see Mendelsohn 1970 and Kligsberg 1974.

13. The "esthetic point of view" is dealt with at length by Miron (1973). Although not unknown in connection with other supposedly inelegant vernaculars during the period of struggle to legitimize them for H functions, the vituperation heaped upon Yiddish in terms of its claimed esthetic shortcomings clearly seems to border on the hysterical. Loathsome, ugly, stunted, crippled, mangled, hunchbacked, gibberish were commonplace epithets. "Away with dirt, with spiderwebs, with *zhargon* and with all kinds of garbage! We call for a broom! And whom the broom of satire will not help, him will we honor with the stick of wrath! Quem medicamenta non sanant, ferrum et ignis sanant!" (*Jutrzenka*, 1862, no. 50, 428). Note however that the esthetic metaphor (e.g., the German Jewish historian Graetz refused to "dirty his pen" with Yiddish or to have his works translated into that "foul tongue"), interesting though it may be in and of itself, must not obscure from analysis more basic social, cultural and political goals and loyalties of those that express them. The Yiddish proverb *nisht dos is lib vos iz sheyn, nor dos is sheyn vos iz lib* (We do not love that which is lovely, rather we consider lovely that which we love) applies fully here. By the time of Tshernovits the full force of invective had begun to pass (although it can be encountered in Israel and elsewhere to this very day; see, e.g., Fishman and Fishman 1978) and the countertide of positive hyperbole had begun to rise, assigning to Yiddish not only beauty but virtue, subtlety, honesty, compassion, intimacy, and boundless depth.

14. While it is certainly inaccurate to consider Mizes's comments as "the first scientific paper in Yiddish on Yiddish," it is not easy to say whose work does deserve to be so characterized, primarily because of changing standards as to what is and is not scientific. One of my favorites is Y.M. Lifshits's *Yidish-rusisher verterbukh* [Yiddish-Russian Dictionary], Zhitomir, Bakst, 1876, and his introduction thereto, both of which remain quite admirable pieces of scholarship to this very day. Other candidates for this honorific status abound, several of considerably earlier vintage.

15. Somewhat positive Zionist stances toward exilic Jewish vernaculars had surfaced from time to time well before Tshernovits. Reference is made here not merely to utilizing such vernaculars for immediate educational/indoctrinational purposes, such usage being acceptable to almost the entire Zionist spectrum, but to allocating intimacy-related and even literacy-related functions to them, both in the diaspora and (even) in Erets Yisroel on a relatively permanent basis. Herzl himself (in his *Diary* 1885), suggests a parallel with Switzerland, such that Hebrew, Yiddish, and Judesmo (Judeo-Spanish) would be recognized. Except in Labor Zionist circles such views were very much in the minority, remained little developed or concretized, but yet provided the basis for claims at Tshernovits that since many Zionists/Hebraists had been careful not to reject Yiddish, so Socialists/Yiddishists should do nothing to reject Hebrew/*loshn koydesh*.

16. Interestingly enough, the Balfour Declaration, issued by the British government on November 2, 1917, favoring "the establishment in Palestine of *a* national home for the Jews, but without prejudice to the civil and religious rights of existing non-Jewish communities" also used the *in*definite (a) rather than the definite article (the) as a compromise between opposite extreme views in the Foreign Ministry.

17. Several of the references and citations in this section are originally found in Rothstein 1977.

18. Just as Yiddish books commonly carried *loshn koydesh* titles until rather late in the nineteenth century, so Yiddish periodicals commonly bore either *loshn koydesh* or German titles even into the present century. The diglossic implications are manifold even at an unconscious level. The people of "The Book" was (and in the more unreconstructed Orthodox circles still is) accustomed to encounter serious H-level writing (and particularly such on intragroup concerns) in *loshn koydesh*. Thus, a Hebrew title for a Yiddish book is, in part, a visual habit, in part a cultural signal, and in part a disguise (vis-à-vis rabbinic criticism and other possibly hostile authorities). Similarly, a relatively ephemeral periodical dealing with the wide world of modern secular events is titled in German for much the same reasons. Neither *forverts* nor *yidishes* nor *tageblat* were parts of commonly spoken eastern European Yiddish by well before the nineteenth century. Nevertheless these were perfectly acceptable components of a journalistic title of those times, particularly in the United States.

19. Ḥasidism: a Jewish movement founded in Poland in the eighteenth century by Rabbi Israel Baal Shem Tov and characterized by its emphasis on mysticism, spontaneous prayer, religious zeal, and joy. The various ḥasidic leaders or masters (singular: *rébi,* plural: *rébeyim,* as distinguished from *rov, rabonim* among non-Ḥasidic) typically instructed their followers through tales. Yiddish was, therefore, their crucial medium and their tales became an early major component of popular Yiddish publishing (many also being published—first, simultaneously or soon thereafter—in *loshn koydesh*). Although much opposed by most rabbinic authorities for almost two centuries (the latter and their followers being dubbed *misnagdim,* i.e., opponents by the ḥasidim), ḥasidism finally became generally accepted as an equally valid version of Jewish orthodoxy and is a vibrant (and the more numerous) branch thereof, as well as a major (but largely unideologized) source of support for Yiddish, to this day.

20. Ausbau languages are those that are so similar in grammar and lexicon to other, stronger, previously recognized languages that their language authorities often attempt to maximize the differences between themselves and their Big Brothers by multiplying or magnifying them through adopting or creating dis-

tinctive paradigms for neologisms, word order and grammar, particularly in their written forms. Thus Ausbau languages are "languages by effort," i.e., they are consciously built away from (ausbau) other, more powerful and basically similar languages, so as not to be considered "mere dialects" of the latter, but rather, to be viewed as obviously distinctive languages in their own right. The ausbau process is responsible for much of the difference between (Landsmal) Nynorsk and Bokmal, Hindi and Urdu, Macedonian and Bulgarian, Moldavian and Rumanian, Belo-Russian and Russian. For the particular difficulties faced in finding, creating, and maintaining ausbau differences, including examples from the Yiddish versus German arena, see Paul Wexler, *Purism and Language,* Bloomington, Indiana University Language Science Monographs, 1974. The original formulator of the term *ausbau* (and of its contrast: *abstand*) is H. Kloss, *Anthropological Linguistics,* 1967, 9, no. 7, 29–41.

21. Some additional useful secondary sources concerning the Tshernovits Language Conference are Goldsmith (1977), Passow (1971), and Lerner (1957). A literally endless list of other journal articles (pre-1928 but primarily post-1928, this being the date of the Yivo's twentieth anniversary volume [Anonymous 1931]) remains to be exhaustively catalogued.

22. For their helpful criticism of an earlier draft of this paper I am indebted to Robert L. Cooper, David E. Fishman, and, most especially, S. A. Birnboym. I alone assume responsibility for any errors of fact or interpretation that still remain and hope to correct them in future studies of the Tshernovits Conference, of Nosn Birnboym, and of other issues in the late functional and focal modernization of Yiddish.

REFERENCES

Anon. *Di ershte yidishe shprakh-konferents* [The First Yiddish Language Conference]. Vilna, Yiddish Scientific Institute-Yivo, 1931.

Birnboym, Nosn. Di konferents far der yidishes shprakh: efenongs re de. *Dokter Birnboyms vokhnblat,* 1908, 1, no. 1, 3–7. Reprinted, in Anon. *Di ershte yidishe shprakh-konferents* [The First Yiddish Language Conference]. Vilna, Yiddish Scientific Institute-Yivo, 1931, 71–74 (also reprinted *Afn shvel,* 1968, no. 4 (185), 3–4).

———. *Gottes Volk.* Vienna, Löunt, 1918.

———. *Selections from His Writings.* London, Hamagid, 1946.

Choseed, B. Reflections of the Soviet Nationalities Policy in Literature. The Jews, 1938–1948. Ph.D. Dissertation: Columbia University, 1968 (University Microfilms, no. 69-15, 665).

E[ste]r, R. [Ester Frumkin]. Di ershte yidishe sprakh konferents. The First Yiddish language conference. *Di naya tsayt,* 1908, 4, 89–104.

Eisenstein, Miriam. Jewish Schools in Poland, 1919–1939. New York, King's Corwin, 1949.

Fishman, David E. Y. M. Lifshits of Berditshev: maskil or yiddishist. Ms. 1978.

Fishman, Joshua A. The phenomenological and linguistic pilgrimage of Yiddish. (Some examples of functional and structural pidginization and depidginization). *Kansas Journal of Sociology.* 1973: 9, 122–36.

————. Yiddish and loshn koydesh in traditional ashkenaz. The problem of societal allocation of macro-functions, in A. Verdoost and R. Kjolseth (eds.) *Language in Sociology*. Peeters, 1975, 39–74.

————. *Nosn Birnboym: A Study in Personality, Ideology and Language*. Ms.

Fishman, Joshua A. and Fishman, David E. Yiddish in Israel: A case study of efforts to revise a monocentric language policy, in J.A. Fishman (ed.) *Advances in the Study of Societal Multilingualism*. The Hague, Mouton, 1978, 185–262.

Goldsmith, E.S. *Architects of Yiddishism*. Rutherford, Fairleigh Dickenson Press, 1976. (See particularly the chapters on Birnboym, Perets, Zhitlovski and the Tshernovits Conference per se.)

Kazhdan, Kh. Sh. An epizod unshtot a gesheyenish (20 yor nokh der tshernovitser konferents) [An episode instead of an event (20 years after the Tshernovits Conference)]. *Undzer tsayt*, 1928, no. 7, 73–77.

————. Tshernovits—Kholem un vor [Tshernovits: dream and reality]. *Undzer tsayt*, 1969, January, 17–21.

Khmurner, Y. Vegn a feler vos khazert zikh iber. [About an error that is being repeated]. *Bikhervelt*, 1928, no. 7, 1–6.

Kisman, Y. Tsum fuftsikstn yoyvl: di tshernovitser shprakh-konferents [On the fiftieth anniversary: The Tshernovits language conference]. *Undzer tsayt*, 1958, July/August, 8–13.

Kligsberg, M. Di yidishe yugnt-bavegung in poyln tsvishn beyde velt-milkhomes (a sotsyologishe shtudye) [The Jewish Youth movement in Poland between both World Wars (a sociological study)], in J.A. Fishman, ed., *Shtudyes vegn yidn in poyln, 1919–1939*. New York, Yivo Institute for Jewish Research, 1974, 137–228.

Lehrer, L. Tsayt tsu shafn a kultur-gezelshaft [Time to organize a culture society]. *Literarishe bleter*, 1928, no. 26, 500–501 and 509.

Lerner, H.J. The Tshernovits Language Conference: A Milestone in Jewish Nationalist Thought. Master's Thesis. Columbia University, 1957.

Lifshits, Y. M. Dir fir klasn [The four classes]. *Kol mevaser*, 1863, no. 21, 323–28 and no. 23, 364–66. Also see the editor's (Alexander Tsederboym's) comments: pp. 375–80 and 392–93).

————. Y.M. Di daytsh-yidishe brik [The German-Jewish bridge]. *Kol mevaser*, 1867, 5, no. 31, 239–41. See nos. 32, 33, 34, 35 and 41 for subsequent comments.

Mark, Y. 60 yor nokh der shprakh-konferents in Tshernovits. [60 years after the language conference in Tshernovits]. *Forverts*, 1968, August 25, Section 2, 11–15.

Mayzl, Nakhmen. Di ershte mobilizatsye. [The first mobilization]. *Literarishe bleter*, 1928, no. 35, 681.

Mendelsohn, Ezra. *Class Struggle in the Pale*. Cambridge, Harvard University Press, 1970.

Miron, Dan. A language as Caliban, in his *A Traveler Disguised*. New York, Schocken, 1973, 34–66.

N[iger], Sh. A yidisher kultur kongres (A Congress for Yiddish culture). *Dos naye lebn*, 1922, 1, no. 2, 1–4.

Passow, I.D. The first Yiddish language conference, in I.D. Passow and S.T. Lachs (eds.) *Gratz College Anniversary Volume*. Philadelphia, Gratz College, 1971.

Pinski, D. Geburt fun der tshernovitser konferents; a bletl zikhroynes [Birth of the Tshernovits Conference; a page of memories]. *Tsukunft,* 1948, Sept., 499–501.

Pludermakher, G. Di tshernovitser konferents un di ufgabn fun itstikn moment. [The Tshernovits Conference and the current task]. *Literarishe bleter,* 1928, 40, 777–78.

Prilutski, N. Nokh di tshernovitser fayerungen [After the Tshernovits Celebrations]. *Literarishe bleter,* 1928, no. 4, 797–99.

Rothstein, J. Reactions of the American Yiddish press to the Tshernovits Language Conference of 1908 as a reflection of the American Jewish experience. *International Journal of the Sociology of Language,* 1977, 13, 103–20.

Roznak, Sh. Hebreyish-yidish (bamerkingen tsu un arum der tshernovitser shprakh-konferents). [Hebrew-Yiddish (comments on and about the Tshernovits language conference)]. *Goldene keyt,* 1969, 66, 152–69.

Shekhter, M. Mir shteyen nit af an ort [We are not standing motionlessly]. *Yiddish.* New York, Congress for Jewish Culture, 1961, 351–63.

Tartakover, A. Di yidishe kultur in poyln tsvishn tsvey velt-milkhomes [Jewish culture in Poland between two World Wars]. *Gedank un lebn,* 1946, 4, no. 1, 1–35.

Tenenboym, Yoysef. Di yidishe shprakh af der tog-ordenung fun der sholem-konferents in pariz, 1919 [The Yiddish language on the agenda of the peace conference in Paris, 1919]. *Yivo-bleter,* 1957/1958, 41, 217–29.

Vays (Slonim), Sh. Oys di tsaytn fun der tshernovitser konferents [From the times of the Tshernovits Conference]. *Fun noentn over,* 1937, 1, 57–63.

Zelitsh, Y. A tsveyte konferents far der yidisher shprakh—60 yor nokh tshernovits [A second conference for the Yiddish language—60 years after Tshernovits]. *Afn shvel,* 1968, 185 (4), 2–3.

Zhitlovski, Khayem. Tshernovits un der yidishizm: tsu dem tsvantsik yorikn yoyvl-yontev fun der tshernovitser konferents [Tshernovits and Yiddishism: In honor of the twentieth anniversary celebration of the Tshernovits Conference]. *Tsukunft,* 1928, December, 735–37.

Zilberfarb, M.A. A shedlikhe iluzye [A harmful illusion]. *Bikhervelt,* 1928, no. 8, 38–43.

Acceleration, Retardation, and Reversal in Language Decay?

Wolfgang U. Dressler

My assignment—to report about language death in connection with nationalistic factors in language spread—at first bewildered me,[1] since, in my opinion, nationalistic factors are not the most important isolable factors in language decay and language death (neither in a quantitative nor in a qualitative way). Before I can show why this is so, I must expound my general views on language decay and language death.[2] I will illustrate my points from five linguistic minority areas:

1) Breton, the Celtic minority language in France,

2) Slovenian as spoken in Carinthia, the southernmost province of Austria, adjacent to the Yugoslav republic of Slovenia,

3) Croatian as spoken in the Burgenland, the easternmost province of Austria, adjacent to Hungary,

4) Bayuvarian German dialects spoken in language islands of Northern Italy,

5) German as spoken in South Tyrol, the northern Italian province of Bozen/Bolzano, adjacent to the Austrian province Tyrol (North Tyrol and East Tyrol).

1.1. Before describing the five minority areas, I must confess to possessing three types of bias. First, in my opinion the preservation of a minority language has to be valued positively, therefore factors endangering language maintenance have at least some negative evaluative features; this bias will oblige me to take a critical view of certain actions and non-actions of past and present governments in Austria, France, and Italy.

Secondly, I understand "nationalistic" in the sense this word family has in Central and Eastern Europe, where language and where culture as mediated by language are more important features of "nation" (and

321

particularly of "nationality") than statehood. And thirdly, I do not understand "minority" only in the sense of an underprivileged group, but also in that of a quantitatively inferior group.

1.2. Even a very short description of the five minorities must comprise the following observations: The French Revolution brought the complete attachment of the hitherto autonomous Brittany to France, whose eastern part (Haute Bretagne) was then already completely francophone, whereas the western part (Basse Bretagne) was monolingually celtophone with the exception of the rather small bourgeoisie, a few linguistically mixed towns such as Douarnenez, and the still much thinner layer of the francicized aristocracy. At the end of the nineteenth century Brittany was fully included in the centralized economy, social, cultural, and national life of France including obligatory French monolingual instruction, military service, monolingual mass media, etc. The church, however, remained Breton.

Although due to high birth rates the total number (ca. 1 million) of Breton speakers remained rather stable (until very recently, when a fatal debretonization has occurred, both in quantity and in quality), there are nearly no monolingual celtophonic Bretons left. Even the oldest generation is using more and more French even in the most conservative areas; there are nearly no children with monolingual Breton primary socialization; and fewer and fewer children have a bilingual primary socialization. On the other hand the attitude of French authorities towards Breton is more tolerant now. Several Breton nationalist movements attract teenagers and people in their twenties to learning and using (standard) Breton;[3] their cultural and ideological impact on the masses is stronger than that of the romantic literary Breton revival of the nineteenth century or than that of the nationalist movement in the thirties. Even when all Breton dialects die, a strong nucleus of nationalistic speakers of standard Breton might subsist.

The history of Slovenian in Carinthia (see Haas and Stuhlpfarrer 1977) is a long history of assimilation to German, particularly since the nineteenth century, accelerating after the First World War and the plebiscite, when a high percentage of Slovenes voted for Southern Carinthia to remain a part of Carinthia (and Austria), thus deciding the outcome of the plebiscite. After a severe repression during the Nazi occupation of Austria (1938–1945), the Carinthian Slovenes obtained a certain number of minority rights (e.g., Slovenian primary and secondary school education can be chosen instead of the ordinary monolingual German education). Still, they have not yet seen fulfilled all the rights that were granted in the Austrian peace treaty of 1955. Within a century the Slovenian population has dropped to a third (about

40,000), of whom the greater part uses German rather than Slovenian as their standard literary language (diglossia). German influence on Carinthian Slovenian dialects is heavy in the lexicon. Very few monolingual Slovenians seem to be left in Carinthia. Even if Slovenian-German diglossia might vanish, a group identifying with Slovenian standard language and Slovenian national values will subsist, helped by the proximity of the Yugoslav republic of Slovenia.

The Croatian villages scattered in the Burgenland have no geographic connection to the Yugoslav republic of Croatia. They were settled by emigrants from Turkish-invaded Croatia in the sixteenth and seventeenth centuries. Their standard language is German and/or Čakavian, whereas the (Serbo-) Croatian standard is based on the very different Štokavian dialects. Outside the church, attempts have been made to adapt the Čakavian standards to (at least orthographic) norms of the (Štokavian) Serbo-Croatian standard. Their number has been halved (now less than 30,000) since the nineteenth century, due to assimilation (rather than to Nazi repression in 1938–1945). No monolingual Croatians seem to exist nowadays. Only in Central ("Mittleres") Burgenland do young children still learn Croatian.

The Bayuvarian language islands in northern Italy, whose presence dates back to settlements in medieval times, are examples of diglossia (Tautsch="Cimbrian" and Italian in the Seven and Thirteen Communes) or triglossia (an equally archaic, nearly Old High German dialect, Friulian and Italian in Sauris and Sappada). German is a very different and, to them, foreign language.

Today only few children seem also to learn the German dialect in Sauris and Sappada and in only three of the Cimbrian villages. The preservation of these idioms seems to be least assured of all the minorities considered in this paper. Decisive historical events for these idioms were the suppression of Cimbrian autonomy in 1797 (after Napoleon's destruction of the republic of Venice) and the expulsion of Cimbrians from their communities (situated very near the battle lines) for the duration of the First World War.

The German minority of South Tyrol is the most comfortable one considered here. South Tyrol became a part of Italy after the First World War; from 1921 to 1971 the germanophone population increased from 193,000 to 260,000, and the italophone population from 27,000 to 137,000, due to the immigration policies of the Fascist government (1923–1945). After the Fascist repression minority rights were increasingly introduced, culminating in the recent establishment of a separate and powerful autonomous provincial government. Many South Tyroleans have an incomplete command of standard German, whereas their competence in Italian has increased. Now a certain lexical influence of Italian is noticeable. The small Ladinian (Retoromanic) minority with South Tyrol gradually assimilated to German rather than to the cognate Italian language, whereas in other Italian provinces it is assimilating to Italian.

2.1. Language decay is relative: e.g., one could say that for French and German the functions of international communication and of the coinage of new terms in science and fashion (in the largest sense) have decayed in favor of English (cf. Kloss 1974). In principle such a "decay" is totally reversible, for (1) only very marginal functions of language are concerned and (2) the specific linguistic systems remain completely capable of performing the above functions, i.e., it is a question of much less frequent performance, whereas the system and the respective competencies of fluent speakers of French and German are not involved.[4] This type of "decay" will not be discussed here.

2.2. On the other pole of the spectrum, we find the case of bilinguals (or multilinguals) who learn the receding language only incompletely, and are thus incompetent speakers of the language. These are individual cases. Here I am interested in the interindividual phenomenon that either all speakers of a language or a whole generation of speakers within a well-definable geographical area of a language possess a reduced language structure which is, in parallel ways for all of these speakers, impoverished in comparison with earlier stages of the language, without any compensating change within the same language. This I call language "decay," and its terminal stage "language death," if at the same time the language becomes (sociolinguistically) dysfunctional, i.e., if the speakers of this variety are unable to use it for sociolinguistic functions which their elders had been able to use it for, and which are still necessary functions of their social activities (e.g., public transactions). Thus, language death and language decay are only two phenomena among the manifold phenomena of language shift, language substitution, and language spread.[5]

2.3. In my opinion the basic mechanism of language decay[6] starts with social change subordinating the respective speech community to another speech community. Speakers reflect this unfavorable change sociopsychologically by a less favorable evaluation of their language. A consequence is a sociolinguistically restricted use of their language, which results in an impoverished linguistic structure for their language.[7] This impoverishment has a feedback on the speakers' sociopsychological evaluation, because the quality for guaranteeing the prestige function and the self-identification function (and hence the unifying/separating functions) of the language has diminished. Also the sociolinguistically restricted use has a parallel feedback effect. Thus a skeleton flow-chart of necessary (but not sufficient!) causes would be:

social subordination → negative sociopsychological evaluation→ sociolinguistic restriction→ linguistic decay   ↑ ↑

Whereas social, sociopsychological, and sociolinguistic changes may involve speakers of all generations, linguistic decay, I hypothesize, occurs predominantly during language acquisition. If children acquire the decaying language simultaneously with, or even after the victorious language and learn to use it only with family members, and if—due to low sociopsychological evaluation—adults exercise weak social control of their acquisition process, the necessary conditions are present for pidginization[8] of the decaying language in its reduced, auxiliary use.

2.4. Phenomena of language decay fit well into the polycentristic approach to language proposed by Dressler (1977a, b), the essence of which is the hypothesis that each language system represents the compromise between conflicting universal tendencies of the semiautonomous components of language:[9] the loss of sociolinguistic functions of a language impairs the fulfilment of semiotic functions of its components, which results in a decay of the respective component; if there is no compensation in another component of the same language, then our definition of language decay is fulfilled.[10]

A very early, though easily reversible, sign of decay is the acculturation of proper names (their semiotic function being identification of individuals). Lower evaluation of one's own language is reflected in using (voluntarily) another language for self-identification (cf. Leys 1974). Christian names in the majority language are also orally used by Cimbrians and quite many Bretons, Austrian Croatians, and Slovenes.

A relatively early, but presumptive sign of decay is the loss of productive word-formation. The semiotic function of "enrichissement lexical" is taken over by the majority language; the minority language retains only the function of synchronic motivation of complex words (synchronic etymology),[11] i.e., speakers can use a word-formation rule to relate two words, but not to form new words. This has been observed for Breton dialects, Austrian Croatian (G. Neweklowsky: personal communication), and the dialect of Sauris (Denison 1977:17). Cimbrian has taken over Italian rules for word-formation (Heller 1975:32).

Sentence semantic functions are signaled either syntactically or morphologically or in both ways. Therefore in diachronic change, the complexity of one of these two components can be restricted only if, by compensation, the other one is elaborated (e.g., by introducing new rules or restrictions). In a decaying language morphological complexity is reduced without compensation,[12] because more complex-sentence semantic relations can be expressed in the majority language. This corresponds to P. Mühlhäusler's (Trudgill 1977:36) definition of reduction as "loss of some part of a component of the grammar without resulting complication of another component to make up for this loss." Simplification (of morphology, phonology, and syntax) may follow the principle of lexical fading (Dressler 1972), i.e., a rule is gradually lost by successive decrease of the number of lexical items it applies to.

One of the main functions of segmental phonology is to make language pronounceable. For this purpose a language has, *inter alia*, its own overall system for a specific basis of articulation. A disintegrating language may lose its own basis of articulation either by adopting the basis of the majority language (as noticed in Burgenland Croatian by Neweklowsky 1978:34) or by relaxing the margins of possible realizations of detailed phonetic rules (or allophones), as observed for Breton (Dressler 1972) and Cimbrian (Heller 1975:33; Schweizer 1939/9), cf. Dressler-Wodak (1977a:9).

2.5. The sociolinguistic restriction by which the decaying language is used in ever fewer types of speech situations results in stylistic shrinkage and finally monostylism (i.e., restriction to a very casual style used with very familiar dialogue partners about restricted topics in routine speech situations). This shrinkage can be measured both in phonology[13] and in syntax.[14] In casual speech one can observe that words are used in a semantically less precise way. A similar semantic vagueness has been observed in dying languages.[15] The phonological, syntactic and semantic imprecision and simplification of casual speech is a result of the more casual behavior and little need for perceptual clarity, and it is compensated for by nonverbal and situational disambiguation (cf. Dressler 1977a:49ff).

When a decaying language has become restricted to this monostylistic use, it is severely dysfunctional. Another source of dysfunctionality is massive lexical impoverishment (see Hill and Hill 1977, Dorian 1973), as observed for Breton by many authors, for Burgenland Croatian by Neweklowsky (1978:46ff), and for Cimbrian where, e.g., in counting, indigenous numbers are not used beyond "four."[16]

Pidginization (see 2.3) seems to be a further stage in certain cases: e.g., monostylistic Breton is utilized by many last-generation speakers only in very few speech-situations; however, in the same situations they also use French, which recalls the phenomenon of "bilingualism without diglossia" among immigrants in the United States (Fishman 1970:83ff). Another well-known sign of extreme language decay is the alignment of inflectional morphology, syntax, semantics, and basis of articulation of the minority language to the respective structures of the majority language. In this case one may safely attribute to speakers a single competence to the differences still existing between the two languages. Reduction in language use may also result in lack of routine in the use of parts of grammar, phonology, and the lexicon, which in its turn may result in noticeable insecurity of norms, fluctuations of speech, and uncertainties of speakers.[17]

3.1. Although nationalistic factors are not the most important ones (see section 2), they play a part in initiating, accelerating, retarding, or reversing language decay. The growing nationalism of European states (especially since the end of the eighteenth century) has probably initiated considerable language decay in the cases of Cimbrians (loss of autonomy), maybe of Burgenland Croatians (first Hungarian nationalism until 1921 and, after the attachment of Burgenland to Austria in 1921, German or Austrian nationalism), and in the case of South Tyrol, where due to the division of Tyrol (in 1919) between Austria (north and east Tyrol) and Italy (South Tyrol and italophone Trentino), German in South Tyrol suddenly passed from the status of the majority language into that of a minority language. In the cases of Breton and Carinthian Slovenian (and maybe Burgenland Croatian) growing state nationalism only strongly accelerated the earlier geographic and social losses of the minorities.

3.2. It is well known that state nationalism (cf. Lemberg 1964; Fishman 1971) has been detrimental to minority languages by promoting growing centralization, unification, and social integration in all respects[18] with resulting acculturation and deethnicization of minorities (cf. Fishman 1966a, b). Particularly the variety called "nationalisme intégral," whose believers consider their nation to be of supreme and absolute value (cf. Lemberg 1964:196ff), endorsed active measures against minority languages, e.g., in the school system (against Breton until the sixties, against Slovenian, Croatian, and German of South Tyrol during the respective Fascist periods).[19] In this way minority languages lost a series of domains (cf. for South Tyrol Egger 1977:20ff).

3.3. Detrimental consequences with respect to language maintenance were:

(a) Diglossia (only now receding in South Tyrol due to recent factual autonomy) with growing or all-pervasive bilingualism (now virtually everywhere with the exception of South Tyrol). This type of diglossia is not a stable one, since political and social factors tend to increase the domains of the dominant language. Thus bilingualism is a transitional stage to monolingualism (in the dominant language).

(b) Use of the majority language as the only standard language (now all Cimbrians, nearly all Bretons, nearly all Croatians, and most Slovenes [with the exception of church language]).

(c) "Schwebendes Volkstum" (Woschitz 1975:136), i.e., identification with state (=majority) nationalism, but maintenance of the minority language for subordinate functions: total among Cimbrians, general among Bretons and Burgenland Croatians, preponderant among Carinthian Slovenes, very rare among South Tyroleans. This means also:

(d) Double linguistic identification, and partial alienation from linguistically expressed minority values due to a role conflict (cf. Dressler-Wodak 1977 a, b).[20] It also means fluctuating loyalties.

(e) The acceptance of majority norms and values may lead to inferiority complexes, shame for, and rejection of minority values (very typical in Brittany, less so in the other cases, nonexistent in South Tyrol) as a converse of general one-sided contempt (only against minority values).

(f) The wish to assimilate also linguistically to the majority: very common in Brittany, Burgenland[21] and Carinthia with a characteristic effect for children in elementary schools: even now only few Bretons send their children to the once-a-week optional half-hour or one-hour Breton course, a minority of Slovenians and Croatians send theirs to Slovenian and Croatian (or rather mixed Slovenian-German, Croatian-German) schools in Carinthia and Burgenland respectively. Cimbrian never had the opportunity of being taught. The majority of "mixed families" in South Tyrol sends their bilingual children to Italian rather than German schools.

(g) Conflict between primary socialization in the minority language and secondary socialization in the majority language (see f) or

(h) Bilingual primary socialization (if not monolingual majority language socialization): total among Cimbrians, general in Brittany, common in Burgenland, preponderant in Carinthia, in South Tyrol only in mixed families.

(i) Folklorization: state nationalism tries to canalize minority ethnocentricity into a folkloristic, very traditional movement, where the minority language plays a small part, if at all—this is true for all five areas in question.

Now "nationalisme intégral" is of less importance in Austria, France, and Italy (here with a dramatic change in the last decade) with the possible exception of a large French-nationalist stream in Brittany and

France (e.g., "Gaullists") and the Pan-German and strictly anti-Slovenian "Kärnter Heimatdienst" in Carinthia, which is an influential pressure group. Still, even now new national factors have come to the fore.

(j) Fusion of small villages into large communities mixes minority villages with majority and mixed villages. Thus—in Brittany, Carinthia, Burgenland, and among the Cimbrians—homogeneous minority villages are deprived of their (minority) mayor (and staff), other "authorities" (if previously existent), priest[22] and school.

(k) Competition for votes in parliamentary democracies disfavors ethnocentric minorities, if they are also quantitatively small minorities in their territories (only in South Tyrol the German minority is a quantitative ethnocentric majority in their province). This is a serious drawback of parliamentary democracies.

Factors (a) and (h) might not be detrimental, if they were the only ones. But their combination with other factors makes them detrimental.

3.4. Minority nationalism generally has a retarding effect on language decay, but not always. For example, in the Bayuvarian dialect islands of Sauris and Sappada, German nationalism is out of the question and awakening anti-Italian Friulian nationalism disfavors identification with local German rather than regional Friulian values. In order to retard language decay, ethnocentric self-identification must pass beyond the stage of folkloric traditionalism and acquiescing "Weltschmerz." Here consciousness and glorification of the distant past is important: this is the case with South Tyrolians and to a certain extent with Slovenians (who are aware of the more recent diffusion of German), and with Croatians and Cimbrians, who take pride in their ancient immigration. On the other hand, many Bretons are unaware of their distant national history, an effect of the French school-system.

Standardization of the minority language is necessary to halt language decay, but the discrepancy between the standard and local dialects makes it difficult to teach the standard. In Brittany, standard Breton is too distant from at least a third of the dialects (particularly from Vannetais). Since very few children learn the dialect, participate in Breton services, or learn a Breton catechism, Breton is losing its function of inter-Breton communication and is in a process of dismemberment.

In the Burgenland the Čakavian standard is used in churches, like Slovenian in Carinthia. But attempts to teach Štokavian Serbo-Croatian, or a mixture of Čakavian and Štokavian, in school have alienated many pupils and parents and decreased attendance of Croatian schools (Benčić 1972:19, 24ff). Here, standardization has—as Fishman formulated it in the discussion of this paper—discredited large numbers of speakers who, before standardization, thought they could speak the language.

There are rare cases of Carinthian Slovenes who frequented the Slovenian high-school in Klagenfurt and replaced there their local dialect with standard Slovenian and then had communication problems in their native villages. Cimbrian never had a standard; and many South Tyrolians are not really fluent in standard German (Egger 1977).

Purification and modernization of the standard have decreased comprehensibility of standard Breton, Slovenian,[23] and Croatian to the respective minorities. This may contribute to widening the gap between authenticity and modernism (see Fishman, this volume). Elaboration of the standard in written or oral literature is nonexistent in Cimbrian (outside of popular traditional songs and poems). It has now only a small public in Brittany (with the exception of recent protest songs). The situation is much better in the other areas due to the existence of a national literature.

The separate function of a minority language is often misunderstood by the majority as separatism. Minority nationalism has reached the stage of separatism only with a few Breton nationalists. Unification with the respective "motherlands," if feasible, would probably be preferred by some Carinthian Slovenians and many South Tyrolians,[24] whereas all Burgenland Croatians seem to have rejected "Yugoslavism" since their attachment to Austria.

Around these separatist kernels there are larger groups who strongly identify with minority language and cultural values. A decaying language has little value for minority self-identification; at least in Brittany there is a growing number of Breton nationalists who pay only lip-service to the maintenance of the minority language and identify with other values more readily.

3.5. Whereas (nearly) all South Tyrolians distinctly perceive themselves as non-Italians and all Cimbrians as Italians, the other three areas show a growing polarization. Among Bretons and (more so) Carinthian Slovenes there is a relatively small, but increasing number of nationalists who identify with ethnocentric values, including the standard minority language, but may sharply disagree as to their political leanings. The major part of the minorities, however, show no sign of giving up the attitudes that result in language decay and language substitution.

In Burgenland only a conservative Catholic minority in the central part of the province is likely to keep the Čakavian standard and the Čakavian dialects up for some time. Thus with the exception of South Tyrol only small layers of the minorities are able to reverse language decay by positively revaluating their ethnocentric language attitudes (cf.

Cooper and Fishman 1974:9)[25] and by giving up their rural dialects in favor of a fairly distant language standard. In South Tyrol, the colloquial German standard has become archaic, partially deficient and/or influenced by Italian during the Fascist regime, but according to the investigations of Egger (1977), it seems possible to modernize, elaborate, and disseminate this standard and approach it to standards used in Austria and Southern Germany.

3.6. Retardation and lasting (?) reversal of language decay may seem to be incompatible with the nationalistic ingredients of modern European states. Fortunately for minorities, European state nationalism has been on the decline since World War II. Moreover, the ideals of European unification and the rediscovery and revaluation of regional traditions have eased conflicts between minority nationalism and identification with the state, e.g., in France and Italy. In Austria two factors dissociate Burgenland Croatians and Carinthian Slovenians from Yugoslavic Croatians and Slovenians. First, within Burgenland and Carinthia there are no historic territorial entities uniquely characterized as Croatian/Slovenian. Immigrant Croatians settled in dispersed villages of West Hungary from which the new region Burgenland was detached in 1921. Carinthia once was totally Slovenian or nearly; later on there was never a distinct Slovenian subentity, no big monolingual town as center for Slovenian activities. The stereotype of "There is only one Carinthia" is accepted also by most Carinthian Slovenians, and the analogically derived "unique Carinthian" should by necessity be germanophone, as is suggested by root-level anti-Slovenian propaganda.

Secondly, whereas Yugoslavia follows the ideals of communism within a one-party state, Austria is a parliamentary democracy of the Western type, in whose elections communist parties receive less than 3 percent of the votes, a percentage which seems to be true also for Carinthian Slovenes.

It is not my intention to make proposals about how national politics should be changed (cf. Kloss 1969) in order to halt or reverse the language decay of national minorities. But it is quite clear that, whereas on the whole the safeguarding of German in South Tyrol is developing in a satisfactory direction, considerable improvements could be made in France and Austria. Still, I do not believe that political measures in the area of nationalistic factors (such as granting maximum regional autonomy for the minority) could do more than retard language decay of part of the speakers concerned.

4. In the discussion following the oral presentation of this paper, Fishman commented that one should distinguish between cases of irreversible language decay, where it is too late for a successful revival,

and cases where the receding language may be salvageable. This has been one of the aims of this comparative study.

In my opinion, the basic question is to what extent social subordination creates negative sociopsychological evaluations of the minority language by its speakers (cf. the flowchart in 2.3). As the various contributions to the volume on language death (*International Journal of the Sociology of Language,* 1977, 12) attest, such evaluations seem to be due, primarily, to socioeconomic and sociopsychological factors quite irrespective of nationalistic factors. Nor does numerical decline play an important role.

For example, because of massive emigration following the Mussolini-Hitler pact, the number of South Tyroleans living in South Tyrol decreased dramatically after 1939. On the other hand, high birth rates of Breton speakers have compensated (or even overcompensated) for the loss of Breton speakers (due to assimilation or emigration) for a long time. Moreover, nationalist repression of German in South Tyrol was much tougher in Fascist Italy than repression of Breton in France during the Third Republic. And even during twenty years of fascism in Italy, the repression of South Tyrolean German was heavier than that of Cimbrian. Still, South Tyrol German decayed much less than Breton, Cimbrian, or Slovenian and Croatian within Austria, where—with the exception of the seven years of Nazi occupation—repression was not as heavy.

Of course, a political upheaval which results in uniting a geographical area A of a threatened minority language with its motherland B will salvage the maintenance of the language (guaranteed in B) also in the area A. This has happened with Slovenian in small southern districts of Carinthia which became part of Yugoslav Slovenia in 1919. Here nationalistic factors have been reversed (and after 1945 German has been virtually eradicated). Thus, nationalistic factors are not the most important agents of language decay. On the other hand the replacement of nationalistic pressures by productive measures may create a situation where the speakers of a minority language may preserve their language intact, if they evaluate their language positively. Both conditions exist in South Tyrol, but not in the other cases discussed here. The spread of an official language (even when favored by state authorities) does not necessarily contradict the preservation of a minority language as an intact, functioning code.

NOTES

1. Therefore this report will be rather short.

2. Here I will go beyond my previous contributions on the subject (Dressler 1972, 1978; Dressler and Wodak-Leodolter 1977a, b) and use the polycentristic approach to language as presented in Dressler (1977 a, b).

3. Still a very small minority among celtophonic Bretons uses standard Breton.

4. Here we must distinguish coordinate bilingualism of emigrants who cannot use German, e.g., for scientific purposes, while they are fluent in German for other purposes.

5. Moreover, they are not necessary components of language shift/ substitution. In my first paper on language death (Dressler 1972) I have dealt with a still much more limited phenomenon, i.e., impoverishment (of the structure of the dying language), which cannot be predicted by the impact of the structure of the victorious/substituting language—since changes in a receding language due to the structure of another language have been amply described before: I have made no larger claims, as Denison's (1977) critique seems to imply.

6. Cf., e.g., Clyne (1976), Denison (1971), Dressler and Wodak-Leodolter (1977a, b), Grassi (1977), Hill (1973), Kloss (1966), Swadesh (1948).

7. Or "knowledge," to use Cooper's terms (this volume), which seem to be useful also for this converse of language spread.

8. Cf. Dressler and Wodak-Leodolter (1977a:8, b:36f, section 2.5. and below), Trudgill (1977).

9. Components are segmental phonology, syntax, lexicon, derivational morphology, etc. The tendencies (such as universal phonological, morphological, syntactic processes or the tendencies towards productivity of rules, towards morphological transparency, towards bi-uniqueness of meaning and form) of each component are based on the semiotic functions of the respective component; in different sociolinguistic domains, marginal conditions (as intervening variables) may be so different that the outcomes of the conflicts between tendencies may differ.

10. Cf. Trudgill (1977), especially p. 36 where P. Mühlhäusler is quoted, and Schlieben-Lange (1977:102) on linguistic dysfunction.

11. Cf. Dressler (1978), Hill and Hill (1977:61), Schlieben-Lange (1977:103).

12. For Burgenland Croatian see Neweklowsky (1978:42ff), cf. Dorian (1973, section 6.2;1977:26f), Trudgill (1977) etc.

13. Breton: Dressler (1972:454ff), Dressler and Wodak-Leodolter (1977a:9; b:36f). Published studies in other languages do not seem to exist.

14. Hill (1973), Hill and Hill (1978), Trudgill (1977:36f), Dorian (1977:27); there are no published accounts on the five minority languages dealt with here.

15. Cf. Hill and Hill (1978), Schlieben-Lange (1977:103), McLane (1977:306).

16. According to Cappellati (1970, 6, note 1).

17. For Breton see Dressler (1972, 8.1.), for Cimbrian Schweizer (1939:9), cf. Dressler-Wodak (1977a:9), Trudgill (1977:35).

18. For Breton it is well-known that suppression started during the French Revolution when nationalism superseded feudalism and that the most detrimental national measures (strictly obligatory elementary school education and mili-

tary service) were introduced and first enforced in the 1880s, when French nationalism rose to its greatest height.

19. Of course, severe nationalist suppression may provoke stiff resistance and minority solidarity as among South Tyroleans and radical Slovenes.

20. In Carinthia these Slovenes are called "Windische" with the false prejudice that their language also differs from the Slovenian of ethnically conscious Carinthian Slovenes: however, the only linguistic difference is that these latter can consciously switch to the use of standard Slovenian terms for concepts usually expressed in German, which the "Windischen" are unable to do (Woschitz 1975:140).

21. Here the socialist party (SPÖ), which represents the majority of Croatians ("Bürgermeisterkonferenz") is an explicit and outspoken protagonist for assimilation because of economic and social reasons.

22. Due to shortages of priests, particularly in Brittany and Burgenland, whereas there are too many Slovenian and too few German priests in Carinthia.

23. Although the traditional Carinthian Slovenian Church language is very puristic and is understood, this does not help the understanding of modernized, purified standard Slovenian, because their respective vocabularies and sociolinguistic functions are quite different.

24. Even the relevant literature is devoid of data; demographic inquiries would be very tricky.

25. A positive evaluation of one's minority language does not guarantee survival of the language, but negative evaluation strongly disfavors it.

REFERENCES

Benčić, Nikolaus. 1972. Abriss der geschichtlichen Entwicklung der burgenländisch-kroatischen Schriftsprache. Wiener Slavistisches Jahrbuch 17.15–28.

Cappellati, Giuseppe. 1970. Auguri in Tautsch al neo Cardinale Bartolomeo Bacilieri. Taucias Gareida 2, 8.6.

Clyne, Michael. 1976. Introduction in: Australia Talks. The Australian National University (Pacific Linguistics D-23) 1–6.

Cooper, Robert L. A Framework for the Study of Language Spread. This volume.

Cooper, Robert L. and Fishman, Joshua A. 1974. The Study of Language Attitudes. International Journal of the Sociology of Language 3.5–19.

Denison, Norman. 1971. Some observations on Language Variety and Plurilingualism. ASA Monographs (London, Tavistock) 157–83.

Denison, Norman. 1977. Language Death or Language Suicide? IJSL 12, 13–22.

Dorian, Nancy C. 1973. Grammatical Change in a Dying Dialect. Language 49.413–38.

Dorian, Nancy C. 1977. The Problem of the Semi-Speaker in Language Death. IJSL 12.23–32.

Dressler, Wolfgang. 1972. On the Phonology of Language Death. Papers from the 8th Regional Meeting. Chicago Linguistic Society, 448–57.

Dressler, Wolfgang. 1977a. Grundfragen der Morphonologie. Wien. Verlag der Österreichischen Akademie der Wissenschaften.

Dressler, Wolfgang. 1977b. Elements of a polycentristic theory of word-formation. Wiener Linguistische Gazette 15.13–32.

Dressler, Wolfgang. 1978. Wortbildung bei Sprachverfall in: H. Brekle and D. Kastovsky (eds.): Perspektiven der Wortbildungsforschung (anlässlich des 70. Geburtstags von Hans Marchand), 62–69. Bouvier Verlag Herbert Grundmann, Bonn.

Dressler, Wolfgang and Wodak-Leodolter, Ruth. 1977a. Introduction. IJSL 12.5–11.

Dressler, Wolfgang and Wodak-Leodolter, Ruth. 1977b. Language Preservation and Language Death in Brittany. IJSL 12.33–44.

Egger, Kurt. 1977. Zweisprachigkeit in Südtirol. Bozen, Athesia.

Fishman, Joshua A. 1966a. The Historical and Social Contexts of an Inquiry into Language Maintenance Efforts. in: Fishman et al. 1966, 21–33.

Fishman, Joshua A. 1966b. Language Maintenance and Language Shift as a Field of Inquiry. in: Fishman et al. 1966, 424–58.

Fishman, Joshua A. 1970. Sociolinguistics. Rowley. Newbury House.

Fishman, Joshua A. 1971. The Impact of Nationalism on Language Planning. Actes du Ier colloque AIMAV, Bruxelles, 15–34.

Fishman, Joshua A. et al. 1966. Language Loyalty in the United States. The Hague. Mouton.

Fishman, Joshua A. Attracting a Following to High Culture Functions for a Language of Everyday Life (The Role of the Tshernovits Language Conference in the "Rise of Yiddish"). This volume.

Grassi, Corrado. 1977. Deculturization and Social Degradation of the Linguistic Minorities in Italy. IJSL 12.45–46.

Haas, Hanns and Stuhlpfarrer, Karl. 1977. Österreich und seine Slowenen. Vienna. Löcker.

Heller, Karin. 1975. Sprachinselforschung aus der Sicht der allgemeinen Sprachwissenschaft—am Beispiel des Zimbrischen. Salzburger Beiträge zur Linguistik 1.25–33.

Hill, Jane H. 1973. Subordinate Clause Density and Language Function. Papers from the Comparative Syntax Festival, Chicago Linguistic Society, 33–52.

Hill, Jane and Hill, Kenneth. 1977. Language Death and Relexification in Tlaxcalan Nahuatl. IJSL 12.55–69.

Hill, Jane and Hill, Kenneth. 1978. Honorific usage in modern Nahuatl. Language 54.123–55.

Kloss, Heinz. 1966. German-American Language Maintenance Efforts. in: Fishman et al. 1966.

Kloss, Heinz. 1969. Grundfragen der Ethnopolitik im 20. Jahrhundert. Wien. Braumüller.

Kloss, Heinz. 1974. Die den internationalen Rang einer Sprache bestimmenden Faktoren. Institut für Deutsche Sprache, Forschungs-berichte, 20, 7–77.

Lemberg, Eugen. 1964. Nationalismus, Reinbek, Rowohlt.

Leys, Odo. 1974. Sociolinguistic Aspects of Namegiving Patterns. Onoma 18.448–55.

McLane, Merrill F. 1977. The Calo of Guadix: A Surviving Romany Lexicon. Anthropological Linguistics 19, 303–19.

Neweklowsky, Gerhard. 1978. Die Kroatischen Dialekte des Burgenlandes. Wien, Verlag der Österreichischen Akademie der Wissenschaften.

Schlieben-Lange, Brigitte. 1977. The Language situation in Southern France. IJSL 12.101–108.

Schweizer, Bruno. 1939. Zimbrische Sprachreste I. Halle, Niemeyer.

Swadesh, Morris. 1948. Sociologic Notes on obsolescent languages. IJAL 14.226–35.

Trudgill, Peter. 1977. Creolization in Reverse: Reduction and Simplification in the Albanian Dialects of Greece. Transactions of the Philological Society 1976–7, 32–50.

Woschitz, Walter J. 1975. Sprachminderheit und Staatsvolk. Grazer linguistische Studien 1.135–41.

Microsociolinguistics of Hungarian-Serbocroatian Bilingualism

Melanie Mikes

When we approach bilingualism from the sociolinguistic point of view, the best way to get to the core of the problem is through one of its forms of occurrence. In this paper we concentrate upon Hungarian + Serbocroatian bilingualism, especially on selected microsociolinguistic manifestations. Such bilingualism, however, is not treated in isolation, but as part of the complex interaction of micro- and macroenvironmental factors.

This approach has grown out of the questions we want to answer. The mere statement that parents communicate with their children in one language or the other is not in itself satisfactory, since a question immediately arises about what their attitudes are toward linguistic communication in one and/or the other language.

The answer to the first question in each case of bilingualism depends a great deal on the answer to the second question. Parents' attitudes, however, never arise in the minds of parents by themselves, independently from happenings in the broader social environment, rather they are conditioned by the historical and social reality of the macroenvironment of which the microenvironment, e.g., the family, is an integral part.

Interaction between micro- and macroenvironmental factors happens in the following way: the subjective and objective factors of the macroenvironment coexert an influence on the particular attitudes in the microenvironment, which—depending on the reality of the microenvironment—alter the microenvironment. Each change in the microenvironment is reflected in the structure of the macroenvironment. By accepting this view of interaction we are obliged to view bilingualism in correlation with the interaction of micro- and macroenvironmental factors.

Hungarian-Serbocroatian bilingualism interactions take place in the following situations:

—ethnolinguistically mixed microenvironment in a predominantly monolingual macroenvironment
—ethnolinguistically mixed microenvironment in a bilingual macroenvironment
—ethnolinguistically homogeneous microenvironment in a predominantly monolingual macroenvironment
—ethnolinguistically homogeneous microenvironment in a bilingual macroenvironment.

Within the above situations we can distinguish the following variants:

Father's language	Mother's language	Language of the social environment
H /Hungarian/	SC /Serbocroatian/	H(SC) /predominantly H/
SC	H	H (SC)
H	SC	SC (H)
SC	H	SC (H)
H	SC	bl (bilingual)
SC	H	bl
H	H	H (SC)
SC	SC	H (SC)
H	H	SC (H)
SC	SC	SC (H)
H	H	bl
SC	SC	bl

Interaction between the micro- and macroenvironmental factors of bilingualism is activated by the socioeconomic relations of the micro- and macroenvironments. The subjective factors of the macroenvironment act by means of institutionalized bilingualism, and together with the sociolinguistic reality of the micro- and macrostructures (father's language, mother's language, the language of the social environment), they influence the formation of parents' attitudes towards bilingualism in their children. The strength and quality of this impact, however, depend on the cultural and economic level of the microenvironment; which means that the effects of individual bilingualism vary according to the differences of the economic and cultural levels of microenvironments. We presume that the motivation cannot be the same in economically and culturally diverse microenvironments, and therefore it cannot have the same stimulative power to promote the acquisition of bilingualism.

Economic and cultural factors are "sensitive" to the phenomenon of bilingualism. In the case of Hungarian-Serbocroatian bilingualism, they are controlled by the pluralistic concept of language policy which is incorporated into the constitution of the Socialist Federal Republic of Yugoslavia, the constitutions of the socialist republics, and the corresponding legislative acts of the socialist autonomous provinces, as well as in the statutes of the sociopolitical communities and self-management acts of organizations of associated labor.

Thus, under Articles Four and Five of the Constitution of the Socialist Autonomous Province of Vojvodina (an autonomous province in the northeast of Yugoslavia) the rights of nationalities (national minorities) are guaranteed:

In the Socialist Autonomous Province of Vojvodina nations and nationalities have equal rights in all the fields of life, labor and creation. Every nation and nationality are guaranteed the right of free development and expression of their national particularities, linguistic, cultural, historical and other features, and therefore the right to establish organizations, and to enjoy other rights stated by the constitution. In the Socialist Autonomous Province of Vojvodina, Serbocroatian/Croatoserbian, Hungarian, Slovakian, Rumanian, Ruthenian and their alphabets enjoy equal rights.

The Development of Hungarian-Serbocroatian bilingualism in the microenvironment, and the acquisition of bilingualism on the whole, does not mean that both languages are used in the family. The process is indeed a form of mother-tongue maintenance and second language acquisition. The neighborhood, common courtyards or playgrounds, the circle of close friends, etc., are also microenvironments where children's bilingualism can be developed.

The examples we shall quote in this paper are intended to serve as illustrations of the characteristics of Hungarian-Serbocroatian bilingualism in the social environments of Vojvodina.[1] We wish to (1) demonstrate some aspects of interactions between the child and the microenvironment in the process of the child's acquisition of bilingualism, (2) indicate certain aspects of interactions between micro- and macroenvironmental factors which possess "sensitivity" to the phenomenon of bilingualism, and (3) conclude by exemplifying some patterns of language use among secondary school students.

1.1. Viewing language as a form of human activity in which the speaker's life experience and social determinants run together, we shall exemplify how these two essential components of linguistic activity are reflected in the speech behavior of the child who acquires early bilingualism in the family. Our starting point is the use of the two languages in relation to the collocators. The empirical material is represented by a corpus containing one thousand verbal interactions registered at the age two to three in the speech of a child who was acquiring bilingualism in an etholinguistically mixed microenvironment.

Distribution of the use of Serbocroatian and Hungarian

	Mother	Father	Sister	Grand-mother	Uncle	Brother
SC	72.28%	0.00%	84.72%	2.70%	23.81%	23.81%
H	2.27	81.54	5.56	83.78	47.62	52.38
SC/H	25.45	18.46	9.72	13.52	28.57	23.81

This table shows that there is a "usual" language of communication with each of the chid's collocators, but there are cases when the child addresses a collocator in the "unusual" language of communication. Thus we need to answer the question: which factors influence the choice of a certain pattern of verbal interaction and cause the appearance of "mixed speech" (marked in the table by SC/H)?

"Mixed speech" is considered to be conditioned: (1) by Hungarian-Serbocroatian structural interference, (2) by the sociolinguistic factors of the microenvironment, and (3) by the close association between the use of a code and the person who represents not only the usual collocator using this code, but also the "teacher" of this language.

Among the variants of "mixed speech" the most interesting for our consideration is "mixed speech with theorizing," e.g., a kind of internalizing of the bilingual situation, for instance:

Child: *Ja ću elcsapti.* (I am going to switch off [television].)
Mother: *Ti ćeš iskopčati.* (You are going to switch off [TV].)
Child: *Nem fogom elkapcsolni, elcsapni.*

In the last sentence the child is explaining to the mother, of course implicitly, why she (the child) has derived the "mixed word" *elcsapti* (H *elcsap* + SC *ti*): the segment *elcsap* (the verb without the infinitive ending *-ni*) does not correspond lexically to the segment *iskopča* (SC verb without the infinitive ending *-ti*). It seems that the child has not yet realized the difference between the virtual and the actual use of a lexeme. In spite of this arguing by the child, the mother's use of the verb *iskopčati* was correct in this sentence.

Some details registered in the *mother-child* dyads are also very interesting, having in mind that these interactions represent 70 percent of the corpus analyzed. The data in the table show that "mixed speech" on the part of the child appears in 25 percent of the interactions with the mother. This occurs most frequently at the age of two and a half, and after that period diminishes rapidly. However, it should be mentioned that "self-correction" appears in the same period, for instance:

ja ću viti // ovo je moja tašna // ja ću odneti tašnicu (I am going to take my bag // this is my bag // I am going to take the bag)

This discourse is organized in Serbocroatian. Only at the beginning the child has used a "mixed word" *viti*, composed of H *vi* + SC infinitive ending *ti*.

Much later, when the child was 3;10, the mother consciously tried to elicit such corrections, for instance:

Child: *Trebam sad úju.* (H *újból* = again)
Mother: *Sta trebaš?*
Child: *Trebam sad ponovo.* (SC *ponovo* = again)

The verbal interaction, as a whole, is organized in Serbocroatian.

In the mother-child dyads the percentage of Hungarian language use is very low (2.27%). It was not before 2;10 that the child began to address the mother in Hungarian too. At the age between 2;7 and 2;8 the word "Hungarian" appeared. For instance, if accidentally the child initiated the communication with her mother in Hungarian, the following comment was made by the child: "I said it in Hungarian." Or, when hearing somebody speaking Hungarian, the child informed the mother: "That's Hungarian."

In the period when the child started to address the mother in Hungarian (2;10), she transmitted her "linguistic meditations" to the mother in Hungarian, too. "Linguistic meditations," however, were implicitly also present in the earlier utterances of the child, for instance:

Mother: *Skočila si.* (You jumped.)
Child: *Nisam skočila, samo ugortam.* (SC *skočila sam*, H *ugortam:* I jumped.)

In the linguistic corpus verbal interactions with two or more collocators were also analyzed. In these interactions the child adjusted the language to the collocators, and so it happened that she switched from one language to the other, for instance:

Mother: *Pitaću nadmamu kad si piškila.* (I am going to ask grandmother when you did wee-wee?)

Child: *Pitaću ja*. (I am going to ask.)
Child (addressing the grandmother): *Mikor pisátam?* (When did I wee-wee?)
Grandmother: *Most köll elöbb pisálni*.
Child (addressing the mother): *Rekla nadmama sad treba da piškim*.
(Grandmother said I should wee-wee now.)

1.2. In the following example our attention will be concentrated on the correlation between the degree of bilingualism between a child and his collocators in an ethnolinguistically mixed kindergarten group and on his use of mother tongue and second language. The average age of the kindergarten group was 5;9. There were 25 children in the group: 10 children from Serbian families, 7 from Hungarian families, and 8 from mixed marriages. We have published a paper on the socialization in this kindergarten group[2] in which we stated that the function of both languages with respect to the nature of interaction had a sociable tendency, from initiating to sharing, and that no important difference was observed in the choice of either language for more or less sociable and friendly interactions.

The children were divided into three groups according to the degree of their bilingualism: bilinguals (Group A), incipient bilinguals (Group B), and monolinguals (Group C). Our observations took place in two examination periods: at the beginning of October and at the beginning of May. We spent 25 hours in October and 27 hours in May on observations. A total of 2,922 interactions in children's mutual contacts were registered.

The degree of the children's bilingualism was measured by a test administered in May. The children had the following linguistic backgrounds: Group A (10 children): 4 from Hungarian families, 6 from mixed marriages; Group B (9 children): 4 from Serbian families, 3 from Hungarian families, 2 from mixed marriages; Group C (6 children): all from Serbian families.

In this kindergarten group there was no Hungarian monolingualism, only Serbocroatian, and this fact was reflected in the distribution of language use.

Language use with respect to the respondent's bilingualism

Language:	SC	H	SC/H	
Group	34–73%	20–60%	4–7%	Children from H family.
A	48–96	5–52	0–8	Children from mixed family.
Group	85–100	0–8	0–3	Children from S family.
B	24–98	2–71	5–6	Children from H family.
	92–95	5–8	–	Children from mixed family.

As children belonging to Group C were not bilingual at all, they communicated with all children only in Serbocroatian.

Verbal interaction use with respect to the bilingualism of the collocator[3]

Interactions with collocators:	A	B	C
Collocators of group A (H)	67%	29%	2%
A (H/S)	47	41	11
B (H)	66	18	16
B (H/S)	57	21	12
B (S)	40	36	20
C (S)	49	32	13

The two preceeding tables show that the use of Hungarian was relatively small in mutual interactions among the children, when compared to the ethnolinguistic structure of the group. This finding was also confirmed by comparison of the state of bilingualism in this kindergarten group at the beginning of the examination period (October) to that at the end of it (May).

Group	October	May
A	42%	46%
B	35	27
C	23	27

It is obvious that in this microenvironment the presence of those macroenvironmental factors which should activate the educational process towards promoting two-direction bilingualism was not felt. As we know the situation in this environment well, we may say that the reason for this state of affairs was the unsuitable organization of the educational process in the two languages and an unlucky choice of teacher. The teacher's knowledge of Hungarian was very poor, so she was handicapped in promoting bilingualism in monolingual children whose mother tongue was Serbocroatian.

The unsatisfactory state of bilingualism in this kindergarten group of mixed ethnolinguistic structure had the following effects. The bilingual children from Hungarian families most often contacted the bilingual children (67% of interactions), while their contacts with monolingual children were scarce, and we know that all the monolingual children were from Serbian families. The monolingual children, however, did not close themselves in their ethnolinguistic group—only 13% of such interactions were observed—rather they contacted all the children who were willing to communicate with them in Serbocroatian. The distribution of the interactions of bilingual children from mixed marriages presents the most favorable picture, because these children found themselves in a situation similar to that in their homes.

The distribution of bilingualism in this kindergarten group shows that the favorable results one might expect on the basis of the macroenvironment can be prevented by an inefficient interaction between the micro- and macroenvironmental factors "sensitive" to the phenomenon of bilingualism.

2.1. The interaction of micro- and macroenvironmental factors in Hungarian-Serbocroatian bilingualism will be illustrated on a sample of 60 children of kindergarten age (5–6 years old). The data were collected in 1968–69 in kindergartens in three ethnolinguistically diverse macroenvironments: predominantly Serbocroatian linguistic environment—SC (H), predominantly Hungarian linguistic environment—H (SC), and bilingual environment—H/SC. We investigated the microenvironmental conditions which made these children bilingual before they entered kindergarten.

Macro-environment	Microenvironment		
	Mixed marriage	*Hungarian family*	*Serbian or Croatian family*
SC (H)	5 children	13 children	-------
H (SC)	13	-------	1 child
H/SC	12	13	3 children

The table shows that, in a predominantly Serbocroatian linguistic environment, the children from Hungarian families most often become bilingual before entering kindergarten. In a predominantly Hungarian linguistic environment, children from Hungarian families do not acquire bilingualism at all before entering kindergarten. In such a linguistic environment children from mixed marriages (or from Serbian or Croatian families) become bilingual before entering kindergarten. In a bilingual macroenvironment, the bilingual children come to kindergarten both from mixed marriages and Hungarian families, and only a small number of children from Serbian or Croatian families acquire bilingualism before entering kindergarten.

We have stated that in ethnolinguistically mixed families, the children most often acquire bilingualism so that one parent communicates with them in one language and the other in the other language: SC (H) 2 children (from the total of 5 from mixed marriages), H (SC) 13 children (all children from mixed marriages), H/SC 7 children (from the total of 12 from mixed marriages).

The other children from mixed marriages have acquired bilingualism in the following ways: one child from SC (H) and two children from H/SC communicated only in Serbocroatian with one parent, and in both languages with the other parent; two children from SC (H) and one child from H/SC communicated in both languages with both parents; one child from H/SC communicated only in Hungarian with one parent, and in both languages with the other parent; one child from H/SC communicated only in Hungarian with both parents.

Fifty percent of the children of this sample have not acquired bilingualism in the conditions of mixed marriage. Of 26 children from Hungarian families, 22 acquired bilingualism in microenvironments outside the family circle, and only 4 in their families. Of 4 children from Serbian or Croatian families, 2 became bilingual in microenvironments outside the family circle and 2 by communicating in Hungarian with some of the members of the household.

The data we have indicated may be considered typical for the state of affairs in Vojvodina some ten years ago. In order to make possible the acquisition of bilingualism in children who live under microenvironmental conditions which do not favor bilingualism, the practice of teaching the second language in kindergartens has been promoted and spread in kindergartens all over Vojvodina. It is quite reasonable to expect that our present investigations will validate this practice, which activates the interaction of micro- and macroenvironmental factors "sensitive" to the phenomenon of bilingualism.

2.2. The following example is an illustration of the influence of a predominantly Hungarian ethnolinguistic macroenvironment on diverse ethnolinguistic microenvironments.

When preparing to test bilingual children in 1968, we gathered data on 146 bilingual children in a predominantly Hungarian ethnolinguistic macroenvironment: 29 children at the age 6–7 (Group A), 22 children at the age 10–11 (Group B), 95 children at the age 15–16 (Group C).

Microenvironment (family)		
Mixed marriage	*Hungarian family*	*Serbian or Croatian family*
Group A	62.07%	20.69%	17.24%
Group B	22.73	68.18	9.09
Group C	5.26	82.11	12.63

These data are revealing when they are read vertically whereas a horizontal reading would give us only the reflexion of the macroenvironmental ethnolinguistic structure in the microstructure. By reading the data vertically, we may perceive a tendency towards bilingual growth in children from Hungarian families, a tendency towards bilingual decrease in children from mixed marriages, and may note the facts that the children belonging to Serbian or Croatian families are mostly bilingual at the age of 7, that thereafter they show a tendency to lose bilingualism, and a tendency to reacquire it at the age 15–16. This positive tendency of reacquiring bilingualism may be ascribed to the influence of macroenvironmental factors in the period from 1968 to 1977.

We checked this assumption on a sample of 124 secondary school students belonging to Serbian families living in a predominantly Hungarian macroenvironment. We investigated whether, when, and with whom these students communicated in Hungarian. We found that in certain situational settings more than 70 percent of these students communicated with their Hungarian friends in Hungarian.[4]

2.3. It is in the nature of the ethnolinguistically mixed microenvironment that it possesses a greater capability of adaptation to the fundamentals of any macrostructure than does a homogeneous microstructure. So it is quite understandable that we are interested in the impact of a predominantly Serbocroatian linguistic macroenvironment on a Hungarian-Serbocroatian linguistic microenvironment. Our investigations, however, do not yet enable us to assess the impact completely. At present we can present an illustration relative to the distribution of the Hungarian and Serbocroatian language use in ethnolinguistically mixed families only in the case in which children have classes in Hungarian, i.e., in cases when one of the macroenvironmental factors "sensitive" to the phenomenon of bilingualism is present.

The sample comprises 23 students aged 14–16 in macroenvironments where the percentage of Hungarians is 8–23 percent. All students are taught in Hungarian.

Language-use distribution in H-SC microenvironments			
Only H or rarely SC	*One parent H, other parent SC*	*One parent H, other parent H/SC*	*One parent SC, other parent H/SC*
16 respondents	3 respondents	1 respondent	3 respondents

2.4. The previous example permits us to make the assumption that the language used in the educational process does influence language use in microenvironments, i.e., that due to the influence of an education in Hungarian, Hungarian has been used relatively much in ethnolinguistically mixed families. As we did not have a control group, we were not able to check this assumption.

In the present example, however, we are able to show the relationship between the language distribution in ethnolinguistically mixed families and the language or languages in which students acquire their knowledge. Our question is: how does a predominantly Hungarian ethnolinguistic macroenvironment influence language-use distribution in microenvironments in cases of diverse efficiency of the educational macrosociolinguistic factor?

The sample serving as illustration of this aspect of the interaction between the micro- and macrosociolinguistic factors comprises 22 students aged 16–18 in a macroenvironment where the percentage of Hungarians is 85 percent. Fourteen students frequent classes taught in Serbocroatian (Group SC), and 8 students classes taught in Hungarian (Group H).

Language-use distribution in H-SC microenvironments

	Group SC	Group H
Only Hungarian	——	7 respondents
One parent H, other parent SC	2 respondents	——
Both parents SC	4 respondents	——
One parent SC, other parent H/SC	4 respondents	——
Both parents H/SC	4 respondents	1 respondent

The table shows that there is mutual influence between the language of education and the use of this language in family. However, it would be superficial to assert that this is a case of one-directional influence, e.g., that a student uses Hungarian or not when communicating with his parents depending on whether he attends classes in Hungarian or not. Fundamentally we are concerned with the consequence of parents' attitudes towards developing bilingualism in their children and the choice of the language they want their children to be educated in. This choice, as we have already seen, depends on the objective and subjective factors of the macroenvironment.

Here the "sensitivity" of the economic factor emerges again. We have already pointed to this factor and we will return to it in section 3.3. However, in treating the impact of the economic factor on Hungarian-Serbocroatian bilingualism we would like to stress that we do not view the relevance of this factor as it is expressed in the Yugoslav language policy, but as it is manifested in the consciousness of people, where remnants of the past have been conserved.

2.5. Finally, we shall illustrate a situation relative to the interaction of micro- and macrosociolinguistic factors in ethnolinguistically mixed microenvironments as parts of a macroenvironment of similar type. The sample comprises 20 students aged 14–16 in a macroenvironment where the percentage of Hungarians is 49 percent. All students attend classes in Hungarian.

Language-use distribution in H-SC microenvironments

Only H or rarely SC	13 respondents
One parent H, other parent H/SC	2 respondents
One parent SC,	
other parent H/SC or both H/SC	5 respondents

The data in this table permit us to conclude that there are great similarities in the language-use distribution in mixed families whose children attend classes in Hungarian, without respect to the ethnolinguistic structure of the macroenvironment.

3.1. The data presented in the former sections had an illustrative character, while the data we shall present in this section are representative. We obtained them by analyzing the material gathered by administering a questionnaire to 700 secondary school students who use Hungarian and Serbocroatian. The sample comprises students from three ethnolinguistically different macroenvironments: SC (H), H (SC), and H/SC; they are Hungarians or they belong to one of the Yugoslav nations; their mother tongue is Hungarian or Serbocroatian.

We were investigating the use of mother tongue and second language. The questions pertain to immediate speech situations (domains): At Home, At School, At a Party, In Public and in Intimate Interactions. Students were also questioned about cultural background: what do the students and their parents read in one or both languages, do they listen to broadcasts in one or both languages, which television programs do they watch, etc. All alternative answers were given in advance, and the task of the student was to mark the question pertaining to his speech behavior.

We approached the analysis of these data on the basis of three fundamental criteria: nationality, social environment and language.

	Constant variables		
1. Scheme	Nationality	Social environment	Language
2. Scheme	Language	Social environment	Nationality
3. Scheme	Social environment	Nationality	Language

3.2. From the complex of these investigations we present some selected patterns of language use as results of the analysis according to the second scheme. The analysis based on this scheme enables us to observe the use of one language in its double function, e.g., in the function of mother tongue, when it is used by native speakers, and in the function of the language of the social environment, when it is used by second-language speakers.

Our attention will be focused on the situational setting (domain) At a Party, because we consider this domain as very indicative for the patterns of language use in students at this age (17–18).

All the students comprised by this sample (376 students) live in a macroenvironment H (SC). They are divided into two groups: Group L 1—mother tongue Hungarian (252 students), and Group L 2—second language Hungarian (124 students).

3.3. The tables below show language use ordered according to frequency. The topic and the category of the collocator appear in combination. In the situational setting At a Party the following categories of collocators are distinguished:

—collocator of Hungarian nationality who speaks both languages well—H (bl)
—collocator of Hungarian nationality who does not speak Serbocroatian well—H
—collocator is not Hungarian, and he speaks both languages well—S (b1)
—collocator is not Hungarian, and he does not speak Hungarian well—S.

Group L 1

Order	Topic / Collocator	H language use in %
1.	actual events / H	90.48
2.	cultural events / H	90.08
3.	actual events / H (bl)	87.30
4.	school life / H	86.11
5.	family life / H	83.33
6.	school life / H (bl)	83.33
7.	cultural events / H (bl)	83.33
8.	intimate life / H (bl)	81.75
9.	family life / H (bl)	78.57
10.	intimate life / H	78.17
11.	cultural events / S (bl)	47.22
12.	intimate life / S (bl)	47.22
13.	actual events / S (bl)	47.22
14.	family life / S (bl)	46.03
15.	school life / S (bl)	44.44

16.	family life / S	25.79
17.	cultural events / S	17.46
18.	school life / S	15.87
19.	actual events / S	13.49
20.	intimate life / S	12.70

Group L 2

Order	Topic / Collocator	H language use in %
1.	family life / H	72.41
2.	school life / H	70.94
3.	cultural events / H	67.24
4.	actual events / H	64.35
5.	intimate life / H	63.72
6.	family life / H (bl)	34.18
7.	school life / H (bl)	27.87
8.	actual events / H (bl)	26.67
9.	cultural events / H (bl)	23.77
10.	intimate life / H (bl)	23.53
11.	school life / S (bl)	21.48
12.	family life / S (bl)	20.83
13.	actual events / S (bl)	18.85
14.	family life / S	18.80
15.	intimate life / S (bl)	17.80
16.	cultural events / S (bl)	16.87
17.	school events / S	15.38
18.	cultural events / S	13.68
19.	intimate life / S	10.43
20.	actual events / S	6.96

The most frequently discussed topic for Group L 1 is *actual events* in Yugoslavia and abroad, when the interactions are with a collocator of Hungarian nationality who does not speak Serbocroatian well (90.48%), while *intimate life* takes the last place when the collocator is not Hungarian and does not speak Hungarian well (12.70%).

The first place in group L 2 is taken by *family life* in the interactions with the collocator of Hungarian nationality who does not speak Serbocroatian well (72.41%), and *actual events* are to be found at the very end of the list when the collocator is not Hungarian and does not speak Hungarian well (6.96%). These data show that topic is a relevant factor in the choice of Hungarian as mother tongue or as second language; namely, *actual events* take first place when Hungarian is used as mother tongue and the last place when it is used as second language.

Both groups use Hungarian to a relatively high degree when the collocator does not speak Serbocroatian well. The main difference between the use of Hungarian as mother tongue and its use as second language is to be found in the criterion *nationality*. Namely, the students whose mother tongue is not Hungarian fairly often use this language in verbal interactions with collocators of Hungarian nationality who do not speak Serbocroatian well (63.72–72.41%), whereas they use it in a much lesser degree with those collocators of Hungarian nationality who speak Serbocroatian well (23.53–34.18%). However, students whose mother tongue is Hungarian use their mother tongue nearly as much with collocators of their nationality who speak both languages well (78.57–87.30%) as they use it with those who do not speak Serbocroatian well (78.17–90.48%).

3.4. If we compare the data presented in this section—especially those pertaining to the group of Serbocroatian native speakers—with the data we presented in the previous sections, we perceive that they give a more favorable picture of the developing two-direction bilingualism, e.g., functional bilingualism (as it is called in the respective Yugoslav literature).[5]

This state of affairs is not to be viewed as a result of spontaneous development, but rather it reflects the efficiency of macroenvironmental factors "sensitive" to bilingualism, primarily the economic factor. That is, the knowledge of Hungarian represents an advantage when one is applying for a post in many enterprises and institutions in Vojvodina. So the acquisition of a second language (the language of the social environment) is not only an existential problem for Hungarians, but also for the other Yugoslav peoples who live and work in Vojvodina.

It is not by chance that we got such data from young people who are coming of age. They are getting rid of the influence of their parents in whose consciousness some remnants of the past (language intolerance, minority complex, etc.) may sporadically be present.

If, summarizing all we have said, we wished to answer the question: *which factors influence the spread of a language,* we would not be able to give a direct answer. We presume that there are micro- and macroenvironmental factors which are "sensitive" to bilingualism and to the linguistic phenomenon on the whole; these are: economic status, cultural level, educational process, etc. There are the fundamentals of the context, as, for instance: the ethnolinguistic structure of the micro- and macroenvironment; there are subjective macroenvironmental factors, as for instance, the organized social and political forces of the macroenvironment. None of these factors per se leads to the spread of use of particular languages or to the restriction and loss of use in languages. The influence of the factors can be made efficient only by their interaction in particular objective conditions.

NOTES

1. According to the census of 1971, the total population of Vojvodina amounted to 1,952,533 inhabitants, of which 423,866 were Hungarians.

2. Melanie Mikes, Janet Tallman, and Lajos Göncz: A contribution to the problem of socialization among bilingual children in kindergartens (in Hungarian). *Papers of the Institute of Hungarian Studies,* 8/1971 Novi Sad, Ujvidék.

3. The frequency of the interactions of particular children with their mates (classified according to the degree of bilingualism of the latter) has been observed. In scoring the results, only collocators with more than four interactions were taken into consideration. Characters in brackets pertain to the family: (H) Hungarian, (S) Serbian, and (H/S) mixed marriage.

4. Ferenc Junger: On the use of Hungarian as second language (in Serbocroatian). *First Congress of the Yugoslav Societies of Applied Linguistics,* Belgrade 1977.

5. M. Mikes, A. Lük, F. Junger: A chapter on bilingualism in Yugoslavia (in Serbocroatian), *Kultura* (in press).

Contributors

Asmah Haji Omar	*University of Malaya*
Bernard Barber	*Barnard College, Columbia University*
Dayle Barnes	*University of Pittsburgh*
Louis-Jean Calvet	*University René Descartes, Sorbonne*
Robert L. Cooper	*The Hebrew University of Jerusalem*
Wolfgang U. Dressler	*University of Vienna*
Charles A. Ferguson	*Stanford University*
Joshua A. Fishman	*Yeshiva University*
Shirley Brice Heath	*Stanford University*
Richard Laprade	*University of Pennsylvania*
E. Glyn Lewis	*Ministry of Education, United Kingdom (retired)*
Stanley Lieberson	*University of Arizona*
Ushari Mahmud	*University of Khartoum*
Melanie Mikes	*University of Novi Sad*
Bal Govind Misra	*The Central Institute of Hindi*
Herbert H. Paper	*Hebrew Union College*
Carol Myers Scotton	*Michigan State University*

Index

354